LSWR Carriages
in the 20th Century

G. R. Weddell

Oxford Publishing Co

CONTENTS

First published 2001

ISBN 0 86093 555 8

All rights reserved. No part of this book may be reproduced or transmitted in any form or by any means, electronic or mechanical, including photocopying, recording or by any information storage and retrieval system, without permission from the Publisher in writing.

© G. R. Weddell 2001

Published by Oxford Publishing Co

an imprint of Ian Allan Publishing Ltd, Hersham, Surrey KT12 4RG..
Printed by Ian Allan Printing Ltd, Hersham, Surrey KT12 4RG.

Code: 0103/AI

FOREWORD

LSWR Carriages, Volume One, published by Wild Swan in 1992, dealt with the development of passenger carriages on the London & South Western Railway from the beginning in 1838 up to the end of the century. It remains to take the story on up to the formation of the Southern Railway at the end of 1922, including several carriage types that were designed and built in LSWR style until 1925. The majority of the carriages described in this period continued in Southern Railway service well into British Railways days, some until the late 1950s and a few beyond that.

When the first volume was written it was the intention to include in this second volume some chapters on those classes of vehicles that were designed to be suitable to run in passenger trains or at passenger-train speeds, such as luggage vans, milk vans, horse boxes, Post Office vans, and so on. However, as work went on it became obvious that this would lead to an undesirably large and expensive book. It has therefore become necessary to split the work between this volume and a third one.

The format of this volume follows that of the earlier one; the chapter numbering follows on from that, and the same simple system of cross-referencing the vehicles is used. Within each chapter every vehicle type has a number which is used for the drawing, the photograph and the place in the appendix. Thus, for example, the suburban bogie block sets, being non-corridor carriages, are found in Chapter 6, the drawings are labelled Figure 6.10, any photos as Plate 6.10a, b, c, etc, and the numbering details are found in Appendix 6 as item 6.10. This avoids the need for any unwieldy cross-indexing, but it can lead to some gaps.

Various rather similar LSWR Committee names are quoted. The structure and responsibilities of committees changed several times over the years. Generally, carriage matters were linked with those of locomotives, but sometimes with wagons, the commercial department or with stores. Occasionally, an *ad hoc* committee was appointed to look into specific carriage matters. Usually, requirements for new or replacement carriages originated with either the Traffic Committee or the General Manager, whose recommendations were referred to the appropriate committee currently dealing with carriage matters, often on the same day.

The decisions of that committee were formally placed before the Board of Directors, again sometimes on the same day but in any case within a few days. They appear to have normally been accepted without comment, the only recorded decisions by the Board being on the rare occasions when they disagreed or required additional information.

The bibliography is substantially the same as was shown in Volume One, but with the following additions concerning Chapter 7:

Electrification on the London & South Western Railway,
   Metropolitan-Vickers Electrical Co Ltd, 1922.
Minutes of Proceedings of The Institution of Civil Engineers,
   Vol CXXXIX, 1900.
The Electrical Review, Vol 45, 1899.
The British Westinghouse Gazette, 1914.
Waterloo and City Railway, by Nigel Pennick, published by
   Electric Traction Publications, 1981.

Since the publication of Volume One a few additional pieces of information (as well as a few errors) have come to light. These are given in 'Volume One — Matters Arising!' before we commence Chapter 6.

Once again I offer sincere thanks to all those who have helped me, in particular to Ray Chorley, Harold Tumilty, the staff of the Public Record Office and to many other people, mainly in the South Western Circle; also to all those who have allowed their photographs to be used. In the few cases where the photographer or publisher is not credited, this is because there is no identification on the photo, I ask them to accept my apologies and thanks.

I must also thank my wife Margaret for her support during the preparation of this work, she must have been very fed up at times.

G. R. Weddell
November 2000

The beginning of the 20th century on the LSWR, August 1901. Adams 'T6' class No 680 with a Pullman express to Bournemouth. The train consists of a 44ft Brake Van, two 48ft Composites, a Pullman, a 48ft Brake Third, then various other short carriages, all non-corridor. *Lens of Sutton*

VOLUME ONE —
MATTERS ARISING!

A few fresh items have come to light, largely as a result of the publication of *LSWR Carriages, Volume One*, which make it worthwhile to provide an addendum to that volume.

There was some discussion of the early trains, their composition and fares. To expand on that there is now appended a copy of the timetable that was printed on 16 August 1840 for introduction on and after 9 November 1840. Not only does this give the train timings but there is also a lot of interesting information about fares, the carriage of Third-class passengers, parcels, horses and so on.

Pages 15 and 86 — use of the company crest on carriage doors. A photograph has recently (1999) come to light showing part of a suburban block set Brake Third of the late 1870s, on which the company crest appears in the lower panel of the door nearest to the centre of the vehicle. This now establishes that the crest was used on at least some carriages of all three classes prior to the decision to cease their use in 1884, though whether all carriages had them is still not certain.

Page 59 — labelling of 'Smoking' compartments. A photo in the *Southern Railway Magazine* for 1938 shows a group of staff at Yeovil in 1884 posed in front of a Composite of c1865. Although etched 'Smoking' labels can be seen in some of the quarterlights to the left of the doors, there is also the word 'Smoking' painted in the lower panel, about 4in below the waist moulding, on the door of a Second-class compartment — not on a separate board as was indicated in the Minutes. The lettering is in a light colour, presumably either white or yellow.

Page 113, Figure 4.14 — 22ft Passenger Guard's Van. From enquiries from model makers I realise that the arrangement of the linkage between the vacuum brake and the Guard's handbrake is unclear and actually lacking a detail. The only way to clear this up is by means of the sketch that is shown here as Figure 4.14b. In the two preceding versions of 30ft Passenger Brake Van, in 1882 and 1884, one had the cylinder on the same side as the handbrake linkage while the other had it on the opposite side, in each case close to the solebar. The 1882 design also had the cross-shaft higher up, with a slightly different brake rodding to clear the centre axle. Unless a clear photograph of the 22ft version can be found it will be impossible to say which arrangement applied, but the probability is that it was the later one.

Mr J. N. Faulkner has kindly sent some further information about Plates 5.3b and 5.4b as follows:

Plate 5.3b on page 151, showing the 'Royal' train — the train is in use as the special conveying the Colonial Secretary, Joseph Chamberlain, from Southampton to Waterloo on 14 March 1903, after his visit to South Africa following the victorious end to the Boer War. It is his portrait which adorns the smokebox of No 773.

Plate 5.4b on page 155 shows the Inspection Saloon No 1s near Durnsford Road, Wimbledon, allegedly in 1935. As Mr Faulkner points out, it was most probably taken on 17 May 1936, with the train being the first to cross the new flyover. While the flyover was being built the down local road was diverted via the Wimbledon Corporation power station siding (at the right of the picture) and the down through was slewed into the down local. The numerous platelayers visible in the picture have probably just completed restoring the original course of the down local and linking the previous down through with the flyover to become the new up local, which the special is using.

Page 178 — 'Eagle' saloons as ambulances in Egypt and Palestine. Mr R. W. Kidner wrote to say that he had heard that six of these carriages were formed into ambulance train No 6 in Egypt in December 1916, followed by another six as train No 9 in June 1917. They were later renumbered as trains 48 and 51 in 1918, and again in 1919 as 48/51 (*sic*). He also mentioned that *Harakavet* for June 1990, a quarterly magazine published in Leeds, had carried more information on Middle East ambulance trains.

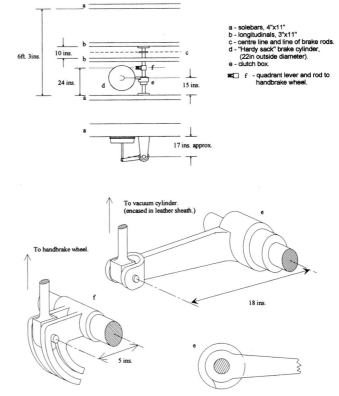

a - solebars, 4"x11"
b - longitudinals, 3"x11"
c - centre line and line of brake rods.
d - "Hardy sack" brake cylinder, (22in outside diameter).
e - clutch box.
f - quadrant lever and rod to handbrake wheel.

Figure 4.14b
Arrangement of brake gear on Passenger Brake Vans of 1884.

Unfortunately, a few errors also crept into Volume One, so the following should put them right.

Page 9 (Southern Railway renumbering list):
  Third class — add 2465-72 L&B (Lynton & Barnstaple Railway).
    Brake Third — amend LSWR to read: 2601-3202
    Brake Third — amend SECR to read: 3234-3547
    Motor Brake — amend to read: 10101-10121

Page 10:
  Horse Boxes — amend SECR to read: 2909-3010

(Note: There were several copies of numbering and renumbering lists held at different offices. It is hardly surprising that they were not all in total agreement, particularly as to dates of changes.)

Page 23, Plate 2.5b. The location is described as Chard Junction, but I have been told that the train is actually in the LSWR bay at Chard Joint Station, the track in the foreground belonging to the GWR.

Pages 93 and 116, Figures 4.4b and 4.16. The scales were drawn 1ft too long; instead of 15ft read 16ft!

Page 119, Fig 4.17. Note 3 states that gas lamps were fitted from about 1908. This is incorrect as regards the central one, as this was fitted only after the July 1919 Traffic Officers' Conference (a monthly meeting). Under the heading 'Passenger Guards Vans' they recorded several decisions on alterations to be carried out to passenger guard's vans as they went into shops. Several were minor, such as details of the provision of a coat-hook, but the main ones were as follows:
(a) Letter racks to be on the partition near to the brake wheel and to be made of wire net instead of solid wood so that the contents could easily be seen;
(b) Vacuum and Westinghouse brake-release wires to be moved away from the entrance to the guard's door to prevent inadvertent release;
(c) '6-wheeled Passenger Guards Vans fitted with a light at each end, leaving the centre where all writing and sorting of letters takes place, in darkness. An additional lamp should be fixed in the centre as in the case of bogie vans, and in order to economise in lighting each gas lamp should be provided with a tap inside so the light can be turned off and on as required, the switch at the end of the vans can then be abolished. This principle should also be applied to electrically lighted vans, which would effect considerably economy in this direction';
(d) 'a little padding to be provided on each side of the lookout where the guard's shoulder rests in order that damage to the men's coats, which accrues from constant rubbing against a wooden surface, should be avoided' (note that the concern was the damage to a uniform coat, not the possible bruising to the guard's shoulders!);
(e) 'Flag socket holders are required, two on each side, in a suitable position in each van to take the guard's flag so that it should be handy when required instead of being dropped in various parts of the van.' There was also a requirement that heaters, where fitted, should be mounted vertically to avoid the dust that normally collected, and should have a ledge to permit keeping tea warm.

Page 139. Charles Long has found further Pullman information since the publication of *Pullman: Travelling in Style* and has advised that my statement that Pullman car *Alexandra* was the former *Victoria*, altered and renamed, now appears to be incorrect. Apparently at that time there were at least two *Alexandra* cars running, one of them on the LBSCR. Naming a third seems unlikely, whilst records at the American headquarters of the company show that *Victoria* was renamed *Prince of Wales*. It thus seems more likely that the *Alexandra* in question was borrowed from the LBSCR services and was returned after the trial.

Page 167, Figure 5.7 — 48ft Brake Lavatory Tri-Composite. The 'American' bogie shown lacks its two swinging links to support the spring tray! See the correct versions in Figures 5.1 to 5.6.

Page 181, Figure 5.12 — 44ft Passenger Brake Van. The end views incorrectly show torpedo ventilators on the roof. These vans had no ventilators — only the lamps shown in the side elevation.

Page 228. In the listing of 42ft Thirds, the building dates of Nos 971 to 977 are shown as 9/81; they should of course be 9/91.

Page 229 — 48ft Brake Tri-Composite No 444; this should read 448.

Page 233 — 44ft Brake Van No 17 (replacement) is shown as having been built 12/1901; this should read 12/1907.

Page 241 — 48ft Third No 1048; the Southern number (shown as 569) should read 595.

Page 243. On the lower diagram showing the conversion of drawing 758 (48ft Composites to 58ft Brake Composites) the lower lookout should not be right at the end of the vehicle, as can just be seen in the distant photograph on page 200. The lookouts on these converted carriages were not opposite each other. The same applies to most (if not all) Southern Railway conversions of carriages to Drawings 650 and 772.

Overleaf: LSWR timetable of London-Southampton services in 1840, the year the line was opened throughout.

LONDON AND SOUTH WESTERN
RAILWAY

On and after November 9th.

HOURS OF DEPARTURE, AND TIME TABLE.

Down Trains.

LEAVE STATIONS.	mixed.	stopping.	stopping.	Fast Train.	Goods.	stopping.	stopping.	mixed.	stopping.	stopping.	stopping.	Fast Mail.	Goods.
	h. m.	h. m.	h. m.	h. m.	h. m.	h. m.	h. m.		h. m.	h. m.	h. m.	h. m.	h. m.
NINE ELMS	7. 0	9. 0	9.30	11.0	12. 0	12. 0	1. 0	....	4. 0	5. 0	6. 0	8.30	8.45
Wandsworth ..	....	9. 8	9.38	....	....	12. 8	1. 8	....	4. 8	5. 8	6. 8	....	....
Wimbledon....	....	9.18	9.48	....	....	12.18	1.18	....	4.18	5.18	6.18	....	....
Kingston......	....	9.32	10. 2	....	12.43	12.32	1.32	....	4.32	5.32	6.32	8.52	9.28
Esher	....	9.41	10.11	....	12.57	12.41	1.41	....	4.41	5.41	6.41	....	9.42
Walton	....	9.50	10.20	....	1.12	12.50	1.50	....	4.50	5.50	6.50	....	9.57
Weybridge	....	9.58	10.30	....	1.26	1. 0	1.58	....	5. 0	5.58	7. 0	9. 9	10.11
Woking	7.57	10.15	....	11.46	1.54	....	2.15	....	....	6.16	7.15	9.24	10.39
Farnborough ..	8.27	10.45	....	12.12	2.37	....	2.45	....	....	6.45	....	9.51	11.22
Winchfield ..	8.46	11. 4	....	12.29	3. 9	....	3. 4	....	....	7. 4	....	10. 8	11.54
Basingstoke ..	9. 7	11.25	....	12.50	3.48	....	3.25	....	....	7.25	....	10.29	12.33
Andover Road	9.39	11.57	....	1.17	4.35	....	3.57	....	....	7.57	....	10.57	1.20
Winchester ..	10. 0	12.18	....	1.34	5.10	....	4.18	....	....	8.18	....	11.14	1.55
SOUTHAMPTON.	10.30	12.48	....	2. 0	6. 0	....	4.48	....	....	8.48	....	11.40	2.45

Up Trains to London.

LEAVE STATIONS.	Mail.	stopping.	stopping.	stopping.	stopping.	Goods.	Fast Train.	stopping.	stopping.	mixed.	stopping.	stopping.	Goods.
	h. m.	h. m.	h. m.	h. m.	h. m.	h. m.	h. m.	h. m.	h. m.	h. m.	h. m.	h. m.	h. m.
SOUTHAMPTON.	2. 0	....	6. 0	....	8.30	10. 0	11. 0	....	1.30	....	....	6. 0	8. 0
Winchester ..	2.29	....	6.34	....	9. 4	10.57	11.29	....	2. 4	....	....	6.34	8.57
Andover Road	2.53	....	7. 0	....	9.30	11.37	11.53	....	2.30	....	....	7. 0	9.37
Basingstoke ..	3.13	....	7.23	....	9.53	12.23	12.13	....	2.53	....	....	7.23	10.23
Winchfield ..	3.32	....	7.46	....	10.16	12.59	12.32	....	3.16	....	....	7.46	10.59
Farnborough ..	3.49	....	8. 5	....	10.35	1.29	12.49	....	3.35	....	....	8. 5	11.29
Woking	4. 7	7.45	8.27	....	10.57	2. 5	1. 7	....	3.57	....	....	8.27	12. 5
Weybridge	4.23	7.57	8.44	10.45	11.14	2.33	....	2. 0	4.16	....	7. 0	8.44	12.33
Walton	....	8. 5	8.51	10.50	11.22	2.46	....	2. 5	4.22	....	7. 8	8.53	12.46
Esher	....	8.13	9. 0	10.58	11.30	3. 0	....	2.13	4.30	....	7.13	9. 0	1. 0
Kingston......	4.41	8.25	9.10	11.10	11.40	3.14	....	2.25	4.40	....	7.25	9.10	1.14
Wimbledon....	....	8.39	9.26	11.24	11.56	....	....	2.39	4.56	....	7.39	9.26	....
Wandsworth ..	....	8.50	9.37	11.35	12. 7	....	....	2.50	5. 7	....	7.50	9.37	....
NINE ELMS	5. 4	9. 0	9.46	11.45	12.16	4. 0	2. 0	3. 0	5.16	6. 0	8. 0	9.46	2. 0

ON SUNDAYS.

Down Trains.

LEAVE STATIONS.	stop.	stop.	stop.	stop.	stop.	stop.	Mail.
	h. m.	h. m.	h. m.	h. m.	h. m.	h. m.	h. m.
NINE ELMS	9 0	10 0	10 30	2 0	5 0	7 30	8 30
Wandsworth ..	9 8	10 8	10 38	2 8	5 8	7 38	....
Wimbledon....	9 18	10 18	10 48	2 18	5 18	7 48	....
Kingston......	9 32	10 32	11 2	2 32	5 32	8 2	8 52
Esher	9 41	10 41	11 11	2 41	5 41	8 11	....
Walton	9 50	10 50	11 20	2 50	5 50	8 20	....
Weybridge	9 58	10 58	11 28	2 58	5 58	8 28	9 9
Woking	10 15	11 15	11 45	3 15	6 15	8 45	9 24
Farnboro'	....	11 45	....	....	6 45	....	9 51
Winchfield	....	12 4	....	....	7 4	....	10 8
Basingstoke ..	....	12 25	....	....	7 25	....	10 29
Andover Road	....	12 57	....	....	7 57	....	10 57
Winchester ..	....	1 18	....	....	8 18	....	11 14
SOUTHAMPTON.	....	1 48	....	....	8 48	....	11 40

Up Trains to London.

LEAVE STATIONS.	Mail.	stop.	stop.	stop.	stop.	stop.	stop.
	h. m.	h. m.	h. m.	h. m.	h. m.	h. m.	h. m.
SOUTHAMPTON	2 0	....	10 0	....	5 0	....	....
Winchester ..	2 29	....	10 34	....	5 34	....	....
Andover Road	2 53	....	11 0	....	6 0	....	....
Basingstoke ..	3 13	....	11 23	....	6 23	....	....
Winchfield	3 32	....	11 46	....	6 46	....	....
Farnboro'	3 49	....	12 5	....	7 5	....	....
Woking	4 7	8 0	12 27	11 0	7 27	6 0	8 0
Weybridge	4 23	8 12	12 44	11 12	7 44	6 12	8 12
Walton	....	8 20	12 52	11 20	7 52	6 20	8 20
Esher	....	8 28	1 0	11 28	8 0	6 28	8 28
Kingston......	4 41	8 40	1 10	11 40	8 10	6 40	8 40
Wimbledon....	....	8 54	1 26	11 54	8 26	6 54	8 54
Wandsworth ..	....	9 5	1 37	12 5	8 37	7 5	9 5
NINE ELMS	5 4	9 15	1 46	12 15	8 46	7 15	9 15

Goods' Trains as on other Days.

☞ London Time will be observed, and the Doors of the Stations closed at the Times given above.

16th August, 1840   *Smith and Ebbs, Printers, Tower-hill, London.*   [SEE OVER.

London and South Western Railway.

The *First Class Train* will perform the journey in three hours, taking *First Class Passengers only*, excepting that accommodation will be afforded for a limited number of Servants in Livery. The Fare will be **20s.** each Passenger; the Fare for Servants in Livery **13s.** each. This Train will not call at any Stations between London and Woking Common, but will take up and set down Passengers at all the Stations between Woking Common and Southampton.

The Fare from London to Southampton by the *Mixed Trains* will be **18s.** First Class; **12s.** Second Class.

The *Third Class* Passengers will be taken by the Day Goods Train only.

The *Mail Trains* call at Kingston, Weybridge, Woking Common, and all Stations to the West of Woking Common. The Fares the same as the Mixed Trains for both First and Second Class Passengers.

The Servants of the Company are prohibited receiving any fee or gratuity.

Passengers are earnestly requested to have their Name and Destination stated in full on their Luggage, and to see that it is put in or upon the proper Carriage, by the Servants of the Company. The Company do not hold themselves responsible for Luggage, unless booked and paid for according to its value, in which case the Company will require it to be in the custody of their own Servants, who will give the Proprietor a Receipt for it, and that Receipt is to be given up when the Luggage shall be received from the Company's Servants.

PRIVATE CARRIAGES, HORSES, &c. should be at the Station a quarter of an hour before the departure of the Trains. Horse Boxes and Carriage Trucks are kept at the Principal Stations on the Line, but in order to prevent disappointment, a day's Notice should be given.

PARCELS may be booked at the undermentioned Offices, and will be forwarded from thence without any additional charge to the Station at Nine Elms. Arrangements have been made by which Parcels will be delivered at the following rates of charge, including Porterage, viz.

		Not exceeding 28 lbs.	Not exceeding 56 lbs.
To or from	Wandsworth	8d.	1s. 0d.
....	Wimbledon	9d.	1s. 2d.
....	Kingston, Esher, Walton, Weybridge, Woking, Farnborough, Winchfield, or Basingstoke	1s. 0d.	1s. 6d.
....	Andover Road, Winchester, or Southampton	1s. 3d.	2s. 0d.

OMNIBUSES convey Passengers to and from the Station near Vauxhall, from the following Coach Offices, viz.—the Spread Eagle, Gracechurch-street; Swan with two Necks, Lad-lane; Cross Keys, Wood-street, Cheapside; White Horse, Fetter-lane; George and Blue Boar, Holborn; Golden Cross, Charing-cross; and Universal Office, Regent-circus.—Fare 8d.

STEAM BOATS convey Passengers to and from the Railroad, from and to Old Swan Pier, Old Shades Pier, Upper Thames-street, Hungerford Market, Waterloo and Westminster Bridges, at 4d.

POST HORSES are kept at the Station, and Carriages are taken to, or fetched from, any part of London, at a charge of 10s. 6d. including the driver.

STEAM PACKETS from Southampton to the Isle of Wight, Portsmouth, Poole, Weymouth, Tourquay Plymouth, Guernsey, Jersey, St. Malo, Granville, and Havre de Grace; from the latter place there is Steam communication to Caen, Morlaix, Rouen, Paris, Rotterdam, Hamburg, &c.

FARES.

Passengers.   **Horses and Carriages.**

Distance	STATIONS.	FAST TR. 1st Class.	MIXED TRAIN. 1st Class.	MIXED TRAIN. 2nd Class.	GOODS TR. 3rd Class.	CARRIAGE	1 HORSE.	2 HORSES.	3 HORSES.
Miles.		s. d.	s. d.	s. d.	s. d.	s. d.	s. d.	s. d.	s. d.
3	London to Wandsworth	..	1 0	0 6	..		not taken	taken	
6	.... Wimbledon	..	1 6	1 0	..		not taken	taken	
10	.... Kingston	..	2 0	1 6	..	10 0	7 0	10 0	12 0
13	.... Esher and Hampton Court	..	2 6	1 6	..	10 0	7 0	10 0	12 0
15¼	.... Walton	..	3 0	2 0	..		not taken	taken	
17¼	.. Weybridge	..	3 6	2 0	..	10 0	7 0	10 0	12 0
23	.... Woking	6 0	5 0	3 6	2 6	12 0	8 0	12 0	15 0
31¼	.... Farnborough	8 6	7 6	5 0	3 0	17 0	11 0	17 0	21 0
38	.... Winchfield	10 0	9 0	6 0	3 6	21 0	14 0	21 0	26 0
46	.... Basingstoke	12 0	11 0	7 0	4 0	26 0	18 0	25 0	30 0
56	.... Andover Road	15 0	13 6	9 0	5 0	31 0	22 0	30 0	36 0
64	.... Winchester	17 6	15 6	10 0	6 0	36 0	25 0	34 0	42 0
76¾	.... Southampton	20 0	18 0	12 0	7 0	42 0	30 0	40 0	50 0

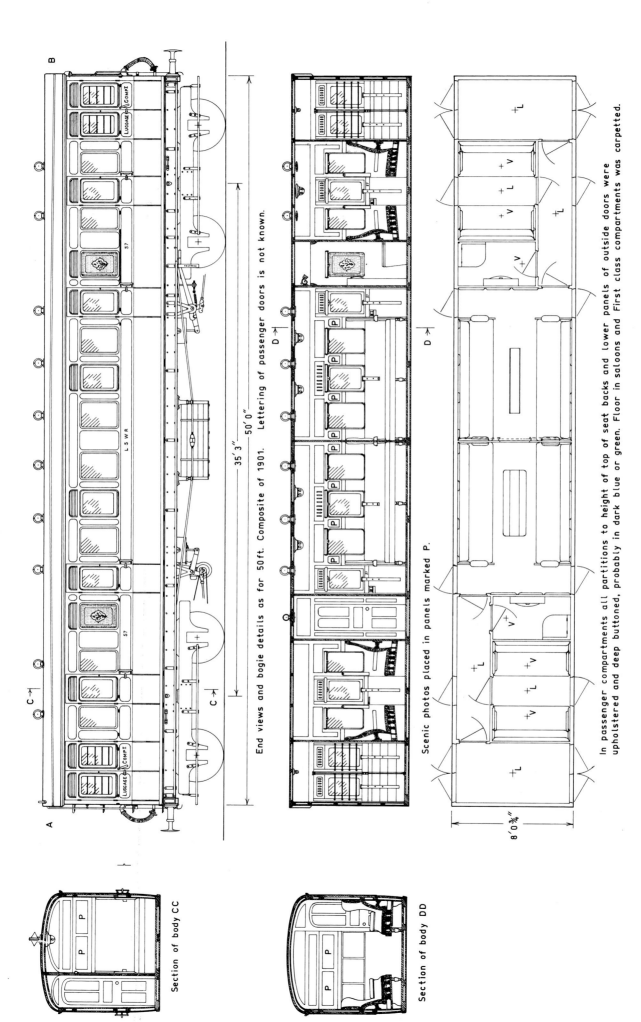

End views and bogie details as for 50ft. Composite of 1901. Lettering of passenger doors is not known.

Scenic photos placed in panels marked P.

In passenger compartments all partitions to height of top of seat backs and lower panels of outside doors were upholstered and deep buttoned, probably in dark blue or green. Floor in saloons and First class compartments was carpetted.

Section of body CC

Section of body DD

Figure 6.1
LSWR 50ft Double Family Saloon of 1900

Chapter 6
NON-CORRIDOR CARRIAGES, 1900-23

In the previous chapter (Volume One, Chapter 5) it was seen how large quantities of bogie carriages were built to a common length of 48ft during the 1890s, with just one new design 50ft long at the end of 1899. Although there were to be some more 48ft vehicles, and indeed some 46ft ones, the trend was towards longer carriages.

The first of these in the new century again followed the South Western's (or rather its customers') fondness for saloons — a pair of 50ft double saloons that were authorised on 31 January 1900 at a cost of £1,086 each. (Figure 6.1) In the Minutes they were called 'Family Carriages', and as built they had two completely separate sections, each comprising a small saloon, a compartment with First-class furnishings, a lavatory and a luggage compartment, thus making them ideal for family travel. However, in October 1905 it was decided that the *four* double saloons were to have a door provided between the saloons. According to the records the present saloons were the only ones that answered this description; all the other double saloons had a lavatory between the saloons with access from both via doors into a side vestibule. In any case, for these two an additional partition was put in, shortening one saloon by a couple of inches, the new door sliding between the partitions. Then, in April 1907, it was decided to provide them with standard gangway connections (as distinct from the South Western's first type of gangway — this will be mentioned again in Chapter 9 on corridor carriages) 'for use with boat traffic'. Whilst

this may have been more convenient for other passengers on the train, particularly if there was a dining car, it must have created resentment and complaints from people who had hired a saloon to obtain privacy. The LSWR drawing, No 919, shows a hand brake on each side; like the 48ft saloons shown near the end of the previous chapter this appears to have been a later addition, and similarly, although the drawing is not explicit on this, it looks as though there was a right-handed lever on one side and a left-handed one on the other. Again, there was a short hand-rail on the upper waist fascia, above the brake handle.

No photographs of Family Saloons are clear enough to show what lettering, if any, there was in the door waist panels.

In December 1900 four more carriage types were authorised: seven 48ft Composites without lavatories, which were mentioned in the previous chapter as dimensionally identical to the 'standard' Thirds; seven 50ft Composites with lavatories; nine 46ft Thirds with lavatories, and five 50ft five-compartment Brake Thirds without lavatories. At first glance this might suggest some uncertainty over policy but it seems most likely that, although not mentioned specifically, the non-lavatory carriages were intended for the short- and medium-distance trains and the lavatory ones for the West of England services.

Another 12 of the 50ft Composites (illustrated at Figure 6.2) were authorised the following August. They were all fitted with electric lighting but the records seem to show that only three of

Plate 6.2 50ft Composite No 115 (Drawing 980) at Whitstone, July 1948. *J. H. Aston*

9

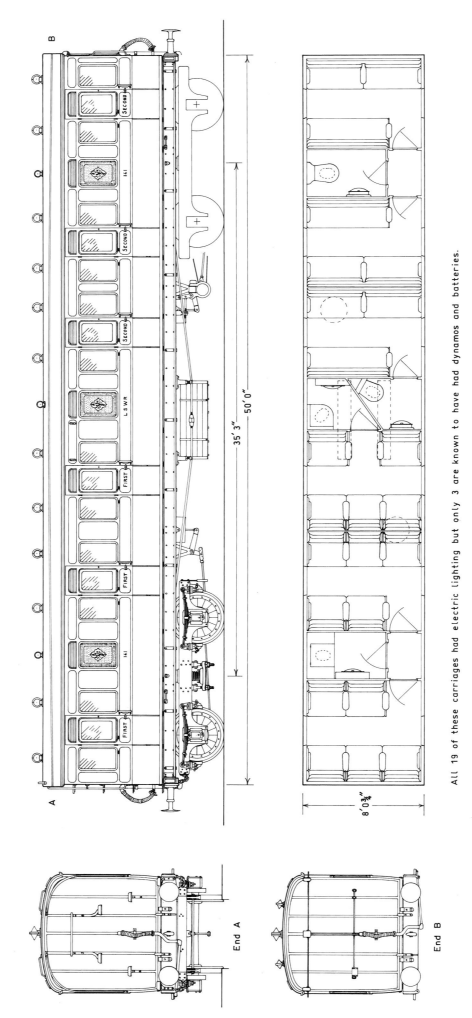

All 19 of these carriages had electric lighting but only 3 are known to have had dynamos and batteries.

20 feet

Figure 6.2
LSWR 50ft Composite (4 lavs) of 1901.

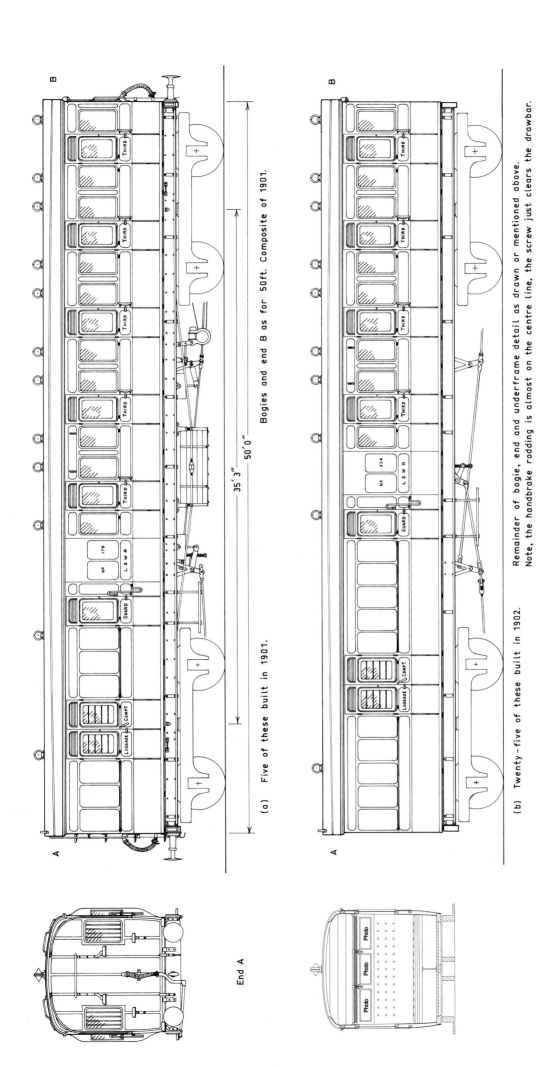

B

THIRD · THIRD · THIRD · THIRD · THIRD · THIRD · THIRD

GUARD · N° 176 L S W R · LUGGAGE COMPT

35′ 3″

50′ 0″

Bogies and end B as for 50ft. Composite of 1901.

(a) Five of these built in 1901.

End A

B

THIRD · THIRD · THIRD · THIRD · THIRD

N° 324 L S W R · GUARD · LUGGAGE COMPT

Remainder of bogie, end and underframe detail as drawn or mentioned above.
Note, the handbrake rodding is almost on the centre line, the screw just clears the drawbar.

(b) Twenty-five of these built in 1902.

A

Photo Photo Photo

0   5   10   15   20 feet

Figure 6.3/6.6
LSWR 50ft Brake Thirds of 1901 and 1902.

the total of 19 had dynamos and batteries, suggesting that most of them had to take their power from an adjacent vehicle. All compartments had access to a lavatory but these were graded, those for the Firsts being fitted out rather more elaborately with more decorative seats over the actual lavatory pans. The tip-up hand-wash basins were enclosed in fitments that provided a small shelf over the top. The doors to the First-class lavatories were 1ft 10in wide, compared with 1ft 8in for the inferior ones. Eight of these Composites finished up as Southern Railway Camping Coaches in the late 1930s.

The order for nine 46ft Thirds (Figure 6.4) was repeated in August 1901. Again, they had lavatory access from all compartments, but the internal doors were only 1ft 6in wide. They were fully provided with dynamos and batteries, but it would be pure conjecture to suppose that they were intended to run with — and supply power to — the Composites.

The batch of five 50ft Brake Thirds (Figure 6.3a) was followed by another batch of 25 that was authorised in July 1901. Whereas the first five were simply repeats of the earlier 48ft version, having a slightly lengthened van, the main batch, which was built in 1902 (Figure 6.3b, Appendix item 6.6), had only four compartments and a larger luggage area. Of the five earlier ones, three had one compartment stripped and added to the luggage space at some unknown date — possibly around 1922 when many of the 48ft ones were altered in this way.

Incidentally, it is noted on many drawings in this chapter that the carriages had the same bogies, ie with 10in-deep sideframes, as those shown for the 50ft Composites of 1901 (Figure 6.2). This is not necessarily true of the bolster springs in all cases. As was remarked in Chapter 5 of the first volume, there were cases where even different batches of a particular type seem to have had differing types of bolster suspension. Apart from original provision, the works had a quantity of spare bogies that could be used to prevent a vehicle from being held out of service awaiting a bogie repair. Thus there do not seem to have been any hard and fast rules on this matter.

Electric lighting on Stone's system had been tried out successfully in a saloon during 1897 and had gradually been adopted for some new carriages from 1898. On 23 January 1901 the Locomotive, Carriage & Stores Committee noted that 276 carriages had already been successfully fitted with electric lighting, whilst 2,600 were gas-lit. It was then decided that all new carriages should be provided with electric lighting. With some exceptions this was put into effect until March 1905, when the General Manager, Sir Charles Owens, started to press for a reversion to gas lighting, and an electrically-lit bogie block set was converted to gas. This was probably for a combination of reasons. The company had made a large investment in gas lighting, both in fixed plant and in stocks of fittings for the carriages. In addition, Pintsch's new system of incandescent lamps was just becoming available. With this system the gas flame was enclosed in a fine fireclay mantle that glowed with an intense white light, giving better illumination for less gas than previously. At the same time, the electric installations, with their heavy batteries and dynamos, had a higher initial cost, and the light given by the early carbon filament bulbs was fairly dim and yellowish. These carbon filaments were also very fragile and the bulbs needed frequent replacement, this apparently giving particular concern on the suburban bogie block trains that experienced so many rather jerky stops and starts.

As an aside regarding Pintsch, during the early part of the 1914-18 War it was reported that the Pintsch firm (of Berlin) was engaged in the development and manufacture of poison gas for use against troops. It was doubtless its product that was later used to horrible effect against Allied troops on the Western Front. Good and bad out of the same pot!

A further refinement for gas lighting was offered by Pintsch and accepted for trial on the gas-lit bogie block train at the urging of Sir Charles Owens during the meeting of 15 November 1905. Hitherto it had been necessary for a porter to enter every compartment of a train to light the lamps; therefore, to avoid great waste of time at stations, the lamps had to be left burning on any train that would be passing through a tunnel, or where the journey would start or end other than in full daylight. In the case of incandescent lamps this method of lighting also caused a high

breakage rate in gas mantles. The modification was the provision of a bypass. Each carriage already had a tap in the gas pipe, mounted at about waist height on the carriage end and operated by a horizontal rod that could be easily reached from the platform, on whichever side that happened to be. An additional pipe was now branched off from just under this tap and led up to the roof lamps, where it was connected to small pilot burners. These pilot burners could be left on all the time a vehicle was in service, using only a small amount of gas, but when the main lights were needed it was only necessary to turn on the tap for all the burners to ignite from the pilots. It was estimated that this bypass system reduced gas consumption by between 50% and 66%. Following trials it was decided, on 31 October 1906, to convert all existing gas-lit stock to the incandescent system with bypass pilots. This involved about 9,000 compartments at a cost of £2 each. The Carriage Register records the conversion date of very many vehicles but it is doubtful if the job was ever completed, because an *Appendix to the Book of Rules and Regulations* dated July 1921 gave very specific instructions for the care and lighting of the ordinary gas lamps, including those with horizontal burners, as distinct from those with incandescent burners.

Meanwhile, at least one more bogie block train had been fitted with the full incandescent gas lighting system, and on 1 May 1907 it was agreed that four more new trains would also be so fitted, when the initial costs for electric and gas installations were quoted as £431 and £135 respectively, with annual maintenance at £33 12s 0d and £19 12s 0d respectively. The cost of the gas consumed was not mentioned!

Despite the General Manager's urging, most of the authorisations for new construction specified electric light, but he again pressed the matter on 17 February 1910, claiming that the adoption of the incandescent system would save £6,000 on renewals and ultimately £4,000 per annum on maintenance. It was then agreed by the Locomotive, Carriage & Stores Committee that all new stock would be fitted with gas lighting. Even so, a pair of saloons was authorised to have electric light on 14 April 1910, and a batch of Brake Tri-Composites similarly on 17 November 1910. Then, on 1 December 1910, the General Manager said that, due to the reduced cost of fitting electric lighting and the improved bulb life resulting from the introduction of metallic filaments, he would recommend that the company continue (!) to fit all new carriages for electric lighting, and this was agreed by the Committee.

Stone's lighting system, introduced by J. Stone & Co of Deptford towards the end of 1895, originally consisted of a dynamo and a 24V battery on each carriage, each battery consisting of twelve 2V cells or accumulators. This arrangement was fitted to some six-wheeled stock (as shown in Chapter 4 of the earlier volume), where there were usually one large and one small battery box containing eight and four cells respectively. Some bogie vehicles also had this system, but with two equal-sized battery boxes, each containing six larger and heavier cells.

The single-battery system had disadvantages, such as the lack of voltage stability when more advanced switchable lighting arrangements were needed in carriages. Stone & Co then developed a two-battery system which, as far as the LSWR was concerned, became the standard. The batteries were contained in lead-lined teak boxes hung from the underframe. The six cells of each battery could have any odd number from nine to 17 plates, according to need, and so sometimes two battery boxes could suffice for two carriages while in other cases three boxes were needed for a single carriage.

Apart from a master lighting on/off switch, all switching was contained within the dynamo housing, in the domed end that can be clearly seen in many photographs. Initially the master switch was on the carriage end where the gas switch had been, but later, and particularly with the introduction of corridor carriages, connectors were provided between carriages so that the lights could be controlled from the guard's compartment — all on, all off or just half of them on.

The dynamo was driven by a cotton balata belt from an 18in-diameter pulley on a main axle, but it was hung from the underframe in such a way that its weight tensioned the belt, the precise tension being adjustable. Thus, once it reached a certain speed, the belt would start to slip, preventing serious over-generation. The dynamo housing contained a rotary switch to

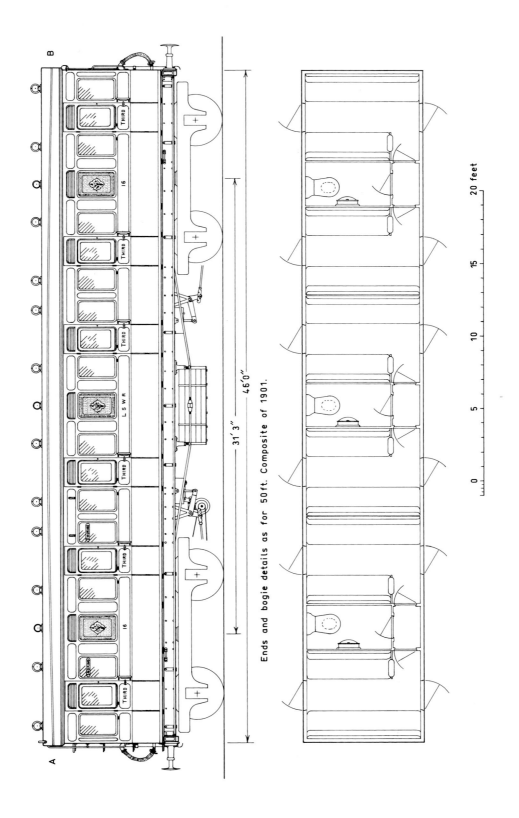

B

THIRD · 16 · LSWR · THIRD · 16 · THIRD

A

31' 3"

46' 0"

Ends and bogie details as for 50ft. Composite of 1901.

0   5   10   15   20 feet

Figure 6.4
LSWR 46ft Third (3 lav) of 1901.

13

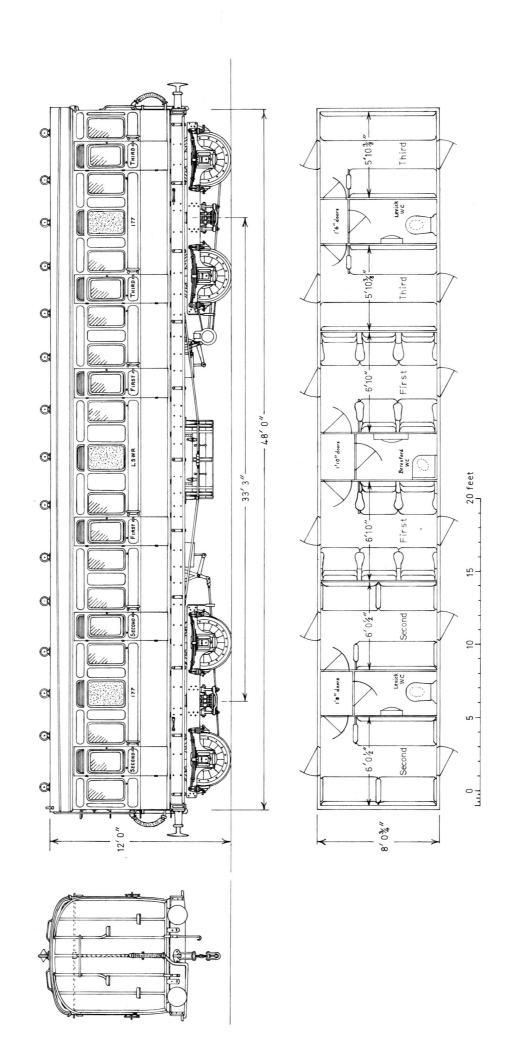

Figure 6.5
LSWR 48ft Composite built 1901/2.

ensure correct polarity, whichever way the vehicle was moving. The two batteries, each of 12 cells, were connected in semi-parallel in such a way that, through resistors, the dynamo polarity and centrifugal switches controlled the charge and stabilised the voltage to the lamps. Travelling in one direction, one battery and the dynamo supplied the lamps while the other battery was charging; then, going the other way, the roles of the batteries were reversed. This equalised the charge-discharge cycle and helped to prolong the life of the cells. (For more details of the dynamo and battery arrangement see Volume 6 of *Modern Railway Working*, published by The Gresham Publishing Co in 1912, though note that the switches are represented by symbols more commonly recognised as capacitors nowadays!)

Communication cords and chains have been mentioned in earlier chapters, but, to recapitulate, the cords of the earlier system ran through thimbles on the roof cornice and were connected from carriage to carriage, terminating on gongs on the tender and in the guard's van. Thus any passenger wishing to call the attention of the train crew had to lean out of a window, grasp the cord, collect in all the slack, and then give tugs to make the gongs sound.

Automatic vacuum brakes (AVB) had been fitted to all passenger vehicles on the LSWR by mid-1894, but it was not until the end of 1899 that the Board of Trade approved the use of communication cords to apply the brakes and recommended that the internal compartment fittings should be standard on all railways.

Shortly after this the LSWR started to fit carriages with internal communication chains. These chains ran in tubes just above door-top level, with a short section exposed in each compartment. The chains were fixed at one end of each carriage, and at the other end they operated a short lever in a small semicircular housing. This lever was attached to a transverse rod passing through a box on the centre line of the carriage. Inside this box was an air valve connected by a small pipe to the main brake pipe. If the chain was pulled it rotated the rod and opened the valve, admitting a limited flow of air so as to cause partial application of the brakes. The rod extended through the two chain boxes, and a small oval plate, sometimes called a 'butterfly', was attached to each end. In the normal position the butterfly was horizontal, but when the chain was pulled the butterfly, which was painted bright red, turned to and remained in the upright position, giving the crew a quick indication as to the carriage where the chain had been pulled.

There is no mention of any specific decisions in Committee Minutes, but from the Registers it can be seen that there was quite a major operation to convert all carriages to this system between 1900 and about 1903. These fittings were normally placed on that end of a carriage that did not have end steps to the roof, both to avoid damage to the apparatus and to avoid tripping any staff climbing on to the roof. The external fittings can be seen in Figure 6.2.

During the changeover, fully-fitted vehicles still needed to have provision for the external cord for some time because of the likelihood of their being marshalled in trains with carriages awaiting conversion. A photograph of a train leaving Bournemouth on 31 May 1902 shows the leading vehicle to be one of the then very new 50ft Brake Thirds mentioned above but clearly fitted with cornice thimbles for the old type of cord.

In the 1911 *Appendix to the Book of Rules and Regulations* it was stated that all the pipes operating brake blocks were painted black, all the pipes not operating brake blocks being painted bright red. This applied to both AVB and Westinghouse brakes. In the case of AVB the engine driver was required to establish the vacuum at 18in and to maintain it throughout the journey. Westinghouse pressure had to be maintained at 70 to 75lb/sq in, and it was noted that a reduction of 25lb/sq in would apply the brakes with full force, but that a reduction of between 5 and 8lb/sq in was to be used for normal stops. There was also a note that Carriage Examiners should check the wear of brake blocks; each brake block should be a minimum of $^3/_{16}$ in and a maximum of $^5/_{16}$ in clear of the wheel. For Westinghouse brakes these clearances were to be $^3/_8$ in and $^1/_2$ in respectively.

Turning again to specific carriages, another variant on the 48ft theme appeared at the end of 1901 with six Tri-Composites to Drawing 1051 (Figure 6.5), followed by another five in mid-1902. This time there were two compartments of each class, each pair sharing access to a lavatory.

Plate 6.6a At Bournemouth Central, 31 May 1902: the leading carriage is a 50ft Brake Third; the third carriage is a Pullman. *Lens of Sutton*

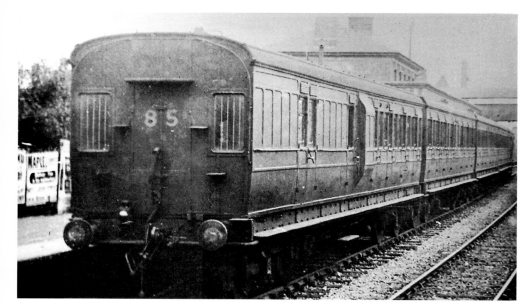

Plate 6.6b 50ft Brake Third to Drawing 1046. *Author's collection*

Plate 6.7 Maunsell 'N15' class No 785 *Sir Mador de la Porte* with a Bournemouth train. The leading carriage is 50ft ex-Second of 1902 (Drawing 1090). *Lens of Sutton*

The next authorisation, on 18 December 1901, included eight Seconds and five Thirds that were to have seven compartments each, but with lavatory access from only four of them. They were all completed by August 1902. Because of their great similarity they are shown together here in Figure 6.7 (Appendix items 6.7 and 6.8 respectively); the Seconds were 50ft long and the Thirds, because of their narrower compartments, were 48ft long. A more significant difference, at least on the official drawings, was that the Seconds were shown to have three battery boxes fitted whilst the Thirds had none. Most drawings of this period showed the dynamo mounting brackets and reinforcing plates, presumably because they would be rather difficult to fit retrospectively, but many of them give no indication of the provision of batteries, although they were definitely electrically lit. Certainly, when the Thirds came into Southern ownership one of them was noted as electrically wired only. Unfortunately photographs only rarely help us over these details.

Another slight increase in length was introduced at the meeting of 14 May 1902 with the decision to build five 51ft Brake Tri-Composites to Drawing 1122 (Figure 6.9); these were completed in the following November. They had two compartments of each class, but gave lavatory access only for the First-class passengers. That they were really intended for the shorter-distance services is

suggested by the relatively short luggage compartment and the definitely suburban size of the Third-class compartments: only 5ft 7in between partitions. There is no evidence of the usual protective bars behind the end windows and droplights in the guard's compartment, again suggesting that they were not expected to be loaded full of luggage like a main-line vehicle. Nevertheless, a photograph showing an 'E10' class 'double single' locomotive hauling a down train to Salisbury has one of these as the leading vehicle. It is particularly interesting that the light yellow colouring of the interior window-frames of the First- and Second-class compartments can be clearly seen; it seems likely that this picture dates from around 1904 to 1908.

The same May meeting also gave approval to the construction of 'thirty-two bogie Composite and Brake Third carriages formed into four block trains'. Although described in this way they were in fact built as eight four-car block trains — a formation that became very familiar to all London-area commuters on the South Western over the next few years. These eight sets were completed by January 1903, each one formed of two 51ft Brake Thirds to Drawing 1129, one 51ft Composite to Drawing 1127 and a 49ft Tri-Composite to Drawing 1128. They are illustrated in Figure 6.10. Seating was for 10 in each Third-class compartment and for eight in the Second-class ones, but there is some uncertainty about the Firsts: the drawings show eight in each, with central dividing

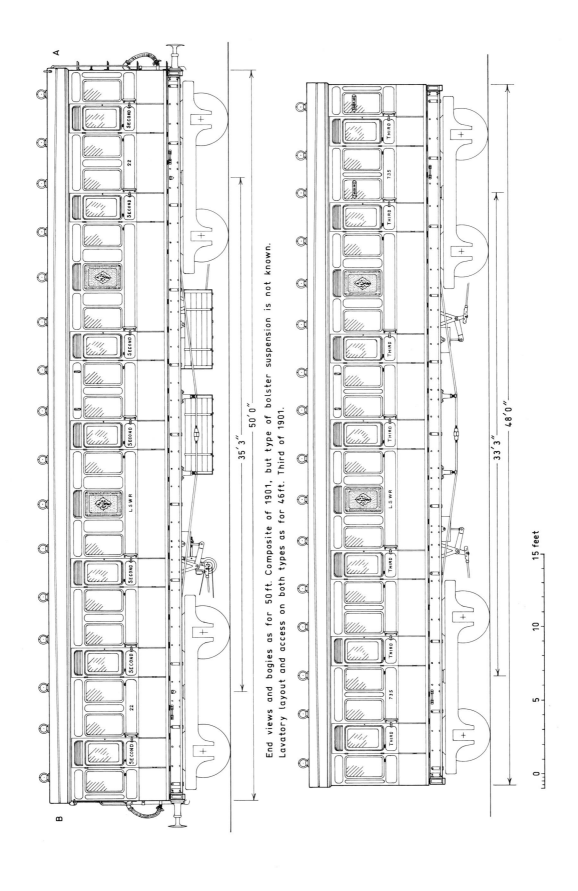

End views and bogies as for 50ft. Composite of 1901, but type of bolster suspension is not known.
Lavatory layout and access on both types as for 46ft. Third of 1901.

Figure 6.7/6.8
LSWR 50ft Second and 48ft Third of 1902.

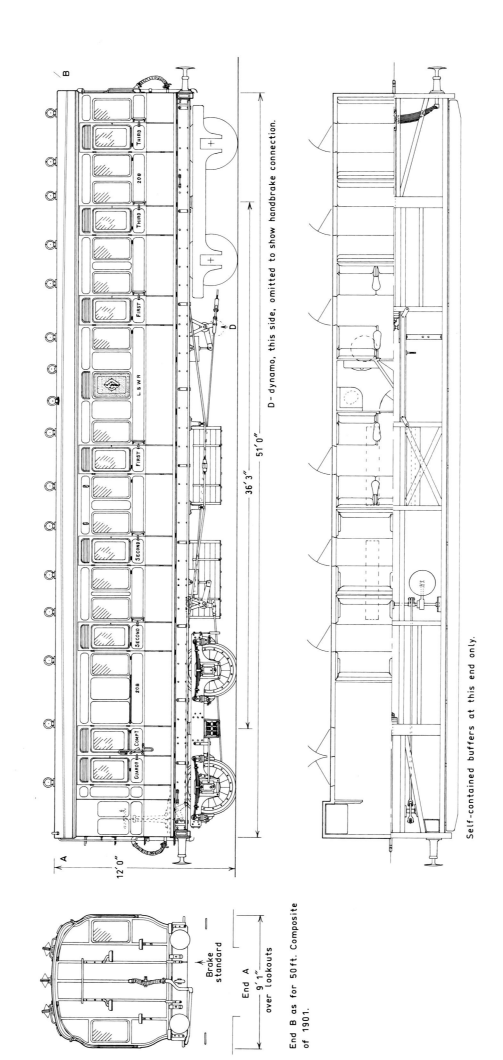

B

THIRD

208

THIRD

FIRST

L S W R

FIRST

SECOND

208

SECOND

COMP¹

GUARD'S

A

12' 0"

D

D - dynamo, this side, omitted to show handbrake connection.

36' 3"

51' 0"

Brake standard

End A

9' 1"
over lookouts

End B as for 50 ft. Composite of 1901.

Self-contained buffers at this end only.

0   5   10   15   20 feet

Figure 6.9
LSWR 50ft Brake Tri-Composite of 1902.

Plate 6.9 'E10' class No 372 near Wimbledon with a Waterloo-Salisbury train. The leading carriage is 51ft Brake Tri-Composite (Drawing 1122). Note the light-colour framing to the First- and Second-class windows. *Lens of Sutton*

Plate 6.10a 'O2' class No 208 with bogie block set No 9B. *Author's collection*

armrests, but the registers show the more usual six — presumably with armrests to every seat.

Between 1902 and September 1912 a total of 145 bogie block sets were built, though there were two variants. The first 73 sets, built up to June 1905, were as described above. The remaining 72 had the same type of Brake Thirds and 49ft Tri-Composites to Drawing 1128, but the 51ft Composite design was altered, by instruction of the Traffic Committee of 17 May 1905, to a Tri-Composite, Drawing 1393, which is also included in Figure 6.10.

It might seem rather strange to go to such a degree of 'fine tuning', and one wonders whether they really did measure the demand so precisely!

The earlier sets all had underframes constructed of timber in the usual way but the later ones — there is no record of the exact date when the change started but it included all of the Drawing 1393 Tri-Composites — had steel channel-section solebars, although they still had timber headstocks and other members. Some of the earlier ones probably also had bogies with coil bolster springs

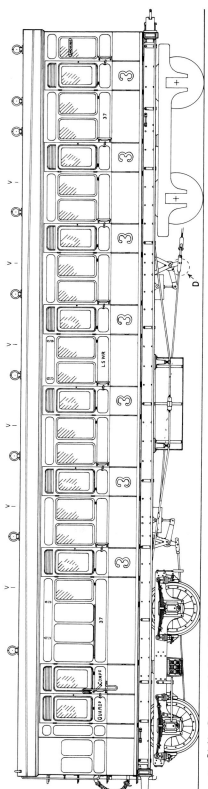

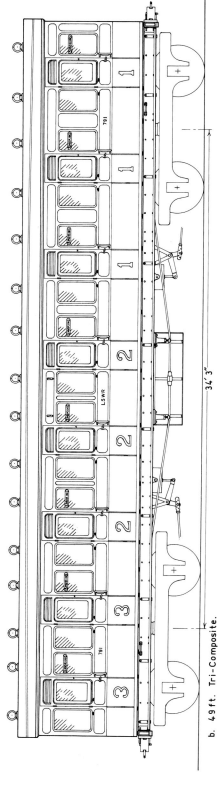

c. 51ft. Brake Third. End view as for 51ft. Brake Tri-Composite. D-position of dynamo, this side, when fitted. Some vehicles had 3 Smoking compts, each with 2 ventilators, some had 2 ventilators to every compt. Alternative positions of destination board brackets are shown dotted. For more detail of block coupling see "Block Sets of 1900/01"(6-wheel stock).

b. 49ft. Tri-Composite.
Bogies as for Brake Third above. In some sets these carriages did not have batteries. The exact shape of the door numerals is uncertain. Destination board brackets were not provided on later carriages.

0   5   10   15 feet

Figure 6.10
LSWR Block Sets of 1902-1912.

20

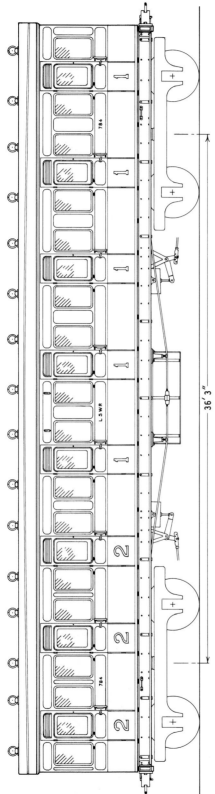

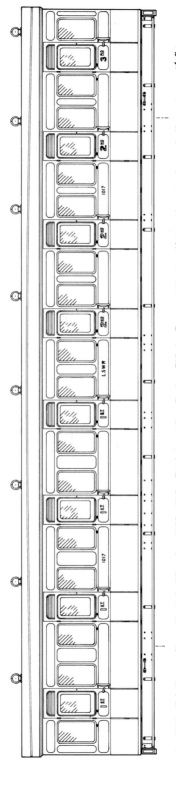

a. 51ft. Composite. This type was used in the first 73 sets, 1902-1905. Bogies as for Brake Third.

36' 3"

d. 51ft. Tri-Composite. Used in 72 sets, 1905-1912. Bogies as for Brake Third. Truss rods, couplings, etc. as above, battery boxes 5'4" long.

The Composites were marshalled with the Firsts nearest to the centre of each set.

0   5   10   15   20 feet

Figure 6.10
LSWR Block Sets of 1902-1912

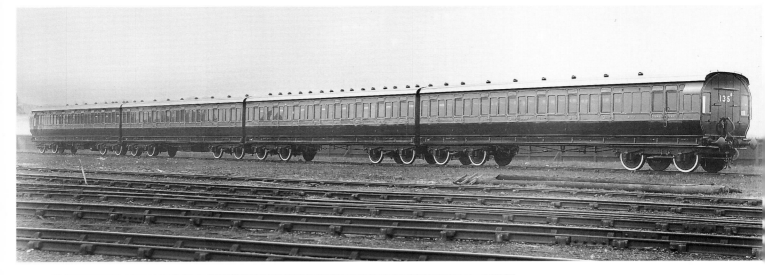

Plate 6.10b Bogie block set 135[B]. Note the dynamos and batteries under the far two carriages only. *National Railway Museum*

Plate 6.10c Bogie block Brake Third (Drawing 1129) at Horsley, 1 June 1925. Note the cover over the electric-light cable. *H. C. Casserley*

Plate 6.10d 'M7' class No 324 with bogie block set. *Real Photographs*

rather than the transverse elliptical ones used later and shown on the present drawings.

These sets had self-contained buffers and normal couplings on the brake ends, like the Brake Tri-Composites illustrated at Figure 6.9, but the four vehicles were virtually permanently close coupled together like the six-wheeled block sets of 1900 and 1901, described in Chapter 4 of the earlier volume and illustrated at Figure 4.36. As with those there was a nearly circular steel block between the headstocks that fixed the distance of 1ft 2in between the carriage bodies. A jointed drawbar passed through this block and was secured at each end, via India rubber shock absorbers, to the stretchers carrying the bogie centre castings. Each headstock was provided with wooden blocks that performed the function of dumb buffers when separated vehicles were being shunted around the works. In effect, the four vehicles formed a single (though flexible) unit, and any snatch or jolt was transmitted harshly throughout the train. It may well be for this reason that they were subject to a speed limit of 40mph.

Due to the close coupling, the brake pipes could not be connected between vehicles using the normal vertical end pipes and swan necks. Between these carriages the pipes were secured just below the headstocks to one side of the coupling, the flexible pipes connecting below the block coupling; this meant that the rest of the fixed pipe, which was secured as usual below the footboard on one side of the carriage, alternated from one side to the other along the set. When, in July 1904, it was decided to start fitting steam heating to these sets a similar arrangement had to be adopted, but of course criss-crossing to opposite sides of the vehicles.

The bogie block sets were allocated set numbers suffixed with a 'B', but unfortunately no actual list linking these numbers to vehicle numbers is available, though it is known that they started at 1ᴮ and ran, presumably, to 145ᴮ.

One very noticeable change was made in the lettering. Instead of the former 'FIRST', 'SECOND' or 'THIRD' on compartment door waist panels, the first few sets had '1', '2' or '3' in 12in-high numerals placed in the centre of the lower panels of the doors. Later on, and probably by 1910, these large numerals were replaced by '1st', '2nd' or '3rd', with the numerals almost filling the height of the waist panels.

Another change that must have been noticeable and welcome to passengers and the repair shops alike was the provision of Kayes' spring locks on the doors. Before this, in most cases, the locks had been simple latches that had to be closed either by a passenger or porter. Slamming such doors did not lock them; it merely damaged the lock and the door frame. The Kaye lock not only allowed the doors to be slammed shut but had a two-step latch, for safety. Whether it was coincidental or to mark this difference is not certain, but the door handles were now made as simple T-bars, though the Guard's doors still had the oval loop handles. Some photos show that the T-handles were not horizontal but were slightly inclined when in the normal locked position, though in much later days they seem to have been horizontal or nearly so.

Most of the sets were built with electric lighting, though the distribution of batteries and dynamos does not seem to have been uniform. This can be seen in the photograph, 6.10b, of set 135ᴮ (built in December 1910), where only one Brake Third and one Composite have batteries, while only one Brake Third appears to have a dynamo. Other photographs show different arrangements and the Appendix shows how vehicles were equipped at the time the Southern Railway took over. Even the LSWR drawings do not agree with photographs in this respect. At first, lighting switches were provided on one end of each carriage in the same fashion as the taps on gas-lit stock, but in November 1903, by which time 48 sets were in service, it was decided to fit switches in each guard's compartment to control all the lights on the train. This was to cost £16 per set for the extra wiring. At least six sets were fitted with gas lighting between 1905 and 1908 in connection with the argument over the economics of the two systems and the need to use up existing stocks of gas equipment, though I have not been able to identify fully which actual vehicles were concerned.

Evidence regarding the communication cords or chains is rather obscure. From the date of first building one would expect all of this stock to have had internal chains linked to the Automatic Vacuum Brake (AVB) system on every carriage, but the original LSWR drawing for the Brake Thirds shows where the holes were to be drilled for an external cord to enter the guard's compartment, just between the lookout and the door. None of the other drawings gives any indication of the system. In photograph 6.10a, set 9ᴮ, which was presumably an early set, in pristine condition and

Figure 6.11
Conversion of bogie block sets into 2-car Pull-Push sets.

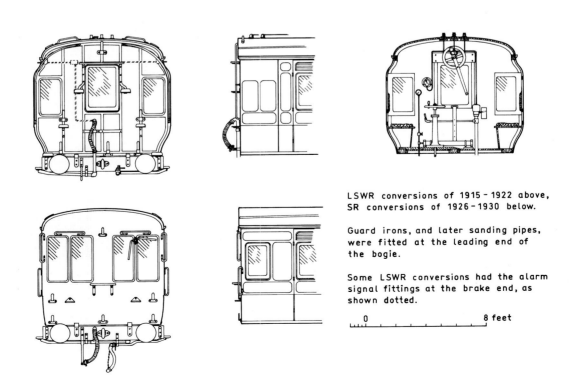

LSWR conversions of 1915 – 1922 above,
SR conversions of 1926 – 1930 below.

Guard irons, and later sanding pipes,
were fitted at the leading end of
the bogie.

Some LSWR conversions had the alarm
signal fittings at the brake end, as
shown dotted.

0   8 feet

displaying the early large class numbers on the doors, seems to have a 'butterfly' at the compartment end of the near Brake Third, but distance prevents any certainty about the others. The photograph of set 135ᴮ, which also appears to be in new condition, reveals no 'butterflies', except, possibly, on the brake end of the distant Brake Third. No explanation can be offered for these apparent inconsistencies. Later photographs definitely show a 'butterfly' on every carriage, but in the case of the Brake Thirds sometimes at the compartment end and sometimes at the brake end. In the latter cases the transverse rod is protected from anyone climbing the end steps by a half tubular cover.

Initially the carriages were fitted with the usual Laycock's 'Torpedo' ventilators, but, possibly around 1906, along with some of the new corridor designs, some sets were provided with Ash's 'Acme' type (sometimes called 'shell') ventilators. By the 1920s these were already being replaced piecemeal by smaller 'Torpedo' ones made of sheet steel.

Planning for electrification started in 1912 and this subject is covered in Chapter 7, but since it was the routes served by the block sets that would be the first to be electrified it was logical to convert the existing vehicles rather than to build new ones. Sixty-three block sets were progressively withdrawn for conversion in late 1914 and through 1915.

The remaining 82 sets were not to remain untouched for long. Two sets were split and formed into four two-car Pull-Push sets in 1915; the drawing for the modification is annotated: 'for Clapham Jct, Ludgate Hill, Kensington and Richmond services, and Cobham line services'. A subsequent note adds: 'and Tooting and Wimbledon line service'. However, a short article and photograph in the *South Western Gazette* for 1 February 1916 states: 'In December last the Company introduced Pull and Push trains on the Clapham Junction-Kensington-Richmond, Windsor-Woking, and Gosport-Fareham services. These trains consist of two-coach bogie set trains with a tank engine.' So the true facts are not quite clear.

The inclusion of Cobham refers to the fact that the 'new' line to Guildford had been electrified only as far as Claygate when World War 1 put a stop to the scheme and short trains were required as a shuttle between there and Guildford. Accordingly, at the end of 1916 two more bogie blocks were similarly treated. Then in 1922 a further block was split to form Pull-Push sets for the Swanage service. Either at the time of this last conversion or very shortly afterwards the two Brake Thirds, Nos 1257 and 1258, were reduced from seven to six compartments, thus providing the extra luggage space that would be required for a service to a holiday resort. The whole section between the double doors and the next remaining compartment was re-clad with seven panels of uniform width. These 10 sets were numbered 1ᴾ to 10ᴾ, and later became Southern sets 351 to 360.

The alteration to the Brake Third ends is shown in Figure 6.11. It followed the principle used for the two-car 'motor train' sets built in 1906 for the Plymouth district, described in Chapter 8. As in those, a duplicate regulator lever was provided. Attached to this was a drum, over which ran wires that then led through the roof, over pulleys and along to the locomotive, where they entered via the cab roof and were attached to a similar drum on the actual regulator. A third wire over the roofs operated the whistle. On the roofs these wires ran through triple guides, offset to pass the ventilators. Braking was effected via the AVB system; the works drawing is not entirely clear, but, in addition to the original guard's valve near one seat, there appears to be an additional valve near the other seat, the former shielded from accidental operation by a small casing. Provision also seems to have been made for some form of battery-and-bell signalling system between driver and fireman. Clearly there had to be close co-operation from the fireman on the locomotive, since the driver had no means of operating either the reverser or the steam brakes.

The most obvious external feature was a large central droplight, though doubtless the driver would often sit on one of the side seats once he had set the regulator. By this date, steam heating had been

Plate 6.11a Ex-block set Brake Third No 163 and Composite No 152, converted to Pull-Push in November 1916. *Author's collection*

Plate 6.11b Half bogie block set as Pull-Push Virginia Water-Weybridge shuttle, at Weybridge, 28 April 1921. The P-P wires can just be seen between locomotive and carriage, the latter a 51 ft ex-Tri-Composite (Drawing 1393). *H. C. Casserley*

Plate 6.11c 4-4-2T No 485 with half of a block set plus a 24 ft luggage van — not Pull-Push. *F. Moore / Ian Allan Library*

Plate 6.11d Bogie block Brake Third No 576 (Drawing 1129), altered to Push-Pull by the SR in 1930. *Author's collection*

provided in the carriages, and so a heater was fitted to keep his feet warm. To accommodate the size of the droplight the position of the end upper footsteps had to be altered. The end lamp brackets were capable of taking either carriage or locomotive lamps, having both a socket and a vertical tang. At least two of the Brake Thirds (No 640 and one of the Swanage ones), like several of the originals, had the brake alarm valve and 'butterfly' rodding at the brake end, whilst others did not.

A photograph of 'M7' class 0-4-4T locomotive No 481 has been published showing how the control wires were led from each end of a locomotive to pulleys on the cab roof. This photograph is a mild photographer's fake in that the locomotive is not coupled to a Pull-Push set but to an ordinary bogie block Brake Third; presumably the control wires were tied off to a ventilator out of the camera's view!

In May 1919, when the electric services were becoming overloaded, it was decided to withdraw six block sets and convert all the vehicles, including the Brake Thirds, to full Thirds, at an average cost of £500 each, and to use them to form twelve two-car trailer sets. This work did not proceed very quickly; probably Eastleigh Works was short of trained staff due to the recent war, and was heavily strained catching up with the backlog of repair work. In any event it was reported on 26 May 1921 that only 10 trailer sets had been completed. It was then agreed to take another three block sets and to convert them similarly. October 1922 saw the withdrawal of three more sets to form another six two-car electric trailer sets to provide for the Shepperton services, making 24 such sets in all.

Of the remaining block sets the Southern converted eight into 16 two-car Push-Pull sets (as they were by then described) between December 1926 and July 1930. The Brake Thirds only from a further block set were also similarly altered in November 1930 and coupled, using normal buffers and couplings, each to a 50ft Composite (LSWR Drawing 861, Volume One, Figure 5.21).

In their conversions the Southern dispensed with the lookouts on the Brake Thirds and rebuilt the end entirely, providing two pairs of tall fixed windows in the new sheet metal end panel and a droplight in each side. This alteration is also shown in Figure 6.11, though the dimensions have been derived by scaling from photographs. From these photographs it appears that the hand brake column was moved from the near- to the off-side (as viewed when driving) and that the vacuum brake pipe was extended so as to place the main brake valve on the driver's side. Incidentally, this end design was also used for Push-Pull conversions of 56ft and 46ft 6ins carriages as well as combination conversions onto 58ft underframes. The eight Brake Thirds that were converted in 1926 were reduced to six compartments so as to extend the luggage compartment, like the Swanage pair, but unlike them the windows, droplight and door vent were merely closed up with wooden panels. In 1924 one of the LSWR conversions, No 1836 (SR 2876), was altered for the Yeovil Junction-Yeovil Town shuttle. Doubtless the number of travellers between this large town and the main line would tend to have more luggage than was usual for a branch line, so two compartments were stripped out and the extended van section had a pair of double doors inserted, the arrangement being lookout, double doors, four panels, double doors, three panels (though Drawing 4245 called for four) and then five compartments.

The wire-control system survived on the LSWR-converted stock until after 1929, but the sets converted by the SR were fitted with the more efficient compressed-air system that had been standardised on the former SECR and LBSCR sections of the Southern. Instead of the wires over the roofs, this system required three flexible hoses passing under the headstocks, marked 'Regulator Control', 'Storage' and 'Back Pressure'.

In all cases where block sets were split, either for Pull-Push (P-P) or as Trailers, it was necessary to replace the close-coupling fittings at the new outer ends with self-contained buffers and normal couplings, similar to those on the Brake Thirds. Later photographs show several Southern P-P conversions of all types with small two-pin electrical sockets next to the lamp brackets.

The rest of the block sets remained on steam-hauled services until the Southern Railway converted them to form electric trains, usually on lengthened underframes, in the late 1920s.

The above is almost certainly not the whole story of the conversion and withdrawal of these block sets, but unfortunately the Minutes books and the Registers do not record all these events and dates in full detail. In particular, it is a pity that no official record has been discovered showing the actual set numbers of LSWR trains; very occasionally, sets are noted in the Registers, but otherwise information can be gleaned only from photographs, accident reports or suchlike.

The four-car block set trains were generally operated using either one or two such sets, but sometimes with one or more additional vehicles between two of them or added to the end. The *Waterloo Train Summary* for 1911/12 shows some examples:

4.50am	one block to Virginia Water with one bogie van to Weybridge
6.5am	two blocks to Kingston
8.25am	two Thirds and two blocks to Hampton Court
9.13am	(Sat excepted) one block to Kingston and one block with one van and one First to Teddington
1.15pm	(Sat only) one block, two Composites (4,4), one block and one van to Teddington
2.28pm	(Sat only) one Third, one First and one block to Guildford, and one block to Ascot
5.58pm	two blocks to Bookham
8.35pm	one block to Haslemere and one block to Guildford

The Waterloo to Haslemere journey is about the longest distance noted.

There is a rather curious minute of the Traffic Committee on 21 January 1903 concerning the half-year renewals of withdrawn stock. It is the first authorisation for corridor stock (28 vehicles that will be discussed in Chapter 9 on corridor carriages) but also includes 'ten bogie Composites with Guards Brake at each end'. The odd thing is that it also includes the statement that 'all thirty-eight vehicles to be 59 feet long and 8 feet 6¾ inches wide, but bases to be as at present'. There is no further reference to the question of length, but in fact all the carriages were built to a length of 56ft and width as stated.

The design for the 10 Brake Composites was shortened to 56ft through having only one Brake end in the usual manner, and they were built as Tri-Composites with two compartments of each class and a separate lavatory to each compartment, illustrated here at Figure 6.12. However, they were unique in being the only non-corridor carriages built at this width of 8ft 6¾ in. In most other respects as well they were similar to the corridor stock; the height of the windows and mid panels, and hence the height from the bottom of the body to the top of the cornice, was reduced by 2in but the total height from rail to centre of roof remained at 12ft. Also, as with corridor stock, the footboards were fixed at the mid height of the solebars instead of at the bottom. The requirement for the 'bases to be as at present' seems a bit meaningless as it presumably meant the underframes, which clearly could not be the same as for 51ft x 8ft 0¾ in carriages; in fact they were built entirely of steel instead of wood, or a wood and steel combination, and were 7ft 7in over the solebars — 4in wider than before. The solebars and headstocks were of 10in x 4in channel section, the transverse members of 10in x 3¼ in channel, together with steel strip and plate cross bracings, gusset pieces and angle brackets. Rather like the 51ft Brake Tri-Composite (Figure 6.9), due to the presence of the hand brake fittings the buffers at the brake end were sprung with Spencer's rubber blocks whilst those at the compartment end had transverse leaf springs. The rubber-sprung type may have been replaced later by self-contained ones.

It is one of these vehicles that is preserved at the National Railway Museum, so it will be seen that, to some extent, it is not typical of LSWR bogie carriages.

As the width over the body was increased, so was that over the lookouts, becoming 9ft 3in overall. Later, as with much of the corridor stock of similar dimensions, it was found that these lookouts were a loading gauge embarrassment, so they were replaced, at an unknown date, by small Southern Railway steel ones that reduced the width to just 9ft. The end itself was not rebuilt, so the end windows finished up narrower than they had been. It was probably at the same time that the width of the footboards was also shaved to give the same overall width.

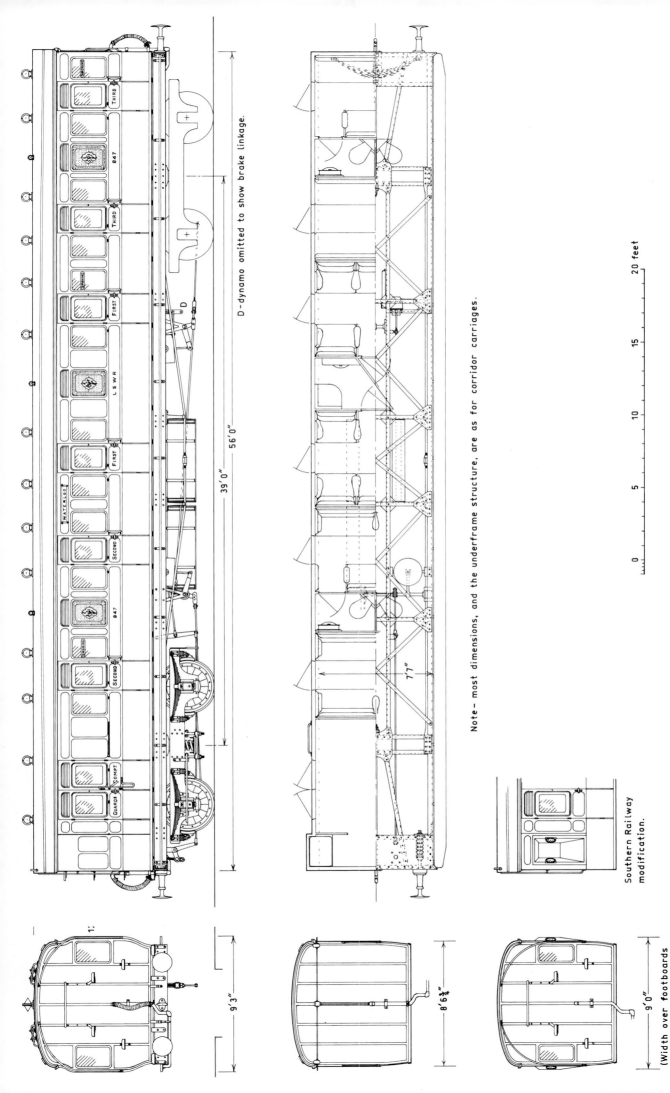

D-dynamo omitted to show brake linkage.

39'0"

56'0"

Note- most dimensions, and the underframe structure, are as for corridor carriages.

7'7"

Southern Railway
modification.

9'3"

8'6½"

9'0"

(Width over footboards
also reduced to 9'0".)

0   5   10   15   20 feet

Figure 6.12
LSWR 56ft Brake Tri-Composite of 1903.

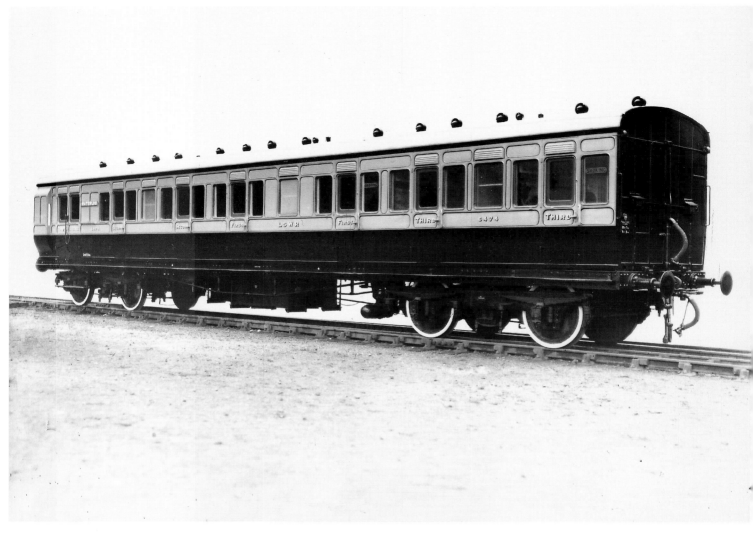

Plate 6.12a 56ft x 8ft 6¾in Brake Tri-Composite No 847 (drawing 1190) as restored by BR. *National Railway Museum*

Plate 6.12b 56ft Brake Tri-Composite (LSWR No 845, Drawing 1190) as BR No S6472 at Fareham in April 1948. Note the modified brake end. *J. H. Aston*

When the former No 847 was 'restored' for the Waterloo centenary, an LSWR-style lookout was stuck on each side but the end was not corrected. The appearance was somewhat odd, since there were both the SR narrowed end windows and the narrow slit windows in the lookouts — which were not even made to line up with the end of the carriage. Apparently it was a 'quick and cheerful' representation that has still (in 2000) not been corrected by the National Railway Museum.

In March 1904 two sets of another type of four-car train were authorised. These were described as 'four coach lavatory bogie block sets for general main line work', but in all further authorisations for this type the word 'block' was omitted. They were not close-coupled.

These sets consisted of two 56ft Brake Thirds to Drawing 1303 (Figure 6.13.I), with one each of the Composites to Drawings 1298 and 1302 (Figures 6.13.III and 6.13.IV respectively). Seven similar sets were authorised in December 1905, but the Brake Thirds were to Drawing 1446 (Figure 6.13.II), the difference being that the guard's position and lookouts were moved from the end to the centre of the vehicle, and the lookouts were made 3ft across instead of the usual 2ft 6in. More of these sets were built until, by the end of 1910, there were 39 of them in service. These carriages provided lavatory facilities for most of the First- and Second-class passengers and for about one third of the Third class. One small detail is that, while some of the earlier vehicles appear to have had lavatory windows incorporating the floral design, the later ones seem to have had frosted glass with either no pattern or a simple stipple. A slightly odd feature is that at least some of the Brake Thirds originally had no roof ventilators over the lavatories, relying solely on the top panel bonnet vents. Some of the later ones had no ventilators over the van section — only over the guard's part. An official drawing has a note that some of these carriages had Ash's 'Acme' ventilators, and one or two photographs show these. By the early 1920s some of the original ventilators had been replaced by smaller steel ones, even mixed on some carriages; still later photographs show some with a similar but 'squashed' type, and also some Brake Thirds with mushroom-headed ventilators over the lavatories.

The original authorisation described their purpose well and they could be encountered almost anywhere on the LSWR other than, generally, the suburban services and some minor country branches. Certainly, some photographs taken between 1905 and 1914 show them on such express services as London to Portsmouth, Bournemouth, Weymouth and North Devon. Most of these photographs show two sets, some with an extra luggage or brake van tacked on the end. However, as corridor stock became more common for main-line services, these sets naturally gravitated to the secondary routes and eventually became known as 'cross-country sets', though whether this was a railway or a train-spotter's term is not known. Referring again to the *Waterloo Train Summary* for 1911/12, here are some examples:

7.40am	four-coach set for Southampton Pier, one Third (Mon only) for Southampton, one bogie van for Bournemouth West, one bogie van for Portsmouth Town via Eastleigh, one Passenger Luggage Van (PLV) for Haslemere, one PLV for Aldershot, one PLV for Guildford, one PLV for Woking, one six-wheeled van for Surbiton
10.25am	four-coach set for Swanage via Bournemouth West, one First for Eastleigh, four-coach set for Salisbury
11.8am	four-coach set, two Tri-Compos, one van for Portsmouth Harbour via Woking, one First for Guildford
11.45am	four-coach set for Alton, one Third and one First for Aldershot, four-coach set for Petersfield
12.10pm	four-coach set for Ascot, one block for Godalming, one PLV for Virginia Water
2.0pm	four-coach set for Swanage, one corr. Third (Fri & Sat only), one corr. Compo (Sat only), four-coach set for Bournemouth West
2.45pm	four-coach set for Exeter, four-coach set and two Thirds (Sat only) for Basingstoke
7.10pm	two four-coach sets for Portsmouth Town via Woking

The only identifiable LSWR set numbers that have become known so far are No 63, which was involved in an accident at Vauxhall in August 1912, and Nos 61 and 66. The vehicles in these sets can be

Plate 6.13a 56ft Brake Third No 612 (Drawing 1303), for the first pair of four-car sets that had end lookouts, seen as No 102s (ex-SR No 2923) at Exmouth Junction, June 1948. *J. H. Aston*

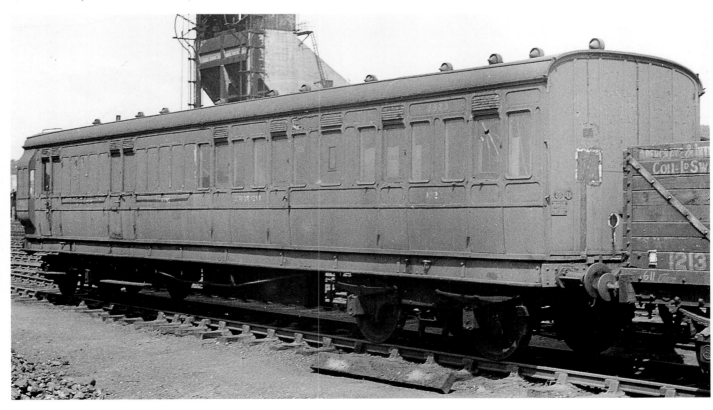

29

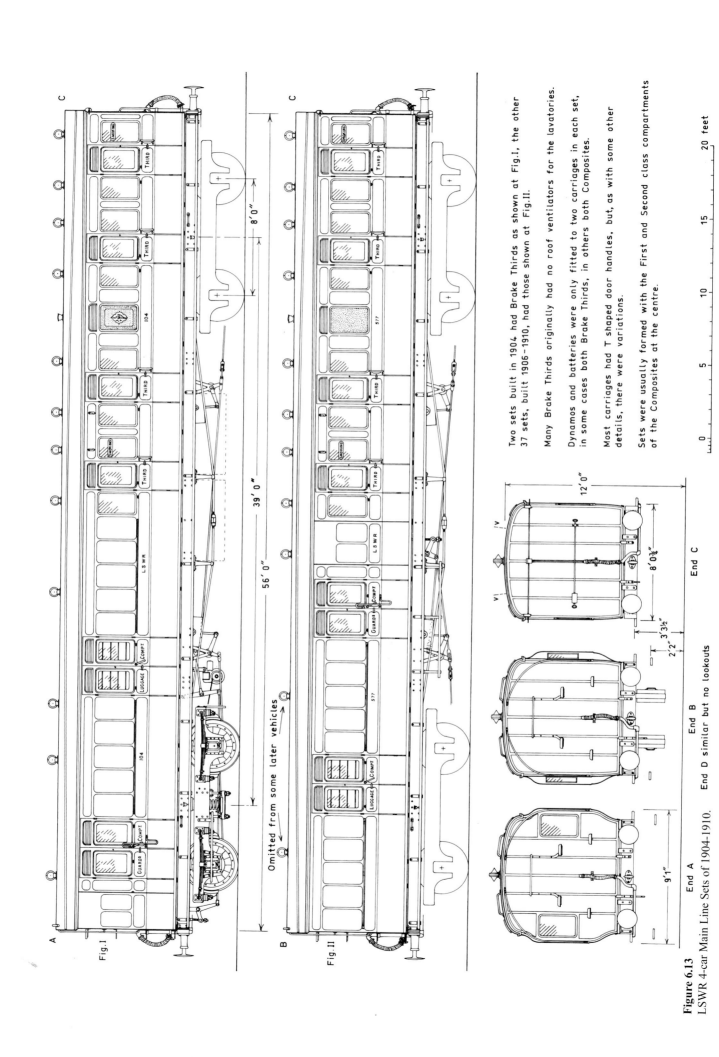

Two sets built in 1904 had Brake Thirds as shown at Fig.I, the other 37 sets, built 1906-1910, had those shown at Fig.II.

Many Brake Thirds originally had no roof ventilators for the lavatories.

Dynamos and batteries were only fitted to two carriages in each set, in some cases both Brake Thirds, in others both Composites.

Most carriages had T shaped door handles, but, as with some other details, there were variations.

Sets were usually formed with the First and Second class compartments of the Composites at the centre.

Fig.I

Fig.II

Omitted from some later vehicles

End A   End B   End C

End D similar but no lookouts

Figure 6.13
LSWR 4-car Main Line Sets of 1904-1910.

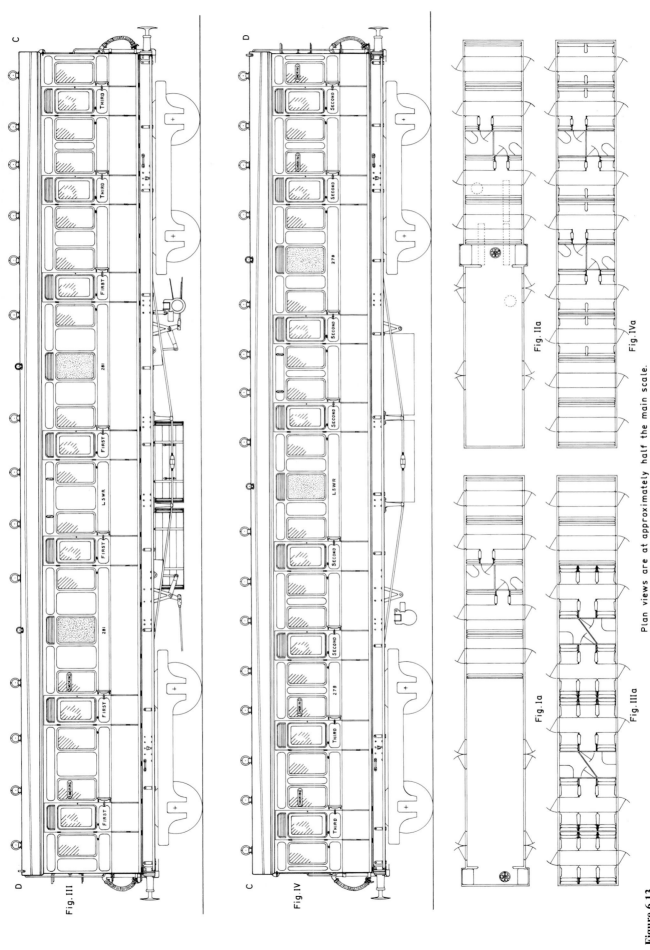

Figure 6.13
LSWR 4-car Main Line sets of 1904-1910.

Plan views are at approximately half the main scale.

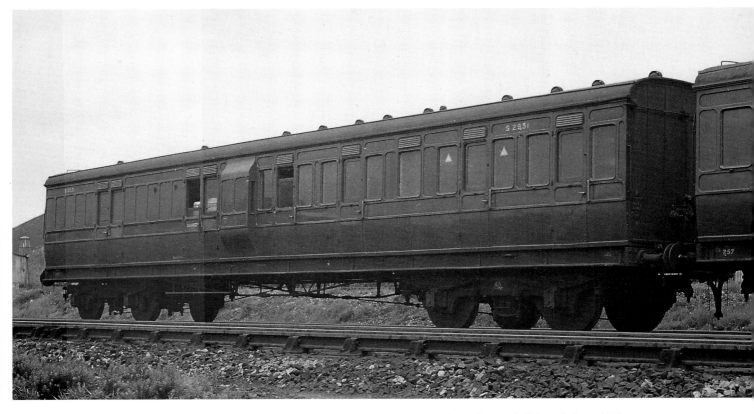

Plate 6.13b 56ft Brake Third No 1381 (Drawing 1446) as BR No S2931 in set 257, at Salisbury in June 1948. Note the lack of dynamos or batteries. *J. H. Aston*

found in the Appendix. It is one of the Brake Thirds, ex-LSWR No 1520 out of set No 63, that survived to be used by the Bluebell Railway as part of a fire-fighting train for many years and is, in 2000, being restored for passenger use with access facilities for the disabled. Some years ago the writer was able to sample the seating in this carriage; the narrowness of the single seat at the side of one of the lavatory doors led to an increased appreciation of the relative comfort afforded by the greater body width of modern carriages!

On 29 August 1912 set No 63 was at the rear of a nine-coach train from Aldershot to Waterloo, standing at the up through platform at Vauxhall. 'T9' 4-4-0 locomotive No 312 was running light-engine, tender first, up to Waterloo, but the driver mistook the signals and passed one at danger. In the resultant collision the tender was derailed and badly damaged, Brake Third 1519 was destroyed and the adjacent Composite, No 385, was considerably damaged. One passenger was killed. Rather oddly, the Brake Third was not written off the Register, the entry remaining unchanged, but photographs in the Hulton Library show it smashed apparently beyond repair. Presumably sufficient parts could be used in the replacement to satisfy the accountants!

One of the Drawing 1298 Composites was still in existence in recent years on the Kent & East Sussex Railway, having finished its British Railways service as a Camping Coach; this prompts the thought that if there was sufficient interest in carriages it would be possible to restore these two and bring them together to give a good representation of an LSWR train.

As with the suburban bogie block sets, only half of the vehicles in each set were provided with dynamos and batteries; in some sets it was both of the Brake Thirds and in other sets it was both of the Composites. The records contain no explanation for this variation. Most of the sets had internal wiring, but one or two high-level photographs taken in the 1930s or later show external wiring, covered by protective battens where it ran along the roofs. Whether some were built like this or whether it was merely the easiest way of replacing decayed wiring is not clear.

Between 1916 and 1920 the Second- and Third-class Composites to Drawing 1302 were all reclassified as entirely Third-class. Apart from this the sets remained in their original formations, at least until around 1936 when the SR set numbers shown in the Appendix were noted by Mr J. Cull and Mr M. F. Galpin. In nearly all cases the building dates of vehicles within the sets match up, so it seems unlikely that much 'swapping' had

occurred. However, at about the same time Mr Cull did notice three of the sets temporarily augmented with a mixed bag of vehicles, bringing them up to nine vehicles in the case of set 311 and to 10 in the cases of sets 313 and 324. Very shortly afterwards, many of the sets had the Third (former Drawing 1302 Composite) removed for a variety of other uses; they then remained as three-car sets until their withdrawal, two sets in fact surviving until as late as 1957. After withdrawal many of these vehicles, particularly the Brake Thirds, were taken into Departmental use, where some survived until the late 1960s.

Back in 1898 there had been trials of steam heating, initially with Laycock's storage system in which steam pipes fed heater elements in each compartment. These elements had an outer steam jacket and an inner tube containing a substance such as strong brine or acetate of soda that would hold heat for a considerable time. A valve admitted steam to heat the radiator and then at a predetermined temperature it closed, reopening when the temperature had dropped to a certain point; thus the maintenance of a steady steam pressure was not critical. Against this, the heaters could not be readily controlled, since they continued to give out heat long after they were turned off. In August 1900 it was reported that trials of the South Western's own system had proved satisfactory, and it was agreed that four trains for the West of England services should be fitted with it before the winter. In one of the Carriage Registers the column for steam heating has the name 'Drummond' against some vehicles; whether this referred to the LSWR system mentioned above or to yet another system is not clear.

Further carriages for specific services were given steam heating in the next year or two, and from 1903 all the new corridor stock was to be so fitted, but there was no mention of non-corridor trains. On 12 December 1906 the Locomotive, Carriage & Stores Committee approved a recommendation that four five-car sets in use for the Portsmouth-Bristol service be fitted with steam heating at a cost of approximately £375. Unfortunately they cannot be positively identified but they were probably the so-called '4½ sets' as described in Chapter 5 of the earlier volume. At the same time the Committee also agreed that all the carriage stock should be heated, but subject to the General Manager's consent! This was obviously given, since new stock was so fitted from about that time, but retrospective fitting naturally took quite a long while to complete. From the notes in the Register the majority of carriages had this work done between about 1908 and 1912.

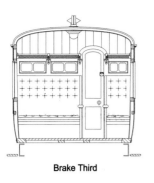

Brake Third

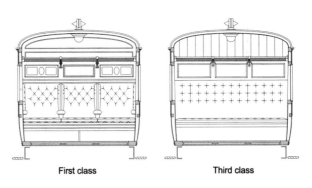

First class

Third class

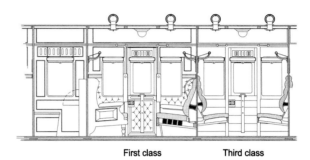

Figure 6.13 Sections

First class

Third class

Plate 6.13c 56ft Brake Third No 1516 (Drawing 1446) as BR No S2971 at Portsmouth, May 1949. *J. H. Aston*

Unlike the vacuum- and (when fitted) the air-brake pipes, which were usually run underneath the footboards, the steam-heating pipes were normally run below or within the underframe, curving round such obstructions as brake cylinders, etc. The main heating pipe was of 1½ in internal diameter with ½ in pipes connected by T-junctions to serve each heater tube, of which there were two in each compartment. All pipes were lagged to preserve the heat, and at least one drain cock was provided per vehicle. At the carriage ends the pipe was set to the right of the coupling (as viewed from the end) and angled downwards, again to assist drainage, and was fitted with a stop cock and flexible connector pipe. The heater tubes each had a control cock on the inlet, controlled through a linkage from a lever fitting on the partition above the seat back.

Each tube was angled slightly downwards from the inlet and a drain cock was fitted at the lower end. The design of the system was intended to give a compartment temperature not exceeding 55°F, but in practice the temperature could vary very widely. Steam pressure was intended to be 25lb/sq in normally, with a maximum of 50lb/sq in.

Heating was only considered necessary between the end of September and the beginning of May in each year, and so the Carriage Department had instructions to remove the flexible connecting hoses during the summer periods. When heating was in use trains were to be warmed up well before departure time, preferably on the empty working from the sidings. The inward locomotive had to remain coupled until the outward one was

33

Plate 6.13d 56ft Composite No 383 (Drawing 1298) as BR No S5048 in set 144, at Portsmouth in May 1949. *J. H. Aston*

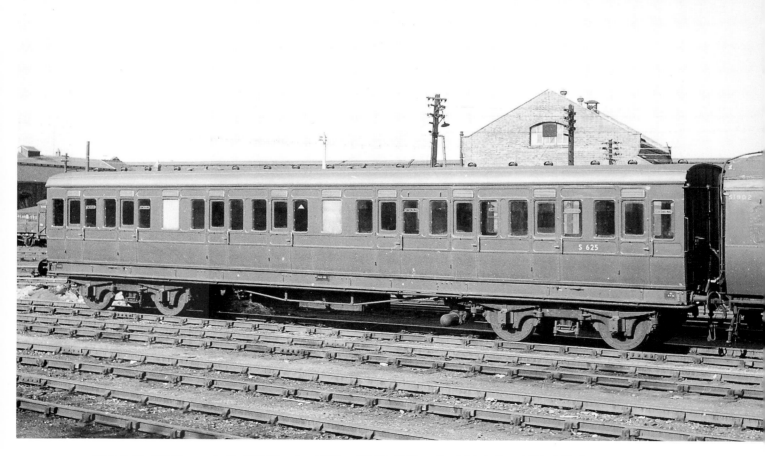

Plate 6.13e 56ft Composite No 389 (Drawing 1302) as BR No S625, at Eastleigh in June 1951. *J. H. Aston*

Plate 6.13f 'N15' No 753 passing Esher on a Waterloo-Bournemouth 'special'. Included in the consist is a four-car lavatory set. *Lens of Sutton*

Plate 6.13g 'U' class No 1796 near Winchfield in August 1937. The train consists of a four-car lavatory set, three 'loose' carriages, a three-car set of 56ft Brake Thirds (to Drawing 1396) and a 58ft rebuild. *Author's collection*

Plate 6.13h Accident at Vauxhall, 28 August 1912. On the right is Brake Third No 1519; on the left is Composite No 385 of set 63. Attending the scene is Nine Elms breakdown crane No 5. *Ian Allan Library*

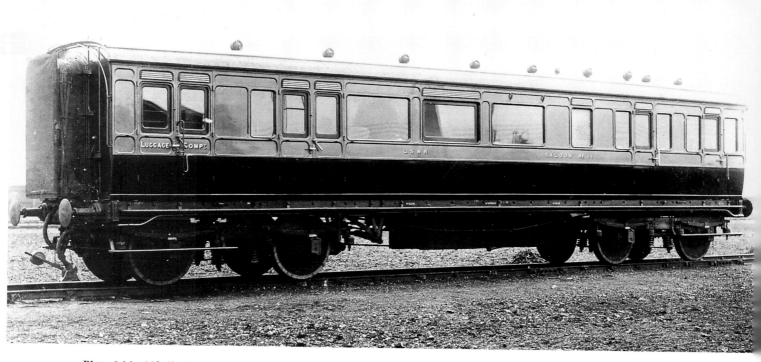

Plate 6.14a 46ft 6in Invalid Saloon No 11 (Drawing 1906). *HMRS*

Plate 6.14b Interior of 46ft 6in Invalid Saloon No 11. *Railway Mechanical Engineer Vol 1*

ready. On first connecting up the heating, the guard had to open the cock at the rear of the last carriage until steam and any accumulated water were discharged, then close it sufficiently to leave just the barest whiff of steam flowing. This had to be checked at station stops to ensure that heating was getting right through the train.

By 1906 it was apparently deemed to be time for some more saloons and so plans for three different types were drawn up. On 13 June 1906 two of the first type were authorised. These were fitted out specifically for the comfort of invalids, and were known as Invalid Saloons. With the intention that they should be able to go anywhere in England, Scotland or Wales (the Tunbridge Wells-Hastings line of the South Eastern & Chatham Railway was forbidden to them), they were built to the same dimensions as the 'Emigrant stock' described in Chapter 9, which is to say with a body length of 46ft 6in, width of 8ft 3¾ in and height from rail to roof of 11ft 8½ in. Of course, they had to be provided with both Automatic Vacuum and Westinghouse brakes, but they also had hand brakes as well. Lighting was by electricity.

The saloon occupied nearly half the length of the carriage, and contained four lounge chairs and a long couch. The ends of this couch could be adjusted to form a bed or support a stretcher; alternatively, if it was considered necessary, there was room to install a normal bed. Double doors with an inside width of 3ft 11in were provided to this saloon to permit moving a stretcher, a Bath chair or an Invalid chair. As with some other Family Saloons there were also compartments for First class, Second class and luggage, as well as a lavatory. The saloon and the First were fully carpeted, and the panelling was of satinwood with oak banding. Figured moquette with a groundwork of old gold colour was used for the upholstery. The Second-class (or attendants') compartment had linoleum and a mat on the floor, whilst the panelling, as in the corridor and lavatory, was in light plywood with mahogany framing. The underside of the body was planked, and the space

between that and the floor was packed with sawdust to reduce noise. The body was mounted on rubber cushions instead of wooden spacers.

The bogie bolster suspension was modified, apparently in an attempt to give a softer ride. The ends of the bolsters rested, through 'U'-brackets, on castings, the ends of which in turn rested on top of coil springs on the swing links. Apart from a few of the Dining Saloons built in 1907, no other carriages seem to have had this suspension, so presumably it did not give the required results. By or during Southern days, these bogies appear to have been replaced by the type used on most other carriages of the 1900s.

Two more Invalid Saloons to substantially the same design were authorised on 14 April 1910, the main difference from the earlier two being the provision of gangway connections (which reduced the seating in the end compartment by two). The two variants were built to Drawings 1593 and 1906 respectively, and are illustrated together in Figure 6.14. Apart from the gangway connections, another small difference was that the earlier pair had Ash's 'Acme' ventilators on the roof whereas the later two reverted to 'Torpedo' ventilators. Lower footboards on both bogies and a waist handrail at one end were fitted to the later pair but not to the earlier ones. One of the second pair, No 11, was transferred in 1938 to the Longmoor Military Railway, where, together with a somewhat similar ex-SECR saloon and a smaller (but exquisite) open-balconied ex-LNWR saloon, it was used as an officers' car until the closure of that line. It then went to the Severn Valley Railway for some years, where sadly it suffered considerable deterioration. Later it was moved to the Kent & East Sussex Railway, where it was restored, and from the mid-1990s was frequently used in a 'Vintage' train.

The other two types, authorised on 16 December 1907, were two 48ft Picnic Saloons to Drawing 1746 and a 51ft Double Family Saloon to Drawing 1758. These were all completed

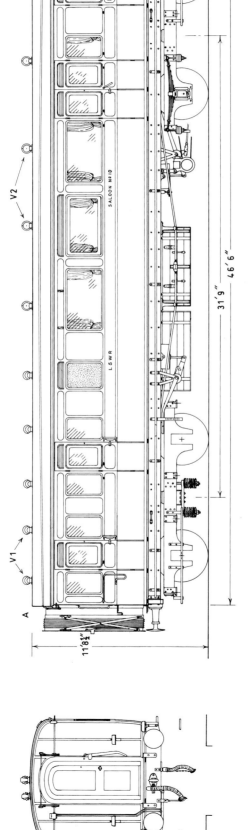

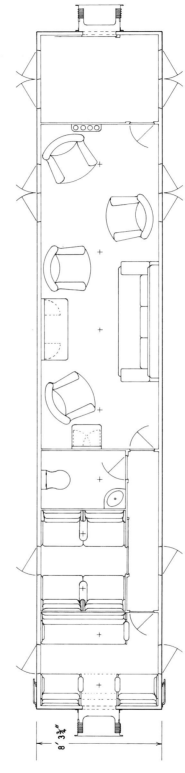

1. This drawing combines features of both the 1907 and 1910 versions.

2. Nos. 9 & 10, built in 1907, had no gangways, no bogie footboards, no handrail at end A, nor grab handles on the luggage doors. They had Ash's "Acme" ventilators, as at V1. The alarm indicator, valve and piping were at end B. 7 Second class seats.

3. Nos. 11 & 12, built in 1910, had gangways, footboards, handrails and alarm indicators as shown. Ventilators were Laycock's "Torpedo" type, as at V2. 5 Second class seats, as shown.

4. Window and panel heights are as for the 46ft. 6ins. corridor stock.

Figure 6.14
LSWR 46ft 6in Invalid Saloons of 1907 and 1910.

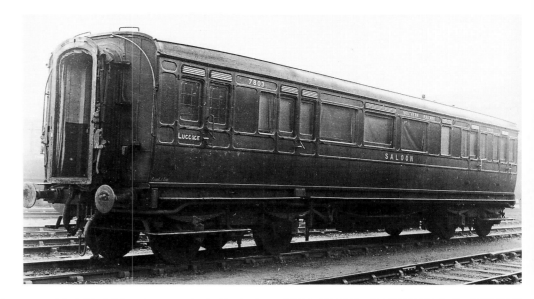

Plate 6.14c 46ft 6in Invalid
Saloon No 11, as SR No 7803.
R. C. Riley

Plate 6.14d 46ft 6in Invalid
Saloon No 11 as BR No 119 at
Longmoor, September 1949.
D. Cullum

Plate 6.15 48ft Picnic Saloon
of 1902, LSWR No 32,
drawing 1746.
J. Tatchell Collection

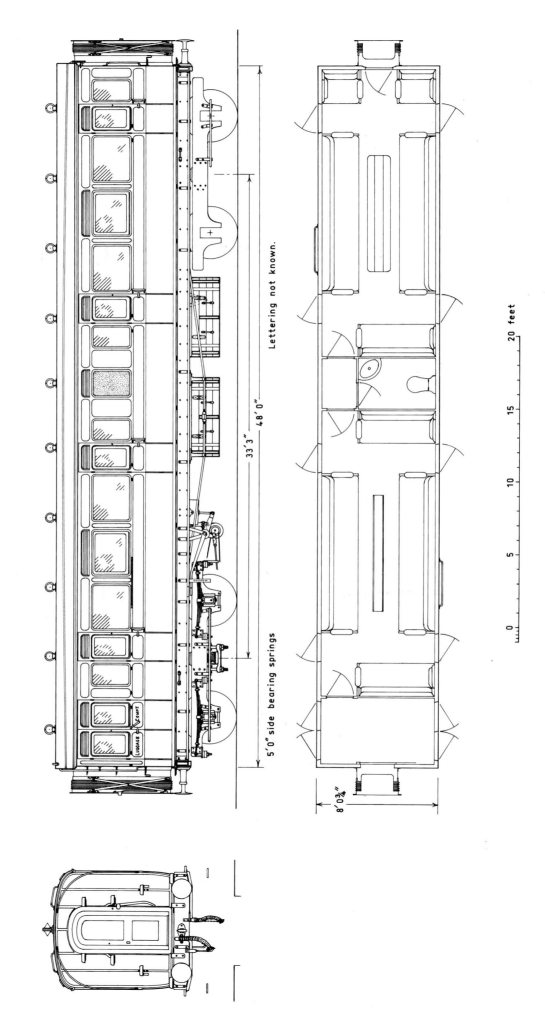

Lettering not known.

48' 0"

33' 3"

5' 0" side bearing springs

LUGGAGE COMPT

8' 0¾"

20 feet

Figure 6.15
LSWR 48ft Picnic Saloon of 1908.

towards the end of 1908. Both types had a sliding connecting door between the two saloon compartments, and also had gangway connections; however, it seems appropriate to include them among non-corridor stock, since there was no separate passageway and they were almost certainly not intended to be placed in the middle of corridor trains where other passengers would be likely to intrude, the purpose of the connecting doors and gangways being to allow the saloon hirers to call the Dining Car attendants, using the bell pushes that were fitted in each compartment.

The Picnic Saloons, illustrated at Figure 6.15, each had only one small luggage compartment and a lavatory shared between the two saloon compartments. The floors were covered with linoleum and the seats upholstered with repp (a thick corded ribbed material of silk or wool, or a mixture of both, used for curtains and upholstery — Waverley dictionary). There were no separate seating compartments, unlike the First-class Double Saloon that is shown in Figure 6.16. It was still the practice of the wealthier large families to hire such saloons for their travels, and for this purpose each saloon compartment had its own associated lavatory, luggage compartment and a four-seat compartment in which presumably the head of the family could get away from the hubbub of the women and children! In this carriage the floor was carpeted and the seats covered in figured moquette. Both types had wooden underframes, were provided with left-handed hand brake levers, were electrically lit and steam-heated, though in this latter respect they did not follow the general scheme as mentioned above in that the steam pipe ran along under the footboard on the opposite side from the vacuum pipe. The only photograph that has come to light so far is Plate 6.15 showing part of 48ft Saloon No 32, but there is nothing to indicate what the LSWR lettering arrangement was.

The next type of carriage to be authorised, on 14 April 1910 along with the gangwayed 46ft 6in Invalid Saloon, was another variant of the 56ft Brake Third, with four compartments and a lavatory. The first batch was of 20, built to Drawing 1936 (Figure 6.17a). Further batches followed, and between December 1910 and February 1912 a total of 50 was built. The first 26, built before the end of May 1911, were gas-lit. From a Minute dated 7 October 1915 it is evident that they were formed into 13 four-car sets (Nos 1 to 9 and 408 to 411), since that Minute specifies the set numbers when requiring that they should be converted to electric lighting. The remainder were built with electric lighting, though the authorising Minute stated that they 'require no lighting plant', so they were intended to rely on the centre vehicles, like many of the other suburban and main-line four-coach sets. Photographs in Southern days show at least some of them with normal battery sets. In the passenger section they were similar to the Drawing 1446 Brake Thirds already described for the four-car lavatory sets, but instead of normal double doors to the luggage compartment they had two large sliding doors on each side, and the lookouts were the usual 2ft 6in across.

Notes in the Carriage Register state that the first eight built were assigned to the Portsmouth to Cardiff service, but there is nothing to show which carriage was in which set.

Although they were built so as to form set trains, no other matching vehicles were ordered at the same time. An official photograph in the National Railway Museum shows two of these new gas-lit Brake Thirds coupled up with a pair of electrically-lit Composites to Drawings 1298 and 1302. I have been unable to find any other evidence of this combination, and it seems almost certain that the vehicles were posed together for the photograph and that the Composites were restored to their normal Brake Thirds afterwards. There are one or two other instances of this type of mild photographic deception, so one has to be wary even of official photographs! In fact, from other photographs, they seem to have been formed into four-car sets using 48ft vehicles, usually Composites to Drawing 650 or 758, or occasionally a 48ft Composite and a 50ft Composite.

As with the preceding four-car sets, these sets seem to have been reduced to three cars in about the late 1930s, and in some cases the centre carriage was lengthened on to a Southern Railway 'standard' 58ft underframe. At about this time the footboards of many of these and similar sets were raised to the same height as those on the SR underframes, ie along the centre line of the

solebars. The existing brackets were retained but wooden blocks were inserted, a detail very evident on several photographs. There is a photograph taken in April 1950, a year before withdrawal, which shows set 111 reduced to just two of these Brake Thirds.

Another authorisation that poses questions as to precise use is that of 17 November 1910 for 10 56ft Brake Tri-Composites with lavatories, 'to form ten two-car set trains to replace the three-coach sets now running', at a total cost of £8,500. The three-coach sets were presumably four- or six-wheelers used on branch lines, possibly Brake Third, Composite, Brake Third. The new carriages were to Drawing 1996 (Figure 6.18) and were followed by an order for six more on 15 May 1911, the completions running from September 1911 to May 1912.

The Second- and Third-class compartments were of the same size, which might suggest anticipation of the abolition of Second class, but the furnishings still differed considerably. In the Seconds the body sides and doors were still upholstered, and armrests were provided at the sides and centre, whereas the Thirds were devoid of armrests except at the seat ends by the lavatory door, the linings of the sides and doors being of painted wood in the usual manner. A class distinction also still existed in the lavatory doors: those from the First class were 1ft 10in wide, from the Second 1ft 8in and from the Third a mere 1ft 6in. Whilst all the lavatories and wash basins were now made of chinaware, the decorative wood casings enclosing them not surprisingly repeated the usual differences of finish in the compartments.

The van section of these vehicles was quite short, but of course most of the bogie Brake Thirds that could have been paired with them, whether 48ft, 50ft or 56ft, had quite large vans. It has not been possible positively to identify any of these two-car sets by numbers, but one photograph taken in LSWR days and another after Grouping show one of the Brake Composites paired with a 48ft Brake Third to Drawing 606, whilst the *Appendix to Carriage Working Notices* for June 1947 shows nine of them in ordinary two-car sets and six as Driving Trailers in Push-Pull sets. All of these are shown as paired with 58ft Brake Thirds rebuilt from 48ft Composites, ex-Drawing 650, although there is a photo of one of them, SR No 6488, paired with an ex-SECR vehicle rebuilt on a 58ft frame. The conversion to Driving Trailers involved the provision of four large windows in the end, removal of the lookouts, and installation of droplights in their place, much like the Push-Pull conversions of bogie block sets described earlier.

Up until 1906 the South Western had generally used Laycock's cast-iron 9in-high 'Torpedo' ventilators, but, as will be mentioned again when dealing with corridor carriages, it then started using Ash's 'Acme' ones for a few years. These were apparently not entirely satisfactory, so it reverted to the 'Torpedo' type, sometimes from Laycock but also using its own, smaller, fabricated-steel version. The original drawing for these Brake Tri-Composites shows the usual large type, but there is a note, confirmed by the overall vehicle height, that the 'shallow ventilators' were to be used instead; in this case they were 6¼ in high. Being of sheet steel they naturally did not last as well as the cast-iron ones, and several photographs of these and other carriages show some ventilators replaced by a later Southern type that has the appearance of having been squashed.

The last type of non-corridor carriage to be designed by the LSWR was another version of the four-compartment 56ft Brake Thirds with lavatories. Between 1910 and 1912 there were at least five authorisations of carriages to this description, but the total number of vehicles mentioned is less than those actually built, and there is no distinction in the Minutes between those previously described and these last ones. However, these carriages were built to Drawing 2040 (Figure 6.17b) and differed from the previous type in having only one large sliding door on each side of the luggage compartment instead of two; otherwise they were very similar. Again, there is no indication of whether they were intended to be made up into specific sets; however, the LSWR *Appendix to Rules & Regulations* for July 1921 details a Metropolitan Railway notice forbidding the use of four-coach lavatory sets with 56ft Brake Thirds — trains numbers 1 to 73 — from working via Ludgate Hill and King's Cross, St Pancras or Kentish Town, as well as some other vehicles and all 52ft, 54ft and 56ft corridor carriages. Since the three types of 56ft non-

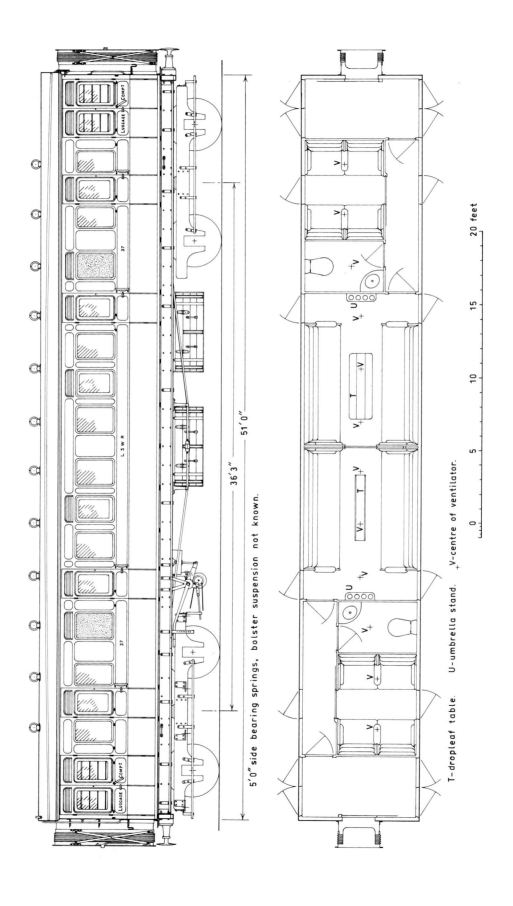

L S W R

37

37

LUGGAGE COMPT

LUGGAGE COMPT

36'3"

51'0"

5'0" side bearing springs, bolster suspension not known.

T-dropleaf table. U-umbrella stand. V-centre of ventilator. +-centre of ventilator.

V   T

V   T

U

U

0   5   10   15   20 feet

Figure 6.16
LSWR 51ft Double Family Saloon of 1908.

Plate 6.17a 56ft Brake Third (LSWR No 650, Drawing 1936) as SR No 3048 in set 108, at Plymouth Friary in July 1948. *J. H. Aston*

Plate 6.17b 56ft Brake Third (LSWR No 84, Drawing 1936) as SR No 3000 in set 108, at Plymouth Friary in July 1948. *J. H. Aston*

Plate 6.17c Ex-SECR 'N' class locomotive with ex-LSWR train. In order, the carriages are: 56ft Brake Third (Drawing 1936), 48ft Bi-Composite (Drawing 758), 48ft Tri-Composite (Drawing 650), 56ft Brake Third (Drawing 1936), unidentified 46ft 6in 'Emigrant' carriage, 48ft Brake Third (Drawing 606), 48ft Tri-Composite (Drawing 650), 51ft Brake Tri-Composite (Drawing 1122) and 46ft 6in 'Emigrant'. *H. G. Tidey / Lens of Sutton*

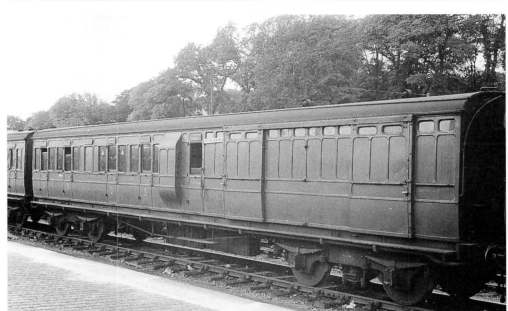

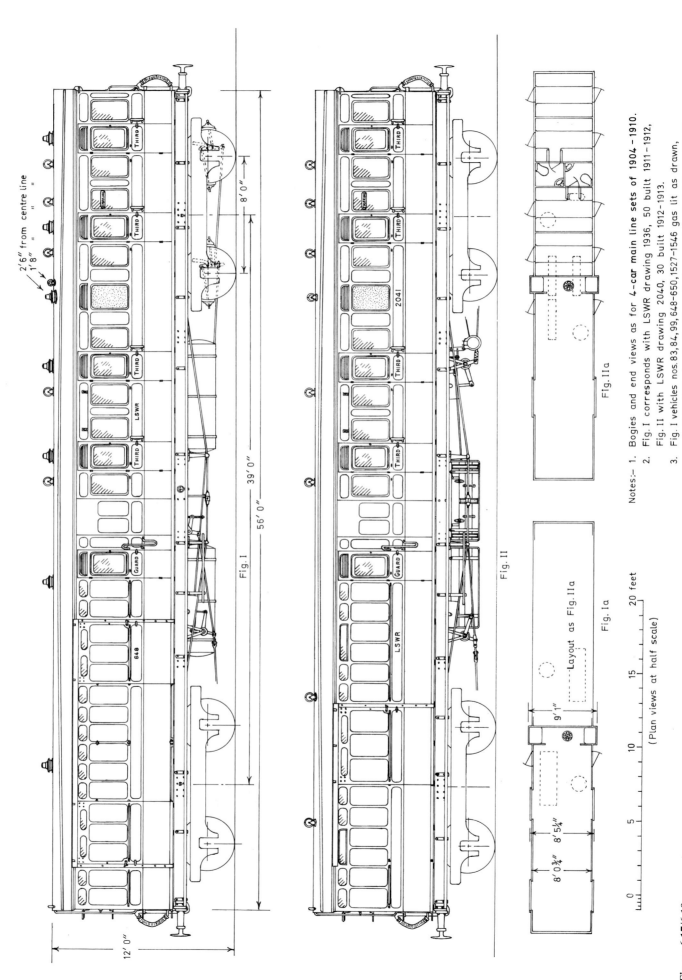

2'6" from centre line
1'8"

8' 0"

THIRD

THIRD

LSWR

THIRD

GUARD

648

39' 0"

56' 0"

12' 0"

Fig. I

THIRD

THIRD

2041

THIRD

GUARD

LSWR

Fig. II

Fig. IIa

Fig. Ia

Layout as Fig. IIa

9' 1"

8' 0¾" 8' 5¼"

(Plan views at half scale)

0   5   10   15   20 feet

Notes:- 1. Bogies and end views as for 4-car main line sets of 1904–1910.
2. Fig. I corresponds with LSWR drawing 1936, 50 built 1911–1912,
    Fig. II with LSWR drawing 2040, 30 built 1912–1913.
3. Fig. I vehicles nos. 83,84,99,648–650,1527–1546 gas lit as drawn,
    nos. 1548–1571 electrically lit, underframe and roof details as Fig. II.

Figure 6.17/6.19
LSWR 56ft Brake Thirds of 1911-1913.

44

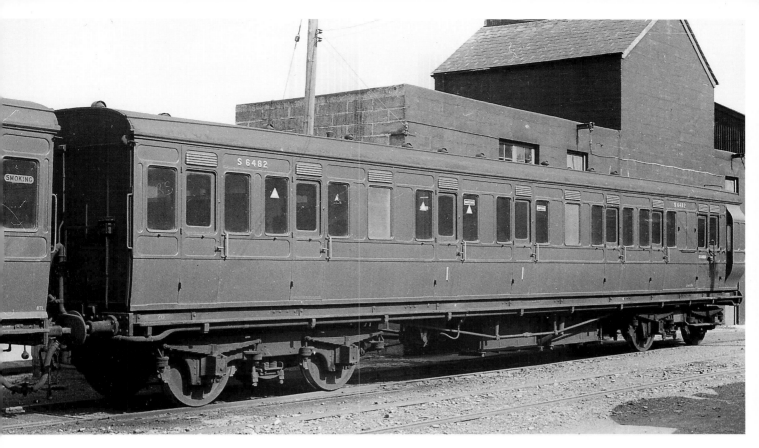

Plate 6.18a and 6.18b 56ft Brake Tri-Composite (LSWR No 408, Drawing 1996) as BR No S6482 at Padstow, 28 May 1950. *Both J. H. Aston*

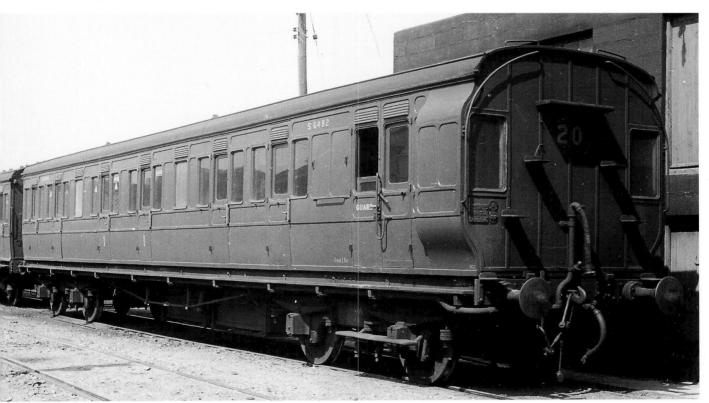

corridor lavatory Brake Thirds totalled 158, it is evident that nearly all were in four-coach sets.

Photographs taken in Southern days show the last type in various forms. These include four-car sets, with two 48ft Composites — one to Drawing 650 and one to Drawing 758 (or in one case a 50ft Composite to Drawing 861 and a 48ft one to Drawing 712) — and three-car sets, with a 48ft Composite to Drawing 1051 or a 58ft rebuilt Drawing 758 Composite.

Six of them were converted to Driving Trailers for Push-Pull working in 1939. For this purpose the sliding doors were removed and replaced by panelling to match the existing panels, four large windows being provided in the driving end as for the SR Push-Pull conversion of some bogie block set vehicles (Figure 6.11). In this form they were paired with 58ft Composites rebuilt from 48ft Drawing 758 Composites. A total of 30 of these Brake Thirds was built between May 1912 and June 1913. After this date all new carriage construction was of corridor vehicles.

Plate 6.18c 56ft Brake Tri-Composite (Drawing 1996) as converted to Push-Pull Brake Composite. *A. E. West*

Plate 6.18d 56ft Brake Tri-Composite (LSWR No 1024, Drawing 1996), converted to Push-Pull in June 1937, as BR No S6488 at Fareham, 24 June 1950. *D. Cullum*

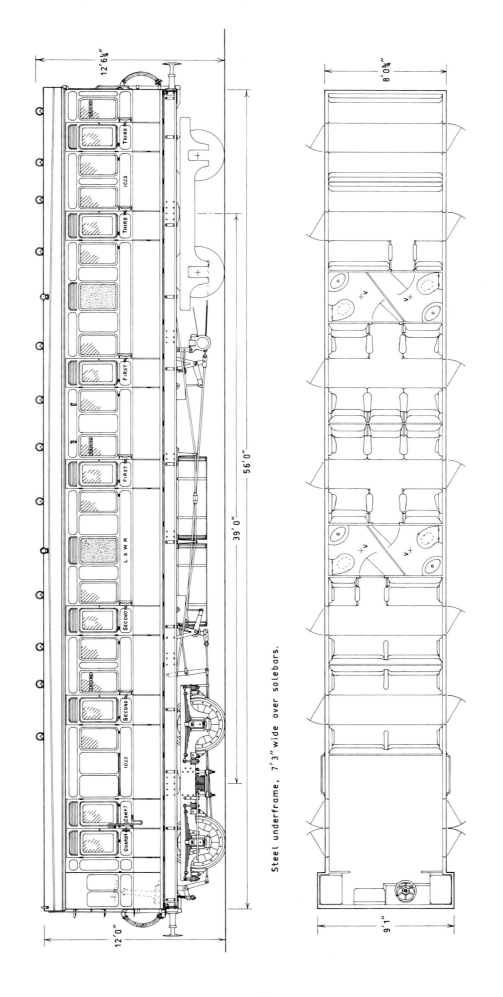

Steel underframe, 7'3" wide over solebars.

Figure 6.18
LSWR 50ft Brake Tri-Composite of 1911.

Plate 6.19a 56ft Brake Third (LSWR No 1586, Drawing 2040) as BR No S3057 at Eastleigh, June 1950. *D. Cullum*

Plate 6.19b 'T6' class No 681 with a train including 56ft Brake Third (Drawing 2040), 50ft Composite (Drawing 861), 48ft Tri-Composite (Drawing 712) and 56ft Brake Third (Drawing 2040). *Lens of Sutton*

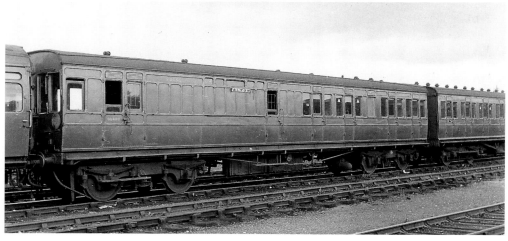

Plate 6.19c 56ft Brake Third (LSWR No 1584, Drawing 2040) as altered to Push-Pull in 1939, pictured at Eastleigh as BR No S3055 in June 1950. *D. Cullum*

Chapter 7

ELECTRIC TRAINS

The first London terminus of the London & Southampton Railway was opened at Nine Elms in 1838. This was partly due to the high cost of getting nearer to the centre of London combined with the uncertain nature of the traffic to be expected. Some provision was made for the connection in the opening notices which announced that arrangements had been made with the London & Westminster Steamboat Co that steamboats would be provided for conveying passengers between Nine Elms, Dyers Hall Wharf (Upper Thames Street) and Hungerford Market. Omnibuses would also be provided between Nine Elms and the 'Spread Eagle, Gracechurch Street, 'Swan With Two Necks', Lad Lane, 'Cross Keys', Wood Street, 'White Horse', Fetter Lane, 'George & Blue Boar', Holborn, 'Golden Cross', Charing Cross, and Universal Office, Regent Circus, Piccadilly.

Pressure to extend nearer to the centre, and particularly towards the City of London, grew quickly and resulted in the extension to Waterloo in 1848, as well as in further plans to extend to London Bridge. These fell through in the slump that followed the period of Railway Mania, but there was always a need to improve the connection between Waterloo and the City. The opportunity came with the development of underground electric railways.

The first underground railways, those of the Metropolitan and District companies, were steam operated, but of course these were sub-surface lines where there could be ventilation gaps to the open air. When deeper tunnels were needed, both to get under the River Thames and to avoid massive expense and disruption of surface streets and buildings, electric traction was the only practicable method, although cable haulage was originally planned for what was later to become the City & South London Railway. This line, opened in 1890, was the first passenger electric underground railway in the world, using small electric locomotives to haul rakes of three carriages.

The City & Waterloo Railway, quickly renamed the Waterloo & City Railway, was set up as an independent company, though it had the strong backing of the London & South Western. At the time it was planned all underground railways needed to follow the line of streets, so far as was possible, in order to minimise the high cost of wayleaves and damage claims from the owners of surface properties. Thus there were (and still are) some rather tight curves on the line which soon caused constraints to be placed on the operation of the trains. When it opened on 8 August 1898 it became the second underground electric railway, but the first to use motor-powered carriages instead of locomotives. Later, in January 1907, after the line had been completed and was operating successfully, it was incorporated into the LSWR.

The only LSWR drawings known to have survived are an outline sketch, apparently prepared late in 1898, showing a proposed conversion of the original motor cars to non-driving trailers, and a general arrangement for the construction of some extra trailers in 1922. There are also the usual LSWR plan diagrams in the Diagram Book. Copies of the sketches that accompanied the invitations to tender still exist but they do not bear a very close resemblance to the vehicles as built. A lot of drawings accompanied the papers placed before the Institution of Civil Engineers by Harley Hugh Dalrymple-Hay and Bernard Maxwell Jenkin in November 1899. These largely cover the tunnel and electrical works but there are several dealing with the

Plate 7.1a Waterloo & City Railway motor car No 1 at Jackson & Sharp's works, Wilmington, USA.
Courtesy of ACF Industries Inc

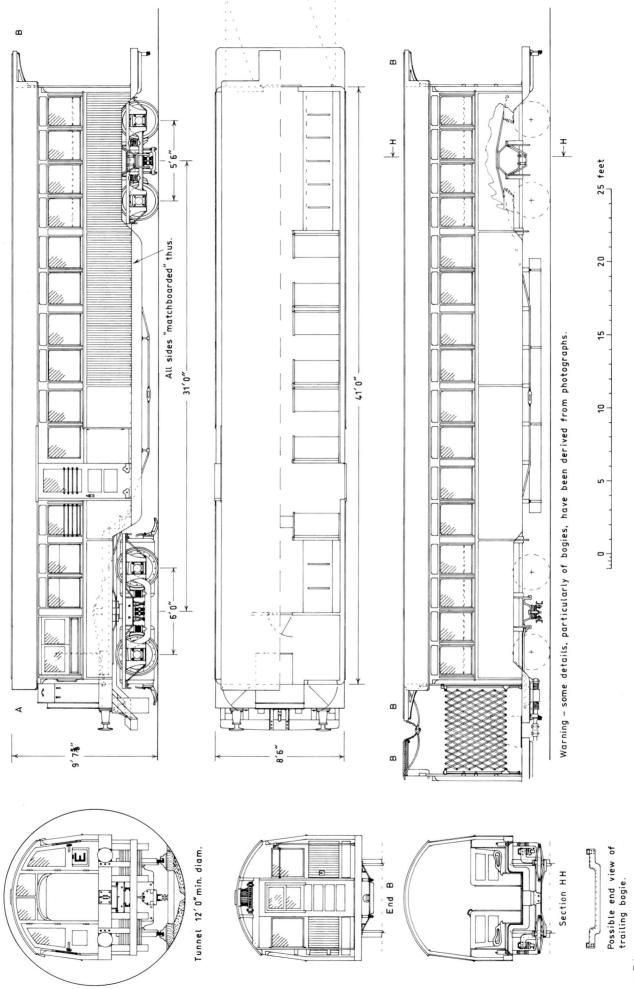

All sides "matchboarded" thus.

31'0"

5'6"

6'0"

9'7⅝"

41'0"

8'6"

Tunnel 12'0"min. diam.

End B

Section H H

Possible end view of
trailing bogie.

Warning − some details, particularly of bogies, have been derived from photographs.

0   5   10   15   20   25 feet

Figure 7.1
Waterloo & City Railway, 1898 stock.

Plate 7.1b Interior of Waterloo & City car No 1 at Jackson & Sharp's works. Note the fitting of luggage racks, not seen in later photographs. *Courtesy of ACF Industries Inc*

rolling stock, though these concentrate on the electrical aspects, and some of the bodywork details are not entirely reliable.

Technical journals of the time, such as *Railway Engineer*, *The Electrical Review* and *Tramway and Railway World*, carried substantial articles about the line, but again mainly concerning the civil engineering, signalling and the electrical equipment, including the Waterloo power station, but with relatively little about the rolling stock, presumably because it was of American design and construction!

The original rolling stock consisted of five four-car trains, with two spare motor cars. One American and seven British rolling stock companies expressed an interest in tendering after the first outline specification was issued in November 1896. Railway Carriage Co of Oldbury, Midland Carriage & Wagon Co, Lancaster Wagon Co, Ashbury Railway Carriage Co and Brown Marshall Co all tendered on the formal specification of March 1897, with prices ranging from nearly £20,000 (excluding brakes) to over £30,000 (but all of them plus more for roller bearings), and deliveries between 11 and 18 months. Jackson & Sharp of Wilmington, USA, got the contract on the basis of its tender of £23,039 inclusive of brakes and roller bearings, with delivery in seven months. On completion, the vehicles were dismantled to kits and sent over to Eastleigh for erection. Nearly all of the electrical equipment, apart from the armature windings, was left off until after final delivery underground at Waterloo. They are shown here as Figure 7.1.

The motor cars had two Siemens 42bhp motors on each of the driving-end bogies. These were direct-drive, with the armatures wound on 6in axles and with very big field windings supported from the bogie frames. For the delivery run the armatures had protective casings that can just be seen in some of the photos, but the field magnets had such a small clearance over the rails that it was probably deemed unsafe to pass them over the surface tracks from Eastleigh to Waterloo.

Speed control was by means of a large controller in each

driving cab. The controllers were connected together by eleven power cables that ran in casings on top of the roofs, via couplers hanging over the platforms between the cars. These cables carried current at up to the full line voltage. The controllers gave eight working combinations of motors and resistors in series and parallel. The resistors were mounted in clear air under the driving-end platforms behind the low-level buffer/coupling beam.

Current was collected, at 530V DC, from a central third rail via cast-iron shoes at each end of each motor bogie, attached to the motor casings. This third rail was formed of an inverted steel channel mounted on porcelain oil insulators. It was at the same level as the running rails, which were used for the current return, so there were wooden ramps at pointwork to carry the collector shoes up and over the running rails. All axles had roller bearings, claimed to be the first railway application in this country.

As a protection against passing a signal at danger, the motor bogies were fitted with a 'slipper' on the leading left side, rather like the later electric train pick-up shoes. The 'slippers' were energised through a breaker circuit in the train control unit. Close to each signal was a short section of what must have looked like an outside electric rail, known as a 'slipper bar'. When a signal was at Clear, showing green, the contact between the slipper and the bar caused a relay to allow the signal spectacle to drop and display the red Stop signal and also to earth the slipper bar. Then, if a following train passed the signal at Danger, the current through the slipper and bar to earth caused the breaker on the train to cut off the traction power.

On entering service the trains were quickly found to be underpowered. This was because the original plan had envisaged that trains could accelerate down the gradients from the terminals and pass round the 5-chain curve under Hatfield Street and Upper Ground Street (later named as Hatfields and Upper Ground) at a speed of 24mph, 30mph having been successfully run during the trials, using this speed to help in climbing the following gradient. Unfortunately the Board of Trade Inspector, Sir Francis Marindin,

Plates 7.1c and 7.1d
Framework of Waterloo & City trailer car at Jackson & Sharp's works. *Both courtesy of ACF Industries Inc*

Plate 7.1e Waterloo & City Railway motor car No 3 on delivery at Waterloo, prior to installation of field magnets and control equipment. The paint scheme appears to be two-tone. *Locomotive Publishing Co*

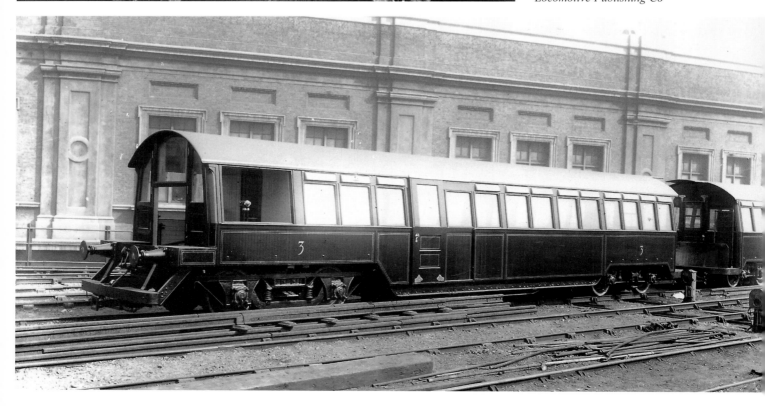

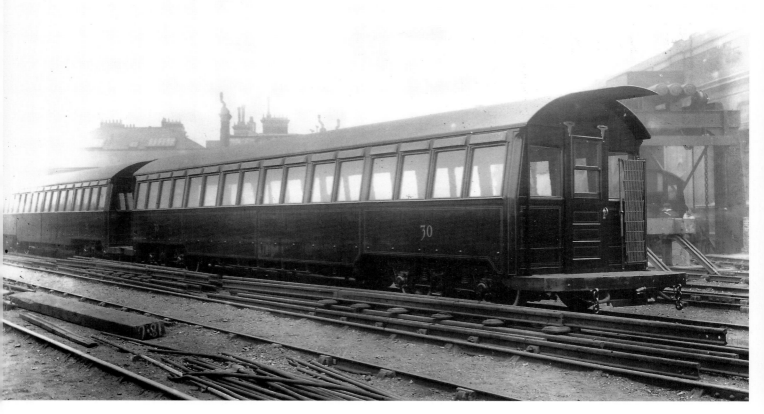

Plate 7.1f Waterloo & City trailer car No 30 on delivery at Waterloo. Note the folding gate, roof extension to carry the power cables, and a motor car on the lift at right background. *National Railway Museum*

insisted on a maximum of 15mph. This meant substantial use of brakes and a much harder pull up the following gradient, increasing the journey time from the intended average of under five minutes to six or just over.

It was therefore proposed to the Locomotive & Stores Committee on 11 October 1898 that a further five motor cars should be built and 'fitted with motors strong enough to move the heaviest trains'; these were subsequently referred to as locomotives. It was presumably at this time that the sketch mentioned above proposing conversion of the existing motor cars to trailers was prepared. However, at the following meeting, on 26 October, it was reported that Messrs Siemens had stated that the motors could be altered to provide greater power, but at a lower maximum speed, allowing the journey to be completed in five minutes. It was agreed that this work should be done, but that a further five double-ended motor cars should be built for use singly during the off-peak periods. These will be described later.

In January 1899 there were reports from the engineers on 'the proposal to work the Waterloo & City Railway by electric locomotives instead of by motor cars as at present'. Plans and estimates were to be submitted 'for two additional electric locomotives and for the conversion of the motors contained in 10 of the existing motor cars into locomotives. Messrs Siemens' tender of £980 for rewinding the motors to be accepted.'

Because of the brevity of some of the Minutes it is not clear how the discussion of the proposed conversion to locomotive haulage proceeded. The only contract recorded was on 16 February 1899 for Siemens to supply eight new motors (ie sufficient for four motor cars, leaving eight unaltered). At the same time it was also decided that the cost of rewinding the existing motors would not be necessary, since the engineers now considered that it would be possible to increase the size of the wheels from 33in to 35in. The last note seems a little strange, but that is what is recorded in the Minutes. Then, in the following December, Mr Jones, the line's Electrical Engineer, stated that a new controller, resistances, etc would be required in order to re-equip the second of the spare motor cars which had been dismantled in order to fit up one of the experimental locomotives, and recommended that spare bogie frames, one motor and one trailer, be put in hand so that all the cars might be kept in running order except while bogies were being changed.

This was approved at an estimated cost of £675.

What actually happened about rewinding the motors and increasing the wheel size remains a trifle puzzling, since in November 1903 the Locomotive, Carriage & Stores Committee approved the General Manager's proposal that 24 pairs of 33in disc driving wheels should be replaced with 35in spoked ones. Whether some trains were faster or more powerful than others in the intervening period is not clear.

No information has come to light regarding the experimental locomotives, and the slight detail mentioned above does not seem to relate in any way to the four-wheeled service locomotive that was used for shunting coal wagons from the bottom of the lift shaft to the power station.

In July the General Manager recommended that the device known as a 'dead man's handle' be fitted to the 12 motor coaches of the four-car trains at an estimated cost of £150, which would enable four Assistant Motormen to be withdrawn, effecting a saving of £148 per annum. This was approved by the Locomotive, Carriage & Stores Committee.

Westinghouse air brakes were fitted to all trains, operated from either driving cab, but there were no compressors on the trains. At Waterloo power station an engine drove pumps to keep a large reservoir permanently topped up, so that the long reservoir cylinders under each car could be recharged whenever necessary. The train cylinders were intended to hold sufficient air for about 20 journeys.

The motor and trailer cars of the set trains had bodies 41ft long and 8ft 6in wide, though the motor cars had a sliding door on each side outside this nominal width. The trailers and the non-driving ends of the motor cars had sliding doors in the ends leading onto end platforms over the buffer/coupling beams; these extended each end by 2ft 7¾in and suited the station platforms which were 1ft 6in above rail level. Small canopies extended the roofs over these platforms and supported the power cables and couplers at a height of 6ft 10in above the platforms. An 'apron' or fall-plate on one end of each vehicle spanned the gap between the end platforms. A folding steel gate was hinge-fitted to one side of each body end. The gates were hooked back to allow passengers on and off, but were opened out and hooked to the body of the next carriage when the train was running. Three guards had to be carried on each train to collect the tickets and operate the gates, and presumably to ensure that passengers remained safely inside

Plate 7.1g Interior of Waterloo & City motor car. *National Railway Museum*

Plate 7.1h Interior of Waterloo & City trailer car. *National Railway Museum*

Plate 7.1i Motor cars being fitted out at Waterloo. *Electrical Review 1899*

Plate 7.1j Motor bogie; note the central collector shoe. *Electrical Review 1899*

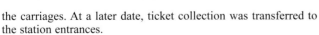

Plate 7.1k Motor unit. *Electrical Review 1899*

Plate 7.1l 1898 motor unit, showing the armature wound directly on the axle. *Courtesy of Railway Gazette International*

the carriages. At a later date, ticket collection was transferred to the station entrances.

The motor end had a 1ft 8in platform over a normal-height headstock. Normal buffers (two types show in photographs) and a coupling hook were fitted for the delivery journeys, but these were removed once the vehicles had been transferred underground. Below this headstock, and extending another 1ft 5½ in, there was a buffer/coupling beam as for the trailers. Mounted on the end platform and projecting into the cab was the cabinet containing the electrical control equipment. The driver's speed control took the form of a large vertical wheel on the rear left side of the controller cabinet, the reversing lever being below and to the right of it. On either side of the cabinet was a

narrow door which could give access to the equipment cabinet or be used as an emergency exit in the tunnel.

The coupling between vehicles, mounted below the buffer/coupling beam, was of the American style, consisting of a heavy bar on each vehicle, contained in a sleeve, which could be linked with that of the next carriage by dropping in a coupling pin. The vehicle end of each bar was constrained between two powerful coil springs. Side chains and hooks were also fitted.

Construction of the carriages was very different from anything experienced previously on the LSWR. The motor cars had massive solebars that appear to have been of 'I'-section steel. These were quite low along the middle of the vehicle but swept up and over the bogies with dropped extensions to carry the end platforms and buffer/coupling beams. These solebars were further supported by truss rods which, after several bends, ended near the ends of the vehicle. The up-sweep was greater over the motor bogies than over the trailing ones to give clearance for the motors and the 33in disc driving wheels. This made it necessary to raise the floor in this area with two steps up to the 'attic', as it was sometimes called. The body was then built on top of this rigid frame and probably could not be separated from it as a normal carriage body could.

The trailer cars were built in a different manner. Here the floor was flat throughout the central section and along the central gangway over the bogies. The main strength was derived from steel channels, acting as solebars, which ran the length of the bodies inside the outer skin above the level of the bogie arches. The wooden side framing was attached by brackets to the top edge of the channels and the floor timbers hung from the channels on metal hangers. Truss rods with adjusters, similar to those on ordinary carriages, supported five of the floor cross-members directly without queen posts. They then ran up inside the body casing, past the internal 'solebar', to strong frames over the ends of the fixed bogie supports, and terminated on the 'solebar' adjacent to the corner pillars. The bogie outside bearing pads thus came out almost to the full width of the body, well outside the bogie frames, and therefore the upper bolster had to be made in a wide flat U-shape passing under the compensation beams.

The body of all cars was double-skinned, the inner layer being planked diagonally and the outer one vertically, producing the 'matchboarding' effect, relieved by one horizontal and five vertical raised narrow strips. The paint scheme is not absolutely certain. In the specification it was stated: 'The materials, construction, finishing and painting of the whole of the woodwork and ironwork of the carriages are to be in accordance with the practice of the London and South Western Railway in every respect.' Some photographs appear to show the two-tone scheme; in others there is no clear distinction. The fact of the lower sides being vertical and the upper parts sloping could cause misleading reflections; also, many photographs of surface stock which was definitely two-tone fail to show the distinction, so at present there is no definitive answer. All that is certain is that the lower sides and ends were very dark and were lined out with double narrow lines, presumably gold, right-angled at the corners.

All the seats were made of moulded plywood on hardwood frames and, according to the *South Western Gazette* for August 1898, 'the coaches are for the sake of cleanliness made without upholstery'. They are similarly shown on the drawing for the 1922 trailer cars. Later, as seen in photographs, they were given a fairly thin upholstery covering. Some seats were fitted transversely in pairs on either side of a central gangway, whilst in the bogie areas they were arranged longitudinally along the sides. The seat backs in the 'attics' over the motor bogies almost blocked out the windows in those sections. All windows were fixed, and eventually many had advertisements pasted on them. Ventilation was through the hoods over the windows and the droplights in the end doors. The motor cars had 46 seats and the trailers 56.

It was noted earlier that five double-ended motor cars were authorised on 26 October 1898. Dick, Kerr and Co of Preston won the contract against tenders from Siemens Bros & Co Ltd (sic), and from The Electric Construction Co. It agreed to commence delivery on 6 September 1899, but suggested a possible delay 'in view of the peculiar construction of the underframes'. In the event they were still promising them in January 1900, and it was not until 2 April that they started test running on the line, and were finally accepted in early May 1900.

These five motor cars, Figure 7.2, appear to have been structurally very similar to the set train motor cars but, unlike those, they had matching bogies at each end, supplied by the Leeds Forge Co, requiring symmetrical underframes. The bogies had 2ft 9in-diameter Kitson wheels on a 5ft 6in wheelbase at 31ft centres. Each bogie had a pick-up, probably ahead of the motor as in the case of the earlier motor cars. The two motors were English Electric type 15L developing 75hp through single-reduction gearing, which suggests that they were intended to act as locomotives, as was originally stated, and not merely for the off-peak services that were their usual employment.

The bodies were 45ft long, 47ft over the buffer beams, and again nominally 8ft 6in wide but with two sliding doors on each side outside this width. The sliding doors had handles on the outside with recessed ones inside, but the latter appear to have been later replaced with keyholes for use by the guard conductors who rode in the cars. They were divided internally into a smoking and a non-smoking compartment by a pair of sliding doors. A total of 50 seats was provided, the longitudinal ones over the bogies being on raised floors. There was no glazing behind these seats but the frames were panelled to match the glazing in the rest of the body. As on the earlier four-car trains, the seats were made of formed plywood without any upholstery, this being remedied in later years. As a means of emergency exit there was a sliding door in each end; this appears to have had a window with an opening light above it when built, but later views show it panelled, with a covered ventilator above it.

Each driving compartment occupied only a corner of the body; the control equipment in these compartments was much more compact than on the earlier motor cars and was very similar to that used on tramcars — hardly surprising in a Dick, Kerr product. Control cables between the cabs once again passed through trunking on the roof.

Westinghouse brakes were again used, with storage cylinders under the cars; these had the capacity for 15 round trips. There was an intention to install motor-driven air compressors, but if and when this was done is not recorded. Two flexible brake hoses were fitted at each end under the buffer beams.

Low-level buffer beams, similar to those on the four-car trains, were provided, but there were no normal buffers or couplings — simply coupling bars of the American type. Side safety chains and hooks were fitted to the buffer beams originally but, as with surface stock, these were later removed.

Two more trailer cars were built by the Electric Tramway Co of Preston in 1904 for use as spares. In February 1920 the General

Plate 7.1m Waterloo & City train on withdrawal in 1940. *Courtesy of The Railway Magazine*

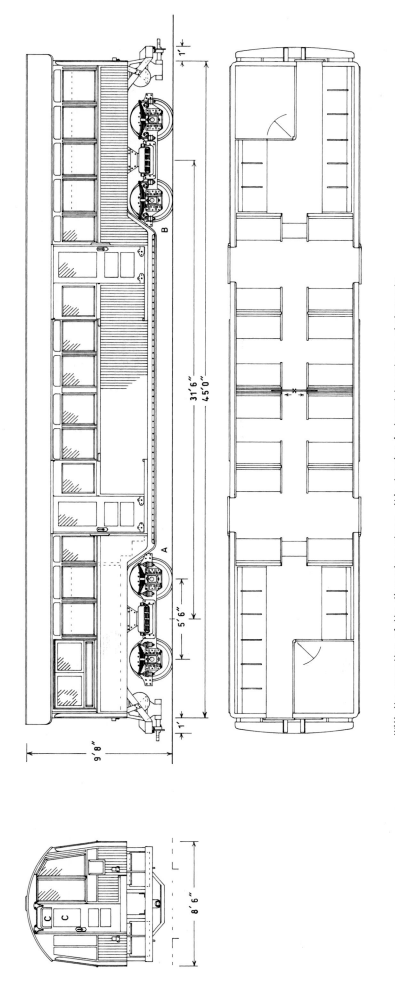

With the exception of the dimensions shown, this drawing is based largely on photographs.

The primary springs were probably 2ft. long (bogie A) but later replaced by 2ft.6ins. ones (bogie B).
The end doors were probably glazed at CC but later panelled and with a hooded ventilator, as shown.
Lamp irons were fitted on the ends, later replaced by electric lamps.

Figure 7.2
Waterloo & City Railway, Motor cars of 1900.

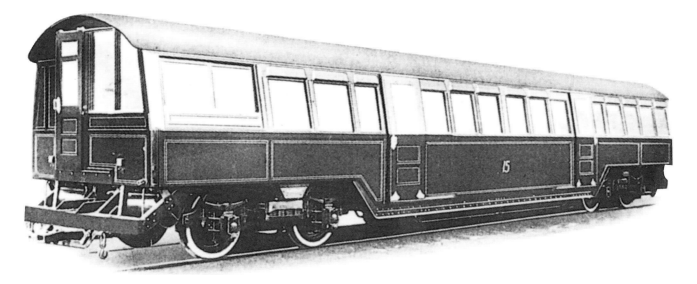

Plate 7.2a Waterloo & City Railway 'either end' driving car of 1900.
Colin J. Marsden collection

Plate 7.2b End of 1900 car. Note the coupling, sidechains, and casings for the resistors.
Tramway & Railway World

Manager referred to the considerable overcrowding that was occurring, and recommended that six all-metal trailer cars should be built so as to extend the existing six four-coach trains to five-coach, and at the same time that all the electrical equipment be replaced in order to speed up the service from 20 trains per hour to 24, thus in all increasing the effective seating capacity by 50%. The estimated total cost would be £75,000. A month later, after discussion by the Board and the Traffic Committee, it was decided to drop the idea of re-equipment and all-metal trailers, and instead to build just four more ordinary trailers at Eastleigh. These, together with the two existing spares, would still permit mainly five-car working.

All these Waterloo & City line vehicles remained in service until 25 October 1940, when the train sets were all withdrawn and

replaced by new stock. The double-ended motor cars were reportedly kept on for a few years. However, some ciné film was taken of the vehicles being raised to the surface which included a shot of one of the double-enders arriving at the top, so this throws some doubt on that report. (This film has been reproduced as part of a programme on Southern electric trains in video-cassette form.) A few photographs were also taken before the stock was dumped in sidings for demolition, there having been little opportunity for more to be taken since the few shots of 1898 and 1900.

By 1900 electric tramways were providing rapid, frequent and cheap transport in many towns and cities. This competition hit the existing local railway services very hard, and many companies considered how they could combat the trams.

Plate 7.2c 1900 car, showing driving compartment at left. *Tramway & Railway World*

Plate 7.2d 1900 car central partition with sliding doors. *Tramway & Railway World*

The first to respond in a big way was the London, Brighton & South Coast Railway (LBSCR), which, under pressure from the London County Council (LCC) tramways in South London, decided to adopt electric traction in 1903 and settled for an overhead-fed supply at 6,600V AC. This was transformed down and rectified in each motor coach to 750V DC. The LSWR held off making such a decision for a few years, possibly hoping that the level of competition from the tramways would stabilise and even decline when the novelty had worn off; if so, it was a forlorn hope, since London United Tramways (LUT) was penetrating more and more of the outer suburban territory that had originally been developed by the LSWR. The railway services had been somewhat leisurely while the only competition was from horse buses, but electric trams running through the busiest streets with frequent stops for boarding and alighting were another matter altogether. Even if trams were at first a little unreliable, at least when they broke down the passengers could readily alight and go on by cab, another tram or even on foot.

Suburban commuter services were never really profitable, so reluctance to make big investments in a new system of traction was perhaps understandable, but in 1912 the Central London Railway (CLR) announced proposals to extend from Shepherd's Bush to Richmond. This undoubtedly would have had a most serious effect on the LSWR. To make matters worse, several local authorities approached the CLR to urge it to extend beyond Richmond and into their districts, and this forced the LSWR Board to face up to the situation.

In his *Report on the Electrification of the London Suburban Lines* of November 1912, the Electrical Engineer (Mr H. Jones) mentioned and dismissed the three-phase AC system, which would require three wires over each track, and then included the following paragraphs:

'Single-phase AC at 6,000V to 11,000V using one overhead wire over each track and the track rails (for the return). This system is particularly suitable for hauling heavy individual passenger or goods trains for long distances, in short the conditions most suitable for steam traction are also most suitable for the single-phase system. It is adapted to the electrification of an extended railway system but is at a disadvantage when operating a heavy service of light trains. The best examples of this system are the New York, New Haven and Hartford RailRoad, operating 73 miles of main line but with no suburban traffic within 15 miles of New York, and the LB&SC suburban lines.

'Having eliminated the three-phase and single-phase system it only remains to consider which form of DC system is most suitable for our requirements.

'Several lines in the United States are operated on DC overhead at 1,500V to 2,400V, and a short length of the Lancashire & Yorkshire is being electrified at 3,500V. The current-carrying capacity of overhead wires is considerably lower than that of a third rail, and the system is not in operation at a sufficiently high voltage to compensate for this difference. It is very suitable for operating a light service such as that of the interurban railways in

Plate 7.2e 1900 car driving controls. *Coutesy of Colin J. Marsden*

Plate 7.2f Interior of 1900 car in later years. *National Railway Museum*

the United States but cannot compare with the third-rail system for heavy work. The third-rail system at 1,200V possesses certain advantages over that at 600V on lines operating a light service of trains, but on a heavy suburban system the annual charges in connection with the extra cost of the 1,200V train equipments and the additional protection of the third rail outweigh the saving that can be effected by spacing the sub-stations further apart as is permissible at the higher voltage. In order to justify the use of 1,200V on a third rail it therefore becomes necessary to show a saving in the cost of power delivered to the line as a result of the use of the higher voltage. With this object in view a complete scheme of power production from diesel oil engine stations supplying the line direct at 1,200V was worked out and was abandoned because it was found impossible to ensure a sufficiently low-priced fuel oil. Small steam-driven power houses are uneconomical, consequently high-tension transmission from one main power house is the only alternative to the diesel oil engine proposal. I therefore recommend the DC third-rail system at 600V is most suitable for use on our suburban lines. This system is well tried, having been in use for 20 years on tube and elevated railways, and for over six years for heavy railway work on the Hudson and Harlem divisions of the New York Central Railroad. It is also in successful operation on the Lancashire & Yorkshire, North Eastern, and West Jersey and Seashore railways.'

No doubt note had also been taken of the cost and construction problems that the LBSCR had encountered in providing its lines with an overhead power feed, including the number of gantries, the clearances in bridges and tunnels, and the disruption to services during the construction. Another consideration was that the District Railway had, since 1905, had running powers over LSWR metals, using the third-rail low-voltage system, reaching Turnham Green, Richmond and Wimbledon, so to some extent the LSWR already had some experience in this field. The decision was therefore taken by the Board in December 1912 to electrify most of its services within 15 miles of Waterloo using the third-rail 600V DC system for the main electrification scheme.

The District Railway found it necessary to add a fourth rail for current return in order to minimise earth currents and their effects on nearby telegraph circuits and metallic water and gas mains. The LSWR, where telegraph and mains services pipes were generally not so close to the tracks, was presumably calculated not to be likely to suffer much of this trouble, so the fourth rail was not provided and the initial installation costs seemed to be relatively low.

Actual work started in the summer of 1913, and the first services commenced in October 1915 between Waterloo and Wimbledon via East Putney, using part of the existing District Line's electric route. This was closely followed by the Kingston loop and the Shepperton branch in January 1916, the Hounslow loop in March, to Hampton Court in June and to Claygate in November 1916. Meanwhile, electrification had of course been completed down the main line from Clapham Junction to Surbiton and to the junctions for Claygate and Hampton Court. This also involved building the flyover crossing at Hampton Court Junction to avoid the need for frequent electric trains to cross the main lines.

To provide the rolling stock for the new services it was not necessary to build anything new. All the lines concerned were already being served by the relatively new four-car bogie block trains (described and illustrated in Chapter 6), which would not find much use if they were replaced by new electric stock. It was therefore decided to rebuild enough of the block sets to form the required number of electric sets. Because of the better acceleration and higher average speed of the electric trains, permitting tighter schedules, it was calculated that conversion of 63 four-car steam sets into 84 electric three-car sets would both carry the existing traffic and allow for the anticipated increase in passengers. This quite soon turned out to be an underestimate, and strengthening trailer stock had to be provided, as will be mentioned later. It was also decided that there would be no Second-class provision in the electric trains.

The contract for the conversion of stock was placed with the Westinghouse Electric & Manufacturing Co Ltd (later Metropolitan-Vickers Electric Co Ltd) in 1913. It provided for the

Plate 7.2g 1900 car at Waterloo. *Southern Railway*

Plate 7.2h Geared motor of 1900 car.
Tramway & Railway World

work to be done by the contractor in part of the LSWR Works at Eastleigh. The LSWR would do the structural alterations to the vehicle bodies, with the contractor doing all the electrical work, consisting of motor bogies, control equipment, cabling, electric lighting and heating, and provision of Westinghouse brake equipment with automatic compressors.

The specification stated that the track pressure would nominally be 600V DC, but could vary between 500V and 630V, with a working average of 575V. The free-running speed on level track was to be 52mph, with acceleration up to 30mph of about 1mph per second, but not initially exceeding 1.1mph per second. Braking retardation was not to exceed 1.75mph per second.

All of the allotted 126 Brake Thirds were converted to Motor Brake Thirds and, to complete the balance of motor cars needed, 42 of the 51ft Composites to Drawing 1393 were similarly altered to form Motor Brake Composites. They are illustrated here in Figure 7.3, which is based largely on the drawings of the original block set carriages, together with LSWR Drawing 1393, some details from the work of the late Ray Tustin, and several photographs published by Metropolitan-Vickers in a

1922 booklet describing the electrification of the LSWR.

For all of the motor cars the outer-end bogie was replaced by a motor bogie having two 275hp motors, one geared to each axle. Each motor bogie was fitted on either side with a wooden beam carrying a collector shoe that could run on top of the outside raised conductor rail. All four collector shoes on a set were interconnected to minimise the risk of the train being caught, in the vicinity of crossings etc, without connection to the power supply. The power cables from the collectors were led up to fuse carriers hung from the solebars, thence passing outside the solebars and in through the side of the body panels — certainly unacceptable in modern practice, and in fact later replaced by internal wiring, probably when the Southern Railway rebuilt the trains. It was doubtless at the same time that the fuse carriers were transferred to the bogie frames.

The Brake Thirds had the brake end and one compartment replaced by a driving compartment, an equipment section and a guard's/luggage compartment. The driving ends were formed as a flattened 'V', with a large window on the driver's side and an outward-opening hinged window on the other side. Between these

Continued on page 67.

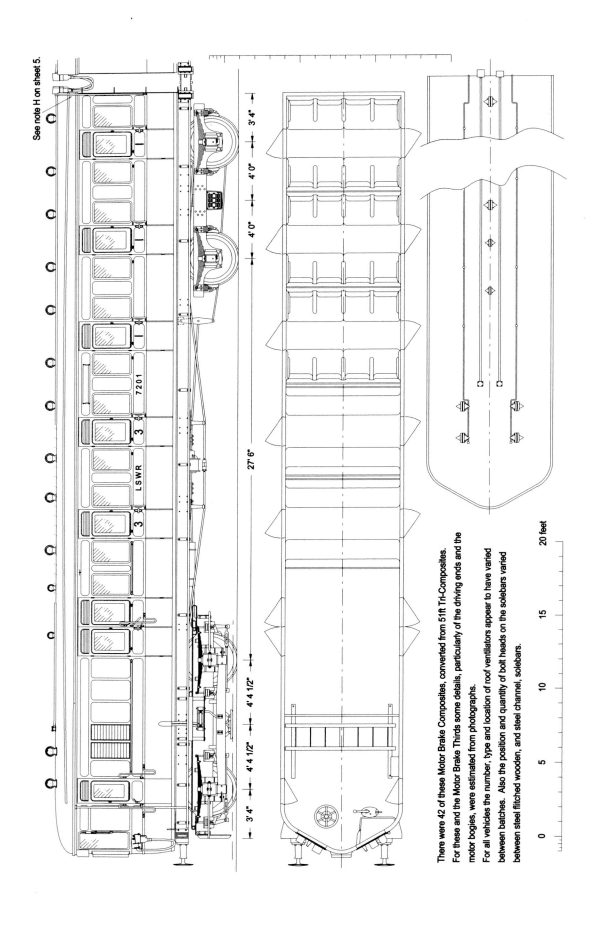

There were 42 of these Motor Brake Composites, converted from 51ft Tri-Composites.
For these and the Motor Brake Thirds some details, particularly of the driving ends and the
motor bogies, were estimated from photographs.
For all vehicles the number, type and location of roof ventilators appear to have varied
between batches. Also the position and quantity of bolt heads on the solebars varied
between steel flitched wooden, and steel channel, solebars.

See note H on sheet 5.

0   5   10   15   20 feet

Figure 7.3
LSWR electric trains of 1915, Motor Brake Composite.

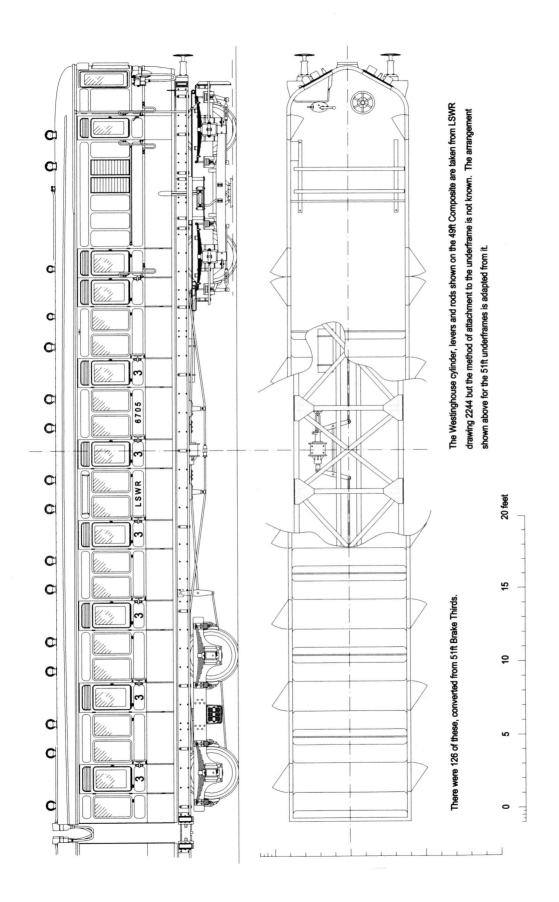

The Westinghouse cylinder, levers and rods shown on the 49ft Composite are taken from LSWR drawing 2244 but the method of attachment to the underframe is not known. The arrangement shown above for the 51ft underframes is adapted from it.

There were 126 of these, converted from 51ft Brake Thirds.

LSWR

6705

20 feet

15

10

5

0

Figure 7.3
LSWR electric trains of 1915, Motor Brake Third.

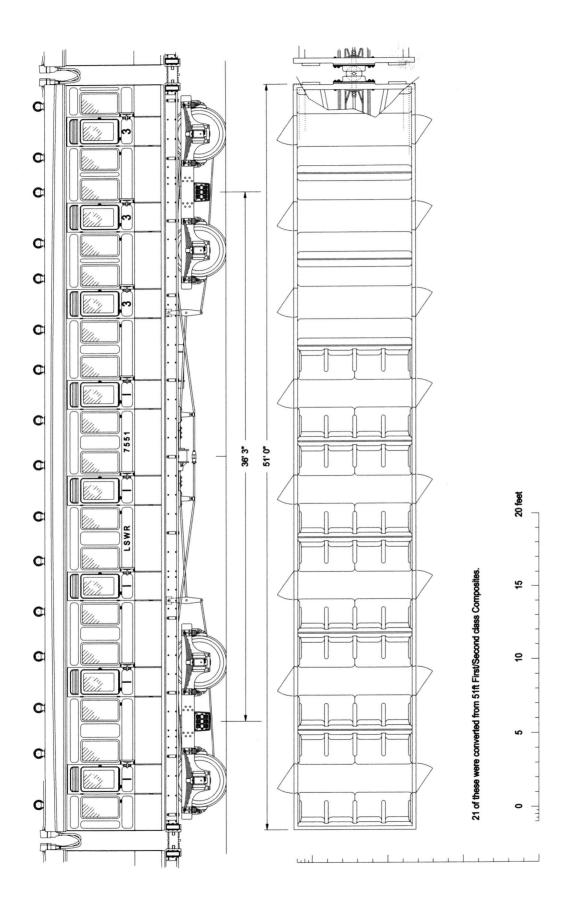

21 of these were converted from 51ft First/Second class Composites.

0   5   10   15   20 feet

Figure 7.3
LSWR electric trains of 1915, 51ft Composite.

64

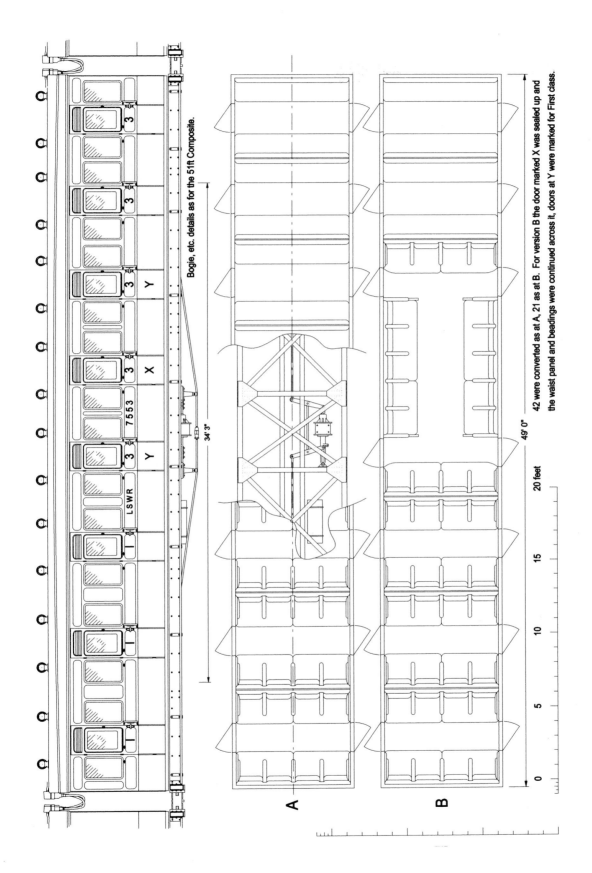

Bogie, etc. details as for the 51ft Composite.

34' 3"

42 were converted as at A, 21 as at B. For version B the door marked X was sealed up and the waist panel and beadings were continued across it, doors at Y were marked for First class.

49' 0"

20 feet

A

B

Figure 7.3
LSWR electric trains of 1915, 49ft Composite.

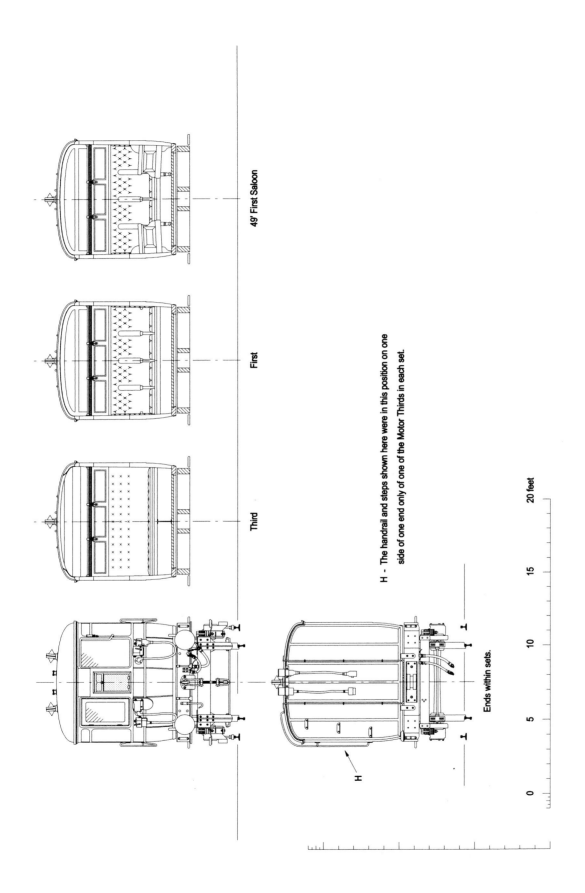

49' First Saloon

First

Third

H - The handrail and steps shown here were in this position on one side of one end and only of one of the Motor Thirds in each set.

Ends within sets.

H

0   5   10   15   20 feet

Figure 7.3
LSWR electric trains of 1915, ends and sections.

Plate 7.3a Set E7 leaving Surbiton. *D. Cullum collection*

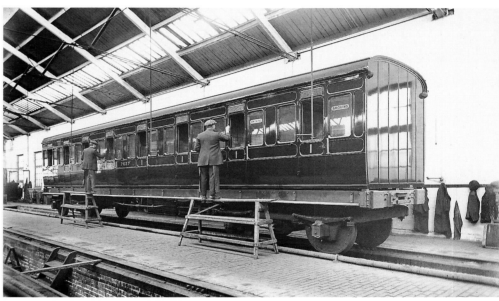

Plate 7.3b 51ft Composite No 776 during conversion to electric Composite No 7627. *National Railway Museum*

windows was a narrow panel housing a destination-indicator frame backed by a piece of opaque white glass illuminated from behind. The driver or guard could reach out of the opening window and attach a metal stencil to the indicator frame; thus the stencilled character would appear white by daylight or illuminated by night. The driver was provided with a hand-operated windscreen wiper. A whistle, operated by air from the brake system, was mounted on the corner at the left-hand side of the driver's window.

The Motor Brake Composites were similarly converted, but in this case the three Second/Third compartments at one end were removed and converted to driving, equipment and luggage compartments. The remaining 6ft compartment and the adjacent First-class compartment were classed as Thirds; however, the LSWR went to the trouble of putting false partitions into the former 6ft 6in First-class compartments so as to reduce them to a width of 6ft.

In both the Motor Brake Thirds and Motor Brake Composites, where the guard's compartment was formed the ordinary window of the former passenger compartment remained, thus making these compartments about the only ones on the LSWR to have such extra light for the guard.

The V-shaped end became widely known as a 'Torpedo' end. One foot of it overhung the headstock, bringing the overall body length to 52ft. The original solid block couplings between all carriages within the sets were retained, but 1in-thick steel packing pieces were inserted between the oval blocks (or buffer balls) and each headstock casting, bringing the distance between the carriage bodies to 1ft 4¾in (1ft 5¾in between headstocks). The original self-contained brake-end buffers were retained, or were fitted in

the case of the Motor Brake Composites. Of course, the existing steam-heating pipes and radiators had all to be removed and Westinghouse had to fit all compartments with two electric-heating radiators under the seats, fed off separate circuits so that half or full heat could be provided. The heaters were to have the capacity to maintain a temperature of 60°F in the compartments with the outside air at 32°F.

One unseen alteration was that, because of the extra acceleration and drawbar pull, the wooden stretchers to which the bogies were attached were replaced or reinforced with steel channel-section stretchers.

The electrical control equipment was housed on a rack across the width of the equipment section, with access from the driving compartment and by flap doors in the luggage compartment. The two upper-body panels on either side of this section were fitted with louvres to provide ventilation, since a considerable amount of heat could be given off by the resistors. The control compartments were lined by the LSWR with fire-resistant material. The control equipments at both ends of each set were connected together by a control cable along one side of the roofs of the carriages and a power cable on the other side, and by jumper connectors — round for the power and flat for the control circuits — between carriages. Jumper connectors were also provided at the outer ends so that two or more units could be worked in multiple from one driving cab. The specification actually required that the control equipments should be capable of allowing up to four train units to be thus coupled together.

The driver, or motorman, was provided with a forward/reverse lever (which he was obliged to take with him if he left the cab for any purpose whatsoever), a controller and a brake handle. This

Plate 7.3c Set E2 leaving Hounslow. *Lens of Sutton*

Plate 7.3d Set E29 arriving at Hounslow. Note the power cables either side of the ventilators, and the lighting cables outside those (see also Plate 7.3e). *Author's collection*

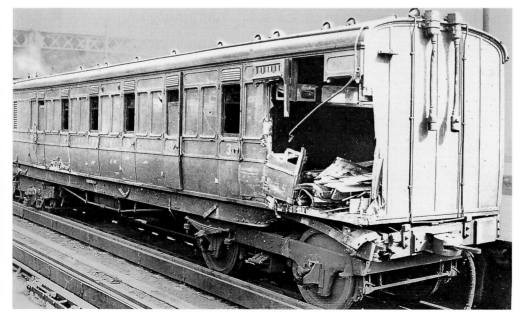

Plate 7.3e An unfortunate incident, but one useful for showing end details of Motor Brake Third No 6769. The two thick cables at the top are power jumpers; note also the block coupling. *J. Tatchell collection*

Plate 7.3f Motor Brake Third No 6754 in 1923. *HMRS*

Plate 7.3g Motor Brake Third, showing the motor bogie, collector beam and shoe, fuse, and cables to control equipment. *Metropolitan-Vickers, courtesy of GEC Archives*

Plate 7.3h Motor bogie. *Metropolitan-Vickers, courtesy of GEC Archives*

controller unit was designed for right-handed operation, the specification requiring that it be placed so that a driver could observe a guard's starting signal on the near side without removing his hand from the controller handle. This handle, often called a 'dead man's handle', was sprung at a slightly upward angle. In order to drive the train, this handle had to be pressed downwards and then rotated from the 'off' to one of the four 'notch' positions; if desired, it could be taken straight to the top position without pausing at the intermediate ones. Acceleration was automatically controlled by a number of relays that clicked quite loudly as they operated, giving rise to the nickname 'nutcrackers' that was sometimes applied to these sets. If the driver released his pressure on the handle it rose due to the spring action. The relays then automatically cut off the power and applied the brakes. Power could not be restored until the driver returned the controller to the 'off' position, pressed the handle down and again rotated it to one of the notches.

The vacuum brake was the standard for LSWR steam-hauled vehicles, but the invitation to tender offered the possibility of fitting either vacuum or air brakes. Westinghouse offered its air brakes and this was accepted. The motor cars were fitted with 14in cylinders and the trailers with 12in ones; all cars had an auxiliary reservoir, with the usual triple valve and release cock.

Each motor car had a compressor pump to charge the system, together with a main reservoir, the pumps being on a common automatic control line. Unlike those on most steam-hauled stock, the main reservoirs were connected through the train as well as the normal brake pipe. Thus there were two flexible pipes at each end of the vehicles: the 1in-diameter train pipe and the ¾in main reservoir pipe. Pressure in the main reservoirs was maintained at not less than 90lb/sq in and the train pipe normal pressure was 70lb/sq in. The intermittent throbbing of the pumps could be heard in the carriages after a brake application or during prolonged stops. A drop of 20lb/sq in was sufficient to achieve maximum braking, but for normal purposes a little over 5lb/sq in was enough. A Duplex pressure gauge was fitted in each driving cab to show the pressures of the main reservoir and train pipe.

Because the motors practically filled the space between the bogie frames, the brake pull rods ran along the tops of those frames, with hanging couplings to the levers carrying the brake blocks. At the inner end of the bogie a transverse beam connected the side rods to the rod from the Westinghouse cylinder. The arrangement for connecting the pull rods to the levers on the ordinary bogies is not known for certain, as side-view photos are rare. However, an LSWR drawing of 1915, despite being mis-titled as a bogie for the motor end, shows a Fox bogie with coil bolster springs, as used on some of the earlier bogie block sets. It has a pair of vertical levers attached to the underframe inboard of the bogie, with connections to the Westinghouse cylinder and to the normal brake rigging of the bogie. On that basis, the present drawings are shown with that arrangement.

The existing communication chains were retained, with the valves adapted for the air brake system, but, whereas the indicator 'butterflies' on the centre cars were in their original place, those on the motor cars protruded through the top moulding at the point where the luggage van section joined the end compartment.

The electric lighting was all renewed, as it had to work off the 600V supply. There were to be two circuits on each coach, supplying 40W metal filament lamps in series. Two lamps were to be fitted in separate fittings in each compartment, fed off separate circuits. Initially the lights for each carriage were separately switched, but later, additional jumpers were provided between cars so that the lights could all be controlled from any guard's compartment. Class distinction was maintained, since the First-class compartments were to have Hollophane bowls (No 6103 Special) supported by oxidised copper fittings, whereas the Thirds were to have Marbella plain or similar glassware supported by similar fittings in black bronze.

Plate 7.3i Control equipment in the driver's compartment, with 'dead man's handle' at right foreground, handbrake wheel at left foreground, and main circuit breaker at centre of view. *Metropolitan-Vickers, courtesy of GEC Archives*

Plate 7.3j Control equipment with covers off. *Metropolitan-Vickers, courtesy of GEC Archives*

Plate 7.3k Rear of control equipment in the luggage compartment. *Metropolitan-Vickers, courtesy of GEC Archives*

The remaining 51ft Composites were unaltered, except for brakes, heating and electrical cabling, as also were some of the 49ft Composites. However, 21 of the latter were altered by having the partitions between the three former Second-class compartments removed, the doors of the middle one sealed up, and some longitudinal seats provided, thus converting them to 18-seat First-class saloons. This alteration was to Drawing 2244. These apparently proved to be quite popular with some regular travellers to Waterloo.

The modifications resulted in three types of electric set being formed:

21 sets: Motor Brake Third - 51ft Composite - Motor Brake Third

21 sets: Motor Brake Third - 49ft Composite (Saloon) - Motor Brake Third

42 sets: Motor Brake Third - 49ft Composite - Motor Brake Composite

The electric sets were numbered in a new series, E1 to E84, as shown in Appendix 7. This set number was painted on a panel above the route indicator at each end; later this panel was altered to form a ventilator hood, still with the set number on it. Inside the cabs were holders for the route stencils, consisting of the letters H, I, O, P, S and V. The route-indicator box had a space above the letter area that could either be blanked off or display a bar or pair of dots, the dots indicating an empty stock working. The original codes were:

H	Waterloo-Hampton Court
O	Waterloo-Hounslow-Richmond-Waterloo
Ō	Waterloo-Richmond-Hounslow-Waterloo
V	Waterloo-New Malden-Richmond-Waterloo
V̄	Waterloo-Richmond-New Malden-Waterloo
I	Waterloo-Claygate
S	Waterloo-Richmond-Shepperton
S̄	Waterloo-Wimbledon-Kingston-Shepperton
P	Waterloo-East Putney-Wimbledon

It was hardly surprising that a bread manufacturer for many years had advertisements in most of the train compartments, depicting five trains viewed head-on with the respective codes H O V I S, together with a slogan 'The route to health — Hovis — Go b(u)y it'.

Advertising was mentioned in the Minutes of the Traffic Committee for February 1921, when the General Manager reported that it was proposed to enter into a contract with Messrs W. H. Smith & Son for seven years from 1 January 1921 [sic] whereby they would have the right to let spaces beneath the racks

Plate 7.3l Coupling motor coaches together. *Metropolitan-Vickers, courtesy of GEC Archives*

Plate 7.3m Ex-LSWR Motor Brake Third No 6736 as rebuilt as SR No 8036. Note where the original cable from the collector has been removed and the entry plated over, also the louvres panelled over. *Author's collection*

Plate 7.3n LSWR electric train controller. *Westinghouse*

Plate 7.3o Set E7 passing Durnsford Road power station, 1923. Note the power and lighting cables each side of the ventilators. *HMRS*

in carriages of the electric trains, and of certain branch line steam trains, for display of commercial adverts; the LSWR would receive 70% of the gross revenue plus an allowance to cover the cost of fixing and changing the adverts.

The electric trains were all painted in a new livery — or rather in the livery of the Directors' Saloon of 1885 — ie dark green, lined out round the panelling with chrome yellow picked out with black. This scheme was carried round the motor ends but the other ends, together with every part of the underframes and running gear, were painted black, the exception being the collector beams which were varnished teak. The roofs were painted with white lead, but of course this very quickly darkened to a mid-grey, tinged with rust from brake-shoe and wheel particles. Lettering was in gold, shaded with black, and was placed in the waist panels. The letters 'LSWR' and the vehicle number were in the two panels nearest to the centre of the vehicle. It has been said elsewhere that the compartment classes were again marked as for the revised scheme on the steam block sets, with '1st' or '3rd' in 6in or 7in characters in the door waist panels; however, the photograph of 51ft Composite No 7627, which was converted for use in set 77, apparently taken during its conversion, shows plain '1' and '3' numerals in the waist panels. Other photographs, though not very clear, appear to confirm this.

As before, dark blue upholstery was provided in the Firsts, with black and red repp in the Thirds, though later many of the Thirds were re-upholstered with black American cloth. It has also been stated that rattan was used for some of them for a time in the early 1920s.

A very useful innovation with the electric trains was the simultaneous introduction of fixed-interval services. This meant that passengers had virtually no need to refer to the timetable, since at any station there were two or three trains per hour throughout most of the day, timed to depart at the same number of minutes past the hour, with a few extras equally spaced between the regular timings during the peak periods. This very convenient system was continued for about 65 years by the Southern and by British Rail until the latter decided that operating convenience was more important than the convenience of passengers, when they introduced a hotchpotch of timings. After privatisation, the new owners rather wisely reverted to something resembling the LSWR system for much of the day.

During the peak periods most trains were formed of two sets working in multiple, but through the rest of the day single sets were generally adequate on most routes. However, by 1919 the increase in passengers was such that overcrowding had reached serious proportions. Twelve more of the steam block sets were authorised for conversion to 24 two-car trailer sets. In fact it was not until May 1921 that the Locomotive, Carriage & Wagon Committee reported that 20 pairs had been created, with four still awaited; these were not recorded as completed until December

1922. The sets were numbered T1 to T24. At the same meeting it was also agreed that six more two-car trailer sets should be formed, but then there was a moratorium on further major electrification expenditure, pending policy decisions for the Grouping. Despite this, in October 1922, the General Manager authorised an order for these sets with Metropolitan-Vickers amounting to £10,000, but there is no evidence that it was fulfilled. The Southern Railway formed most of its similar two-car trailer sets from ex-LBSCR and ex-SECR carriages.

The Brake Thirds had the van ends rebuilt to form three more Third compartments, very slightly larger between the partitions, whilst the Composites were re-upholstered and lettered as entire Thirds. Thus half of the two-car sets consisted of two 51ft Thirds whilst the other half had one 51ft Third and one 49ft Third. The centre block coupling was retained between the two carriages but normal buffers and couplings were fitted to the outer ends. The brake systems were changed to Westinghouse and through cabling and jumper connectors were provided as for the three-car sets. Peak period train formations then consisted of two three-car motor sets with a two-car trailer set between them. Since the two-car sets were entirely Third-class, a few services where there was a high demand for First-class seats had to be formed of three three-car motor sets. The alterations are shown as Figure 7.4 and their formations are listed in Appendix 7.

After the Grouping the Southern Railway decided to adopt the LSWR third-rail system, so the LBSCR stock and track had to be converted, this being completed by 1929. The South Eastern & Chatham Railway (SECR) system was still in the advanced planning stage, so this was changed relatively easily. Apart from the lettering there was little change to the appearance of the LSWR stock. The 'LSWR' and number disappeared from the waist panels and were replaced by 'SOUTHERN RAILWAY' in gold characters about 3½in high in the two top panels nearest to the centre of the vehicle, with the number in similar characters in the top panels at each end of the vehicle. The classes were again denoted by the figures '1' and '3' in the door waist panels.

As the Southern Railway extended electrification so there was a need both for a lot more electric trains and, eventually, for increased capacity on the existing trains. The new stock is beyond the scope of this book, but one batch is of interest. In 1925 26 more three-car sets were built which resembled the existing LSWR sets very closely in appearance, having similar 'Torpedo' ends and wood mouldings on steel panels. They were somewhat longer, at about 60ft each vehicle, and were 8ft 6in wide over the bodies. The Motor Brake Thirds had seven compartments, whilst the Composites had six Firsts and three Thirds. The LSWR sets E1 to E84 had been renumbered 1201 to 1284; the new sets continued the range with 1285 to 1310. In the Southern classification system these became known as 3-SUB sets. All the other new electric stock differed more noticeably from the LSWR type.

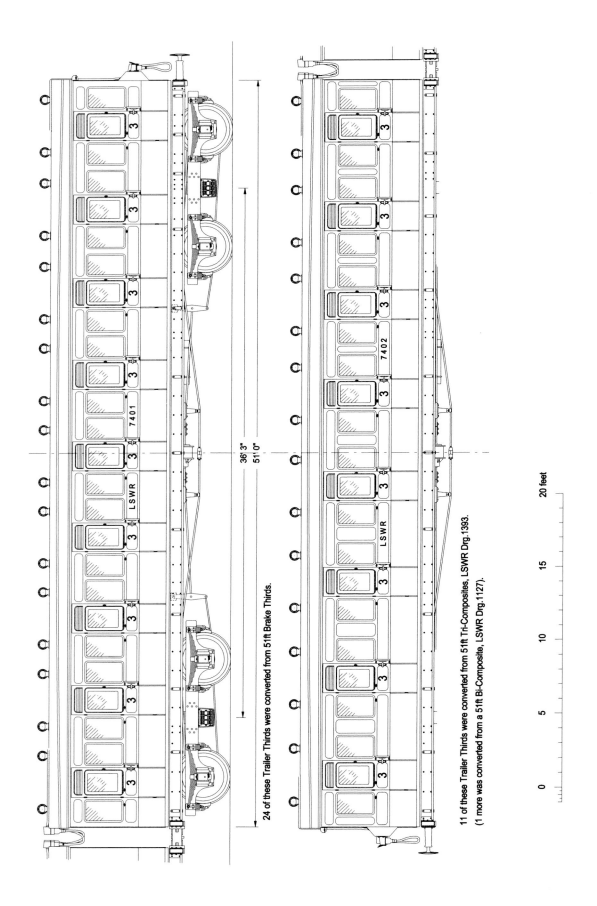

24 of these Trailer Thirds were converted from 51ft Brake Thirds.

36' 3"
51' 0"

11 of these Trailer Thirds were converted from 51ft Tri-Composites, LSWR Drg.1393.
(1 more was converted from a 51ft Bi-Composite, LSWR Drg.1127).

0   5   10   15   20 feet

Figure 7.4
LSWR 2-car electric Trailer Sets o0f 1920.

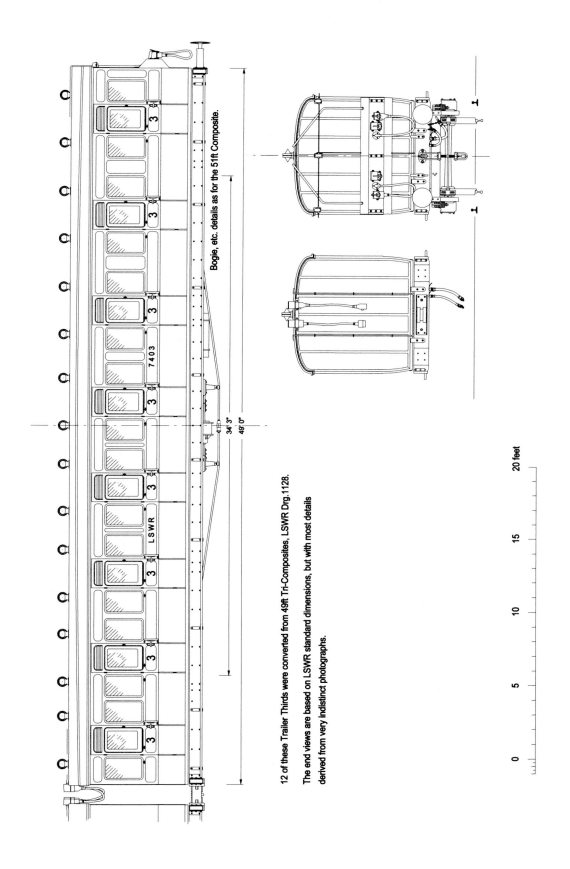

Bogie, etc. details as for the 51ft Composite.

34' 3"
49' 0"

12 of these Trailer Thirds were converted from 49ft Tri-Composites, LSWR Drg.1128.

The end views are based on LSWR standard dimensions, but with most details derived from very indistinct photographs.

0   5   10   15   20 feet

Figure 7.4
LSWR 2-car electric Trailer Sets of 1920.

The 1925 sets, Nos 1285 to 1310, were built with a guard's lookout on one side only of the motor cars; looking from the rear of the train it was on the left side of the last car. However, due to the width of the bodies, they caused route restrictions, and were replaced by roof periscopes in about 1929. The reason for mentioning them is that the original LSWR sets did not have them when built, but photographs show that they acquired them, at least by the time the new stock was built. In their case, however, because of the narrower bodies, they then retained lookouts for the rest of their lives, though in some instances replaced by a modified pattern at a later date.

The Southern was adopting longer body lengths for new stock for the Central and South Eastern sections, and it was becoming increasingly necessary for trains to be interchangeable between the sections. Therefore, between 1934 and 1940, all the original 84 LSWR sets were taken in for lengthening onto 62ft underframes. In fact, only 82 new sets were formed from them, the remaining six vehicles being used for parts or with other types of vehicle. Most of the Motor Brake Thirds had an extra compartment and a half compartment, called a coupé, inserted between the existing compartments and the van section, though some had the van section shortened and two compartments added. The Motor Brake Composites had two compartments inserted. The 51ft Composites had a First-class saloon inserted between the First and Third sections; the 49ft Composites without saloons had two more First compartments added at the First end. The 49ft Composites with a saloon had two more Firsts added at the First end with the existing saloon being shortened to create an extra Third class compartment at the Third class end. At this stage the sets still retained their 1923 numbers; the two sets not used were Nos 1202 and 1210.

It was probably at the time of this rebuilding that, as earlier mentioned, the external cables from the collector shoes to the equipment bays were replaced internally, and the original ventilation louvres were replaced by normal panels.

Photographs show that, presumably at the time of lengthening, the lookouts were rebuilt. Previously they had extended from halfway up the top panel to halfway down the waist panel; on the lengthened carriages they extended only from just below the top panel, giving the effect of a very deep panel there, to about one third of the way down the waist panel. Even if the lookouts needed replacing for weatherproofing reasons, it is hard to see a reason for altering the top and waist panels.

Later, additional capacity was again required, and between 1942 and 1948 these sets were augmented with an extra trailer car made from an ex-LSWR carriage lengthened onto a 62ft underframe. The sets were then renumbered into two series: 4131 to 4171 and 4195 to 4235. Withdrawals commenced just about as the last sets were being completed, but the last of them remained in service until 1956. The augmented sets came into the '4-SUB' classification.

The original two-car trailer sets also underwent changes in Southern hands. They were split up around 1929, the carriages being lengthened onto 62ft underframes and then paired off with ex-SECR carriages. Later still they were used, as mentioned above, to strengthen the lengthened original motor sets. Quite a number of other steam-hauled carriages were similarly lengthened for use as electric trailer cars.

Many of the 48ft Thirds, 46ft Firsts and six-wheelers of 1900/1 were also rebuilt to make electric stock, as already covered in Chapters 4 and 5 of the original volume.

At the introduction of electric trains in 1915 the LSWR issued two Notices to Staff advertising the jobs of Motorman and Electric Train Guard, listing the conditions of service. For motormen the pay during training was 30s (£1.50) per week of 60 hours gross, averaging 10 hours gross per day with 60 minutes per day for meals. After that and during the first year pay would be 36s per week, rising at annual intervals through 37s 6d, 39s, 40s 6d, and two years at 42s, reaching 43s 6d in the seventh year; after three years at that level it would rise to the maximum of 45s (£2.25p) per week. Annual leave with pay was six days after 12 months' service. Electric train guards started at 24s per week, rising through a longer scale to 34s (£1.70) per week in the 17th year. Weekly hours were the same, but paid annual leave was only three days in years 1 to 5, then rising to reach six days after 10 years' service.

The introduction of the new trains brought with it the need for a substantial number of new instructions and changes to existing ones. The Southern Railway version of these, issued in June 1925, was in the form of a pocket book running to 64 pages. It seems most likely that this was mainly a reprint of a similar LSWR publication. Much of it was taken up with the safety measures for staff working on or near electrified lines and included directions for resuscitation after electric shock, but a lot was also concerned with rules for the action required following breakdowns, including the measures for disconnection of track power, the procedure for the use of an assisting train, and so on.

One of the details was that, apart from the illuminated headcodes already mentioned, special electric trains were to carry additionally a black and white disc by day and a purple light by night. They all had to carry a normal tail light as for steam trains. When coupling two trains, after the main couplings and brake pipes had been connected, it was particularly instructed that the power jumper (the round one) be connected before the control-cable jumper (the flat one); this sequence was to be reversed when disconnecting the trains.

A motorman was strictly forbidden to leave his train without (a) opening the circuit breakers, (b) removing the reversing handle, and (c) putting on the hand brake hard. He was also forbidden from relinquishing his reversing handle at any time when on duty, with the sole exception of the requirement to hand it to the motorman of an assisting train following a breakdown.

Because AVB was the normal brake system on the LSWR, there were also quite detailed instructions for the operation and testing of the Westinghouse system, although they were of course very similar in essence, apart from the actual pressures quoted and the use of the stop cocks on the end pipes.

Chapter 8

RAILMOTORS AND VESTIBULE CARS

By the turn of the century the operating costs of some of the branch lines had been causing some concern and one solution appeared to be to resurrect the ideas for steam-powered railcars that had been expounded by William Bridges Adams in the late 1840s. Dugald Drummond had a design prepared for such a railcar, or railmotor, and the South Western, together with the London, Brighton & South Coast, decided to try two vehicles of this type on the short, jointly-owned Fratton to East Southsea branch. The construction of the engine units and the bogies was carried out by the South Western at the Nine Elms works to order K11, while the body sections were built at Eastleigh carriage works, ready for trials in April 1903.

As built, these first railmotors suffered a lot of shortcomings, some of which were overcome later in these two examples and also in two later types built by the LSWR alone, the 'H12' and 'H13' classes. They were used not only in competition with tramways but also to try to rejuvenate some uneconomical country branch lines. However, some of the disadvantages were inherent from the physical combination of locomotive and carriage in one vehicle, and eventually the type was abandoned in favour of small locomotives operating short trains of lightweight trailer cars.

The development of the railmotors, considered as locomotives, is covered in detail, with some fine photographs, in D. L. Bradley's *LSWR Locomotives — the Drummond classes*, published by Wild Swan Publications Ltd in 1986, and readers are recommended to refer to that work for all technical details of the engines and for notes on their service history.

Figure 8.1 illustrates the LSWR/LBSCR Joint Committee railmotors Nos 1 and 2. No 1 was built with a small vertical boiler that immediately proved quite inadequate, so Dugald Drummond instructed that on No 2 the boiler should be extended to as tall as practicable; No 1 was later altered to match. The steam supply was still inadequate and so, in September 1903 and June 1904, Nos 1 and 2 respectively were fitted with larger boilers and fireboxes of a more conventional horizontal design.

In these and all subsequent railmotors the boilers appear to have been directly bolted to the bogie frames as in normal locomotive practice, avoiding the need for flexible pipes under steam pressure but giving the enginemen the discomfort of having the firebox door and most of the controls continually moving and shaking about.

It seems curious that a design in 1902 should still include a low arc roof for the passenger section, but this was no doubt slightly

Plate 8.1a LSWR/LBSCR Joint railmotor No 2 with enlarged boiler. *D. J. Bailey collection*

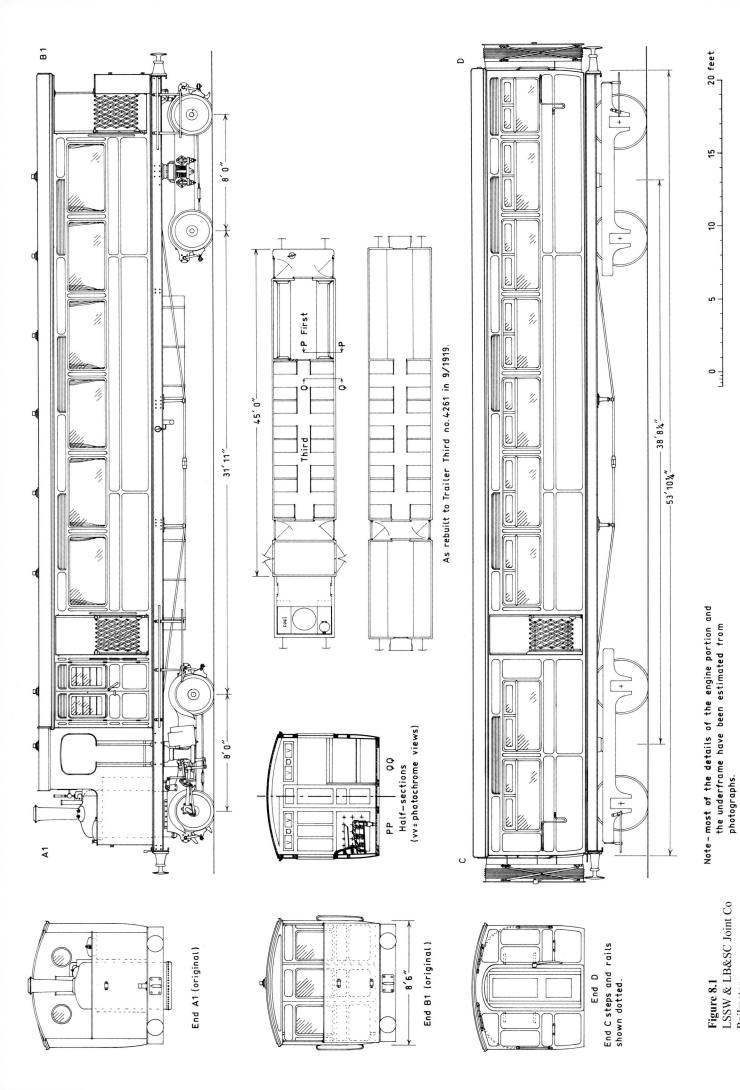

B1

A1

End A1 (original)

QQ

PP

Half-sections
(vv = photochrome views)

End B1 (original)

8'0"

31'11"

8'0"

8'6"

P First

Third

Q

Q

P

P

45'0"

coal

As rebuilt to Trailer Third no.4261 in 9/1919.

D

C

38'8¼"

53'10¾"

End D

End C steps and rails
shown dotted.

Note – most of the details of the engine portion and
the underframe have been estimated from
photographs.

Trailer Third 4261 was electrically lit from the batteries of an adjoining carriage.

0   5   10   15   20 feet

Figure 8.1
LSSW & LB&SC Joint Co
Railmotor.

Plate 8.1b LSWR/LBSCR Joint railmotor with final form of horizontal boiler. *D. J. Bailey collection*

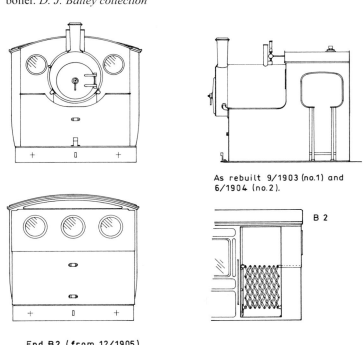

As rebuilt 9/1903 (no.1) and 6/1904 (no.2).

B 2

End B2 (from 12/1905)

Plate 8.1c Rare overhead view of LSWR/LBSCR Joint railmotor No 2, showing the coal bunker this side and the water tank on the far side. *Kenning Collection*

simpler, cheaper and lighter than the current LSWR semi-elliptical roof, and of course it conformed with then-current Brighton practice. There seem to be some doubts about whether oil or gas lighting was intended, but photographs of both No 1 and No 2, taken in April and June 1903 respectively, show gas lighting actually fitted. The open gallery for the driver at the alternative driving end was virtually a throwback to the early days, doubtless placing driver comfort and safety as less important than cost- and weight-saving. In December 1905, and probably after considerable complaints from enginemen, the weatherboarding was extended to full height with three locomotive 'spectacle'-type windows, as shown.

Another curiosity is that vacuum brakes were not fitted. For braking it was necessary to rely on manual brakes applied from either the cab or the trailing end; it is not clear whether there was

any connection between the brakes at each end. The trailing end contained no actual controls apart from the hand brake and an 'over the roof' wire to the whistle. The driver indicated his wishes to the fireman on the footplate by means of an electric bell system. The trailing bogies were, like all the rest of the construction, of an extremely lightweight design, with no pretensions to smooth riding.

Only First and Third classes were catered for, and, since the Third-class seats were of unupholstered plywood construction, as were those of the later railmotors, it was probably a blessing in disguise that the top speed possible or permissible was only around 30mph! Such a low level of comfort was nevertheless quite comparable with that on the competing tramcars, and may well have been acceptable for the short runs between Fratton and East Southsea, but it assumed more importance on

Plate 8.2a 'H12' class railmotor No 1. *British Railways*

the later railmotors that were employed on substantially longer runs.

On both vehicles the engine portion, solebars, bogies and alternative driving end weatherboard were painted in Drummond's locomotive livery but with full lining out only on the engine unit. No 1 had the bodywork painted in LBSCR umber and white livery with the fascias edged in (presumably) gold, whilst No 2 was painted in a variant of the normal LSWR passenger-stock livery. Normally the raised fascias, or mouldings, were painted with the body salmon colour but with dark brown on the rounded edges and with a fine red line edging the brown on the fascia surface. On this vehicle and the subsequent railmotors all of the fascias appear to have been painted with the lower panel dark brown, the rounded edges of all fascias, including those below the waist, being painted gold but without the red lines.

Despite the problems that were having to be overcome with the Joint railmotors, the LSWR decided to build two more, to an improved design, to work the Alton to Basingstoke line. This was an uneconomic line, built only to prevent Great Western encroachment into LSWR territory, and it was essential to operate it as cheaply as possible. Railmotors appeared to be the ideal answer. These two were built to locomotive order H12, the bodies being to LSWR Drawing 1273 and the machinery to LSWR Locomotive Department Drawing 8469. They were put into service in May and June 1904, but unfortunately, even with their increased power, they could not reliably cope with the gradients under all conditions and were quickly transferred to other services.

It can be seen in Figure 8.2 that the general style of the bodies was similar to the LSWR/LBSCR Joint ones, though the compartment layout was substantially changed. The cab was slab-sided and 8ft wide, built on an 8ft 6in-wide footplate, just like an ordinary locomotive, whilst the carriage section had a more or less normal carriage profile, though 8ft 6in wide, mounted on the underframe in the usual way on rubber pads, so there was again a very clear structural as well as colour difference between the two sections.

The underframes and bogies were very similar to the earlier ones, though the bogies had deeper frames and 3ft-diameter wheels, compared with 2ft 9in on the 'K11s'. The driving bogies had larger cylinders with 9in bore and 14in stroke. As compared with the re-boilered 'K11s', the boiler was turned round and completely enclosed in the cab, so now the driver was right at the leading end, with his back to the boiler. One effect of this was that, to get access to clean out the smokebox, the unfortunate fireman or cleaner had to climb over the tank or bunker and squeeze into the narrow space between the smokebox and the bulkhead. Two small smokebox doors were provided, but there was an ash chute from the bottom of the smokebox to below the bogie. As virtually

no light could penetrate to this tiny space a small hatch was fitted to the roof, but working there must have been most unpleasant.

The drawing office seems to have assumed the employment of very tall drivers, since the centre of the driver's windows was 6ft above the footplate. No allowance for the usual timber floor was made, since the firebox door and the shovel hole in the coal bunker were both drawn at footplate level. However, photographs show that a raised floor was in fact fitted, and it can just be seen that the firebox door was raised to match it.

The guard's compartment was provided with large end windows, a regulator lever and a whistle pull-wire in addition to the normal hand brake. Attached to the regulator lever was a large pulley wheel, on which was secured a pair of wires that passed up through the roof and over guide pulleys to the roof of the locomotive section, where the ends passed down and were attached to the regulator lever proper. The whistle wire similarly led over the roofs to the locomotive whistle.

Once again they had gas lighting, including a lamp in the driving cab, though as the lamps were only of the single- instead of the usual double-burner type the lamp tops were slightly smaller than usual. Also, as on the 'K11' class, they at first only had hand-operated brakes. Vacuum brakes were installed before the end of 1904, probably at the insistence of the Board of Trade; this of course included provision of a vacuum-brake control at the alternative driving end.

Car No 2 was converted to electric lighting in December 1905 using a De Laval 'XD'-type 1½bhp turbine generator supplied by the Glasgow Railway Engineering Co Ltd. This was mounted in the left-hand front corner of the motor compartment, protected by a wooden cover. Steam was fed from the top of the boiler and the exhaust was led up to an outlet inside the outer chimney. At the normal turbine speed of 4,000rpm it generated 1kW at 110V, feeding 11 lamps. The head and tail lamps, with 8in red or white interchangeable lenses, were detachable and provided with screw plugs, the bulbs each being of 50 candlepower. One 16-candlepower lamp was fitted in each of the driving compartments, the remaining lamps being of 25 candlepower, five in the passenger compartment and two in the cross vestibule. The whole installation cost £92 2s 5d (£92.12).

When first built they, or at least No 1, had no roof ventilators, the only ventilation being via the concealed grilles in the top panels. As with the brakes, one can only conjecture as to whether this was a cost- or weight-cutting economy; in any case, within a few months they were provided with 10 'Torpedo' vents and the large windows were altered so that each had two outward-opening sections at the top. In the First-class compartment the seats were upholstered with the usual blue cloth and there was a carpet on the floor, but in Third class the seats were just varnished birch plywood whilst the floor was covered with linoleum.

Plate 8.2b Another view of 'H12' class railmotor No 1. *Author's collection*

Plate 8.2c Railmotor No 2 at Cliddesden. *Bucknall Collection / Ian Allan Library*

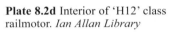

Plate 8.2d Interior of 'H12' class railmotor. *Ian Allan Library*

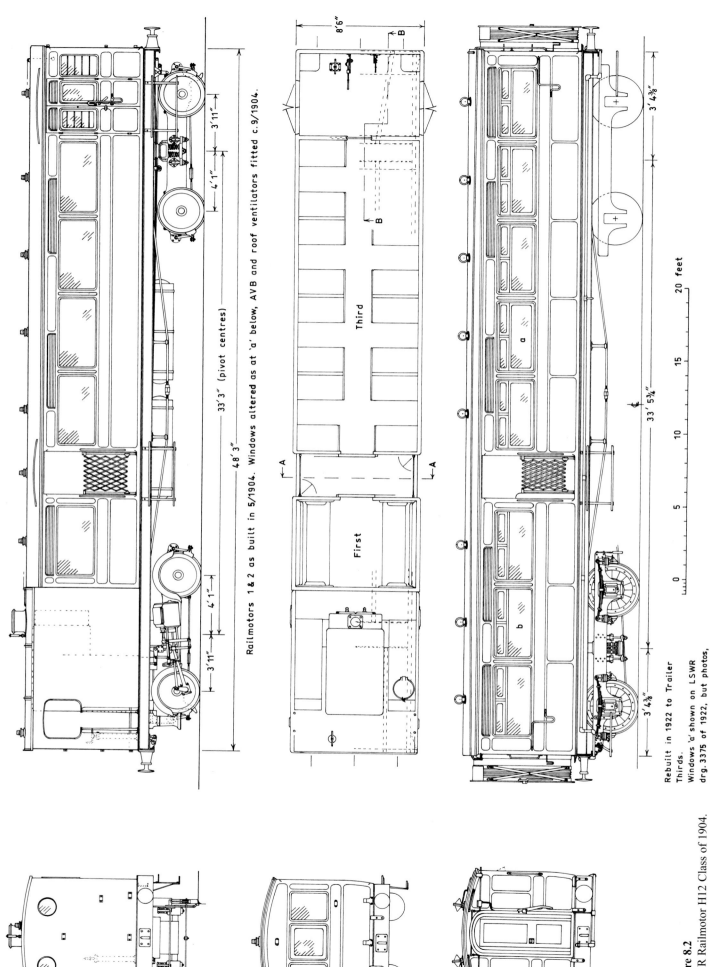

Railmotors 1 & 2 as built in 5/1904. Windows altered as at 'a' below, AVB and roof ventilators fitted c.9/1904.

3'11"

4'1"

33'3" (pivot centres)

48'3"

4'1"

3'11"

8'6"

B

B

A

A

Third

First

33'5¾"

3'4⅜"

3'4⅜"

a

a

b

0   5   10   15   20 feet

Rebuilt in 1922 to Trailer Thirds.

Windows 'a' shown on LSWR drg. 3375 of 1922, but photos, thought to be c.1932 and c.1947, show type 'b'.

Bogie positions taken from SR diagram book, tanks and

7'6"

Figure 8.2
LSWR Railmotor H12 Class of 1904.

Plates 8.2e and 8.2f Ex-'H12' class railmotor No 2 as rebuilt to trailer car.
Both J. Tatchell collection

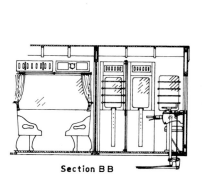

Section BB

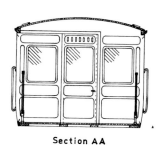

Section AA

The numbers, 1 and 2, may have caused a little confusion, but of course these were in a new LSWR railmotor number list whereas the earlier ones belonged to the LSWR/LBSCR Joint Committee. As with those, the engine compartments and bogies were painted and lined in passenger-locomotive livery, whilst the bodies were as described for Joint car No 2.

Even though these two vehicles showed many of the problems and shortcomings of the Joint ones, there seemed to be promise that further improvements in design could produce a satisfactory result. Thus in May 1905 it was agreed that a further seven should be built for various services, but it was required that they should be capable of hauling a 15-ton trailer car (which did not then exist other than in the form of an ordinary carriage) at 25mph.

These seven, Nos 3 to 9, were built to locomotive order H13 and carriage drawing 1415, and are illustrated at Figure 8.3. With the engine section enclosed within the carriage-style bodywork, they were certainly more elegant than the earlier ones, and looked more like other LSWR carriages. Ventilation and light were provided in the boiler area by louvres and droplights. Boilers and cylinders were again larger, but otherwise they were mechanically very similar to the 'K11s'. Both the driving and trailing bogie were finished in locomotive green, edged black with white lining, whilst the body livery was in the modified style already described for Joint car No 2.

Perhaps surprisingly, in view of the electric lighting installation in 'H12' No 2, all of the 'H13s' were provided with gas lighting. It is mere speculation that the extra drain of the 100lb of steam per hour, or the extra resistance of a wheel-driven dynamo, might have been considered just too much.

A feature peculiar to the 'H12' and 'H13' railmotors, and to the later 'Gate' trailer cars, was that the vertical corners at the ends

and porches were rounded off except at the extreme top and bottom. Also, in the 'H13s' and the later 'Gate' trailers, the height of the sides was increased by 2in, allowing deeper ventilator windows in the top section. As the overall height was maintained at 12ft, this meant that the roof curve was slightly flatter than for other carriages.

The floors of both saloons were linoleum-covered, but in First there was the added luxury of a horsehair mat displaying the Company's monogram. Possibly it had proved difficult to keep the cloth seats clean in the First-class compartments of the 'H12s', because in the 'H13s' these seats were upholstered in blue-coloured leather, but those in the Third class were again of moulded plywood. Smoking was not allowed in either saloon. The luggage compartment was designed to hold up to one ton of passengers' luggage.

Whether or not these cars could in fact haul the trailer specified has been the subject of some debate, but at least two, Nos 10 and 11, and possibly Nos 14 and 15, were provided with gangways at the guard's end, though there is no evidence of these being put to any use. These gangways were of the early LSWR pattern, ie narrower than the standard ones that were being introduced on main-line carriages at about the same time.

In an appendix to the *Book of Rules and Regulations* for January 1911 it was stated that a trailer carriage or two horse boxes, or two other four-wheeled vehicles, could be attached in rear, provided they had vacuum automatic brakes. When a trailer carriage was attached, the conductor-guard was to ensure as far as possible that passengers joining at unstaffed halts went in the railcar in order to simplify and speed the issue and checking of tickets; he was also to ensure that passengers did not ride in the gangway (presumably meaning the entrance vestibule) between

Continued on page 89.

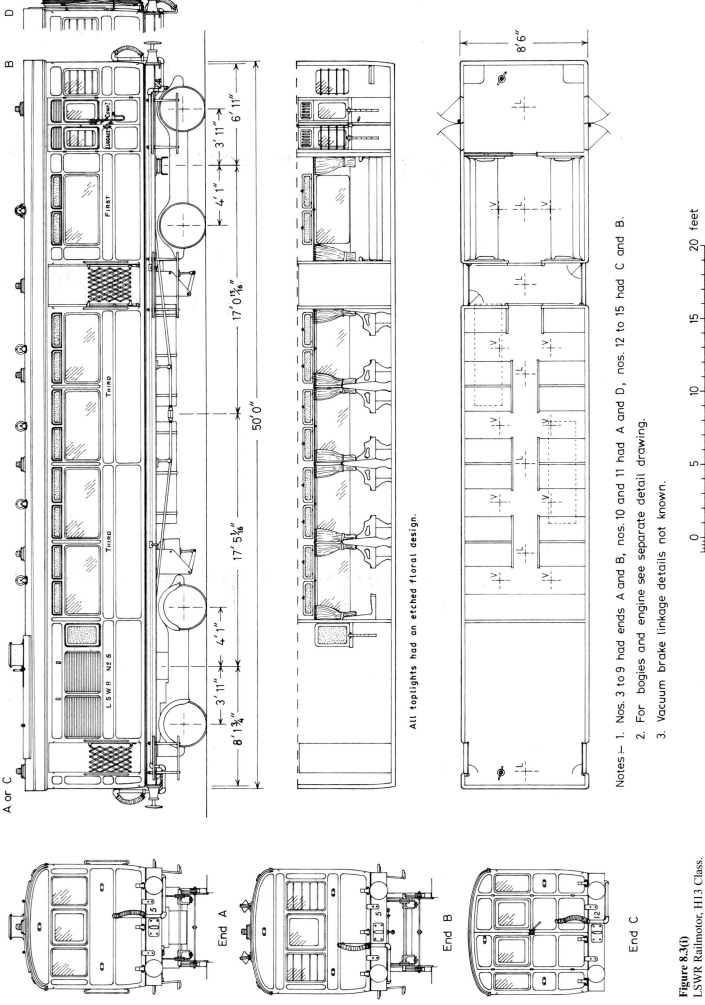

D

B

A or C

LUGGAGE COMP.

FIRST

THIRD

THIRD

L S W R № 5

8' 1¾"   3' 11"   4' 1"   17' 5⅕₁₆"   50' 0"   17' 0⅕₁₆"   4' 1"   3' 11"   6' 11"

All toplights had an etched floral design.

8' 6"

Notes :- 1. Nos. 3 to 9 had ends A and B, nos. 10 and 11 had A and D, nos. 12 to 15 had C and B.

2. For bogies and engine see separate detail drawing.

3. Vacuum brake linkage details not known.

0   5   10   15   20 feet

End A

5

End B

End C

12

Figure 8.3(i)
LSWR Railmotor, H13 Class.

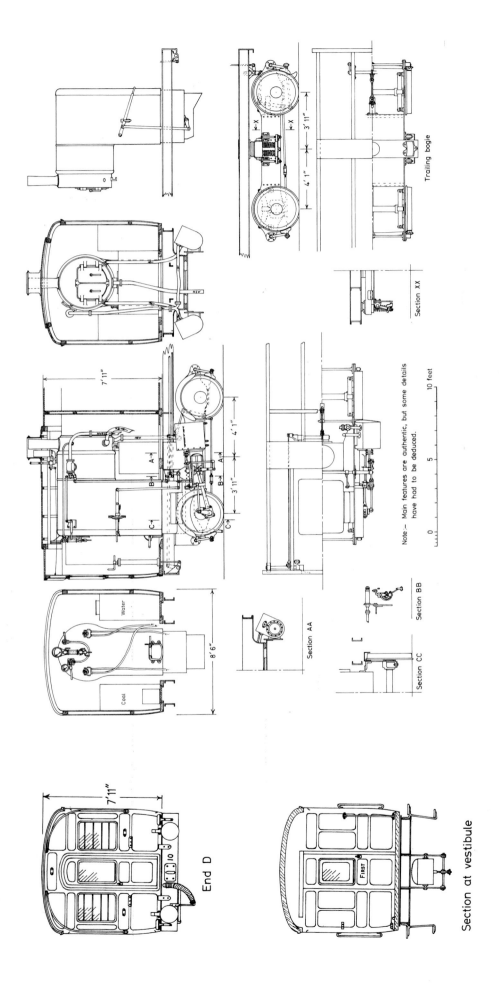

Figure 8.3(ii)
LSWR Railmotor, H13 class engine unit and trailing bogie.

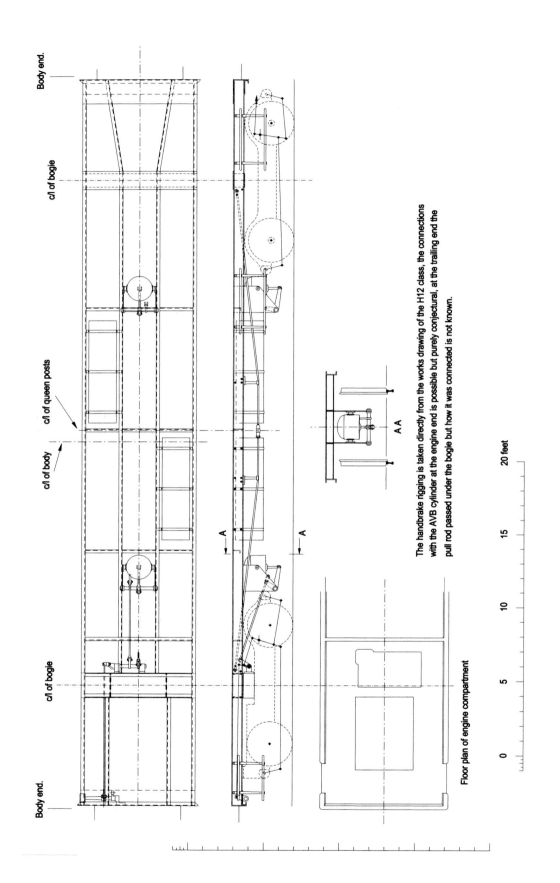

The handbrake rigging is taken directly from the works drawing of the H12 class, the connections with the AVB cylinder at the engine end is possible but purely conjectural, at the trailing end the pull rod passed under the bogie but how it was connected is not known.

Body end.

c/l of bogie

c/l of queen posts

c/l of body

c/l of bogie

Body end.

A

A

A A

Floor plan of engine compartment

0   5   10   15   20 feet

Figure 8.3(iii)
LSWR Railmotor, H13 class.

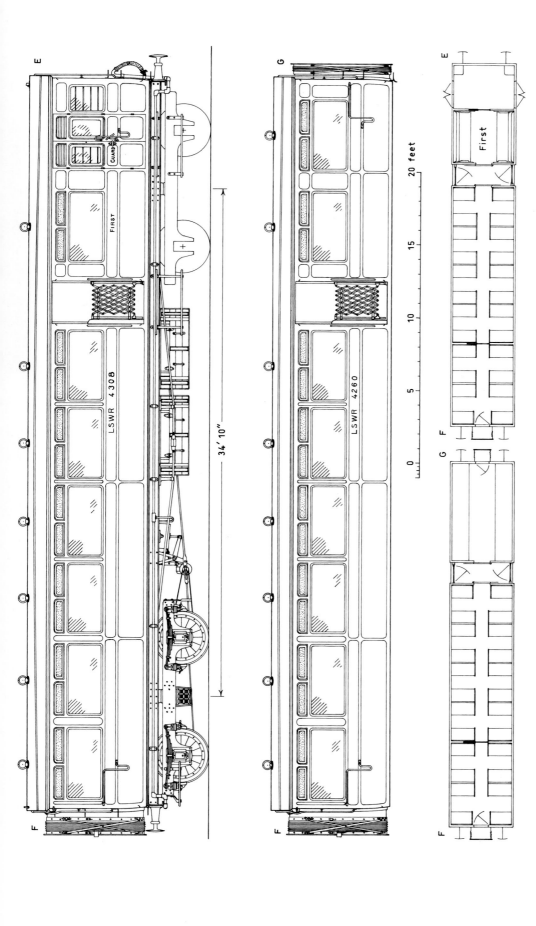

E

G

20 feet

15

10

5

0

GUARD

First

LSWR 4308

34' 10"

LSWR 4260

F

G

E

First

F

G

F

Twelve H13 Railmotors were converted in about 1919 to 2-car
Push-Pull Brake Composites nos.4306-4317 and the remaining
one to Trailer Third no.4260.

SR records suggest that only one car in each pair had a full
set of dynamo and three battery boxes.

Some end and underframe detail has only been estimated
from photographs.

Figure 8.3(iv)
LSWR Railmotor, H13 Class – rebuilds.

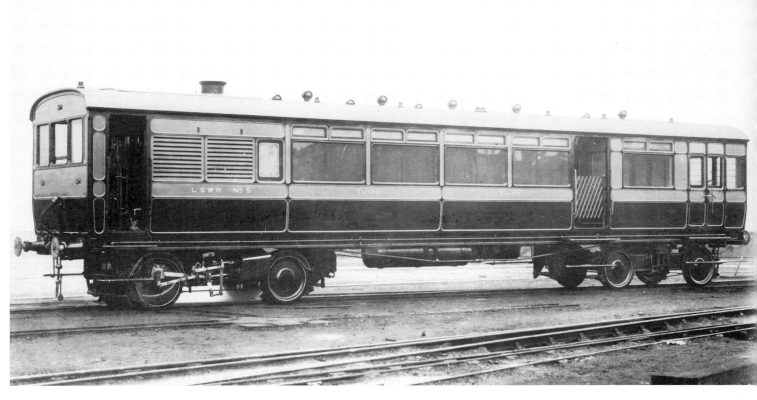

Plate 8.3a 'H13' class railmotor No 5. *Real Photographs*

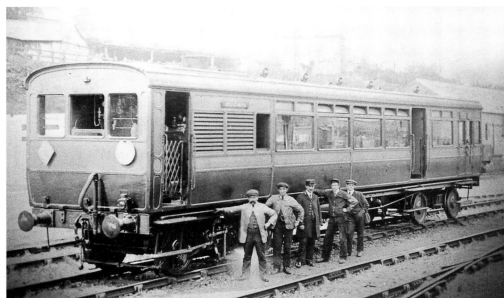

Plate 8.3b 'H13' class railmotor No 8 on the Bodmin-Wadebridge service. *J. Tatchell collection*

Plate 8.3c 'H13' class railmotor No 9 leaving Hounslow. *Lens of Sutton*

Plate 8.3d Former 'H13' railmotor No 4 as SR Driving Trailer No 6557. *J. H. Aston*

Plate 8.3e Former 'H13' and 'H12' railmotors and a two-car trailer set (SR No 731) near Easton behind 'O2' No 213. *Kenning Collection*

the saloons. Second-class tickets were not to be issued, but passengers with such tickets from a connecting service were to be allowed to travel in the First-class saloon. The driver was always to travel at the leading end of the car, and if he wanted the assistance of the brakes worked from the other end he was to give three or more short, sharp whistles.

One major disadvantage of the railmotor concept was the need to separate the two sections for major locomotive maintenance. In the case of the 'H13s' the boiler had to be lifted off the power bogie through a large hatch in the roof before the bogie could be run out for attention. When another four railmotors, Nos 12 to 15, were built on orders A14 and B14 (two on each) they were provided with double doors at the driving end and a removable section of floor and removable headstock, so that the motor unit could be drawn out complete. Of course, there was then no need for the large hatch in the roof.

It was common in the case of locomotives, where a number of separate orders was placed for substantially the same type of locomotive, to refer to the class in general by just one of the order numbers. Thus, in the case of the railmotors, since the H13, A14 and B14 orders were mechanically virtually identical, they were all referred to as 'H13s'. Figure 8.3 shows the main batch together with the detail variations for the A14 and B14 orders. An

interesting feature of the underframes of both the 'H12s' and the 'H13s' is that hardly anything was symmetrical! The bogies were not equidistant from the vehicle ends, nor were the queen posts, and the bogies did not pivot about the centre of their wheelbase. Some of the dimensions on the original drawing were quoted to sixteenths of an inch, which seems rather an optimistic standard of accuracy.

The vacuum-brake hangers appear to have been of sheet steel instead of the usual 'V' shape, and were both arranged the same way round and on the centre line, instead of reversed and offset to the sides, as on most vehicles. How the vacuum brakes were coupled to the floating fulcrum arrangement on the bogies is not known, as photographs have the linkage in deep shadow.

By 1916 the poor economics of operating the railmotors was accepted, and on 5 October the Traffic Committee recorded: 'In view of the fact that the fifteen Railmotors cannot be used economically on any section of the railway, except between Wadebridge and Bodmin, it was ordered that twelve of the cars be dealt with by converting the carriage portion into open corridor vehicles ... at an estimated cost of £260 a car, and scrapping the mechanical portions, providing a credit of £170 for each loco so scrapped.' The retained vehicles, presumably to work the Wadebridge and Bodmin services, were 'H13s' Nos 4203, 4204 and 4210. The two LSWR/LBSCR Joint cars had already been laid aside in August 1914. On 18 December 1919 the Locomotive, Carriage & Wagon Committee ordered that the three remaining railmotors and one of the Joint LBSCR ones be similarly converted. The rebuilding and further use of these cars will be dealt with later.

Before that, in February 1906, it was decided to build three 'motor trains' for use between Plymouth and Tavistock. Each train was to consist of a railmotor, to be built at Nine Elms, and a trailer, to be built at Eastleigh, equipped so that the train could be driven from each end. These sets were to be equipped with Stone's electric lighting. However, at the next meeting, in March, a report from Mr Drummond described the way in which the Great Western was operating 'motor car' trains, and as a result the previous order was cancelled and it was decided to build six vestibule cars at Eastleigh and 10 four-coupled 'motor' engines at Nine Elms. Also at Mr Drummond's urging, it was agreed that the carriages should be fitted with incandescent gas lighting.

The three 'motor train' sets each consisted of two 48ft by 8ft 6in carriages, connected by gangways, one being all Third and the other a Brake Third with driving controls, both shown here at Figure 8.4. The gangways were again of the narrow pattern, possibly recovered from the earlier main-line carriages that were, by then, having their gangways replaced with the standard type. The gangway connections permitted conductor-guard working at unstaffed halts without the restriction mentioned earlier for the railmotors.

Somewhere along the line the order for 10 four-coupled 'motor' engines got translated into a new class of small 'Motor Tank' locomotive, the 'C14' 2-2-0T. Like the railmotors, these were soon found to be somewhat lacking in power, particularly when other and heavier carriages were fitted with Pull-Push equipment, so later on some other locomotives of the 'O2', 'T1', '415' and 'M7' classes, as well as the two ex-LBSCR 'Terrier' tank engines, were also fitted for this type of work.

A very obvious feature of the railmotors and these 1906 Pull-

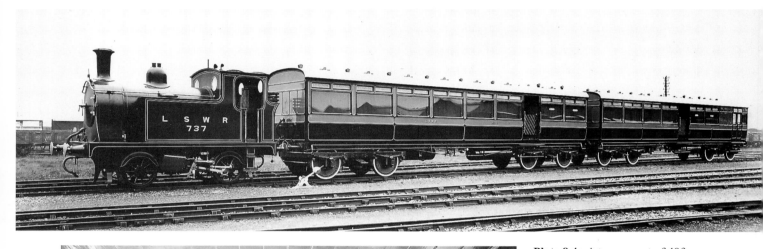

Plate 8.4a A two-car set of 48ft trailers in the company of 'C14' 2-2-0T No 737, 1906.
National Railway Museum

Plate 8.4b Interior of a 1906 two-car set. Note the perforation pattern on the plywood seats.
National Railway Museum

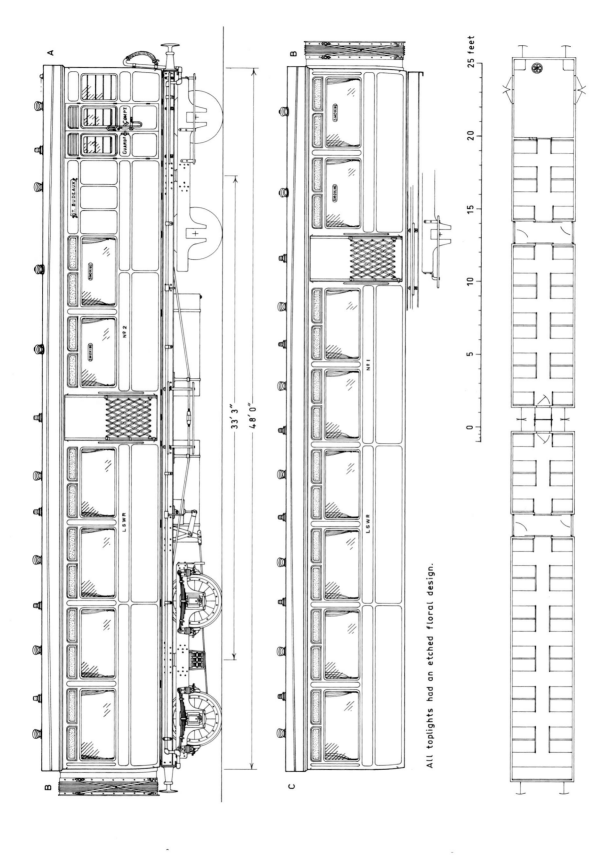

All toplights had an etched floral design.

Figure 8.4
LSWR 48ft 'Motor Train' stock of 1906.

Push sets was that passenger access was by way of Bostwick-type folding and hinged lattice gates, leading on to a transverse vestibule from which sliding doors opened into the saloon compartments. It is from this feature that all the similarly-equipped lightweight trains and railmotor conversions came to be widely known in later years as 'Gate Stock', although the LSWR Carriage Register and the *South Western Gazette* called them 'Vestibule Cars'.

Internally they were similar to the railmotors, the general finish being polished mahogany; the seats were of preformed and polished three-ply birch with patterns of holes, presumably intended to provide ventilation and some roughness to prevent passengers from sliding about. They were thus light in weight, cheap and easy to keep clean. The end and vestibule bulkheads carried coloured photochromes of places of interest fixed in mahogany frames. Lighting was originally by Pintsch's incandescent gas with bypass pilot lights but, like the later ones, they were converted to electric lighting after 1916. Steam heating was fitted along the floor edge on either side, the pipes being enclosed behind polished brass grids — though it is doubtful for how long the brass remained polished! Curtains were provided to the side windows which had, above them, toplights with a frosted floral pattern. These were hinged to open inwards at the top so as to give more ventilation than that obtained through the Ash's 'Acme' ventilators on the roof. The underframes were of channel steel with solebars 9in x 3in x ⅜in.

The guard's compartment was fitted with the same type of controls as the 'H12' and 'H13' railmotors, but in this case the wires passed over the roofs of both carriages and on via pulleys on the cab roof of the locomotive. By this means the driver could control the train from either end, according to whether the locomotive was pulling from the front or pushing from the rear; hence this method of working came to be known as 'Pull-Push', though this later often got turned round to 'Push-Pull'. This form of control lasted on the LSWR and the Western section of the Southern Railway until 1929, when the SR standardised on the compressed-air system that had been adopted by the LBSCR.

It has been said above that these sets were intended for use between Plymouth and Tavistock. The Register shows them as allocated there in 1918, in rather curious detail as two sets to Plymouth-St Budeaux and one set to Plymouth-Turnchapel — limitations which seem a little unlikely. These sets were converted to compressed-air control in about 1929 and used with similarly-fitted 'O2' class 0-4-4T locomotives. They remained in that area until their withdrawal in 1939/40.

The Portland branch was jointly owned with the Great Western, with each company taking turns to operate it. The LSWR was due to take the responsibility in 1910, so on 22 July 1909 it was decided to build three cars for the line, 'to be worked by a small locomotive', at a total cost of £2,500. These three cars were each 56ft long but were otherwise based on the design of the 48ft two-car sets. This time the order consisted of two Brake Composites (First and Third class) with driving control at one end and a gangway at the other, to Drawing 1830, entitled '56 Feet Brake Composite Trailer Car, Weymouth-Portland Branch', and one Trailer Third, with a gangway at each end, to Drawing 1831, illustrated at Figure 8.5. Although the entrance gates looked much like the earlier ones, they were now rigid and hinged instead of folding, and were less than the full width of the wider vestibule openings. There is no record of any LSWR set number having been allocated. Since both Brake Composites were equipped for driving control, it was, as Philip Barnes (South Western Circle) once described it, 'like a fish with two heads'. If it was used for Push-Pull in this form there must have been some unusual arrangement for the control wires to permit connection to a locomotive at either end.

Their early use is uncertain. It seems probable that the set was used as intended in 1910, but there is a report that twice during that year and the next it was replaced for a time by railmotor No 12, but whether for comparisons or during maintenance periods is not known. There is a mention in the Register that the cars were working the Portland branch in November 1918, but not in Pull-Push mode. Certainly the set was split into two parts for some of its existence, with two cars forming SR set 370 and the other one working on its own or coupled to something else. It is not known whether the control equipment was used later, but it was not finally removed until October 1933. The original gas lighting was converted to electric in July 1919, only the Brake Composites having batteries and dynamos. So far, no good photographs of these vehicles have come to light — only one showing little more than one driving end and another where the three-car train is a tiny part of a panoramic view of Portland.

Three more two-car Push-Pull sets of 56ft vehicles, rather similar to the 1909 ones, were built in 1914 following a recommendation from the Carriage & Wagon Stock Committee in

Plate 8.5 LSWR 'O2' class 0-4-4T No 189 with the 56ft three-car trailer set of 1909. Note the conductor-guard.
Author's collection

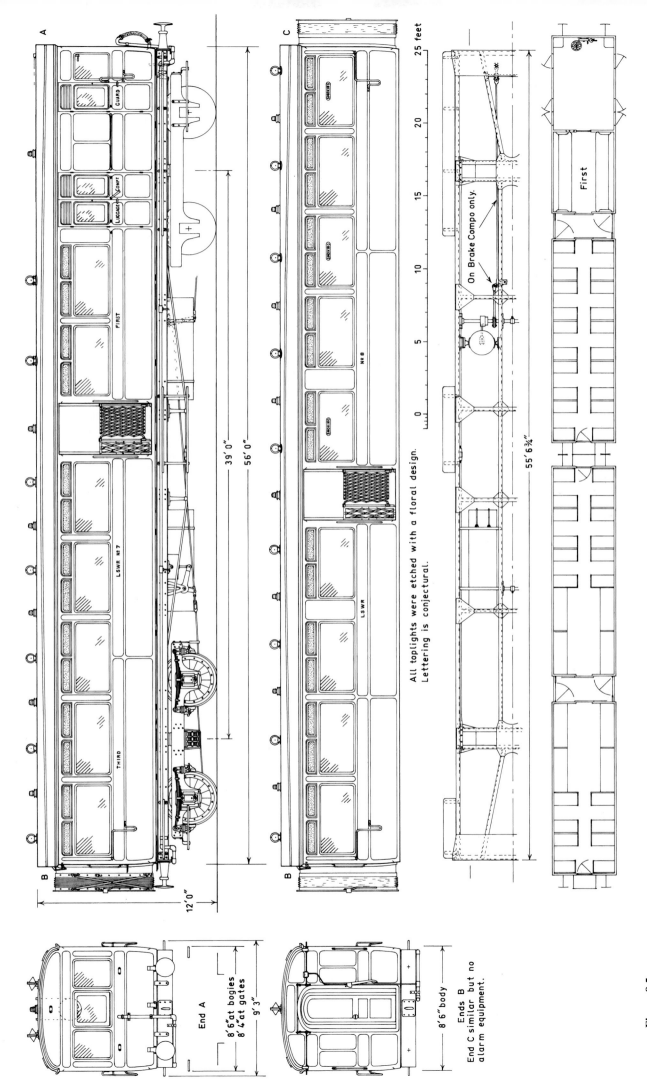

GUARD

LUGGAGE COMPT.

FIRST

LSWR Nº 7

THIRD

End A

8'6"at bogies
8'4"at gates

9' 3"

End C similar but no
alarm equipment.

8'6" body

SMOKING

SMOKING

SMOKING

Nº 8

LSWR

All toplights were etched with a floral design.
Lettering is conjectural.

On Brake Compo only.

First

First

25 feet

20

15

10

5

0

39' 0"

56' 0"

12' 0"

55' 6¾"

Figure 8.5
LSWR 56ft Brake Composite and Trailer Third of 1909.

June 1913 that three new motor trains be ordered for working branch-line services.

The Brake Composites with control equipment were to Drawing 2296 and the Trailer Thirds to Drawing 2295, here illustrated at Figure 8.6. This time the bogies used were of the swinging-link suspension type. The most obvious differences from the earlier ones were the changed position of the vestibules in the Trailer Thirds, the use of hinged ornamental gates instead of the Bostwick type, and the provision of noticeably taller windows in the driving ends of the Brake Composites. Less obviously, the saloon dimensions of the Brake Composites were altered very slightly to permit the inclusion of a sliding door partition in the Third saloon; this might have been to separate smokers from non-smokers, but evidence on this is lacking. Some photographs in Southern days suggest that the door itself had been removed. Unfortunately it is not recorded whether the seats were upholstered or still made of formed plywood as before.

Gas lighting was installed originally, but this was converted to electric in 1919 and 1920. When this was done, batteries and dynamo were fitted to only the Brake Composites, with jumper wires to the Trailer Thirds. It might be in connection with the original gas outfit that full-height handrails and end steps were provided on one of the Brake Composites, No 4303, which were still present in 1938, though the other two had only short rails and the waist-level step when photographed at about the same period, so there is some doubt about this detail.

The ends of all of the 'Gate' stock and the vestibule sides, as well as the trailing ends of the railmotors, were finished in the same two-tone livery as the sides, lined out round the lower as well as the upper panels with either gold or pale yellow in place of the usual very dark brown, the fine red line apparently being omitted.

A photograph (Plate 8.6d) taken by Mr A. E. West at Eastleigh in July 1950 is particularly interesting as it shows the body of SR No 2623 lifted off the underframe, showing very clearly how much the underframe has bowed upwards when relieved of the weight of the body, clearly demonstrating the function of the bottle screws in the truss rods.

It was possibly around 1929 or 1930, when the decision was taken to abandon the three-wire Push-Pull control system in favour of air control, that the driving brake ends were rebuilt by the Southern Railway to its 'standard' Push-Pull design. The three connecting pipes were not needed at this end — only between the cars and at the far end of the Trailer Third. The entire end panelling and windows were removed and replaced with a sheet-steel end having four tall windows; however, the original corner pillars with their rounded-off corners for all but the top and bottom few inches were retained, although covered with a thin metal strip, beaten to follow the original shape and just wide enough to seal the panel joint. On the driver's side there was a hand-operated windscreen wiper that swept both windows, and also a whistle. Sanding pipes led from a sandbox in the driver's area to the leading wheels of the forward bogie. Six two-way sockets were fitted near the lamp irons to permit the use of electric headcode lamps.

It was recorded above that on 5 October 1916 the Traffic Committee ordered 12 of the 'H13' railmotors to be converted to open-corridor vehicles. It has never been very clear just when the conversion work was done, and there have been strongly conflicting views. However, the Minutes for 26 October 1916 state: 'The twelve Railmotors that have been converted into open corridor carriages are to be fitted with electric light at an estimated cost of £165 a pair.' The words 'have been converted' are debatable.

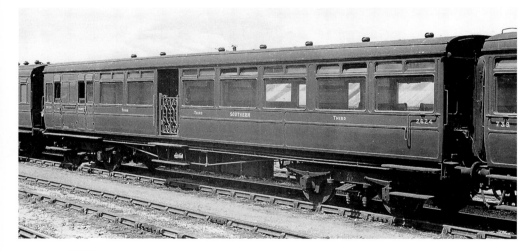

Plate 8.6a 56ft Brake Composite (driving) No 4305 (Drawing 2296) as SR No 2624 at Bere Alston, July 1948. *J. H. Aston*

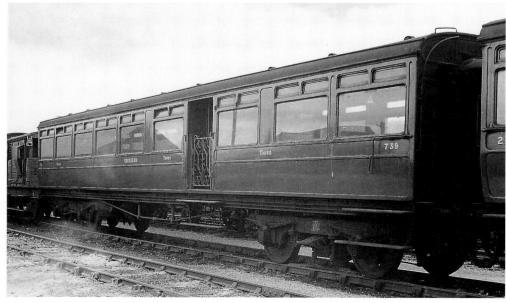

Plate 8.6b 56ft Trailer Third No 4257 (Drawing 2295) as SR No 739 at Bere Alston, July 1948. *J. H. Aston*

Plate 8.6c Gate of 56ft Trailer Third (Drawing 2295). *A. E. West*

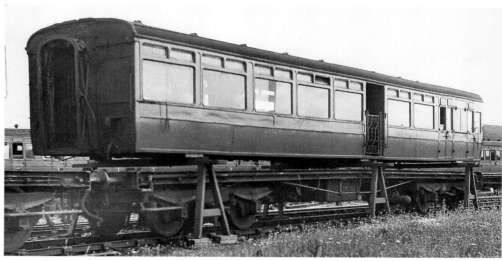

Plate 8.6d 56ft Brake Composite No 4304, altered to Brake Third (SR No 2623) in October 1939. Note the upward bow of the underframe in this July 1950 view at Eastleigh. *A. E. West*

The Register shows 12 as withdrawn in November 1916. Their renumbering dates to Brake Composites are shown as 1919. However, two that were given higher vehicle and set numbers than some of the others are shown as converted in December 1916. This difference seems to suggest that the 12 conversions were all carried out around the end of 1916 but that the cars were not renumbered until 1919 when the remaining three were ordered to be converted to Trailer Thirds. According to the Register the ex-'H13', No 4210, was done then, but the two ex-'H12s' were left (or at least not renumbered) until 1922.

The 12 that became Brake Composites were formed up in pairs connected by standard gangways, including the former No 11, which had its gangwayed secondary driving end rebuilt like the others. These six two-car units were initially intended to work as Pull-Push trains — Nos 11ᵖ to 16ᵖ — using the three-wire control system. Rather unusually, full-height handrails were fitted to both ends of each car. At the gangway ends the steps gave access to the roof, presumably for attention to the control wires, although a climber had to be careful not to trip on the alarm signal rodding. The upper step at the driving end was only high enough to permit attaching a lamp or disc to the top bracket. Previously, the only way of reaching this was by stretching out of the central droplight, which must have been a bit of a stretch for a short man, particularly when the extended tongue was added to the lamp brackets.

Though not mentioned in the records, it may well have been at this time that the seats were at long last all upholstered. It is not certain whether control equipment was retained in all driving cabs, thus permitting the attachment of a locomotive at either end; that this was so might be inferred from a note on one drawing to the effect that double wire guides were required on each side of the roof. The original provision appears to have been double guides along one side of the centre line (and lamp tops) with

single guides on the other side. The Push-Pull equipment was removed in 1932/3, although in some cases the roof pulleys remained in place for a long time afterwards. There does not seem to be any evidence that they were converted for the air-control Push-Pull system, rather that they were used as ordinary two-car sets or just singly.

The authorisation for electric lighting and the SR records after 1923 show that only one vehicle in each pair was provided with a dynamo and batteries. One of the 'wired only' ones, No 4306 (SR 6548), appears in a photo dated in 1935, seemingly without batteries and in use as a single-car train at Torrington and bearing its set number, 361. Other 'wired only' ones show up in photos in the 1950s with anything from a single battery box to a full set of three plus a dynamo, so policy seems to have been variable.

The former No 10, by now Trailer Third No 4260, retained its original narrow gangway in position, though the end windows were panelled in and the luggage compartment was altered to be an extension of the former First-class compartment. The side benches were extended and two oak rails with straps were suspended from the roof to cater for standing passengers in a manner familiar to bus and London Underground users but rather unusual on a surface railway. At the other end a standard gangway was fitted.

In all cases the vestibule gates were modified: the opening was reduced by fitting a gate post to one side and the gates were made rigid by riveting steel strips across their backs. Possibly this was to avoid occasional damage to the framing of the sliding doors when open, or to prevent accidents to passengers' fingers or clothes in the folding lattices.

All of the rebuilt cars were given normal 8ft wheelbase Fox's bogies with leaf bolster springs. It seems quite likely that these bogies were spares recovered from the rebuilding of bogie block set Brake Thirds as described earlier. As 'H13s', the bogie centres

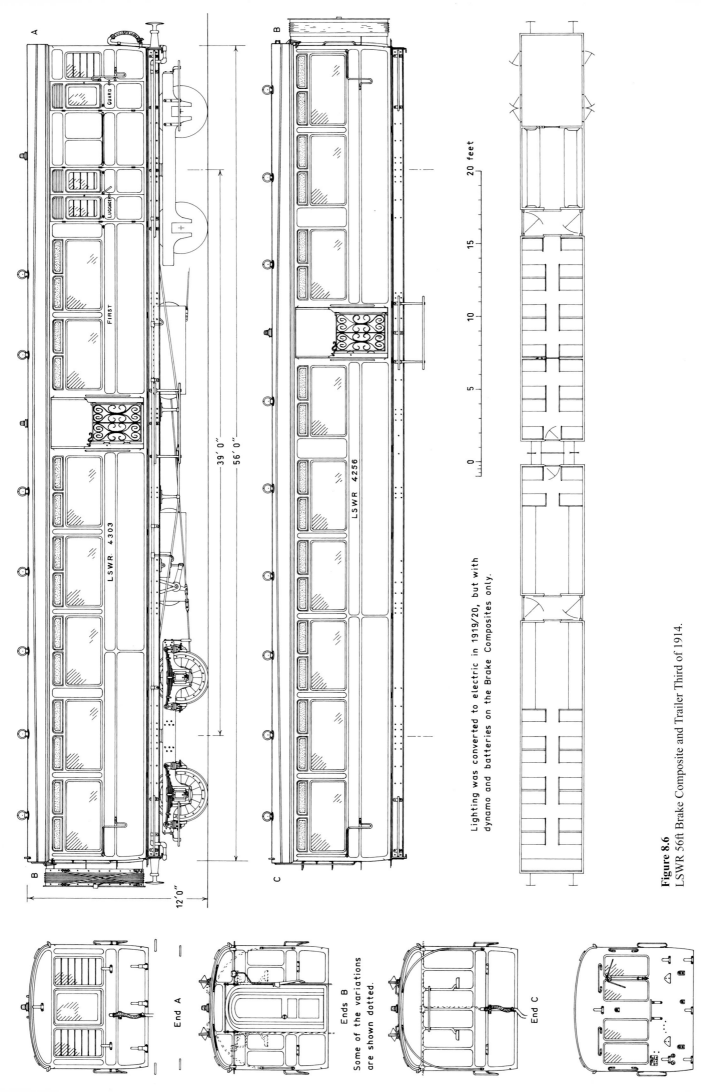

20 feet
15
10
5
0

39' 0"
56' 0"
12'0"

GUARD
LUGGAGE
FIRST
LSWR 4303

LSWR 4256

Lighting was converted to electric in 1919/20, but with
dynamo and batteries on the Brake Composites only.

Figure 8.6
LSWR 56ft Brake Composite and Trailer Third of 1914.

End A

Ends B
Some of the variations
are shown dotted.

End C

SR end A

Plate 8.6e 56ft former Brake Composite No 4305 at Eastleigh, July 1948. *A. E. West*

were not equidistant from the ends, but when rebuilt the centre mountings were adjusted to be symmetrical and this seems to have also involved adjusting the queen posts and truss rods. It was probably also at this time that the original buffers were replaced with normal carriage ones.

Like the other Pull-Push sets, they seem to have wandered far and wide, though largely west of Exeter, and latterly sometimes as single cars. Unlike the 56ft 'Gate' stock, they appear not to have had their ends rebuilt to SR Push-Pull style.

The decision in 1919 to convert the remaining railmotors included one of the LSWR/LBSCR Joint cars, the other one being handed over to the Brighton company for scrapping. The converted one (and there is some disagreement as to which it was) was quite extensively rebuilt as Trailer Third No 4261. The former luggage compartment was removed and this end was built out to the end of the underframe as another side-bench saloon. At the other end the former First saloon was similarly built out to the end in Third-class style. Both ends were given the same turn-under as the other trailer cars and converted 'H13s'. Standard gangways were installed at each end. The windows were altered in the same way as those of the 'H12' railmotors had been much earlier, so that each would have two outward-opening lights at the top for improved ventilation. The overall wheelbase was altered from 47ft 11in to 46ft 8¼in using Fox-pattern bogies as in the other conversions.

As already mentioned, the two remaining railmotors, Nos 1 and 2 of the 'H12' class, were left until 1922, when they were converted as trailer Thirds on the original underframes, with standard gangways at each end. Again, Fox's bogies with leaf bolster springs were used. The former First saloon was extended and reconstructed as Third to take up the space where the engine had been, whilst the luggage and driving compartment at the other end was turned into an extra bay for the main saloon. Electric lighting complete with batteries and dynamo was installed. There are photographs of both of them on the Portland line in 1929. One, the former No 2, lasted right up until March 1956.

The use of all the 'Gate' or 'Vestibule' vehicles is a very complex subject and is not specifically documented in official records. Mr P. E. Barnes wrote some articles on this subject for the

South Western Circle in 1973, and Mr M. King provided supplementary information in 1979 relating to Southern days. For the following I have leaned heavily on their researches, but any errors or omissions are my own fault.

We know from LSWR records for which services many of the carriages were officially intended, but, apart from photographs and recollections of enthusiasts, there is little or no record until the SR Carriage Working Notices of September 1931. Even after that not a great deal of detail is known.

The two-car sets of 1914 that were intended for branch-line services seem to have moved around quite a lot. It has been reported that in 1915 the Exeter-Topsham railmotor was replaced by one of these sets, and the service extended to Exmouth; also that in 1916 another set, working the Seaton branch, was augmented by the insertion of one of the former 'Eagle' saloons that had been re-classed as Third No 72. This set was recorded in the Register as working the Lee-on-Solent Branch in November 1918. It is not known when the ex-'Eagle' was removed from the set, but according to the Register it was restored to First class in July 1925. Also in November 1918 the other two sets were on the Fratton-Southsea and Exeter-Honiton services, the latter not using Pull-Push, presumably because of concern over the safety of operating the long and steep banks with the engine at the 'wrong' end. The Lee-on-Solent set was photographed on the last day of operation, 31 December 1930, still as two cars, bearing a temporary set number 377 on a disc on the top lamp bracket.

The Brake Composites were re-classed to Brake Thirds in late 1939 and the sets were sent to the Plymouth district to replace the three 1906 sets. They worked there for a time but were later seen at Seaton, Yeovil, Swanage and Salisbury, lasting right up to 1956-60.

The only LSWR set numbers recorded are 11ᴾ to 16ᴾ for the six two-car sets of former 'H13' class railmotors. It will be recalled from Chapter 6 that sets 1ᴾ to 10ᴾ were the two-car Push-Pull sets formed from ex-bogie block four-car sets. The SR set numbers that included all the 'Gate' type cars ran from 361 to 374, but their formations varied from time to time.

The SR Carriage Working Notices dated 21 September 1931 set out the open Push-Pull sets in the form of duties:

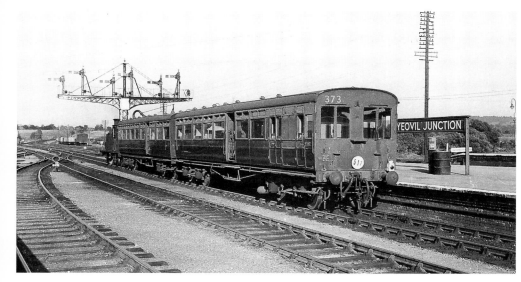

Plate 8.6f 56ft Brake Third (ex-Brake Composite No 4303, Drawing 2296) and 56ft Trailer Third (LSWR No 4265, Drawing 2295) at Yeovil Junction in BR days. *Author's collection*

Duty No	Set or type	Area of use	Berthed at
126	362-4	Bere Alston	Callington
127	367-9	Turnchapel branch	Plymouth Friary
128	367-9	Plymouth-Tavistock	Tavistock or Plymouth Friary
129	367-9	Plymouth-Tavistock	Tavistock or Plymouth Friary
130	1 Brake Compo (Tlr)	Bodmin-Padstow	Wadebridge
131	1 Brake Compo (Tlr)	Torrington-Halwill	Torrington
132	1 Brake Compo (Tlr) (part set 372-4)	Seaton branch	Seaton
133	1 Brake Compo (Tlr) (part set 372-4)	Bishops Waltham branch	Botley
134	372-4	Guildford-Farnham-Bordon	Guildford
135	(unspecified)	Guildford-Farnham-Ascot (included trip to Witley)	Guildford
136	361 + 2 Trailer Thirds	Weymouth-Easton	Weymouth
137	370 + 371 coupled	Weymouth-Easton	Weymouth
138	1 Brake Compo (Tlr)	spare	(unspecified)
139	(unspecified)	spare	(unspecified)

At some time in the 1930s it appears that the set formations were:

Set No	Cars	Withdrawn
361	B/C ex-'H13' 6548, T/Third ex-'H12' 741	3/56 (see Note 1)
362	B/C 6549 & 6551, both ex-'H13' set 11P	10/47 (see Note 2)
363	B/C 6546, T/Third 737, both 56ft set of 1914	11/58 (see Note 3)
364	B/C 6550 & 6552, both ex-'H13' set 12P	10/42 as part of set 362
365	B/C 6558 & 6559, both ex-'H13' set 15P	4/56 and 12/46 respectively
366	B/C 6556 & 6557, both ex-'H13' set 16P	12/39 and 4/56 respectively
367	B/Third 3201, T/Third 733, both 48ft set of 1906	6/39
368	B/Third 3200, T/Third 734, both 48ft set of 1906	12/39
369	B/Third 3202, T/Third 735, both 48ft set of 1906	4/40
370	B/C 6543 & 6544, Third 736, 56ft set of 1909	(see Note 4)
371	B/C 6554 & 6555, both ex-'H13' plus T/Third 742, ex-'H13', & T/Third 740, ex-'H12' }	after bomb damage at Weymouth 4/5/41
372	Unknown	(see Note 5)
373	B/Third (ex-B/C) 2622 & T/Third 738, 56ft set of 1914	10/60
374	B/Third (ex-B/C) 2624 & T/Third 739, 56ft set of 1914	7/56

Notes:

1. An H. C. Casserley photograph shows No 6548, marked set 361, working singly at Torrington, 26/5/35. Another photograph shows both together at Bere Alston, 8/47.

2. Set 362 had at some time included the cars of set 364, ie a four-car set. A Casserley photograph shows No 6551 working singly at Okehampton, 28/8/45.

3. Withdrawn 11/58, but used again for a Railway Enthusiasts' Club excursion in 1959.

4. Set 370 had several changes and its formation at any one time is uncertain. The SR Register shows No 6543 withdrawn 10/37 at the same time as the ex-Joint car Trailer Third No 743, but war damage reports list this, as well as Brake Composite No 6553, ex-'H13', as part of set 370 when it was damaged beyond repair at Weymouth 4/5/41.

5. Set 372 just might have been a single-car set using No 6543 at a time when No 370 was a two-car set, consisting of Brake Composite No 6544 & Trailer Third No 736, both sets on the Portland branch, date unknown. The rebuilt railmotors also moved around a lot, both as pairs and singly, sometimes Push-Pull and sometimes not.

The Appendix to Carriage Working Notices for 16 June 1947 shows sets 363, 373 and 374, by then entirely Third class, as working Turnchapel, Plymouth Friary, Bere Alston and Callington. The ex-'H13' Brake Composite trailers, Nos 6549, 6551, 6557 and 6558, were shown to work these daily commencing services — the 4.50am freight Barnstaple Junction to South Molton Road, two to work the 7.18am Callington to Bere Alston and one for the 9.47am Callington to Bere Alston — leaving a bit of a puzzle about what happened to them for the rest of the day.

Chapter 9

CORRIDOR CARRIAGES (PANELLED)

There is a distinction between corridors and gangways, although the terms are sometimes confused, even in railway records. Strictly, a corridor is simply a passageway within a carriage; in the period under review it was often at one side and partitioned off from the compartments. A gangway is a flexible passageway, usually enclosed, linking two carriages. Perhaps this seems a little pedantic, but the South Western built several corridor carriages that either had no gangways at all or had a gangway at only one end. There were also several carriages that had gangways but no corridors — mainly saloons, as we have seen in Chapter 6 — where there was either an open central passageway or where two saloon compartments had a door between them, but in this case there was probably no intention of allowing passengers from other carriages to pass to and fro.

In a sense the first corridor vehicles on the South Western were the Pullman cars, in that one could walk the complete length of each vehicle, and also between vehicles if two were coupled together. Of course, the first one, the *Alexandra* (mentioned in Chapter 5 of the earlier volume), was really intended as a Parlour Car, and there was nothing else on the South Western permitting through passage. The later ones, introduced from 1890, will be mentioned a little further on.

In Chapter 5 there was a description of the 47ft 6in 'Eagle' saloon carriages, and it was stated that, early in 1901, 14 of them were converted to form three corridor dining trains for the West of England services, where they remained in use for the North Cornwall Express until 1907. Initially no gangways were provided at the outer ends of a set, so each train was essentially self-contained. The same thing applied to the first sets of vehicles

that were designed as corridor trains, but later, between 1905 and 1909, additional gangway connections were fitted at the guard's van ends. The absence of set-end gangways appears to have been a considerable, and possibly deliberate, contributing factor to the demise of Pullman cars on the London-Bournemouth service. These first gangways, whilst of the Lansdowne pattern and similar to those of many other companies, were apparently designed to suit LSWR requirements, without much thought about coupling up to those of other lines. Shortly after Mr Surrey Warner was appointed Carriage & Wagon Superintendent in 1906 it was stated, on 30 May 1906, that 85 vehicles were fitted with the old-type gangways, and it was agreed that these should be replaced with the 'standard' type at a cost of £4.10s (£4.50) per vehicle.

A gangway can perhaps be considered as consisting of three main elements. Fixed to the carriage body by a continuous flange was a kind of steel porch about 12in deep. The top was curved and the shape of this curve appears to vary slightly on different LSWR drawings, though always of an approximately semi-elliptical form. On the outer end of the porch there were brackets for a pair of 'scissor arms' on each side that supported the second element, a flanged frame of similar shape to that of the porch. The lower brackets on both porch and frame provided just pivots, but the upper brackets permitted their pivots to move up and down slightly; thus the arms allowed a limited extension movement. The bottom member of the outer frame had a floor plate that was long enough always to rest on the floor of the porch, even with the arms fully extended. The outer frame had a clip on the right-hand side as viewed end-on. This clip and the similar one on the other vehicle were used to secure the two frames when vehicles were

Plate 9.1a Corridor train of 1904, comprising 56ft Brake Third, 54ft Composite (Drawing 1214), 54ft Composite (Drawing 1225) and 56ft Brake Third. *National Railway Museum*

coupled together. Connecting the fixed porch to the moveable frame was the third element, a 'bellows' that was usually made of leather and which often in later years was provided with an extra leather cover over the curved top.

The earlier LSWR gangways had a width between the angle plates of the moveable frame of just under 2ft 2in and a height of about 6ft 3½in, though the actual door in the end of the body was 1ft 10in wide in a 1ft 9in doorway. Coil springs were fitted above and below the bellows in order to keep the latter extended and the end plates in contact, rather like the Pullman system. The standard gangways adopted from 1906 measured 2ft 9in wide and about 6ft 5in high, but the opportunity to widen the actual doorway was not taken until the introduction of the 'Ironclad'-type stock from 1921, and even then the doorway was widened by only 1in. In the case of those saloons that had sliding doors, the doorway was 2ft 2in, though the opening was still only about 1ft 10in because of the protrusion of the edge of the door when open. The coil springs to extend the gangway were no longer provided. It seems probable that those vehicles fitted with the earlier type only needed new moveable frames, accounting for the small cost for the conversion. As on most 'standards', the new frames did not then remain unaltered. Before long, an extra arc of steel had to be welded to the top curve of the outer frame in order to accommodate variations in the shapes used by other companies, and in particular to make it possible to couple up to Pullman cars. These had substantially larger gangways that were designed to press firmly together. This made it necessary for vehicles that might be coupled to them to have two additional special clips fitted to their outer gangway frames.

The carriages at the front and rear of a train would have had the end door and the interior of the gangway exposed to sparks, dirt and rain, so they were provided with covers. At first, and again later, these were made of wood and, when not in use, were stored inside the corridor or the guard's van. However, for a time around 1911 the South Western adopted a roller-blind arrangement, where the roller was attached vertically at the left side so that the canvas blind could be drawn across the opening and secured to catches on the right side. Although they looked rather flimsy, many of them survived for a very long time, even into British Railways days.

Instructions to staff required that the gangway hoods be always securely fastened down, and that gangways be hooked back and covered by the dust screens when not in use. Evidence from photographs suggests that these instructions were not rigorously obeyed.

Because of the obstruction caused by the gangway, instructions were issued that the rear carriage of a train had to carry two rear lamps by day and night — one on each side of the gangway — except where an extended bracket was fitted, usually on the first step above the headstock, when only one lamp was needed.

The first LSWR carriages to be designed to form corridor trains were authorised in January 1903 by the Traffic Committee in order to make up four trains for improved West of England services. A similar train was ordered, to serve Bournemouth and Weymouth. The improved services were actually started from June 1903, before the new trains were ready, using from six to eight non-corridor carriages or the converted former 'Eagle' carriages (with corridors) and a Kitchen Brake. The new timing from Waterloo to Exeter was 3¼ hours — 92min to Salisbury, and, after this stop, 98min non-stop to Exeter (99min on the up journey). There was a nominal 20mph restriction through Yeovil before rebuilding, but apparently 40 to 45mph was the usual speed.

The first four new corridor trains, consisting of two Brake Thirds, a Third and two Composites, were described in *Railway Magazine* for May 1904 in an article describing the development of the Ocean Quay at Plymouth (Stonehouse Pool) as a terminal for the American Line's transatlantic services. The article described both the train and the inaugural run from Plymouth to Waterloo with passengers from the SS *St Louis*. Naturally, this run, which was accompanied by various senior officers of the LSWR, was planned to be a particularly fast one, the only intended stop being for a change of engines at Templecombe (118 miles), since there were no water troughs on the line. In fact, they encountered what was implied to be a deliberate delay at

Exeter St David's while the Great Western train from the SS *St Louis*, carrying the mails, was allowed to pass! Despite this and a 7min signal stop, the 230 miles 5 chains were covered in 4hr 24½ min. This kind of delay had been a common cause of complaint over the years and led, in October 1905, to the Traffic Committee's sending a recommendation to the Board that the Resident Engineer and the Solicitor should at once proceed with plans and notices to construct an avoiding line from Exeter Queen Street to Cowley Junction. Whether that was simply dismissed by the Board or whether they discussed the matter with the Great Western and were satisfied by assurances is not recorded.

Who knows — perhaps if that line had been built, taking physical control out of Great Western hands, the ex-Great Western influence within British Railways that contributed largely to the virtual destruction of the ex-LSWR/SR network west of Exeter, and still prevents electrification from reaching Exeter and thus competing with services from Paddington, might have been far less effective, leaving much of the West Country with better rail connections than now exist.

The Plymouth boat trains continued to run as and when required, with timings to be as good as the conditions and the drivers could make them, still with only the stop at Templecombe, until after the disaster to one of them at Salisbury in 1906, after which the Templecombe stop was replaced by scheduled timings and stops at Exeter and Salisbury.

As authorised, the new corridor vehicles, together with an assortment of 13 others, were all to have been 59ft long and 8ft 6¾ in wide. There is no mention of altering the planned length, but in fact those that were built varied according to type. The Composites were 54ft long and all the others were 56ft — this length remained the maximum on the LSWR until 1920. The overall width of 8ft 6¾in (9ft 3in over lookouts) also remained the standard for corridor stock until the introduction of the 'Ironclad' stock in 1921. With the increased width there was a reduction of 2in in the mid-panel and window heights and also a modification of the roof curvature, as compared with the non-corridor stock. Footboards were fitted at about the mid-height of the solebars instead of at the bottom of them as previously. These were also the first new carriages to be built without side coupling chains, it having been agreed to dispense with these at the Locomotive, Carriage & Stores Committee meeting on 29 April 1903. These trains, and all the later corridor stock, were fitted with steam heating.

The First-class compartments were finished with polished walnut fascias and sycamore and Hungarian ash panels, with lincrusta linings inside the roof. The seats were upholstered in blue cloth with silk lace trimmings. The Second- and Third-class interiors were similarly finished, but had polished mahogany fascias, instead of walnut, the former being upholstered with brown plush and the latter with brown repp. The corridors of the Composites were finished in mahogany with lincrusta panels, whereas the Thirds and Third Brakes had teak framing with mahogany bottom and pine top panels. In all the corridors there was a brass handrail at half height along the outer windows. All compartments had an electric bell-push to communicate with the Dining Car when this was included in the train, though this provision slightly anticipated the actual authorisation of the Dining Cars.

All corridor vehicles were electrically lit, normally having three battery boxes and a dynamo. A question mark hangs over the cabling to the lights. The official photographs of the first batch of vehicles in 1904 shows that the cabling was external on the roof, protected by (presumably) wooden casings. There are very few other clear photographs of carriages in LSWR condition to confirm whether this was regular practice, but photographs taken in both Southern and British Railways days tend to confuse the matter, since, whilst some have the casings, most have clear roofs where the wiring is obviously internal. General Arrangement drawings give no guidance on this subject. It is purely a personal impression that cabling was probably external on new carriages between 1903 and the end of the decade but was internal after that, though possibly replaced externally if or when rewiring became necessary.

Another detail about which evidence is lacking is the lavatory windows. It has already been mentioned that six-wheeled and non-

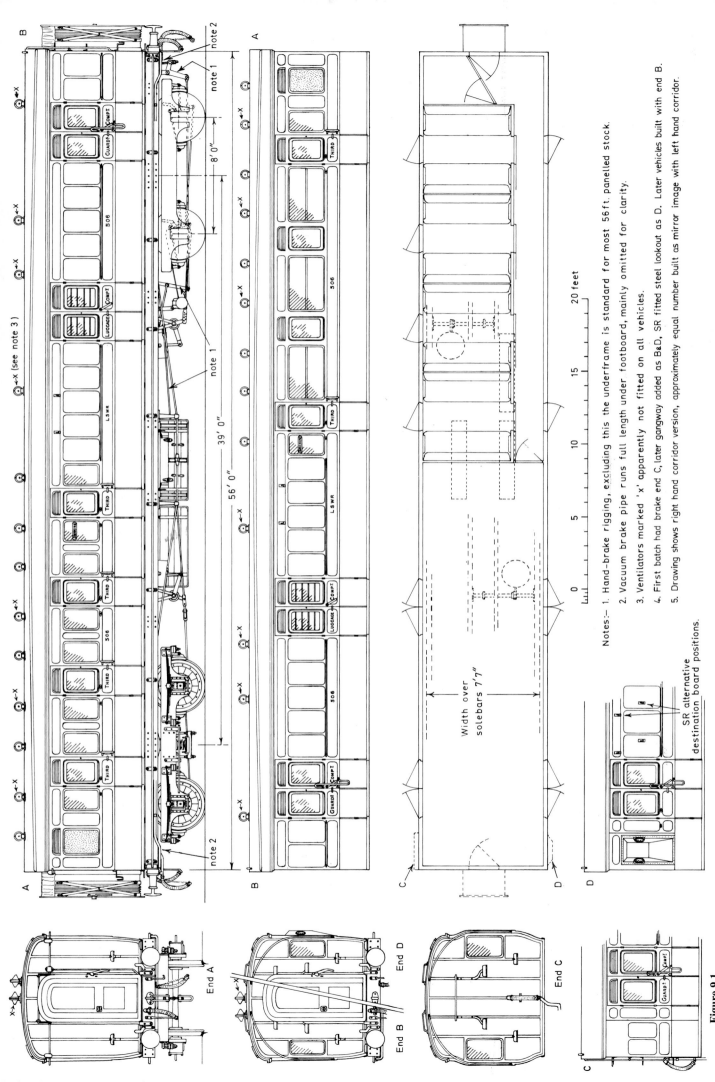

Notes:– 1. Hand-brake rigging, excluding this the underframe is standard for most 56ft. panelled stock.

2. Vacuum brake pipe runs full length under footboard, mainly omitted for clarity.

3. Ventilators marked 'x' apparently not fitted on all vehicles.

4. First batch had brake end C, later gangway added as B&D, SR fitted steel lookout as D. Later vehicles built with end B.

5. Drawing shows right hand corridor version, approximately equal number built as mirror image with left hand corridor.

Width over solebars 7'7"

20 feet

GUARD COMPT
LUGGAGE COMPT
THIRD
506
LSWR

Figure 9.1
LSWR 56ft 0in x 8ft 6¾in Corridor Brake Third.

End A

End B

End D

End C

SR alternative destination board positions.

GUARD COMPT

corridor stock often had a floral design within a kind of cross between an ellipse and a diamond, surrounded by an outer border, etched in the frosted glass. The official photographs of the original corridor vehicles of 1903 and 1904, and of the Sleeping Saloons of 1908, show that there was a similar pattern in the lavatory windows and the corridor side windows opposite the lavatories, but instead of a floral design the central part was in the form of an 'L&SWR' monogram, slightly similar to that used on some passenger locomotives after about 1893, though with the 'S' at the centre rather larger than the flanking 'L' and 'R', and with the ampersand and the 'W' almost lost between them. Dining Saloons, including the high-roof ones of 1913, had a similar design in the large droplights in the kitchen and in one large fixed window in the corridor opposite the kitchen or pantry door. As with the roof cabling, there are insufficient good photographs of carriages in LSWR condition to establish the standard practice, but an official photograph of a Brake Third built in 1910 shows a plain frosted window. Once again, it is purely a personal assumption that the monogram patterns were abandoned for ordinary vehicles some time before 1910 on the grounds of unnecessary expense. In most photographs the angle and contrast make it impossible to decide whether a pattern is present. All photographs taken post-Grouping appear to show plain frosted or 'hammered' glass.

The first type of corridor Brake Third was to Drawing 1227 (illustrated in Figure 9.1) and had the usual LSWR ogee-pattern end lookouts that brought the total width to 9ft 3in. In later years this width limited their route availability, and so this style of lookout was replaced by small pressed-steel ones, bringing the width down to 9ft 1in. However, some of these carriages had already been modified in March 1907, when six of them had the lookouts removed completely and brake-end gangways were fitted, according to a note on LSWR Drawing 1227. Judging from photographs, others were also dealt with similarly. The alterations were detailed on Drawings 1523 and 1533, and were then incorporated in a new vehicle drawing, No 1568 (referred to again later), which was otherwise almost identical to the original drawing, No 1227. A detailed drawing of the underframe for the Brake Thirds, and applicable to most of the other corridor vehicles apart from the handbrake rigging, appeared in *Modern Railway Working,* Volume 5.

Figure 9.1 shows, in the two main side views, the modified vehicles mentioned above or equally the later version built between 1907 and 1911 to LSWR Drawing 1568. End views A and B apply to this version. The original type, built in 1904 to Drawing 1227, was similar in all respects except that the brake end appeared as shown in end and part-side views C. The Southern Railway replacement lookouts are shown as end and part-side views D.

Plate 9.1d 56ft Brake Third (Drawing 1227) — probably No 729 or No 732 — without lookouts. *A. E. West*

Plate 9.1e 56ft Brake Third (ex-LSWR No 14, Drawing 1227) as SR No 3089 in 1948, with SR replacement windows. *J. H. Aston*

Plate 9.1f A Waterloo-Plymouth luncheon-car express near Surbiton, headed by 'D15' class 4-4-0 No 466. *E. S. C. Betteley, courtesy of The Railway Magazine*

Eight of the non-lookout vehicles were taken over during World War 1, seven for United States Ambulance Train No 62, and one for a War Department Continental Ambulance Train, probably No 35. This last carriage, No 1475, was returned after the war and became a Passenger Brake Van, SR No 330. The US Ambulance cars were also returned and were similarly converted to PBVs as shown in the Appendix. Drawings of the van versions have been left for inclusion with the vans.

The two types of 54ft Composite were built to LSWR Drawings 1214 and 1225, which are illustrated in Figure 9.2. The former had four First-class compartments, seating four in each, and three Second-class, seating six in each. Eighteen of these were built, between December 1903 and April 1908. The other type, of which 11 were built, all in 1904, had three First-class and four Second-class compartments, each with the same capacity as before. Later on, when Second class was abolished, the Seconds were altered to seat eight Third-class passengers in each compartment.

There is a minor mystery here. The LSWR drawing for the first batch shows alternate doors and large windows on the corridor side, but a photograph of one of the first three built, No 859, shows two small windows and a panel at the point where there was probably a door dividing the First- and Second-class corridors, though a photograph taken inside the corridor of one of

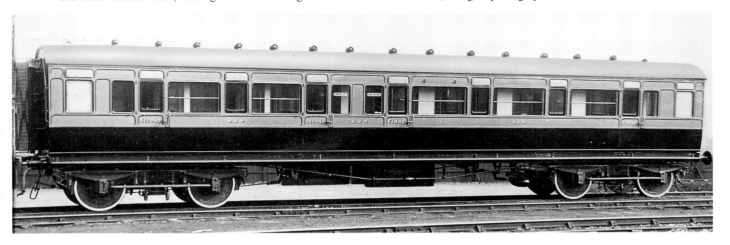

Plate 9.2a 54ft Composite No 589 (Drawing 1214). Note the panel at the door dividing the two sections of the corridor. *HMRS*

Plate 9.2b Corridor of 54ft Composite (Drawing 1214). *National Railway Museum*

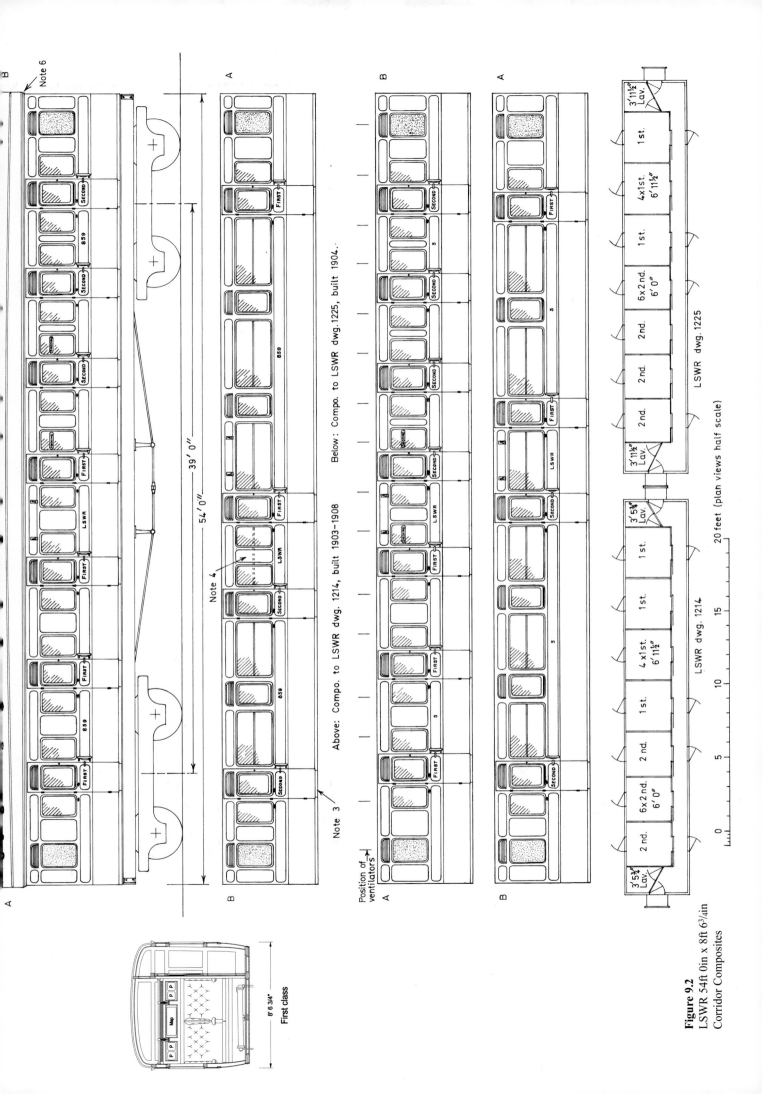

Note 6

A

B

B

A

B

A

Note 4

Note 3

Position of ventilators

859

859

859

859

SECOND SECOND SECOND FIRST FIRST LSWR FIRST SECOND FIRST

FIRST LSWR SECOND LSWR FIRST SECOND

SECOND 5 SECOND FIRST LSWR SECOND FIRST

FIRST SECOND 5 5

39' 0"

54' 0"

Above: Compo. to LSWR dwg. 1214, built 1903–1908

Below: Compo. to LSWR dwg. 1225, built 1904.

8' 6 3/4"

First class

P P Map P P

| 3'5¾" Lav. | 2 nd. | 6 x 2 nd. 6'0" | 2 nd. | 1 st. | 4 x1st. 6'11½" | 1 st. | 1 st. | 3'5¾" Lav. | 3'11½" Lav. | 2 nd. | 2 nd. | 2 nd. | 6 x 2 nd. 6'0" | 1 st. | 4 x1st. 6'11½" | 1 st. | 3'11½" Lav. |

LSWR dwg. 1214

LSWR dwg. 1225

0   5   10   15   20 feet (plan views half scale)

Figure 9.2
LSWR 54ft 0in x 8ft 6³⁄₄in
Corridor Composites

them shows the small windows but no trace of a door. Photographs of later vehicles in this batch are as the drawing. On the other hand, the later drawing shows such a panel and traces of where the door detail has been erased, but photographs of this batch just show large windows! It is quite likely that lockable doors were originally provided as a legacy of the earlier segregation of the classes; also one Southern register specifically notes that the last four to Drawing 1214 did not have a door across the corridor.

The 56ft Thirds are illustrated in Figure 9.3. Forty-four of these were built between 1904 and 1916, but although they all looked the same externally there were in fact three variants. The first batch was built to LSWR Drawing 1226, from 1904 to 1907; two more were built in May and June of 1910 to Drawing 1872, followed by a further 14 of the same between October 1911 and July 1913. This drawing showed the door openings carried right down to the bottom of the body, so that the doors closed into recesses in the bottomsides (the wide and thick timbers forming the foundation of the body). The last batch was built in 1915 and 1916 to Drawing 2390, which was similar to Drawing 1872 except that the sides were now clad with steel panels instead of wood. The new drawing was needed because many of the body framing dimensions had to be slightly altered. As for the Composites, the tare weight was around 27 to 28 tons. Eleven of these vehicles were converted for use in ambulance trains in World War 1, mainly in United States train No 62, as shown in the Appendix.

Shortly after authorising the first five trains, on 27 May 1903 the Traffic Committee sanctioned a further three trains of five vehicles each for the Bournemouth services, and two trains of six vehicles for the West of England. For use on the latter services, eight loose Brake Thirds were also approved. The initial formation of these trains was to be:

Vehicle	Drawing No	Compartments		
		1st	2nd	3rd
Five-car sets				
56ft Brake Third	1227	-	-	4
56ft Third	1226	-	-	8
54ft Composite	1214	4	3	-
54ft Composite	1225	3	4	-
56ft Brake Third	1227	-	-	4
Six-car sets				
56ft Brake Third	1227	-	-	4
54ft Composite	1214	4	3	-
56ft Brake Third	1227	-	-	4
56ft Brake Third	1227	-	-	4
54ft Composite	1225	3	4	-
56ft Brake Third	1227	-	-	4

Since these Brake Thirds had no gangway at the brake end, from the passengers' point of view the six-car sets were really two three-car sets.

The first complete sets were arranged so that the corridors alternated from side to side of the train. This meant that equal numbers of left- and right-handed Brake Thirds had to be built.

It was earlier mentioned that the absence of gangways at the brake ends affected the Pullman cars, so it is worth looking briefly at that story. At the beginning of Chapter 5 reference was made to the short-lived trial of the Pullman car *Alexandra* on the Waterloo-Exeter service in 1880 and which was apparently withdrawn because of poor support from passengers. In January 1889 the Pullman Car Co approached the South Western again, and in June a 10-year agreement was signed. Minutes of the LBSCR for October 1889 record a request from the Pullman company that the Brighton workshops erect two cars for use on the LSWR in addition to the two which were to be erected for the LBSCR.

Plate 9.3a 56ft Third (LSWR No 1609, Drawing 1872), later SR No 663. *Lens of Sutton*

Plate 9.3b 56ft Third (LSWR No 883, Drawing 2390) as SR No 692. *F. Foote*

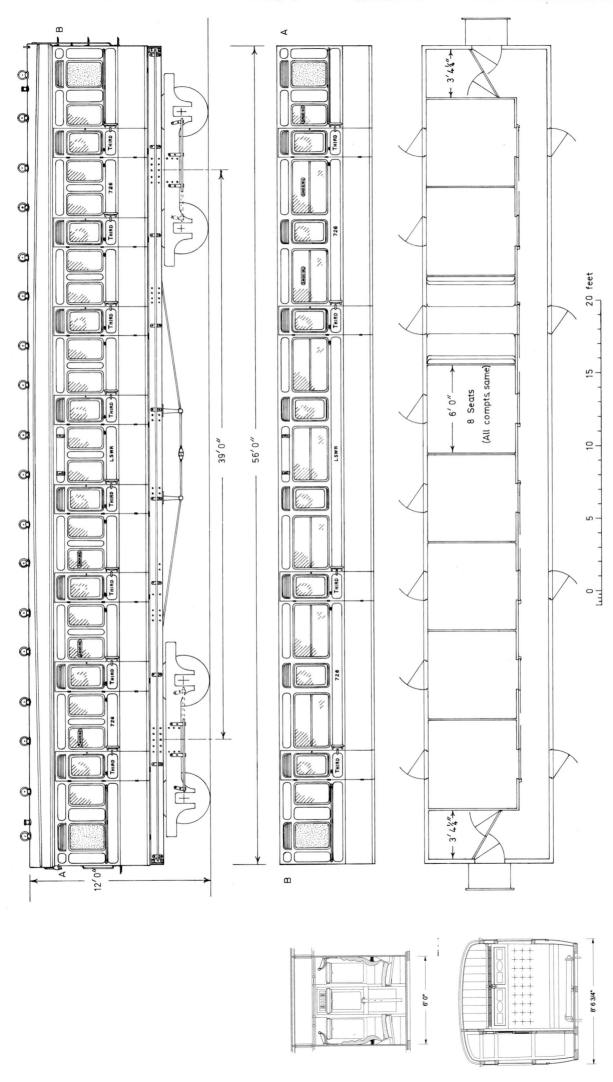

Figure 9.3
LSWR 56ft 0in x 8ft 6¾in Corridor Third.

Notes:— 1. Underframe and bogie details as for 56′ Brake Third, without hand brake rigging.

2. Ends and gangways as A and B ends of 56′ Brake Third, but no windows in end B.

3. Location of roof ventilators and filler caps estimated. (Photos indicate variations).

4. Longer bogie footboards, as shown dotted, usually fitted on compartment side only.

Pullman 'Vestibule Parlor Cars' on the LSWR. *Duchess of Fife* of 1890 at Bournemouth. *C. H. Eden*

The Brighton company replied that the application would have to be made by the London & South Western and that the Pullman company would have to give an indemnity against all risks or consequences! Both conditions were met and the kits of parts were assembled at Brighton, entering service on or about 21 April 1890 as the *Duchess of Fife* and the *Duchess of Albany*. With these it was possible to run up to four services in each direction per day between London and Bournemouth. Because the cars were not owned by the South Western there is no reference to them in the rolling-stock records.

Apparently the Pullman cars were popular enough, because two more kits of parts were brought over in 1893 and assembled at Eastleigh, under the supervision of John S. Marks of the Pullman company, to form the *Duchess of Connaught* and the *Princess Margaret*. The *South Western Gazette* for April 1893 includes a description in which it states that they were 58ft 8in long overall, the body being 52ft long by 8ft 7in wide. The exterior was handsomely painted dark brown, embellished with scrollwork and mediflval designs in gold. Internally, the saloons were finished in vermilion wood, whilst the smoking compartments, passages and buffets were mahogany. The swing seats and stools were covered in old-gold velour velvet and the curtains were crushed-strawberry-coloured damask. They were brilliantly lit with Pintsch's gas lighting.

At this time, of course, there were no other corridor vehicles running on the South Western and so, from a photograph of *Duchess of Fife* at Bournemouth in 1901 and *Duchess of Connaught*, it appears that the Pullman gangways were closed off with an end panel containing a droplight. When the South Western first introduced corridor trains, not only were the gangways incompatible with the Pullman type but, as already stated, they were not provided at the brake ends. At first this probably did not matter much, but when, as the General Manager had put it, Dining Saloons were built to complete these corridor trains, there was a strong disincentive to the use of Pullmans. Whether this omission of brake-end gangways was deliberate or a failure to see their potential usefulness can now only be a matter for conjecture. What is certain is that, according to South Western officials, Pullman usage fell off dramatically.

In June 1896 the Traffic Committee received a report from the Pullman Car Co stating the numbers of passengers travelling in its cars in each year ending in April as: 1891 – 6,843; 1892 – 7,649; 1893 – 8,723; 1894 –12,702; 1895 – 13,844; 1896 – 14,068. Unfortunately no further figures are recorded, but in April 1905 the Traffic Committee received a recommendation from the Superintendent of the Line that 'as corridor trains are now running between London and Bournemouth, and as very few passengers use the Pullman cars, those cars be withdrawn from the 7.50am Up train and the 12.30pm Down train', which was approved. A similar recommendation on 29 November 1905 led to the withdrawal of Pullmans from the 11.10am up and the 6.55pm down. In the following February there was a protest from the Pennsylvania Railroad Co on behalf of the Pullman Car Co, and of some petitioning passengers, in which it was suggested that an opening be made (presumably meaning a gangway) to allow Pullman passengers access to the Dining Cars. There was no direct response to this latter part, but the American company was assured that Pullman cars would continue to run in the 9.12am and 1.55pm up and the 2pm and 4.50pm down trains.

The decline in Pullman passengers seems to have continued, because in November 1908 it was reported that between the previous June and September there had been very few travelling on the 9.12am up and the 2pm down, so these also ceased. By this time the South Western Dining Cars were well established and many Brake Thirds had 'standard' end gangways, but there is no mention of any adaptors to match the Pullman gangways. The end came in June 1911 when it was stated that there were now very few passengers on the remaining 7.50am up and the 4.50pm down, so it was agreed to withdraw the service altogether and terminate the agreement with the Pullman Car Co. It will be noted that the 7.50am and 1.55pm ups seem to have been switched, but there is nothing about this in the Minutes. The decision to terminate the service presumably could not be effected immediately because the 1911/12 Waterloo Train Summary still showed the 4.50pm down as comprising a four-coach set plus one Pullman (Mondays excepted), one corridor First (Fridays and Saturdays only) and one Composite (3,3) (Fridays only), all to Bournemouth West, with another four-coach set for Weymouth.

In May 1904 the General Manager recommended to the Traffic Committee the construction of 10 cars with kitchen

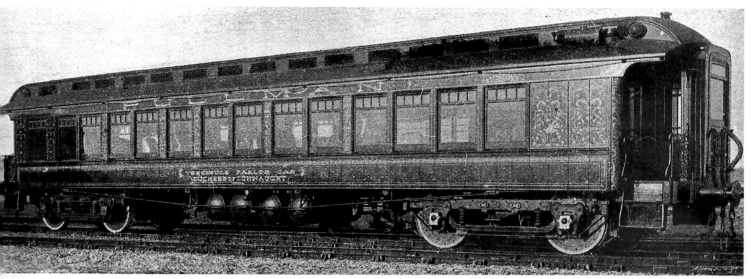

Pullman 'Vestibule Parlor Car' *Duchess of Connaught* of
1893. *Our Railways 1894*
Note the retracted gangways with end windows, also
buffers and brake pipes to match the LSWR carriages.

Interior of Pullman 'Vestibule Parlor Car' *Duchess of
Connaught. Illustration from Our Railways 1894*

accommodation and seats for 28 passengers — to 'complete' the
corridor trains recently ordered — at an estimated cost of £1,300
each, excluding the cost of electric light. This seems to imply that
they were originally intended for these new trains but were not
mentioned at the time either because the design was not completed
or possibly so as not to jeopardise authorisation of the main stock
on cost grounds — my own speculation, but a tactic not unknown
in other spheres! Be that as it may, the Traffic Committee cut the
cost a little by agreeing to have only eight built. They were later
valued in the Carriage Register at £1,375 each.

These Dining Saloons were quite outstanding vehicles, both
internally and externally. The most noticeable external feature was
the clerestory roof which was not used on any other LSWR
vehicle except the rebuilt Royal Saloon, No 17. It was presumably
intended to improve ventilation, particularly in the kitchen area.
Internally they were provided with a very well-equipped kitchen,
intended to permit about 60 luncheons at one sitting, and two
dining compartments. The kitchen was fitted with two electric
fans, and, instead of doors to the corridor, Bostwick gates (folding

lattice) were provided. An 80gal water tank was installed above
the pantry.

The carriages were quite heavy, at over 34 tons tare, so a
number of strengthening improvements was made in the course of
building the four batches. The first saloon, No 59, was built in
November 1904 with underframe and bogies similar to the other
corridor vehicles, but the rest of the batch of eight, which were
completed between March and May 1905 to Drawing 1319, had
an extra truss rod fitted to each side outside the solebars. To take
these, the queen posts were placed slightly further out under the
solebars and had inverted-'T' lower ends to take the double truss
rods.

Another 11, starting at No 67, were built between May 1907
and August 1908. A fresh drawing, No 1601, had been prepared.
Apart from some minor internal changes the truss rods were
replaced by flat 3in x 1in steel bars without adjusters. Between the
two batches there were at least three variations of bogie bolster
springs, but the only record of which vehicles had which type was
in the *South Western Gazette*, which stated in May 1907 that

109

Nos 7, 68 and 69 had Timmis' differential section of coil springs. In Figure 9.4 these parts of the drawings and notes are based on photographs.

In the first batch (Drawing 1319) there is some slight uncertainty about the usage of the two compartments; the drawing does not indicate classes, but what was later the First class was upholstered in blue buffalo hide and the other in soft fabric, probably moquette. This rather suggests a single class, but smoking and non-smoking respectively.

From the second batch (Drawing 1601) onwards one compartment was certainly for First-class passengers and the other for the Second and Third classes. The First-class section was finished with wainscot oak fascias (though the *South Western Gazette* said walnut) and satinwood panels, the seats being trimmed in figured moquette. The Second- and Third-class saloon was finished with polished mahogany fascias and plywood panels. The seats were upholstered with brown plush. In the kitchen the stoves were supplied by Slater & Co.

So far, although the saloons were very comfortable, the window views were rather restricted by the ordinary compartment-type quarterlights and droplights. These droplights were provided with dust excluders. Above each droplight frame and resting on it was a gauze screen in a frame, so that if the glass was lowered part-way the opening was filled by the gauze. Thus chimney ash could to some extent be prevented from falling into the diners' meals. If desired, the gauze could be hooked up out of sight to leave the window open.

In order to improve the steadiness in running, from part-way through the second batch the Dining Saloons were mounted on new bogies that had additional outer side frames. These permitted the bolster beams to be longer and the friction pads steadying the body to be placed 2ft 2in further apart than on earlier vehicles. A detailed illustration of these bogies is shown at Figure 9.5. At this time (mid-1907) the growing naval might of several countries,

Continued on page 118.

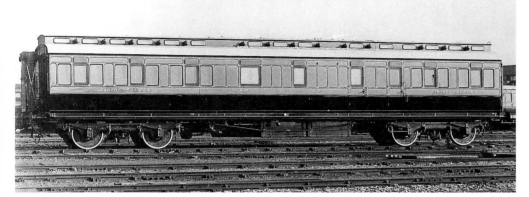

Plate 9.4a The first 56ft Dining Saloon, No 59, to Drawing 1319. *British Railways*

Plate 9.4b 56ft Dining Saloon No 67 of the second series (Drawing 1601), showing the altered bogie springing, flat-bar truss rods and the extra supports for the battery boxes. The gas filler valve cover and the steam pre-heating connection cover can be seen more clearly here than in many views. *National Railway Museum*

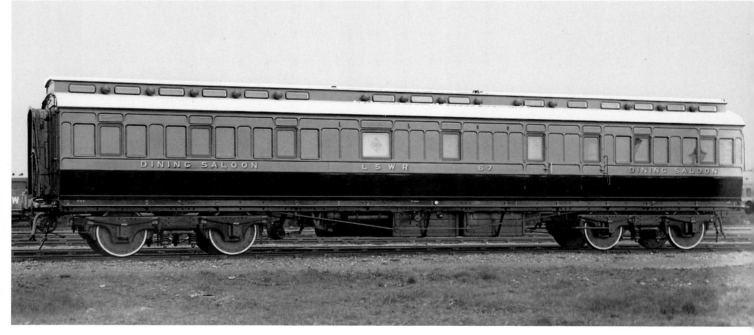

Plate 9.4c Corridor side of 56ft Dining Saloon No 69, built May 1907 to Drawing 1601. *Courtesy of The Railway Magazine*

Plate 9.4d 56ft Dining Saloon No 79 of the third series (Drawing 1869), showing the large windows by each table, and the 8ft wide-framed bogies. *National Railway Museum*

Plate 9.4e First-class section of Dining Saloon No 59, upholstered with dark blue buffalo hide. *National Railway Museum*

Plate 9.4f First-class section of Dining Saloon No 67. *National Railway Museum*

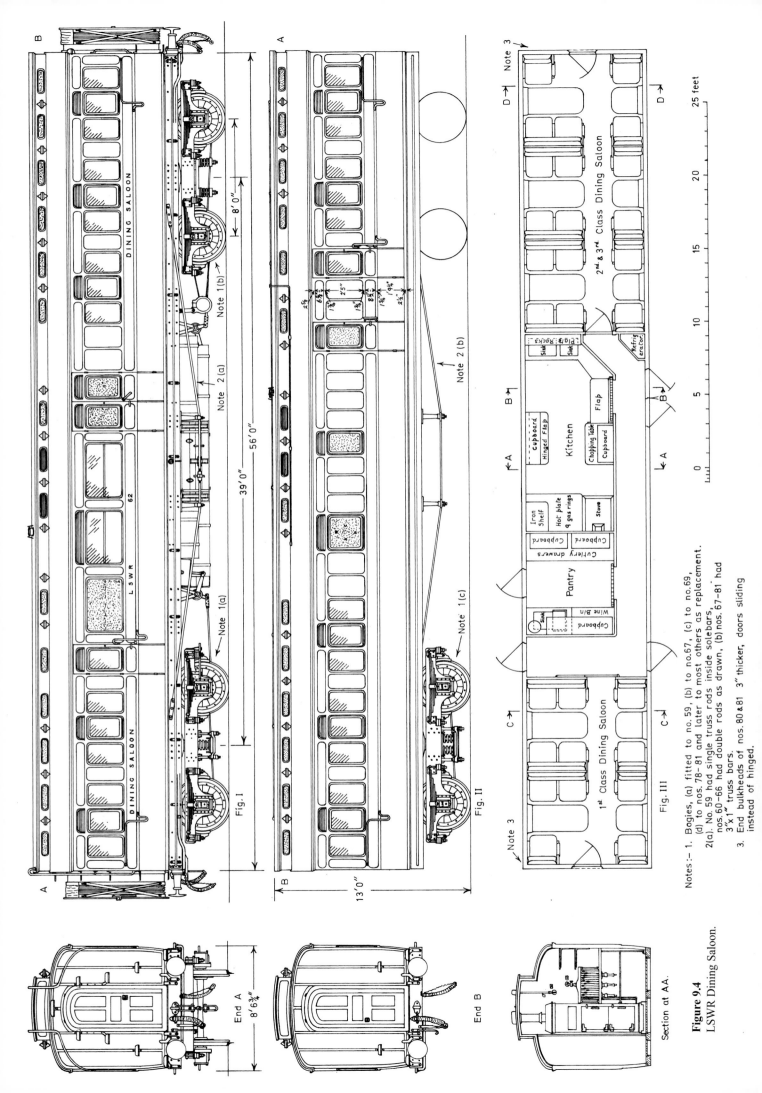

DINING SALOON

L S W R

62

DINING SALOON

8' 0"

39' 0"

56' 0"

Note 1(b)

Note 2 (a)

Note 1(a)

Fig. I

End A

8' 6¾"

End B

13' 0"

Note 2 (b)

Note 1(c)

Fig. II

2¾
6¾
1⅜
2⁵
1⅜
8¼
1¾
9¾
2½

Section at AA.

Note 3

Note 3

Cupboard
Hinged Flap

Kitchen

Iron
Shelf

Hot plate
9 gas rings

Stove

Cupboard

Cupboard

Cutlery drawers

Pantry

Cupboard

Sink

Wine Bin

Chopping table
Flap

Cupboard

Flap

Sink

Sink

Racks

Plate Racks

Refrigerator

2ⁿᵈ & 3ʳᵈ Class Dining Saloon

1ˢᵗ Class Dining Saloon

A
B

A
B

C

C

D

D

Note 3

Note 3

Fig. III

0   5   10   15   20   25 feet

Notes:- 1. Bogies, (a) fitted to no.59, (b) to no.67, (c) to no.69,
(d) to nos. 78–81 and later to most others as replacement.
2(a). No. 59 had single truss rods inside solebars,
nos.60–66 had double rods as drawn, (b) nos. 67–81 had
3" x 1" truss bars.
3. End bulkheads of nos. 80 & 81 3" thicker, doors sliding
instead of hinged.

Figure 9.4
LSWR Dining Saloon.

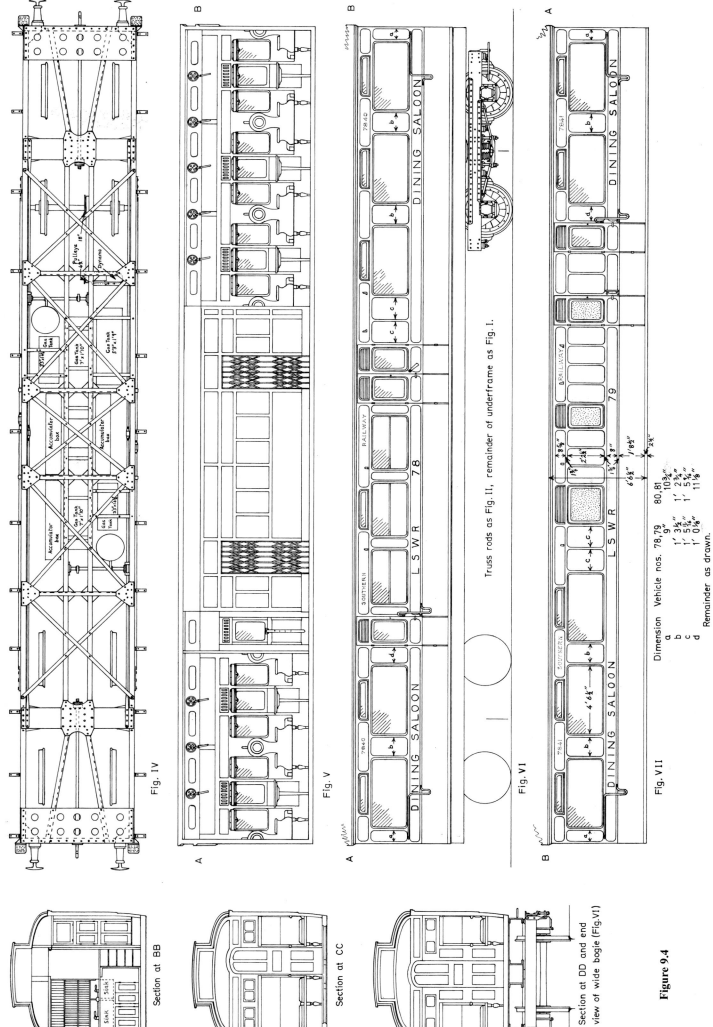

Section at BB

Fig. IV

Fig. V

Section at CC

Fig. VI

Truss rods as Fig. II, remainder of underframe as Fig. I.

Section at DD and end view of wide bogie (Fig.VI)

Fig. VII

Dimension	Vehicle nos. 78,79	80,81
a	9"	10¾"
b	1' 3½"	1' 2¾"
c	1' 5½₁₆"	1' 5 ¹⁄₁₆"
d	1' 0⅛"	11⅛"

Remainder as drawn.

Figure 9.4

Fig. VIII

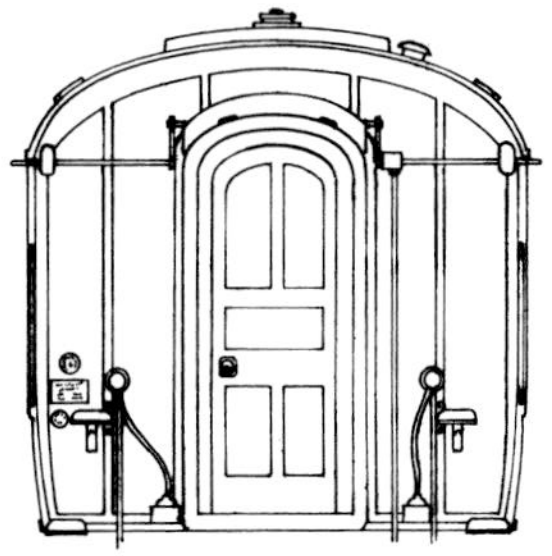

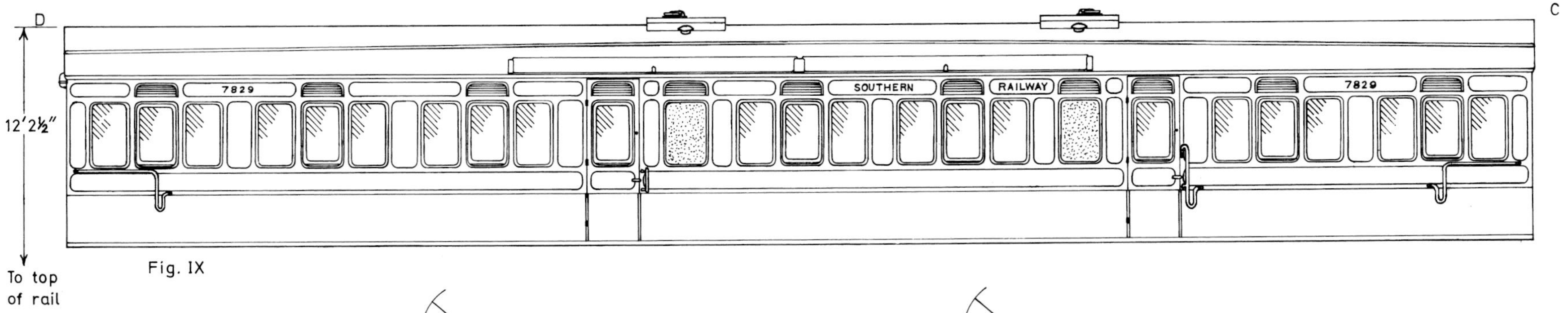

Fig. IX

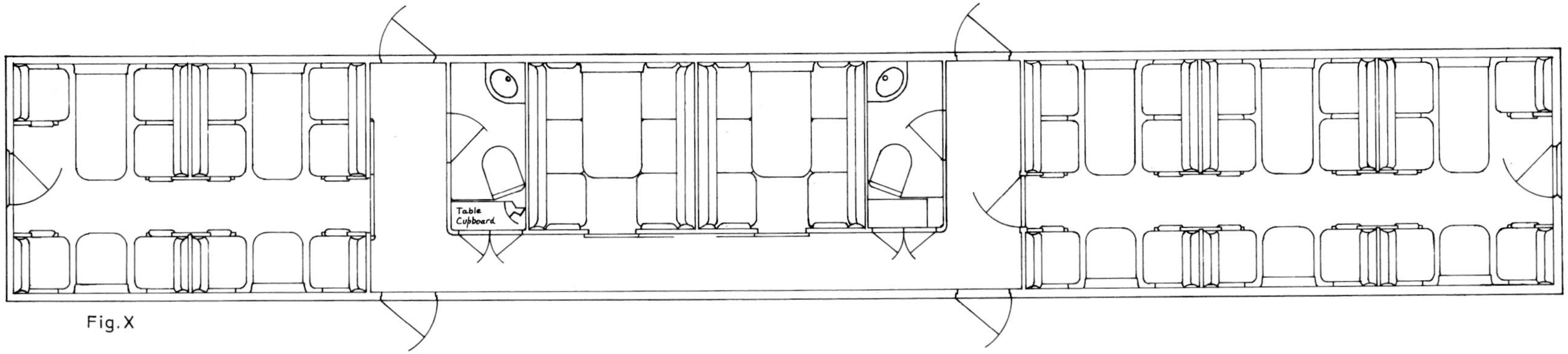

Fig. X

End C

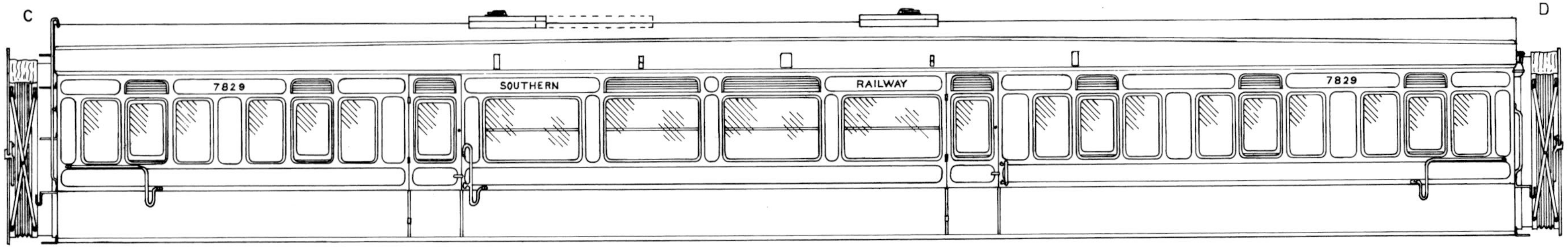

End D

SOUTHERN RAILWAY

7829

12'2½"

To top of rail

Figs. I to V cover vehicles nos.59 to 66 (LSWR dwg.1319) and 67 to 77 (LSWR dwg.1601), with variations as shown in notes 1 & 2. Figs. VI & VII covers vehicles nos.78 & 79 (LSWR dwg.1869), also 80 & 81, figs. III & IV also apply with variations in notes 1 to 3. For nos.80 & 81 the two saloons were slightly shorter, requiring the altered panelling. Fig. IV also applies with modified windows.
End views A & B, and sections AA to DD, apply, with minor interior variations, to figs. I to VII.
In 1931 all Dining Saloons had new roofs as shown in figs. VIII, IX and end views C & D. Nos.59–70, 72 & 76 (by then SR 7821–7832, 7834 & 7838) were altered to Nondescript (i.e. unclassed) Saloons as shown in figs. VIII–X, the remainder retained their original layout.

Figs. XI–XIII show no.7828 as converted to a Naval Ambulance in 1943. Other vehicles were converted for the War Department and the U.S. Transportation Corps. External appearance was generally similar but the interior layouts varied.

Figure 9.4

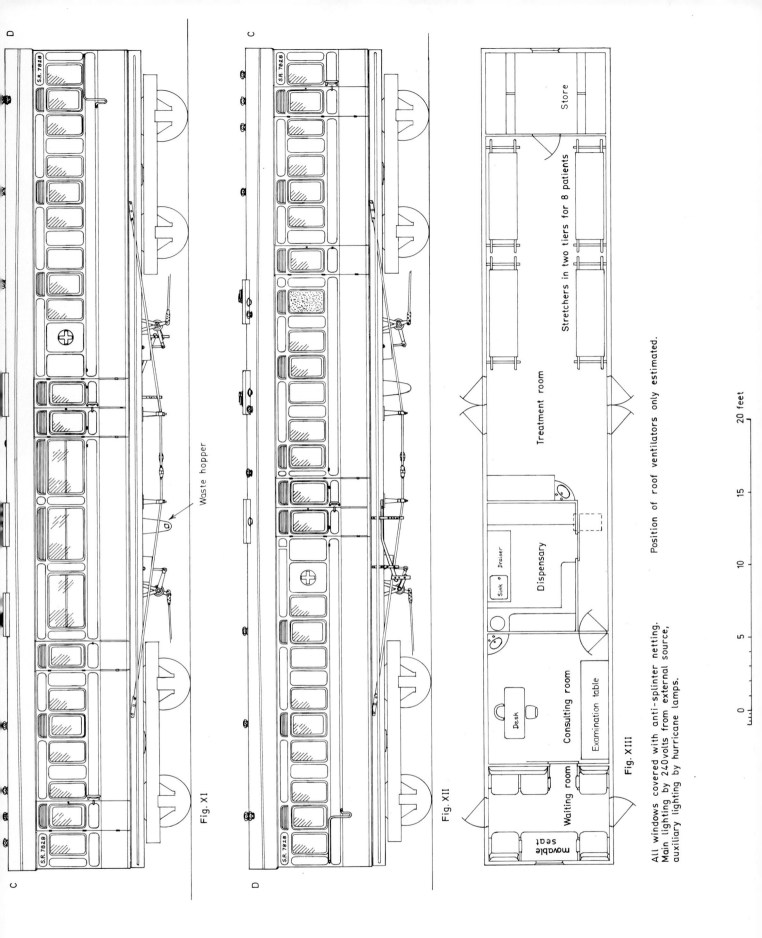

Waste hopper

Fig. XI

Fig. XII

Store

Stretchers in two tiers for 8 patients

Treatment room

Sink Drainer

Dispensary

Desk

Consulting room

Examination table

Waiting room

Movable seat

Fig. XIII

All windows covered with anti-splinter netting.
Main lighting by 240 volts from external source,
auxiliary lighting by hurricane lamps.

Position of roof ventilators only estimated.

0   5   10   15   20 feet

Figure 9.4

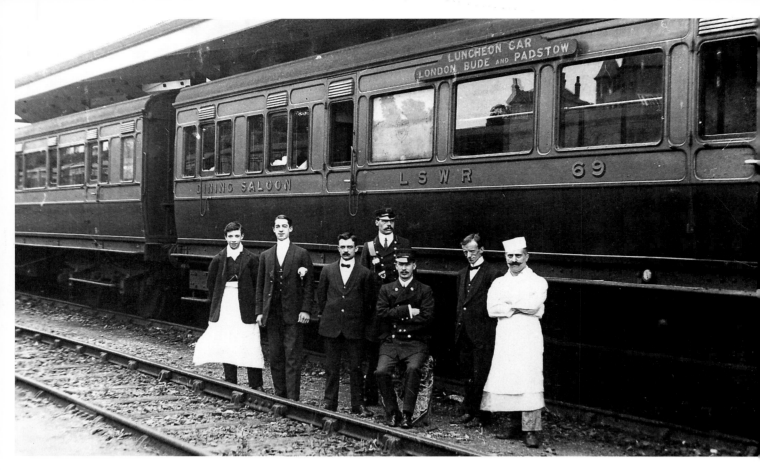

Plate 9.4g Dining Saloon No 69 with staff, including the guard. Note the large style of lettering with the original number.
J. Tatchell collection

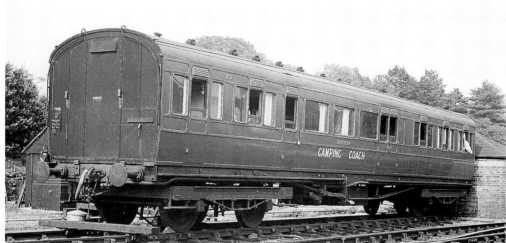

Plate 9.4h Former LSWR Dining Saloon No 66, later SR No 7828. The double truss rods can just be discerned. *J. H. Aston*

Plate 9.4j Former LSWR Dining Saloon No 77 (later SR No 7839), seen in 1958 following use in a mobile office train. *J. H. Aston*

Plate 9.4k Dining Saloon No 72, in later guise as SR No 7834. *J. Tatchell collection*

Plate 9.4l Advertisement for dining-car services commencing 1 October 1912.

Plate 9.4m 'T9' class 4-4-0 No 119 near Claygate with the first luncheon-car train to Portsmouth, October 1912. *E. S. C. Betteley, courtesy of The Railway Magazine*

LONDON & SOUTH WESTERN RAILWAY

You can travel any class between

LONDON (WATERLOO) & **PORTSMOUTH**

and obtain meals en route.

CORRIDOR **EXPRESSES**

BREAKFAST — LUNCHEON — DINNER

WATERLOO	9·10 am	12·45 pm	6·40 pm
PORTSMOUTH	11·10 "	2·34 "	8·26 "
PORTSMOUTH	7·55 am	12·0 noon	7·0 pm
WATERLOO	9·54 "	2·26 pm	9·6 "

DIRECT ROUTE TO THE **ISLE OF WIGHT.**

Figure 9.5
LSWR wide frame ('Dreadnought') bogie.

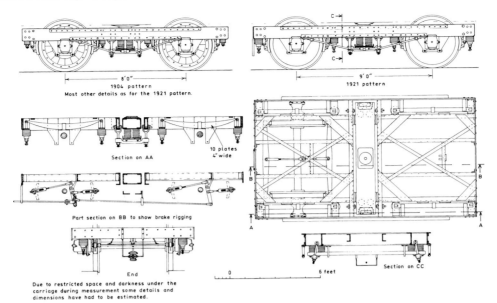

8'0"
1904 pattern
Most other details as for the 1921 pattern.

9'0"
1921 pattern

10 plates 4" wide

Section on AA

Part section on BB to show brake rigging

End

Due to restricted space and darkness under the carriage during measurement some details and dimensions have had to be estimated.

0   6 feet

Section on CC

particularly Germany, was causing a lot of public concern, so there was great interest in the launching of Britain's new battleship, HMS *Dreadnought*, in 1906. It is therefore not surprising that the new bogies, with their massive and heavily-riveted appearance, were soon nicknamed 'Dreadnoughts'.

The final four Dining Saloons, two to each of Drawings 1869 and 2077, improved the view by having large fixed windows the full width of each seating bay. The first two, Nos 78 and 79 which were built in mid-1910, were described in Volume I of *Railway and Travel Monthly* as intended for the Bournemouth to Birkenhead and Sheffield through service via Basingstoke and the Great Western Railway. Incidentally, it was also noted that LSWR locomotives worked through to Oxford with these trains. Shortly after this a further modification was made for the last two cars, Nos 80 and 81, which were built in 1912. This time, the hinged doors in the ends were replaced by sliding ones. The extra thickness for the door casings necessitated slight alterations to the seating-bay dimensions and hence to the exterior panelling. The luggage racks and interior decoration were also altered at the same time.

All 23 vehicles remained as Dining Saloons until 1931, when the Southern Railway removed the clerestories and rebuilt the roofs to approximately the same shape as those of the 57ft 'Ironclad' stock which will be described later. At the same time, 14 of them had the kitchen removed and replaced by two compartments and two lavatories; they were thence described as 'Nondescript' saloons, ie they could be used for either First or Third class according to need. The remaining nine continued as dining cars until World War 2, when one was appropriated to provide staff meals and based at Redhill, whilst three others were allocated to Casualty Evacuation Trains Nos 332, 333 and 334. The other five, including all four large-window cars, remained as diners until 1943, when three were altered to Mess & Tool Vans. One went on until 1945 and the last, as SR No 7840, was not withdrawn until May 1946.

One of the Nondescript saloons, No 7828, was rebuilt as an Ambulance for the Admiralty in 1943, but retained its SR number. After the war this one was again converted, this time to Camping Coach No 25. Many of the other cars were also altered, using rather different layouts, for use as Ambulances by the War Department and the United States Transportation Corps, whilst the rest went into Departmental use, some as First Aid Dressing Vans and later as Mess & Tool Vans. At least two ended up as engineering department Dormitory Vans. Two of these were still

in use at the Ministry of Defence military depot at Bicester as late as 1973, and were later moved to the Mid-Hants Railway at Ropley.

The actual catering on these vehicles was contracted out to Messrs Spiers & Pond Ltd, which already had the contract for most of the station restaurants on the LSWR. An article in the *Railway Magazine* for May 1910 stated that around a quarter of a million customers a year were being served in these cars, and that on some of the most popular trains the demand was such that meals were having to be served on portable tables in adjacent carriages. Although the kitchens were designed to serve about 60 at a sitting, they were in fact having to cater for upwards of 100 on some of the Bournemouth trains, with consequent strain on the chef and staff. A typical menu is quoted as follows (*see opposite*):

Breakfast, luncheon, tea and dinner were served, as appropriate, on the 6.10am, 8.50am, 11am, 1pm, 3.30pm, and 5.50pm West of England trains (12.30pm and 4pm on Sundays) and on the 12.30pm and 7.20pm down trains to Southampton and Bournemouth (12.30pm and 6.40pm on Sundays), and also on corresponding up services. These services were sometimes augmented in the summer months. No catering was provided on the Portsmouth line, other than for specials.

From November 1904 it became the practice to insert these Dining Saloons in the sets as and when required. For the West Country services they were taken out of the down trains and inserted into up trains at Exeter. By the end of 1909 gangways had been fitted to the outer ends of all Brake Thirds, and it was then more normal to insert the Diners between sets or between a set and some loose vehicles.

The next group of vehicles to be described were again quite distinctive since they were built to a size that would allow them to run on virtually any standard-gauge railway in Britain. For a very long time emigration had been a major business at some ports, notably Liverpool, Plymouth and Southampton. Back in 1844 the LSWR had been negotiating special rates with the Emigration Office for the carriage of emigrants from London to Southampton; then in 1848 the Southampton Dock Co applied for — and obtained — the agreement of the Lords of the Treasury Emigration Commissioners to have Southampton formally established as an emigration port. It seems likely that at this time the main emigration was to British colonies, but of course there was an increasing flow of people from all over Europe, many of them refugees, to the United States of America. It was probably in connection with these refugees that the Commercial & Traffic

Committee decided, in February 1853, that drying and disinfecting rooms should be built at the Nine Elms and Southampton emigration depots. This might imply that these people had to travel in the open Third-class carriages!

By late 1866 the situation had changed, and in December Mr Scott recommended to the Traffic Committee that notice should be given to terminate the contract with the Emigration Commissioners and with Mr Lungley (presumably a contractor for the traffic), as the emigration traffic had practically ceased in recent years. There was thus unnecessary expense entailed in keeping an emigration depot open at Southampton. It was agreed that Notice be given accordingly. It is not clear what happened then, but later the traffic revived very vigorously.

In Chapter 5 it was mentioned that the American Line adopted Southampton as its main British terminal in 1892 and that the LSWR built special First-class saloon stock in 1893 to form Boat Trains. The American Line also bought up the Inman Line in 1893 and transferred Inman's services from Liverpool to Southampton. The Inman Line had for a long time carried a large proportion of the emigrant traffic from Liverpool to America, so this traffic was also transferred to Southampton. In 1900 the total of emigrants leaving British ports for the USA was around 180,000, and by 1906 this had risen to well over 300,000. Although some of these people were British, the majority came from various other European countries, travelling in large groups under 'package' arrangements. A number of European countries were then actively developing their transatlantic services, but they naturally tended to go for the prestige end of the market first. Thus the contractors who arranged the parties of emigrants found it most economic to use the railways or smaller shipping companies of Europe to bring the people to Britain, which already had highly-developed transatlantic services catering for every category of passenger and freight.

The emigrants might therefore arrive at almost any UK port that was convenient to the organising contractor, but mainly at Hull from Northern and Eastern Europe, and at Liverpool from the Mediterranean. Thus it had been largely the North Eastern Railway and the Great Northern Railway that had carried the traffic to Liverpool, but in 1894 the Inman Line asked for arrangements to be made for the carriage of emigrants from Hull to Southampton via London. Doubtless the stock was initially provided by the northern companies, and it is recorded that some traffic passed over the Midland & South Western Junction Railway.

It is not known when the LSWR started taking an active part in the renewal of this traffic, but a notice to staff was issued on 7 June 1898 stating 'the following five vehicles are provided with Westinghouse brake and must be used for emigrant traffic only, being returned to Southampton immediately after use'. The vehicles concerned were 42ft bogie Third No 956, 34ft six-wheeled Third No 633, 32ft Brake Third No 303 and Passenger Luggage Vans Nos 37 (22ft) and 65 (24ft).

To handle the increasing quantity of emigrants, the LSWR decided, in July 1904, to build a train of five Thirds, a Composite and two Brake Thirds, all with lavatories and internal corridors, but without connecting gangways. The vehicles were built to the Metropolitan loading gauge so as to be suitable for use over virtually any line serving a passenger port in the UK. They were to be low-roofed and electrically lit, and to have Westinghouse as well as automatic vacuum brakes. Understandably there had to be an unusually high proportion of Third class seats. There was no provision for Second class. In the Composite there was no communication between the First- and Third-class sections. The First-class compartments were upholstered with buffalo leather, whilst the Thirds had dun-coloured sealskin, these materials being adopted for ease of cleaning in view of the somewhat unhygienic travelling conditions that many of the passengers may have been subjected to immediately previously, and not overlooking the popularity of garlic among those from some countries — an odour that was particularly difficult to remove from fabric upholstery.

All of the carriages were 46ft 6in long, 8ft 3¾in wide and 11ft 8½in high, weighing around 23 to 24 tons, and were completed in March 1905. It was presumably this train that was referred to in the following item in the *South Western Gazette* of 1 May 1906: 'The largest number of emigrants landed at Southampton by one of the Company's steamers arrived from Havre by the SS 'Vera' on the morning of 25 March. The total amounted to 400, 120 of which were for the White Star Line and 280 for the American Line steamer sailing from Liverpool. The whole party travelled through to Liverpool by special train.' The actual official seating of the train was 393, so perhaps there was some journalistic licence!

A further, similar train, augmented to six Thirds and a 'spare' Brake Third, was authorised in December 1906 and completed in July 1907. The Brake Thirds cost £869 16s 5d each, the Composite £994 16s 0d, and the Thirds £960 10s 1d each. Again there was a mention in the *South Western Gazette*, in August 1907, that 10 new low-roofed carriages for emigrant traffic were now in

Plate 9.6a 46ft 6in Brake Third (non-gangwayed) at Fullerton Junction with 'A12' class 0-4-2 No 614. *Author's collection*

service, the first journey for seven of them having been on 20 July from Plymouth to London. A third train with the same formation was ordered in February 1908 and completed in November 1908. These latter two trains had gangway connections throughout. Like the first one, they were dual-braked, though the drawings mention only Westinghouse brakes but do not show how they were installed. In addition to the provision of gangways the layout was changed between the first and second batches, requiring rather a lot of drawings in Figure 9.6 to illustrate this relatively small group of carriages.

A small detail change for the 1907 and 1908 trains was the use of Ash's 'Acme' ventilators. This, together with the decision to fit Dean and Churchward brakes to a batch of wagons, seems to have been among the first obvious manifestations of Surrey Warner's appointment as Carriage & Wagon Superintendent. Mr Panter was due to retire on 31 December 1905, having reached the age of 65. Mr Warner, at the time employed by the Great Western Railway at Swindon, was selected and appointed to replace him from 1 January 1906 at a salary of £700 per annum, but at Mr Warner's request the appointment was delayed until 1 February 1906.

It is open to question whether changing to Ash's ventilators was a good idea; certainly the GWR and some other companies had been happy with them, but on the LSWR they seem to have deteriorated fairly rapidly. Between 1906 and 1910 Mr Warner had them fitted to quite a lot of carriages — both new designs and repeat orders for existing types such as bogie blocks and four-car lavatory sets — but they appear in only a few photographs, taken mainly before about 1920. Even by that date they were being replaced piecemeal by cast-iron 'Torpedo' ones, although the carriages themselves were able to last another 30 or 40 years. Some photographs taken before and shortly after the Grouping show carriages with both types intermixed. Compared with this, a lot of the cast-iron Laycock's 'Torpedo' ones, in both sizes, still survive (in 2000) in excellent condition on some of the preserved railways.

During World War 1 one of the 'emigrant' Brake Thirds was loaned to the War Office for use in ambulance train No 21. This train had been formed by the LNWR in 1915 but the LSWR carriage was assigned to it in February 1916, so possibly it was required as a replacement for a damaged vehicle. There do not seem to have been any modifications, and it was returned to traffic at the end of the war.

With the exception of the one 'spare' Brake Third, which was withdrawn in 1933, the Southern kept the three trains in substantially their original formations, as sets 337, 473 and 474, until 1935. At that time a lot of LSWR carriages were lengthened and placed on new steel 'standard' 58ft underframes (see the Appendix to Chapter 5 of the earlier volume). 'Standard' has been placed in quotes because, although the main dimensions, construction and appearance were standard, there were apparently many differences in detail. In view of this policy it seems a little strange that the Southern Railway did not similarly lengthen these short carriages but instead had a batch of a shortened version of the 'standard' underframes built by the Birmingham Carriage & Wagon Co and transferred nearly all of these carriages to them. Whether the Westinghouse brake had been removed earlier is not

clear, but it was not provided afresh on the new underframes.

All of the Ash's ventilators seem to have disappeared by this time, having been replaced by cast-iron 'Torpedo' ones, probably recovered from scrapped vehicles, or by Southern sheet-metal 'Torpedo' ones of both the round and the 'squashed' type. Again, some photographs indicate a mixture on particular carriages until quite late on.

All of the Brake Thirds had their original South Western lookouts removed, but whether it was done at this time or earlier is not certain. The lookouts were not replaced by the Southern sheet-steel ones, but the section between the carriage end and the guard's door was neatly panelled in original style. Minimal changes were made to the actual ends, so the end windows finished up a trifle under 8in wide instead of the original 12in.

Also in 1935, four of the original non-gangwayed Thirds were altered to Driving Brake Composites for Push-Pull working on the All Hallows branch from Gravesend. For this a driving and guard's compartment was created at one end in place of the lavatory and one compartment. The end panel was formed of three plain steel sheets with four large windows, the one on the driver's side having a windscreen wiper. The driver was provided with a droplight on his nearside but the other side, which of course became the nearside when the locomotive was leading, was designated as the guard's side, and had his seat but no droplight. The two compartments at the other end were refurbished as Firsts, while the four in the middle remained as Thirds. Lockable swing doors were provided in the corridor to divide the First-class from the Third-class section and also to divide the Third-class smoking from the non-smoking section.

A whistle was fitted just below the windscreen wiper, and sandboxes were installed with flexible pipes feeding down to the leading wheels. The driving-control equipment used the Southern compressed-air system, so, in addition to the vacuum-brake pipe that ran under the footboard on one side as usual and the steam-heating pipe running under the centre of the frame, there were three pipes on the other side, two against the solebar and one under the footboard. At the non-driving end the control connection pipes were painted blue, green and yellow for identification of the regulator control, storage and back pressure respectively.

Each Driving Brake Composite was paired with a 58ft Third that had been contrived at the same time by lengthening a 48ft Tri-Composite (LSWR Drawing 861, see Chapter 5, Figure 5) onto a 'standard' Southern 58ft underframe. Control through pipes were provided, in a similar manner to those on the Brake Composite, so as to connect the driver's controls to the engine.

The logic of converting Thirds to Brake Composites so as to pair them with Composites converted to Thirds seems most curious, and the sets always had a rather 'hotchpotch' appearance by virtue of the differing body styles; they nevertheless lasted in this form until between 1959 and 1962.

Most of the other 'emigrant' carriages were altered to Push-Pull in early 1943. Seven of the gangwayed Thirds were altered to Composites, with two First-class compartments and four Thirds. These, together with the two built as gangwayed Composites, were paired with the remaining four of the gangwayed Brake Thirds and

Plate 9.6b(i) Non-gangwayed 46ft 6in Third (ex-LSWR No 602) after 1935 alteration to Push-Pull driving Brake Composite. At left is SR Third No 1, ex-LSWR 50ft Tri-Composite No 20.
Lens of Sutton

Plate 9.6b(ii) Non-gangwayed 46ft 6in Third (Ex-LSWR No 652) after extensive 1935 alteration to Push-Pull driving Brake Composite (SR No 6431), seen at Hailsham.
Lens of Sutton

another five Brake Thirds converted from Thirds. All of these Brake Thirds were fitted out with driving ends in a similar way to the 1935 ones, but, unlike those earlier sets, the pairs in the 1943 sets had a harmonised appearance. The gangways between the two vehicles in each set were retained, but that at the locomotive end was removed and two new panels inserted from top to bottom, these being slightly wider than the existing panels. A full set of steps was provided at this end from one side only. It appears that in all cases the lavatories were stripped out and left as luggage or standing space, the frosted glass windows being replaced by plain glass and two protection bars placed across each.

According to a footplateman of the time, on at least some branch services in early BR days the crew did not bother to connect up the three control pipes, only the electrical bell connection. In Push mode the driver used the bell or handsignals for starting and left it to the fireman to drive the train; of course, he had the AVB under his control if it was necessary. Since it also seems that a shotgun was a fairly common item of footplate equipment, presumably the driver could thus keep a good lookout for rabbits!

A detail variation between vehicles was that originally the windscreen wiper was pivoted near the top of the window and cleared a section at about the right height for a standing driver, but probably in the late 1940s some, if not all, of the wipers were re-positioned near the bottom to sweep a lower area suitable for a seated driver. Apart from this there were also several other small end-panel differences between vehicles, such as the form of the window mouldings, position and angle of grab irons, position of whistle, electric light sockets and so on, which were not design matters but due to convenience in the workshops.

Photographs suggest that these Push-Pull sets could turn up on branch lines almost anywhere on the Southern system. Although a Carriage Working Notice for 1947 shows the allocations to set numbers and services, as recorded in the present Appendix, it is by no means certain that sets were not occasionally rearranged due to the need for repairs.

After the first of the 'emigrant' trains was ordered the next authorisation by the Locomotive, Carriage & Stores Committee was, on 14 December 1904, for two rather odd designs, but unfortunately there is nothing to account for their unusual

Continued on page 134.

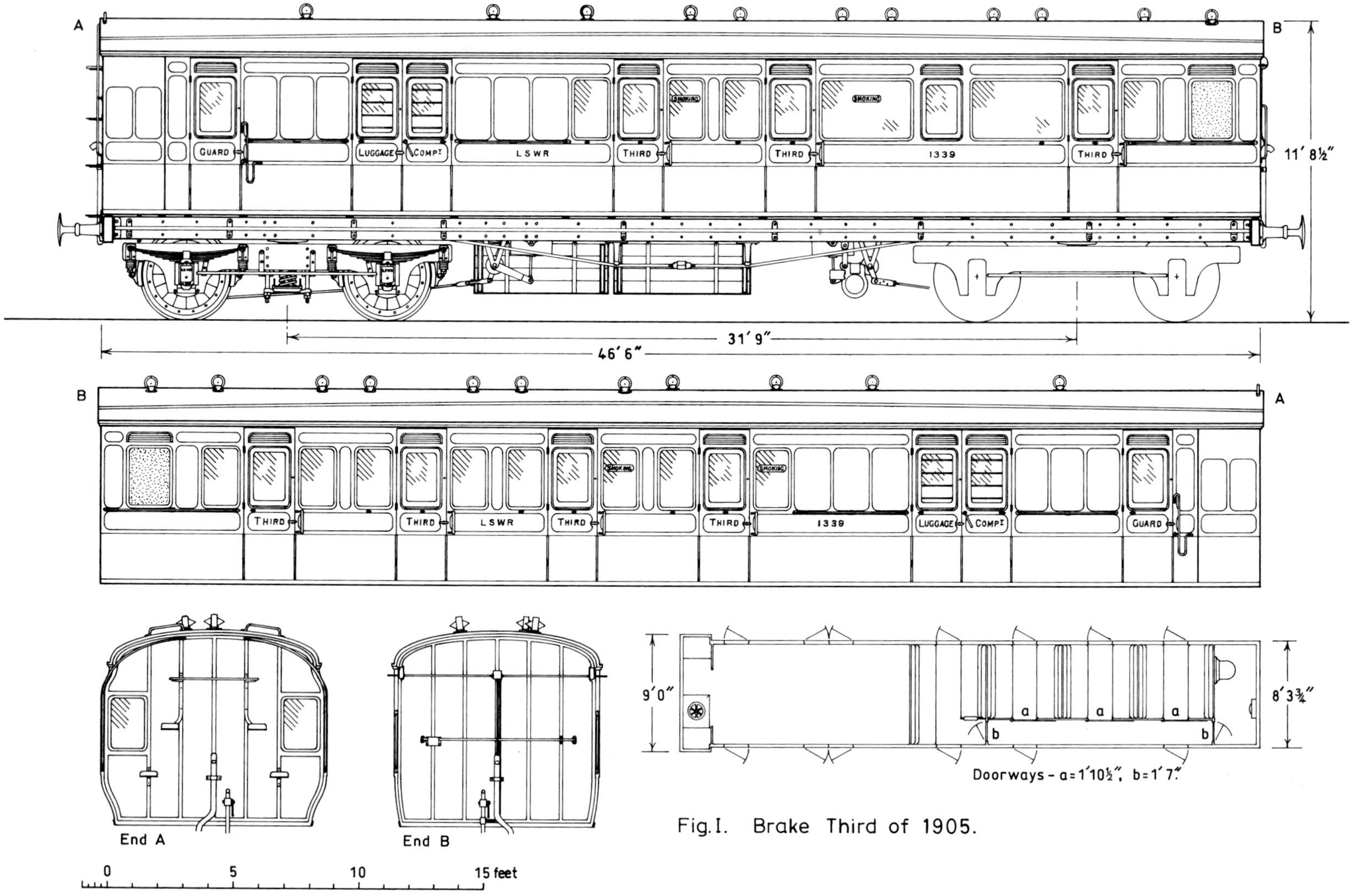

Fig. I.   Brake Third of 1905.

Figure 9.6
LSWR 46ft 6in 'Emigrant' Stock

122

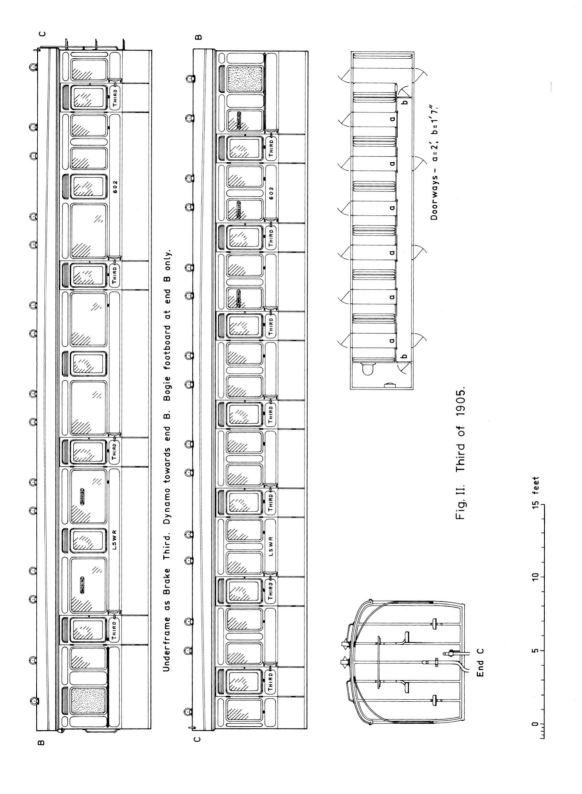

Underframe as Brake Third. Dynamo towards end B. Bogie footboard at end B only.

Doorways – a=2′, b=1′7″.

Fig. II. Third of 1905.

End C

0 ——— 5 ——— 10 ——— 15 feet

Figure 9.6
LSWR 46ft 6in 'Emigrant' Stock

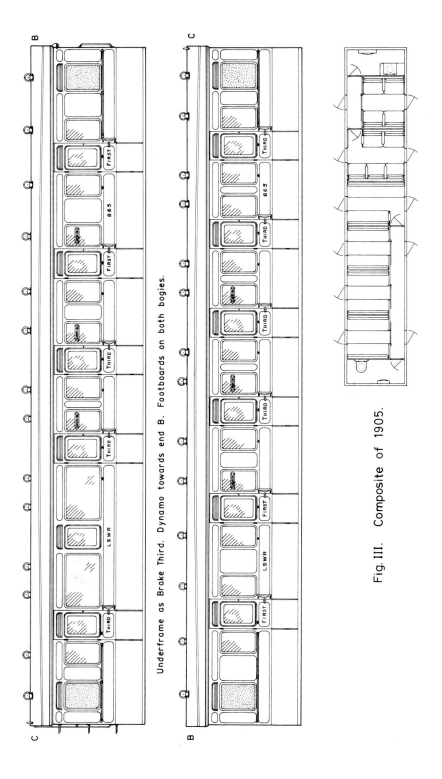

C
B
THIRD
LSWR
THIRD
THIRD
SMOKING
SMOKING
FIRST
SMOKING
865
FIRST
Underframe as Brake Third. Dynamo towards end B. Footboards on both bogies.
B
C
FIRST
LSWR
FIRST
SMOKING
THIRD
SMOKING
THIRD
SMOKING
THIRD
865
THIRD
Fig. III. Composite of 1905.
0
5
10
15 feet

Figure 9.6
LSWR 46ft 6in 'Emigrant' Stock

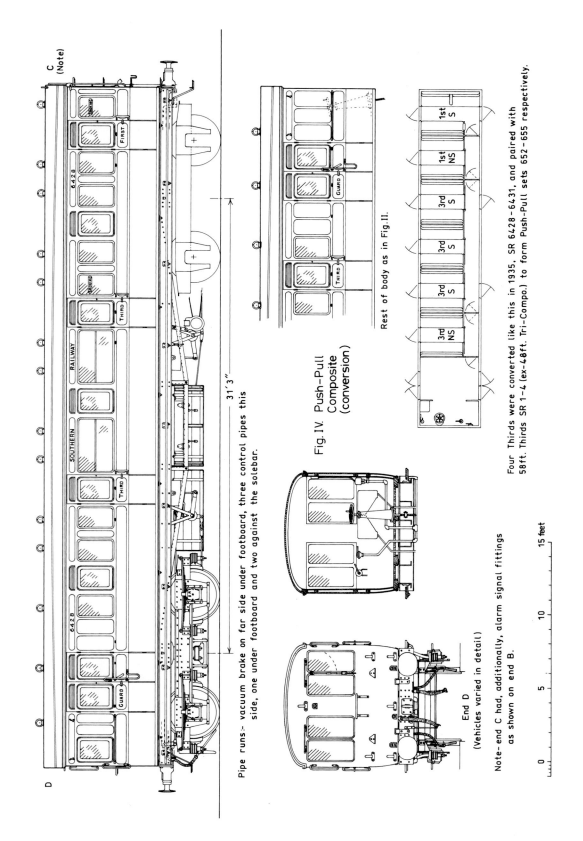

Pipe runs:- vacuum brake on far side under footboard, three control pipes this side, one under footboard and two against the solebar.

Fig. IV. Push-Pull Composite (conversion)

Rest of body as in Fig. II.

Four Thirds were converted like this in 1935, SR 6428-6431, and paired with 58ft. Thirds SR 1-4 (ex-48ft. Tri-Compo.) to form Push-Pull sets 652-655 respectively.

End D
(Vehicles varied in detail)

Note- end C had, additionally, alarm signal fittings as shown on end B.

0   5   10   15 feet

Figure 9.6
LSWR 46ft 6in 'Emigrant' Stock

125

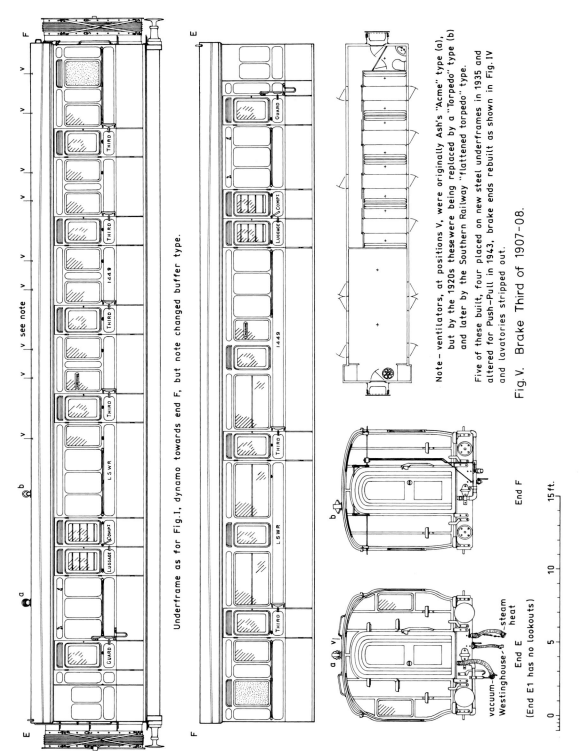

Undeframe as for Fig.I, dynamo towards end F, but note changed buffer type.

Note – ventilators, at positions V, were originally Ash's "Acme" type (a), but by the 1920s these were being replaced by a "Torpedo" type (b) and later by the Southern Railway "flattened torpedo" type.

Five of these built, four placed on new steel underframes in 1935 and altered for Push-Pull in 1943, brake ends rebuilt as shown in Fig.IV and lavatories stripped out.

Fig.V. Brake Third of 1907-08.

vacuum-
Westinghouse-
End E
(End E1 has no lookouts)

End F

—steam
heat

0   5   10   15 ft.

Figure 9.6
LSWR 46ft 6in 'Emigrant' Stock

126

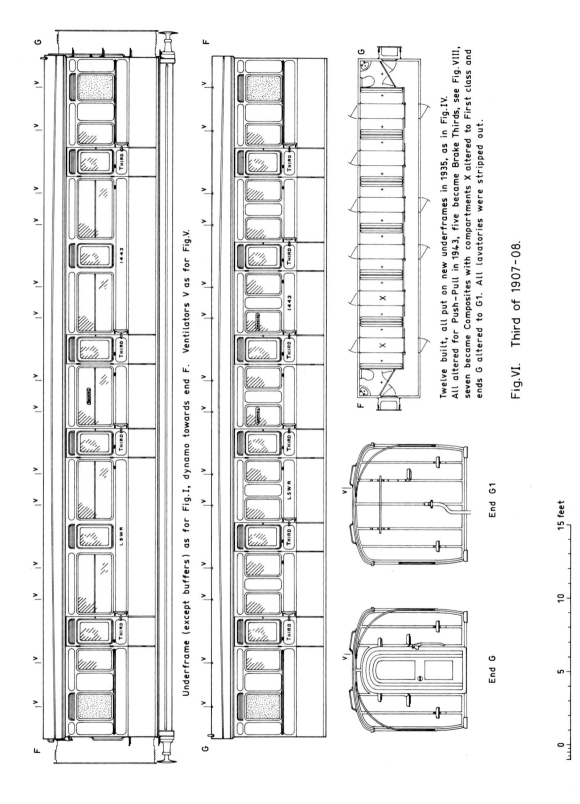

Underframe (except buffers) as for Fig.I, dynamo towards end F. Ventilators V as for Fig.V.

Twelve built, all put on new underframes in 1935, as in Fig.IV. All altered for Push-Pull in 1943, five became Brake Thirds, see Fig.VIII, seven became Composites with compartments X altered to First class and ends G altered to G1. All lavatories were stripped out.

Fig.VI. Third of 1907-08.

End G1

End G

0   5   10   15 feet

Figure 9.6
LSWR 46ft 6in 'Emigrant' Stock

127

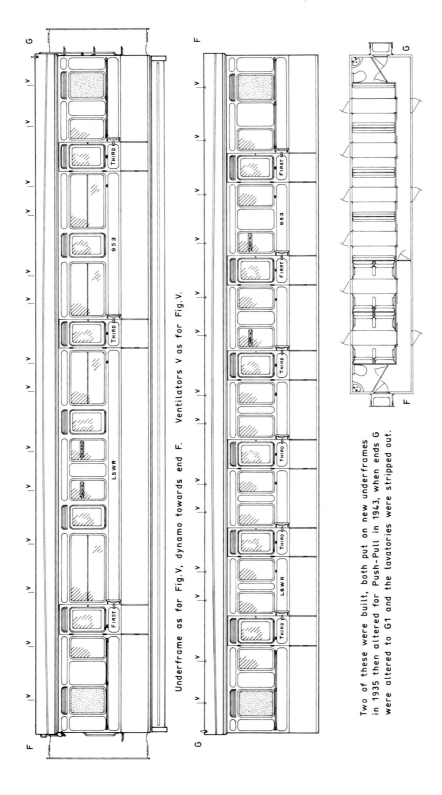

Underframe as for Fig. V, dynamo towards end F.   Ventilators V as for Fig. V.

Fig. VII. Composite of 1907 – 08.

Two of these were built, both put on new underframes
in 1935 then altered for Push–Pull in 1943, when ends G
were altered to G1 and the lavatories were stripped out.

0   5   10   15 feet

Figure 9.6
LSWR 46ft 6in 'Emigrant' Stock

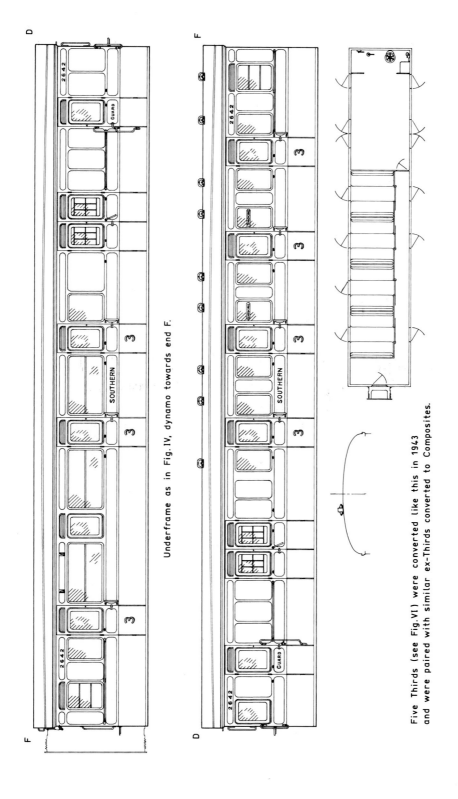

Underframe as in Fig.IV, dynamo towards end F.

Five Thirds (see Fig.VI) were converted like this in 1943 and were paired with similar ex-Thirds converted to Composites.

Fig. VIII. Driving Trailer conversion (1943).

0   5   10   15 feet

Figure 9.6
LSWR 46ft 6in 'Emigrant' Stock

Plate 9.6d(i) 46ft 6in Brake Third (gangwayed) in original condition. *H. V. Tumilty collection*

Plate 9.6d(ii) 46ft 6in Third (gangwayed) in original condition at Waterloo on a train of 54ft/56ft corridor carriages. *Lens of Sutton*

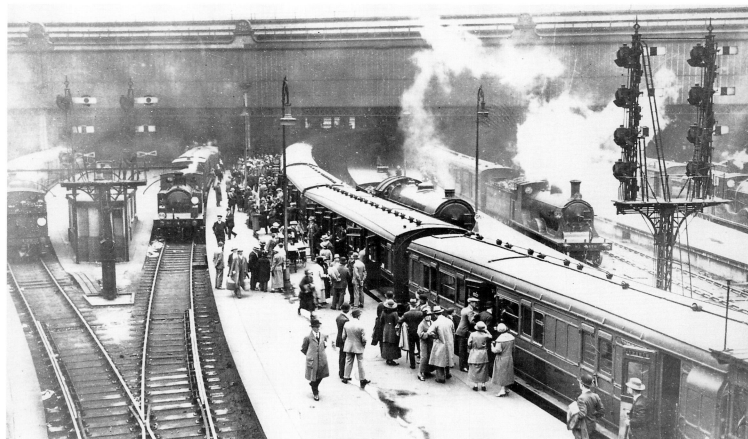

Plate 9.6d(iii) 'O2' class 0-4-4T No 223 at Exeter with an Exmouth branch train. Leading is a 46ft 6in Brake Third (gangwayed), followed by a 48ft Composite (see Vol 1, Fig 5.19) and another 46ft 6in carriage. *H. V. Tumilty collection*

Plates 9.6d(iv) and 9.6d(v) 46ft 6in Brake Third No 1488 after 1943 conversion to Push-Pull driving Brake Third (SR No 2647), at All Hallows in BR days. *Author's collection*

Plate 9.6e(i) Two LSWR 46ft 6in Thirds (gangwayed) and an LSWR 18ft luggage van on the GNR at Peterborough. *Author's collection*

Plate 9.6e(ii) 'N15' class No 456 *Sir Galahad* near Weybridge on a down Portsmouth train. The leading carriage is a 46ft 6in Third (gangwayed); the rest of the train is 57ft stock. *Real Photographs*

Plate 9.6e(iii) 46ft 6in Third, originally gangwayed LSWR No 1485, as altered to Push-Pull Composite (SR No 4762) in 1943. *Author's collection*

Plate 9.6e(iv) Two gangwayed 46ft 6in Thirds (that nearer the camera being ex-LSWR No 1447) as altered in 1943 to Push-Pull Brake Third and Composite, at Gravesend West in 1953. *Author's collection*

Plate 9.6f 46ft 6in Composite (gangwayed), ex-LSWR No 982. *D. J. Wigley*

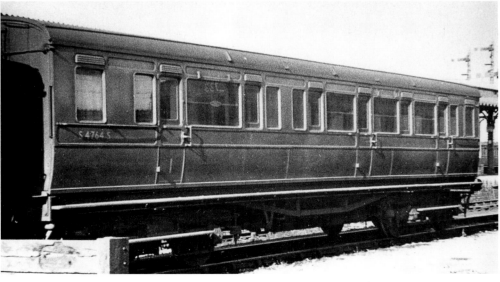

133

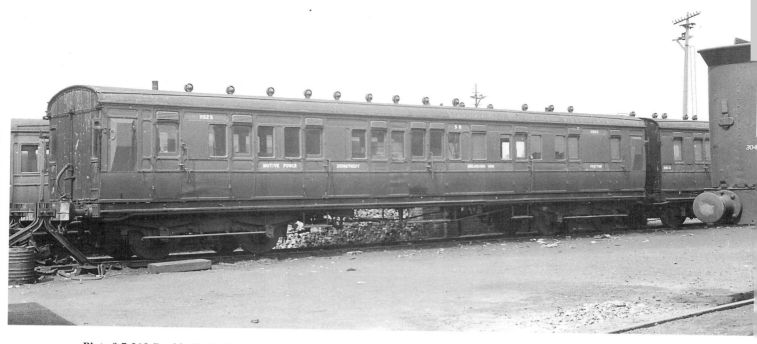

Plate 9.7 56ft Double-Brake Tri-Composite (ex-LSWR No 891, Drawing 1363) at Fratton, June 1950. *D. Cullum*

features. The first was intended for the West of England services, and only one was built. This was a 56ft Brake Tri-Composite with a guard's compartment at each end. Built to Drawing 1363 (Figure 9.7), it was completed in June 1905. Rather like the small corridor Composites already mentioned, it had corridors in the First class and in the Second/Third class, each connecting with a lavatory, but no communication between the two sections nor with either of the guard's compartments, so of course no end gangways were provided. The body width and all main dimensions were as for the other 52ft to 56ft corridor carriages. The original lookouts were the usual ogee pattern, but overall width was 9ft 3in. Thus the double brake ends gave a distinctly odd look to the vehicle. As with most other wide brake ends, the Southern replaced these with their small-pattern lookouts that reduced the width to 9ft 0in. Westinghouse brakes were fitted in June 1907 to permit it to be used for a Plymouth-Brighton service. The tare weight was 28 tons 6cwt.

The other design, of which two examples were built, was also for a corridor Brake Composite without gangways, but this time the drawing, No 1372, showed a small guard's compartment at one end and a luggage compartment at the other. They were stated to be 'for the Paris, Havre and St Malo traffic', and are illustrated at Figure 9.8. There were three First-class and two Second-class compartments, with a corridor and lavatory to each class. These gave a body length of 50ft. Despite the corridors, they were built

to non-corridor dimensions, ie 8ft 0¾in wide (9ft 1in over the lookouts) with the appropriate window and panel heights. The underframes were of composite construction, ie with channel steel solebars but wooden headstocks and other cross-members. Like several other brake-ended carriages of this period the buffers at the brake end were either self-contained or had rubber block springs, since the handbrake linkage prevented use of the normal transverse leaf springs. The buffer casings were longer than usual, and the travel was only 4in instead of the usual 7in. Both vehicles were withdrawn in September 1936 and put into use as Mess & Tool Vans; at least one of them was converted to gas lighting, presumably at that time.

There are no LSWR records of the actual vehicle numbers in corridor sets, and, judging from photographs, the make-up varied as individual vehicles were taken for repairs. In one SR Register there were notes of SR set numbers for some carriages, and some of them had been in three or even four different sets within only a few years. The concept of set formations for corridor stock seems to have been far more flexible than for some suburban workings, and it became quite common to see three-, four- and five-car trains formed of almost any variety, often including two different types of brake vehicle in a set.

On 2 May 1906 the Locomotive, Carriage & Stores Committee ordered the construction of seven more four-car corridor trains — four of one formation and three of another. The first four consisted

Continued on page 139.

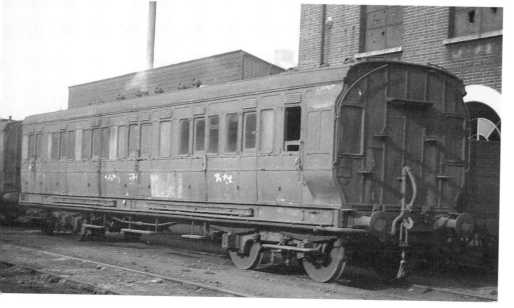

Plate 9.8 Former LSWR 50ft x 0¾in Brake Composite (semi-corridor) No 882, seen as SR service vehicle No 995s at Brighton locomotive shed in March 1946. *R. E. Tustin*

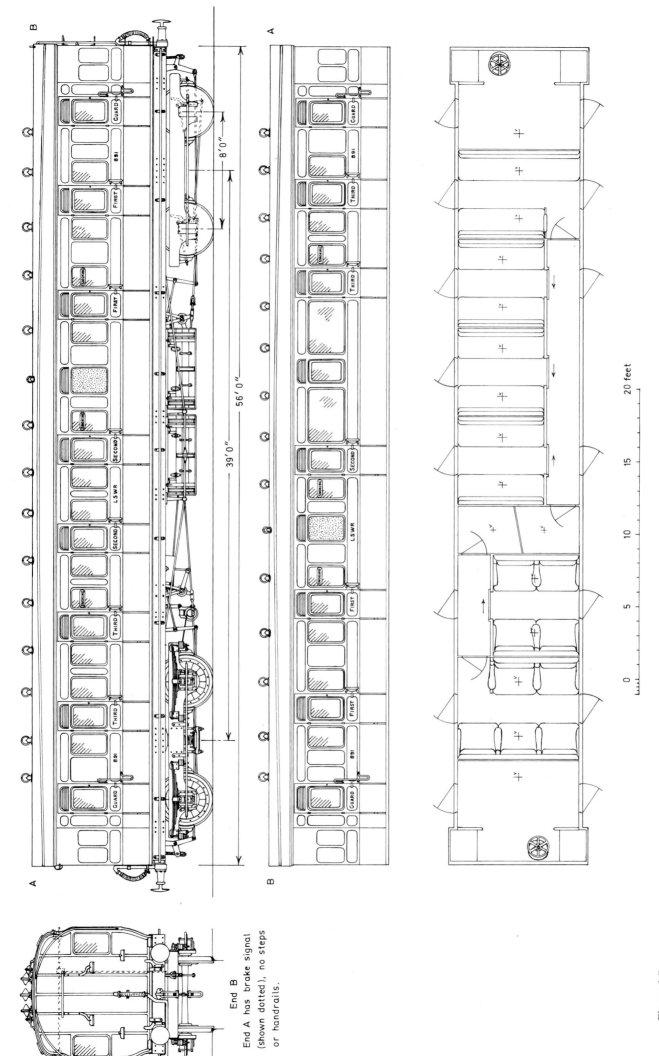

Figure 9.7
LSWR 56ft Tri-Composite Double Brake.

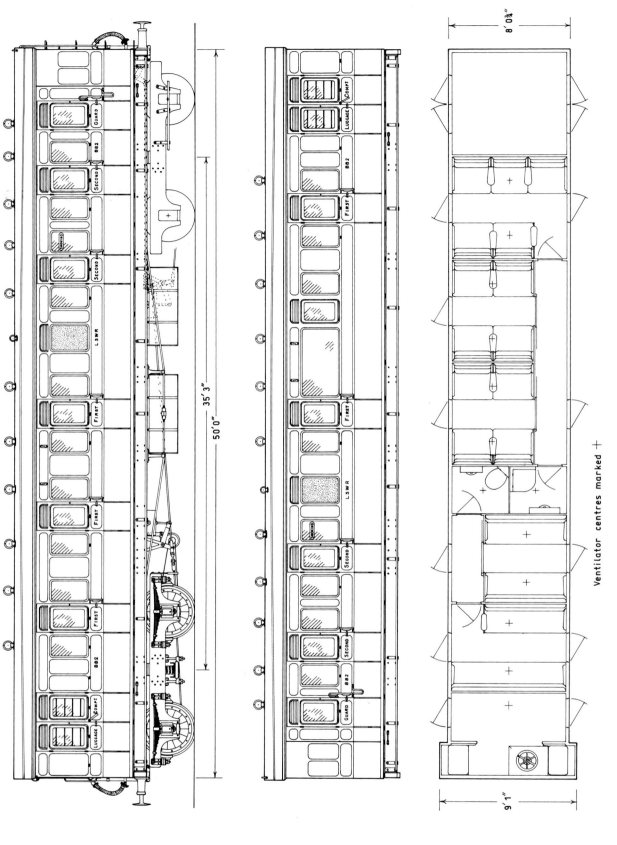

M = Mirror or Map
P = Photo

Ventilator centres marked +

End views as for 4-car main line sets (non-corridor) of 1904–1910.

0   5   10   15   20 feet

Figure 9.8
LSWR 50ft Brake Composite of 1905.

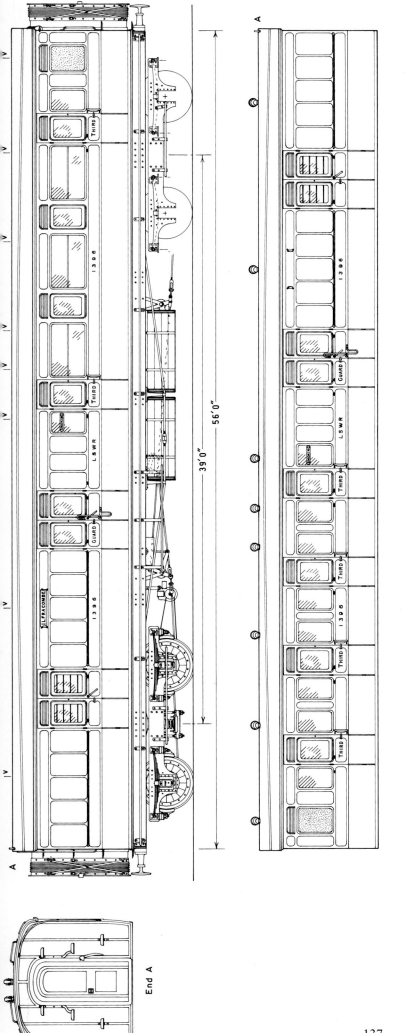

End A

Bearing springs at van end were 4'6" long, those at the compartment end were 5'0" long.

Eight of these were built in 1906/07. All were sold to the War Department in 1917 for use in a Continental Ambulance Train.

0   5   10   15   20 feet

Figure 9.9
LSWR 56ft Brake Third of 1906.

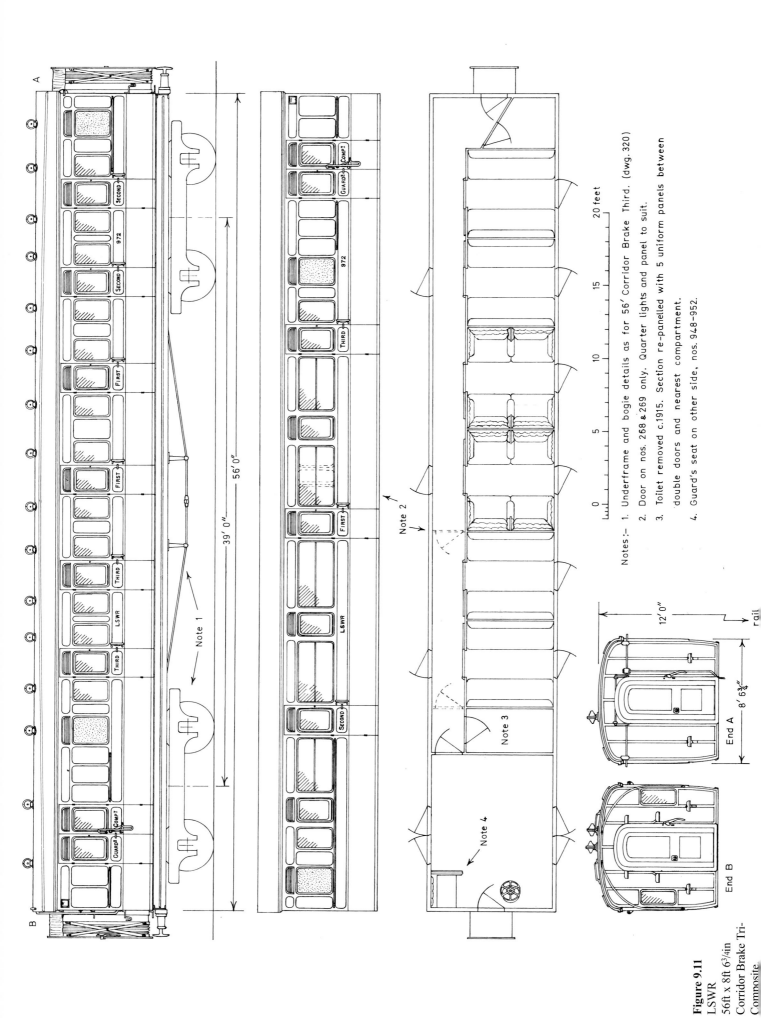

Notes:- 1. Underframe and bogie details as for 56' Corridor Brake Third. (dwg.320)

2. Door on nos. 268 & 269 only. Quarter lights and panel to suit.

3. Toilet removed c.1915. Section re-panelled with 5 uniform panels between double doors and nearest compartment.

4. Guard's seat on other side, nos. 948-952.

Note 1

Note 2

Note 3

Note 4

972

972

End A

End B

56'0"

39'0"

12'0"

8'6¾"

rail

0   5   10   15   20 feet

Figure 9.11
LSWR
56ft x 8ft 6¾in
Corridor Brake Tri-
Composite

Plate 9.11a 56ft Brake Tri-Composite (LSWR No 972, Drawing 17326) as SR No 6509, at Bere Alston in July 1948. *J. H. Aston*

of two Brake Thirds to Drawing 1487 (Figure 9.9), a Composite to Drawing 1214 (Figure 9.2a) and a Third to Drawing 1226 (Figure 9.3). These Brake Thirds were to have the guard's seat and handbrake wheel next to the passengers' compartment. For the first time the guard was not provided with any kind of lookout, so he could no longer monitor the driver's observance of signals, watch for open doors, for anything falling from the train, and so on, as had been his traditional duty. The drawing shows signs that lookouts were originally intended at the centre but that they were erased; there is no evidence as to whether they were actually fitted.

This Drawing 1487, which pre-dates the second batch of 'emigrant' carriages mentioned earlier, was the first new design to show Ash's 'Acme' ventilators.

All eight of these Brake Thirds were sold to the War Department in October 1917 and converted to Ambulance cars, presumably to form Ambulance Train No 35. According to notes in the Register they were intended for use in France, though evidence of their transfer across the Channel is lacking. After the war they were bought back by the LSWR but were not refitted for passengers. Instead they were converted to plain Brake and Luggage Vans and, as such, are illustrated among the Passenger Vans.

The other three trains were each to have two Brake Thirds and two Tri-Composites. This time the Brake Thirds were built to Drawing 1568, which was mentioned when discussing the original corridor Brake Thirds shown as Figure 9.1. They were almost identical to the originals but without the end lookouts; they are not, therefore, illustrated again here, though they are listed as Appendix item 9.13. The Tri-Composites were built to Drawing 1488 and had two First-, three Second- and two Third-class compartments, although the Seconds and Thirds were of exactly the same dimensions. They are listed as Appendix item 9.10 but are not illustrated at this point as they were, except in only one respect, the same as those built in 1913 to Drawing 2138, which are illustrated at Figure 9.20. The difference seems to have been that the later version had three Third-class and two Second-class compartments. Not surprisingly, both batches were grouped together by the Southern Railway under Diagram 280 as

having two First-class and five Third-class compartments.

On 27 June 1906 it was decided to build two Brake Tri-Composites for the West of England services, to Drawing 1503. They are illustrated in Figure 9.11. Once again there is the hazy suspicion of end lookouts having been drawn and then erased. Both this drawing and the similar No 1736, mentioned below, show a sidelamp casing in the top panel of the guard's compartment, and this can be seen in a photograph of one of the carriages. The first two carriages originally had a door in the corridor between the Third-class section and that of the First and Second classes; this was to be provided with a London & North Western Railway private lock. This door necessitated two small windows and a panel in the side at that point. When a further carriage was built in October 1907 as part of the replacements for some withdrawals, this door was omitted and a second large corridor window was placed between the doors. For this alteration a new drawing, No 1570, without sidelamps, was prepared. The drawing was again revised and re-issued as No 1736, though with no apparent significant differences, other than having sidelamps again, and another 17 vehicles were built to it between May 1908 and June 1909. All of these carriages apparently originally had two lavatories — one at the end to serve the First and Second classes and the other between the Thirds and the van portion to serve the Third class. However, all three drawings show the Third-class lavatory erased at some date (possibly c1915), to permit the extension of the van area. The lavatory and matching corridor windows appear to have been replaced with panels.

The provision of the fixed sidelamps on all except the third and the last five built was most unusual for an LSWR carriage. However, they were similar to those used on the London & North Western Railway, and, taken together with the reference to LNWR door locks on the first two, they tie up with contemporary reports that the LSWR was providing most, if not all, of the stock for Bournemouth West to Manchester through services from 1907. Restaurant cars were provided only on the LNWR section, and the service ceased in 1910.

Ten 56ft First-class carriages were built in 1907 to Drawing 1527, and are illustrated at Figure 9.12. On the drawing it was

Plate 9.11b 56ft Brake Tri-Composite to Drawing 1736; note the LNWR sidelamp on the guard's compartment. The next carriage is a 56ft Brake Tri-Composite to Drawing 1832. *H. V. Tumilty collection*

Plate 9.11c 'N15' class No 737 in Clapham Cutting. The leading carriage is a 56ft Brake Tri-Composite to Drawing 1736; next are two 56ft Brake Tri-Composites to Drawing 1832, then a 56ft Brake Third. *Author's collection*

Plate 9.11d 'G14' class No 456 with an Exeter-Waterloo breakfast-car express at Surbiton. The train includes a 56ft Brake Tri-Composite (Drawing 1570), a Dining Saloon (Drawing 1601) and a 56ft Brake Third (Drawing 1227). *E. S. C. Betteley, courtesy of The Railway Magazine*

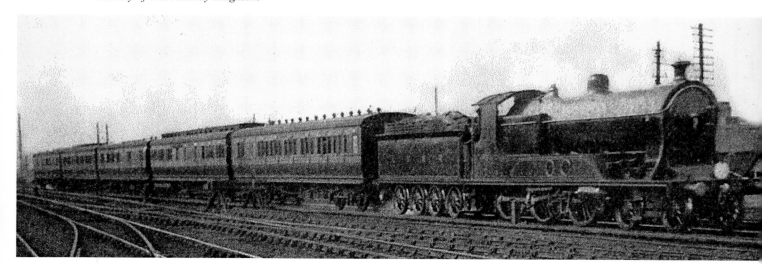

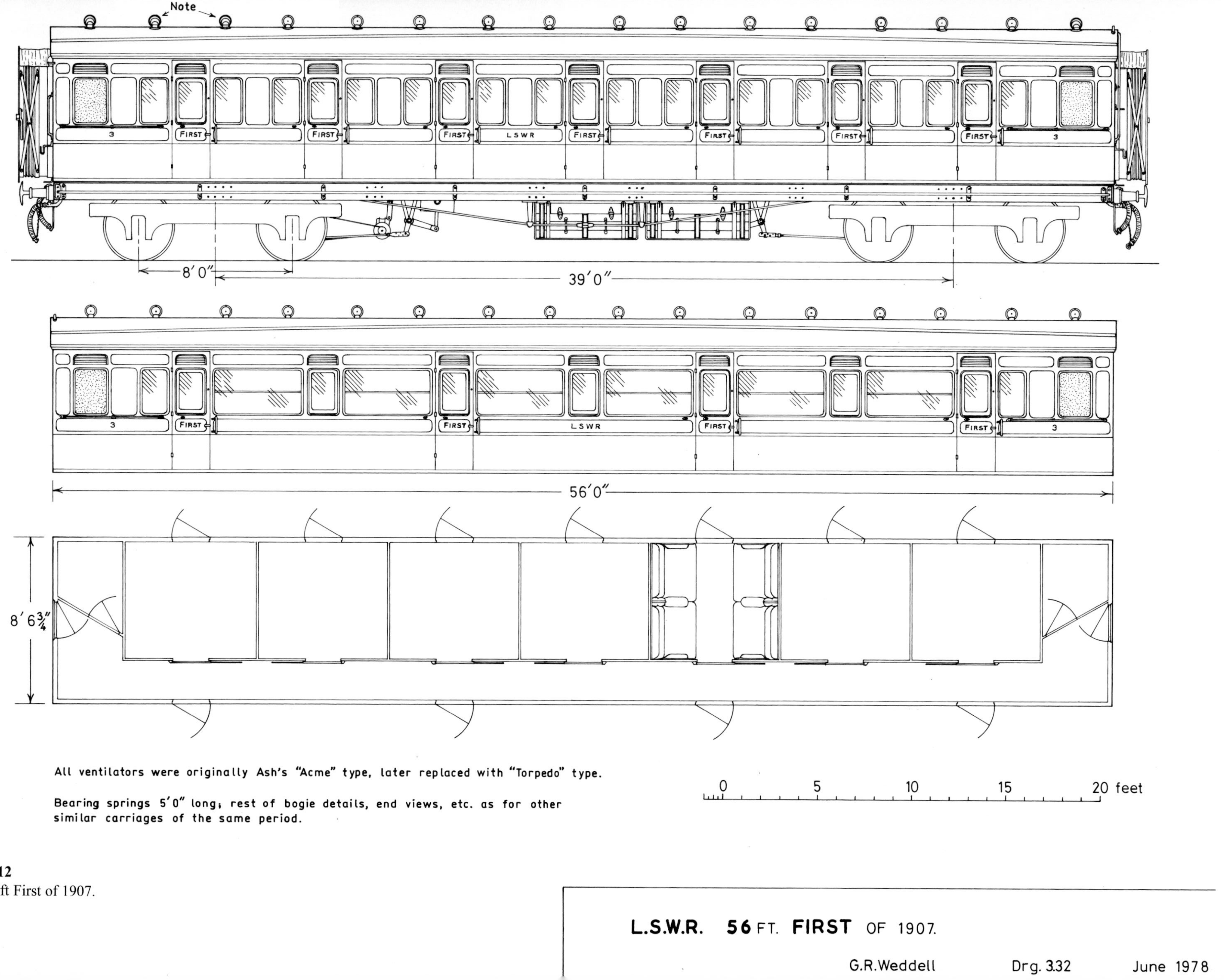
Note
3
FIRST
LSWR
8′ 0″
39′ 0″
56′ 0″
8′ 6¾″
All ventilators were originally Ash's "Acme" type, later replaced with "Torpedo" type.
Bearing springs 5′ 0″ long; rest of bogie details, end views, etc. as for other similar carriages of the same period.
0 5 10 15 20 feet
L.S.W.R. 56 FT. FIRST OF 1907.
G.R.Weddell
Drg. 3.32
June 1978

Figure 9.12
LSWR 56ft First of 1907.

stated that two were built as replacements of two carriages destroyed in the Salisbury accident — it will be recalled that these were 47ft 6in 'Eagle' Saloons. These two, Nos 20 and 24, were to have two 'Smoking' compartments at one end. The other eight, which were built on the Capital account, were to have two 'Smoking' compartments near the centre of the carriage. This Capital account authorisation of December 1906 called for 'two corridor trains of eight carriages each, with gangways throughout', but by study of the completions it is evident that these two trains, if they ever actually ran as such, each consisted of two Brake Thirds to Drawing 1569 (Figure 9.14), four of these Firsts and two Composites to Drawing 1214 (Figure 9.2a). However, since these were the only corridor full Firsts built by the South Western, apart from the 'Ironclads' of 1921, it seems quite likely that they were soon distributed among the more important trains between London and the West Country.

The Brake Thirds to Drawing 1569 were yet another variant on the Brake Third theme. As will be seen in Figure 9.14, these had only three compartments, and an even bigger luggage van with two sets of doors in addition to that for the guard, who again had to manage without any lookouts. Only four were built, so they rarely appear in photographs, particularly since all four were used in Ambulance trains during World War 1 and were converted to full vans on their return to civilian use.

On 1 May 1907 Surrey Warner submitted plans for a new Royal Saloon, but a decision was deferred. The subject was raised again on 17 November 1910, when it was agreed to build a Royal Train consisting of a corridor Brake Composite, a corridor Saloon and a corridor Royal Saloon. Although there is no further explanation in the Minutes, this was not proceeded with, and on 11 January 1912 the order was rescinded.

Shortly after the American Line started to use Southampton Docks, it was realised that a lot of time could be saved for passengers and the Mails if they were set ashore at Plymouth to complete the journey from there to London by train, using the modified 'Eagle' stock (described in Chapter 5), plus luggage vans. This, of course, led to rivalry with the Great Western, and what really amounted to races between the two companies. These came to a head with the disaster at Salisbury on 1 July 1906. The up American boat Train, headed by 'L12' class locomotive No 421 and consisting of a brake van, three 'Eagle' saloons and a Kitchen Brake, with 43 passengers on board, passed through Salisbury at something in excess of 60mph, despite a permanent speed limit of 30mph. On the 8-chain curve at the east end of the station, the locomotive appears to have rolled so far that it hit a van on the adjacent track. Twenty-eight people, including the driver and fireman, were killed, and all the carriages except the Kitchen Brake were destroyed. (Further details of this accident are given in *The London & South Western Railway* by O. S. Nock, published by Ian Allan, and in *The South Western Railway* by Hamilton Ellis, published by George, Allen & Unwin.)

After this things seem to have calmed down a bit. Nevertheless, to cater for evening arrivals of ships at Plymouth, it was decided in August 1907 to build four Sleeping Saloons at an estimated cost

Plate 9.13a 56ft Brake Third (LSWR No 1524, Drawing 1568) — right-hand corridor. *National Railway Museum*

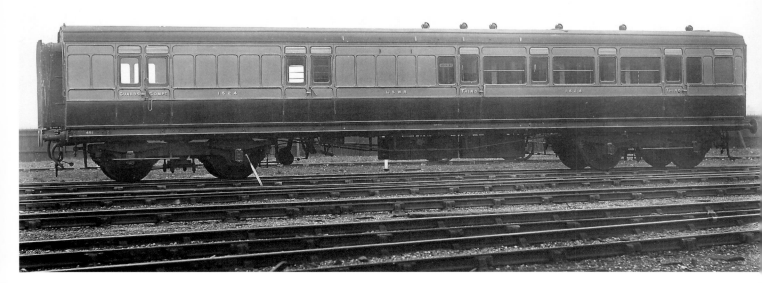

Plate 9.13b 56ft Brake Third (LSWR No 657, Drawing 1568) as SR No 3127 — left-hand corridor. *F. Foote*

Plate 9.14a 'E10' class No 369 on a down Bournemouth train. This is one of the very few photographs to show a 56ft three-compartment Brake Third to Drawing 1569 (second carriage). The leading carriage is a 48ft non-corridor Third; the rest are corridor.
Real Photographs

Plate 9.14b 'T14' class No 447 passing Raynes Park on a down Cornwall express. The leading carriage is a three-compartment 56ft Brake Third (Drawing 1569).
E. S. C. Betteley, courtesy of The Railway Magazine

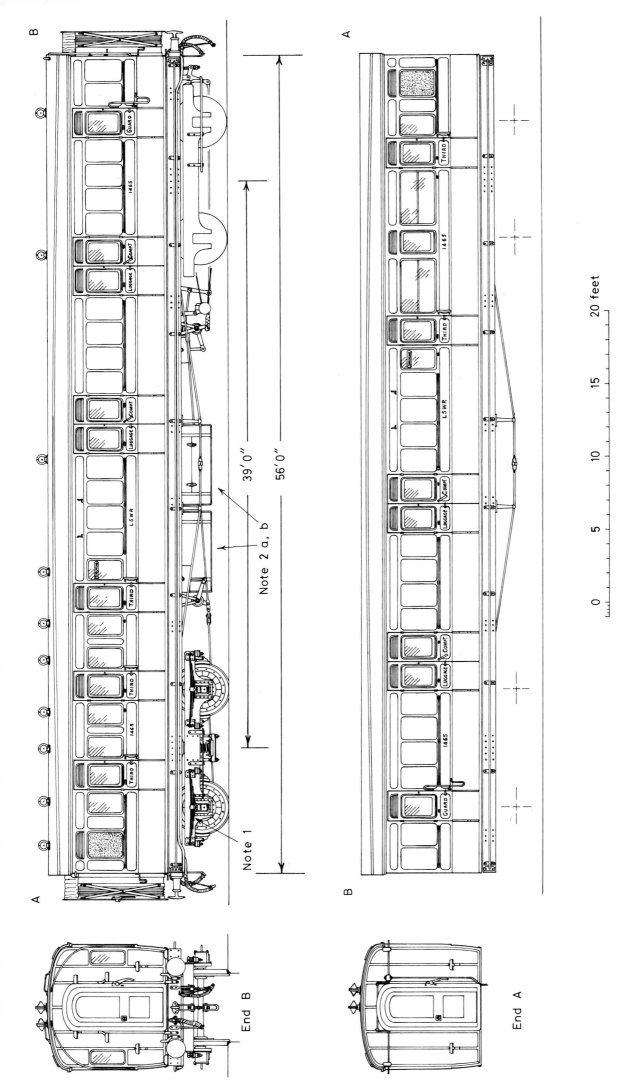

Notes :- 1. 5'0" springs at end A, 4'6" ones at end B.
2. Battery box on far side at 'a', on both sides at 'b'.

Figure 9.14
LSWR 56ft x 8ft 6¾in Brake Third of 1908.

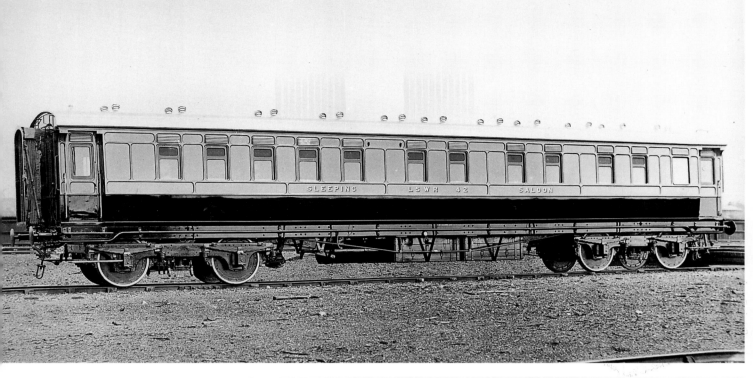

Plate 9.15a 56ft Sleeping Saloon No 42 — compartment side. *J. Tatchell collection*

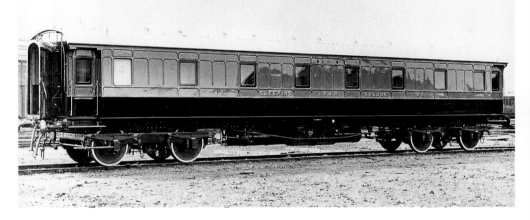

Plate 9.15b 56ft Sleeping Saloon No 42 — corridor side. *HMRS*

of £1,400 each, or £5,600 in total. The actual cost on completion in 1908 came to a total of £6,138 6s 4d. They were built to Drawing 1633, and are shown here at Figure 9.15.

The bodies were to the now common length of 56ft, but, to give room for the beds, the width at the waist was 9ft, tapering in to 8ft 8¾ in below the cornices. An unusual feature for the LSWR was that the entry doors at each end were inset, rather in Pullman fashion, and opened into mahogany-panelled vestibules from which doors led into the corridor. The corridor was panelled in polished plywood with oak framing, and was fitted with a hair carpet.

To call the carriages 'Saloons' seems a little odd, as anything more remote from the usual idea of a saloon is hard to imagine. There were seven single and two double compartments, measuring 4ft 2¾ in and 6ft 7¾ in wide respectively, together with a lavatory and a windowless compartment for an attendant. The beds were more or less ordinary domestic brass-mounted bedsteads. Each compartment was provided with a Brussels carpet and had a wash basin and a small folding writing table; in the case of the double berths this was formed by a part of the wash basin cover. The wash basins, which were of white ware decorated with gold and topped with a marble surround, were supplied with hot and cold water, the former from a gas boiler in the attendant's compartment. Two gas tanks were therefore attached to the underframe as well as the normal electrical equipment.

The panelling in the berths was done with Hungarian ash veneers, and the framing with polished oak. The roof lining was painted as white panels lined out with gold. Two 10-candlepower lights were fitted more or less over each writing table, so, by using

one or both, two levels of lighting — bright or dim — could be selected. In addition there was a reading lamp, again of 10 candlepower, over each bed head. The steam-heat control for each compartment was placed within the reach of a passenger in bed.

A virtue was made of having the minimum of soft furnishings by pointing out that it was thus possible to avoid the accumulation of dust. Partly to this end and partly to reduce the risk of fire from locomotive cinders, the droplights were fitted with fine-mesh brass gauze screens in upper extensions to their frames. Unlike the similar screens in the Dining Saloons, these ones could not be hooked up to leave a window completely open. They were in addition to the usual gauze screens permanently fitted behind the louvre ventilators. The roof ventilators, two to each compartment, were to Ash's 'Acme' pattern.

Although they were very attractive vehicles, the Sleeping Saloons were already being overtaken by events. The outcry that arose after the Salisbury disaster caused both the LSWR and the GWR to give serious thought to the wisdom of continuing to compete so vigorously. This resulted in an agreement under which the LSWR ceased to run the Ocean Specials in 1911, the traffic going by the shorter GWR route. As part of this arrangement, the four Sleeping Saloons were sold to the Great Western for £700 each, though their bogies, dynamos, accumulators and brake gear were retained by the LSWR. Two of the sleeping cars were destroyed in a fire in about 1912, but the other two continued in use until 1928 and 1931.

Five more four-car trains were ordered on 18 December 1907. The 10 Brake Thirds were again to Drawing 1568 (Figure 9.1),

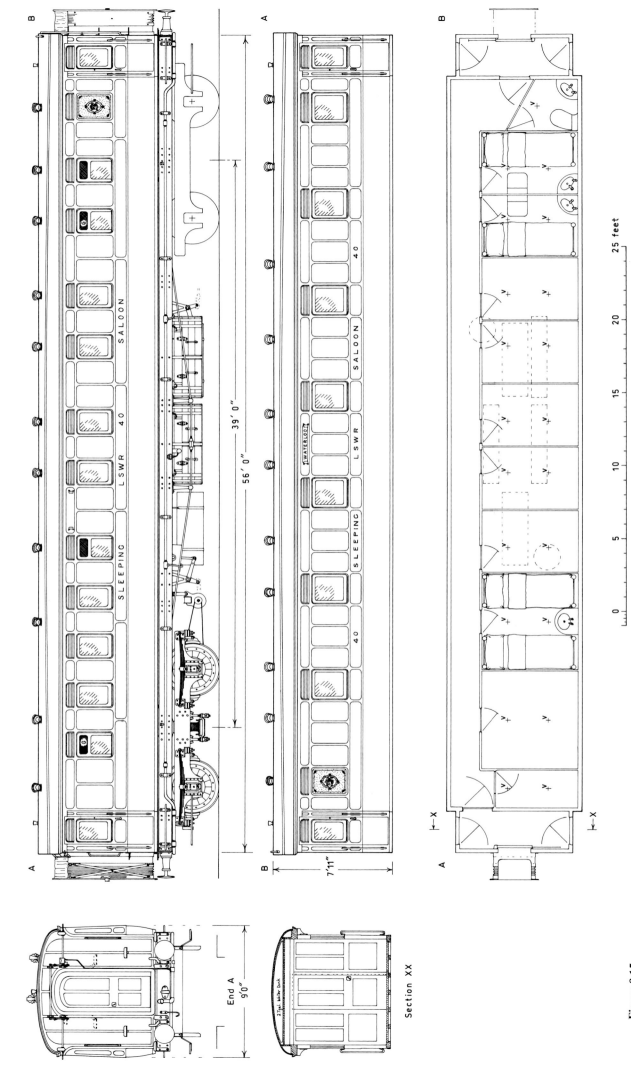

Figure 9.15
LSWR 56ft Sleeping Saloon of 1908.

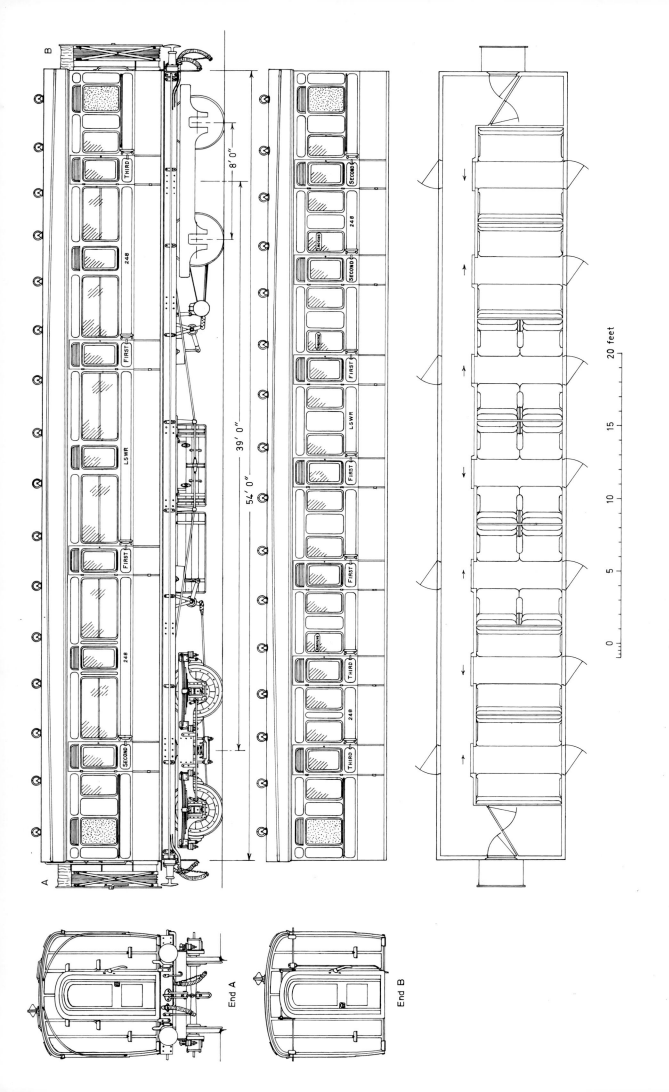

Figure 9.16
LSWR 54ft Corridor Tri-Composite.

whilst the 10 54ft Tri-Composites were to Drawing 1690 (Figure 9.16), having three First-, two Second- and two Third-class compartments.

Next we come to a group of vehicles of which eight were authorised in April 1909, another five in the following August and a final six in April 1910. These were some 56ft Brake Tri-Composites to Drawing 1832 (Figure 9.17). Once again there were no lookouts. The First-class compartments were finished with walnut banding and had two 16-candlepower Osram lamps in a single fitting, whereas the Seconds and Thirds were finished in mahogany and had fittings containing two 12-candlepower Osram lamps. The corridor was panelled with plywood above the waist, below the waist being mahogany, as was the banding above. Previously the door openings had extended down to slightly below the floor line, level with the external shell moulding; now the bottomsides were cut away to allow the door opening to continue right down to the bottom of the body, giving passengers a little more toe room as they stepped up from the footboard.

Drawing 1832 once again shows 'Torpedo' ventilators, though apparently made of sheet steel instead of cast iron, so presumably Surrey Warner had by now been persuaded that Ash's 'Acme' type was proving less than satisfactory. Certainly, several photographs taken before the Grouping show carriages of this period with a mixture of ventilator types on the roof.

The first two batches were not built together with any other vehicles, other than block sets and vans, and there is no mention of any particular service for which they were needed, but, of course, LSWR main-line trains served many West Country branch lines with through services. For these branches one or more Brake Tri-Composites formed the ideal train. They would start out from Waterloo at the rear of a train; the passengers could use the corridor for access to the Dining Saloon, but successive carriages could be uncoupled at appropriate junction stations to continue to

Plate 9.17a 56ft Brake Tri-Composite (LSWR No 1021, Drawing 1832) still in SR guise as No 6534 at Stewarts Lane in August 1950. *A. E. West*

Plate 9.17b 56ft Brake Tri-Composite (LSWR No 992, Drawing 1832) as BR No S6523S at Barnstaple Junction in September 1956. *H. C. Casserley*

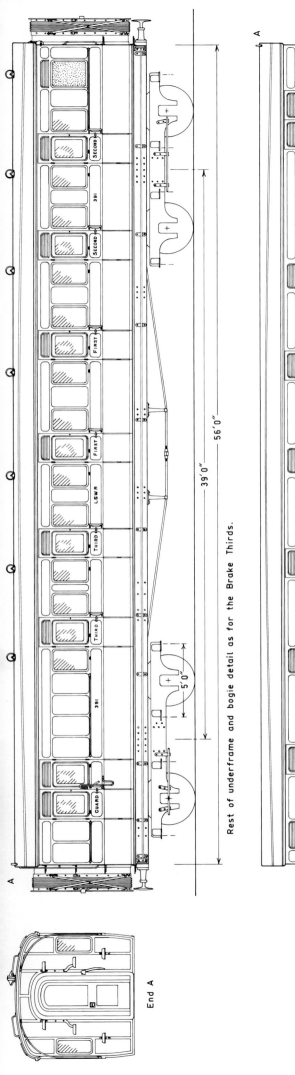

End A

Rest of underframe and bogie detail as for the Brake Thirds.

56'0"

39'0"

5'0"

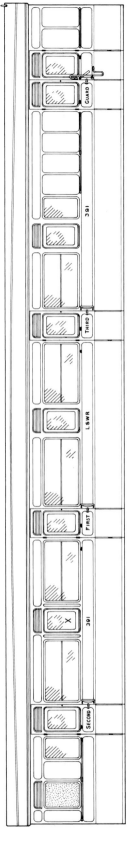

Droplight X was not exactly opposite a compartment door.

0   5   10   15   20 feet

Figure 9.17
LSWR 56ft Brake Tri-Composite of 1910.

their destinations as local trains. The reverse would then take place for the up journeys. Those were the days when it was important for passengers to look carefully at the destination board carried on each carriage! The last batch of six was ordered at the same time as six Brake Thirds (with left-hand corridors) to Drawing 1568 (Figure 9.1), and so it might be that they were intended to form two-car sets.

Two of this final batch of Drawing 1568 Brake Thirds, SR Nos 3127 and 3141, were fitted with Westinghouse brakes, in addition to the normal automatic vacuum ones, in September 1923 for use on the Dover-Birkenhead service. Two more, SR Nos 3126 and 3128, were, according to a Southern Railway Register, transferred in February 1946 to the East Kent Railway, where they were renumbered 5 and 6 respectively, but there is also a suggestion that they were used between Headcorn and Tenterden, so there seems to be some confusion between the EKR and the K&ESR; in any case, they were both condemned in October 1948.

At the same time that the second batch of Brake Tri-Composites just mentioned was authorised, another train of eight vehicles was ordered. This was to consist of four types of carriage:

Two 56ft Brake Thirds	Drawing 1568	Figure 9.1
Two 56ft Thirds	” 1872	” 9.3
Two 56ft Composites	” 1862	” 9.18
Two 54ft Tri-Composites	” 1866	” 9.19

The two Composites and two Tri-Composites were the only ones built to their respective designs. Although the Thirds to Drawing 1872 had full-height doors with cutaway bottomsides — like the Brake Tri-Composites to Drawing 1832 — the rest of the vehicles still had the usual type. There is no record of the service for which this train was intended, nor for how long the vehicles remained together. Works Drawings 1862 and 1866 are rather lacking in detail, but there are interesting notes that the Composites were to have one lavatory fitted and finished in First-class style and the other in Second-class style. The Tri-Composites were to have a First-class lavatory, but the other one was to be finished in Second-class style but with a Third-class wash basin and WC. Judging by the lavatory layout in other drawings this may have been established practice, but it is not recorded whether the lavatory doors had First- and Second-class markings, and one might ponder on what action a guard could take if he found a Third-class passenger entering or leaving one of the superior-class lavatories! After withdrawal in 1949 the underframe of 54ft Composite No 1000 (SR No 5097) was shortened and re-used under the body from the 1885 Directors' Inspection Saloon, by then numbered DS 1.

The next type of corridor vehicle to be authorised was a batch of six Tri-Composites which were recommended to the Traffic Committee by the Officers' Committee on 2 May 1912. These carriages were to be 52ft long with two First-, two Second- and three Third-class compartments. Presumably, by now somebody

Plate 9.17c 'L12' class No 430. The leading three carriages are 56ft Brake Composites (to Drawings 1832, 1736 — no LNWR sidelamps — and 1832 respectively), followed by a Dining Saloon. *Ian Allan Library*

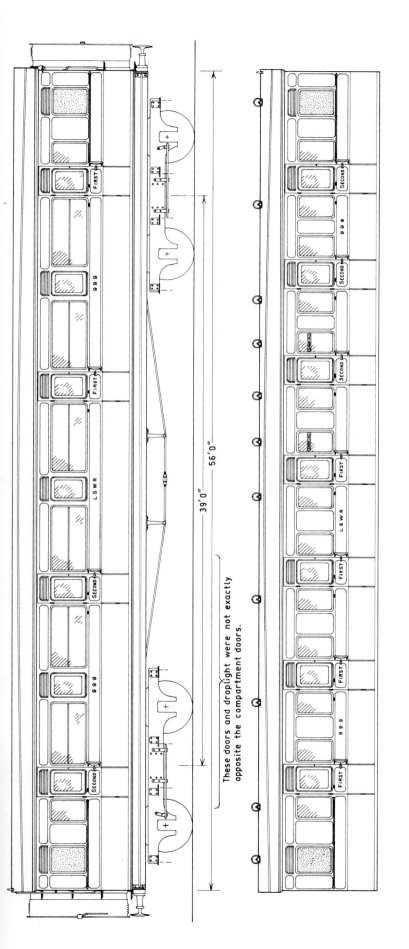

These doors and droplight were not exactly
opposite the compartment doors.

56' 0"

39' 0"

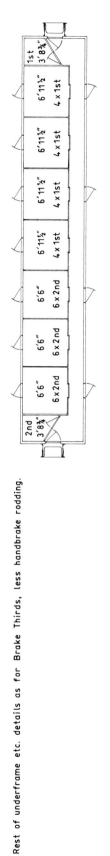

Rest of underframe etc. details as for Brake Thirds, less handbrake rodding.

2nd 3'8¾"	6'6" 6 x 2nd	6'6" 6 x 2nd	6'6" 6 x 2nd	6'11½" 4 x 1st	6'11½" 4 x 1st	6'11½" 4 x 1st	6'11½" 4 x 1st	1st 3'8¾"

0   5   10   15   20 feet

Figure 9.18
LSWR 56ft Composite of 1910.

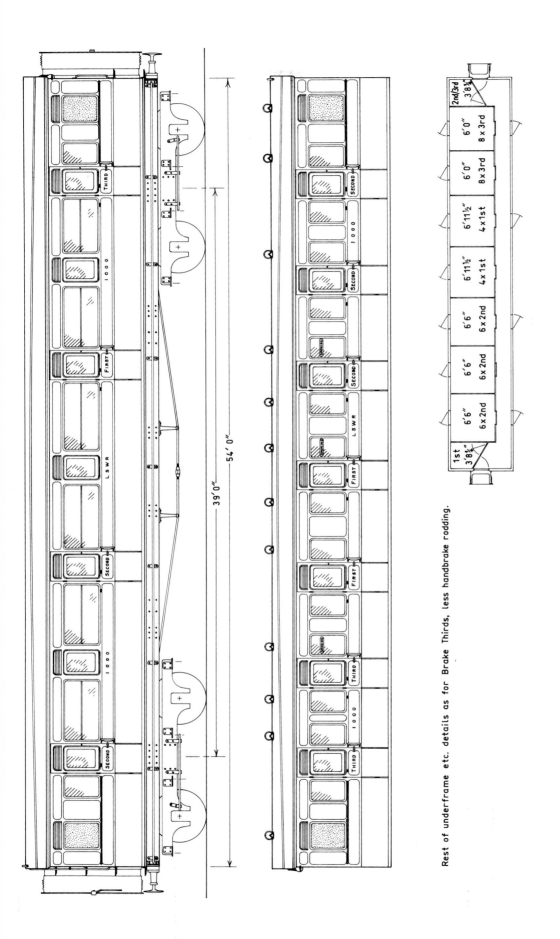

Rest of underframe etc. details as for Brake Thirds, less handbrake rodding.

0   5   10   15   20 feet

Figure 9.19
LSWR 54ft Tri-Composite of 1910.

Plate 9.19 54ft Tri-Composite (LSWR No 1000, Drawing 1866) seen as SR No 5097 while being cut up at Eastleigh c1949. The underframe was then shortened for Directors' Saloon DS 1. *F. Foote*

was looking ahead to the abolition of Second class, which had already taken place on some other railways, since the Second- and Third-class compartments were built to exactly the same width — 6ft between partitions. The drawing number was 2138 (Figure 9.20). By the time they were completed in March 1913 the new 1912 numbering scheme had been implemented, so they took their numbers in the new range and in the new lettering style, with 4in-high characters and having both the company

letters 'LSWR' and the numerals close together as near to the centre of the vehicle as would look balanced.

The same meeting that authorised these six Tri-Composites also sanctioned six new Dining Saloons, which were then built to Drawing 2158 (Figure 9.21) and completed between April and July 1913. These Saloons were clearly developed from the earlier 'Diners' but with some distinctive changes. The kitchen and pantry were much the same as on the earlier version, but they

Plate 9.20 52ft Tri-Composite (LSWR No 2408, Drawing 2138) as SR No 5106. *J. L. Smith*

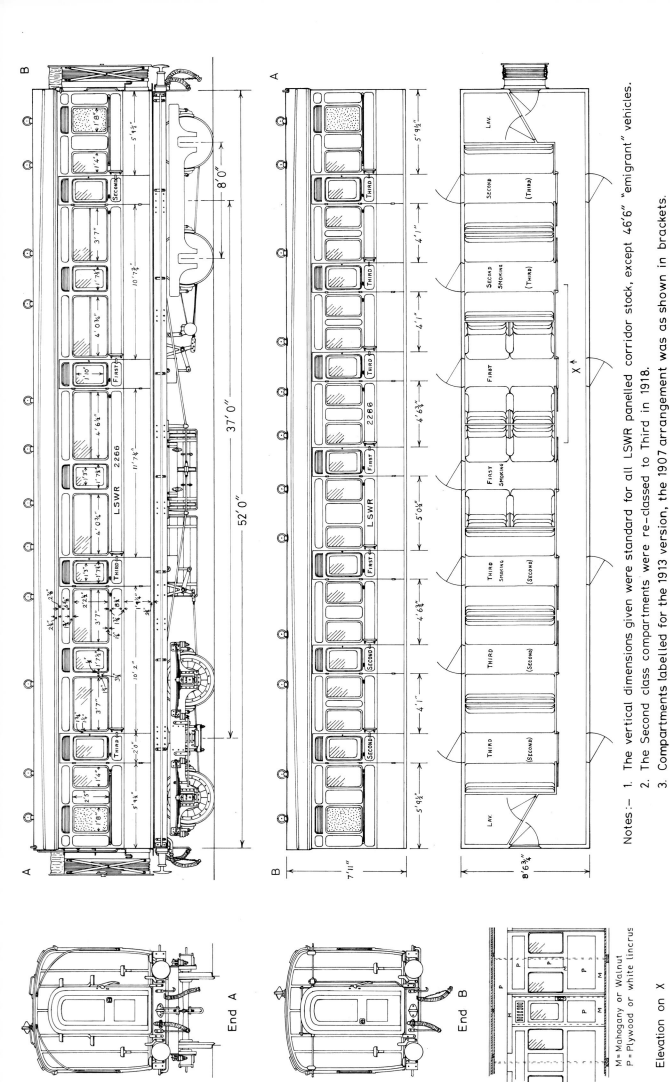

Notes :— 1. The vertical dimensions given were standard for all LSWR panelled corridor stock, except 46'6" "emigrant" vehicles.

2. The Second class compartments were re-classed to Third in 1918.

3. Compartments labelled for the 1913 version, the 1907 arrangement was as shown in brackets.

End A

Elevation on X

End B

M = Mahogany or Walnut
P = Plywood or white lincrus

Figure 9.20
LSWR 52ft Tri-Composite of 1907 and 1913.

were moved from the centre of the vehicle, which had required the staff to split their attentions in two directions, to one end. There were still two separate saloon sections separated by a glazed partition; thus they could be treated either as single-class or two separate classes. Two features copied from the final version of the earlier 'Diners' were the large windows and the outside-framed 'Dreadnought' bogies. However, the most obvious change was a new roof shape, which appears to have been half a true ellipse. Whereas existing 8ft 6¾in-wide corridor stock had a rail-to-roof height of 12ft, the new roof shape took the height up to 12ft 6in, giving the ventilation advantages of the clerestory roof without the structural and weatherproofing problems. To aid the ventilation there was an external trunking along part of the roof, drawing air from the saloon to an exhauster fan in the roof of the kitchen.

Not quite so obvious, until one compares these carriages closely with other ones, is that the heights of the panels were altered, resulting in the top panels being 2in deeper than usual, thus permitting the provision of toplights over each of the big windows; these opened inwards at the top, and appear to have been fitted with glass that had been etched with floral designs.

Fairly logically, it was assumed that passengers would only need to enter the Dining Saloon from adjacent carriages, so the only external doors were intended for staff use. Presumably it was to indicate this that they were glazed with embossed or frosted glass. The two doors to the end vestibule gave access from the ground using steps on the bogie; for loading stores there was a pair of double doors on the corridor side and a single door into the pantry on the non-corridor side. There were steps on the bogie at the other end of the carriage, but in this case they were to allow staff to reach and reset the alarm indicator or to attend to the gangway connection.

The interior of the saloon was finished in mahogany and satinwood, with blinds and curtains at all windows. In the corridor, the framing was of teak; the sides below the waist were panelled with mahogany and above with plywood. The inside of the roof was painted white and lined dark pink. Like the earlier Dining Saloons, the floor of the kitchen, pantry and side corridor was covered with sheet lead for ease of cleaning. Lighting was by electricity, the saloon having a cluster of three 16-candlepower bulbs on the centre line of each seating bay and a single lamp over each toplight, directed towards the table below. Gas cylinders were also fitted, to supply the cooker. Steam-heating elements ran along each side of the saloon floor and were protected by perforated brass covers.

All six remained in service as dining cars until World War 2, when such services were withdrawn. Their use in the early years of that war are not recorded, but two were converted to Ambulance Cars for the United States forces in 1944. Three were grounded for use as offices or stores at (rather curiously) Wembley in 1945, whilst the last one became a Mess & Tool Van in 1947.

Eight more Brake Thirds were authorised on renewals on 5 December 1912. For this batch the hinged luggage doors were replaced by sliding doors and lookouts were re-introduced, this

Plate 9.21a 56ft Dining saloon No 49 (Drawing 2158). *Author's collection*

Plate 9.21b 'N15' class No 737 passing Esher with an express for Plymouth. The leading carriage is a 56ft Dining Saloon to Drawing 2158. *H. L. Salmon*

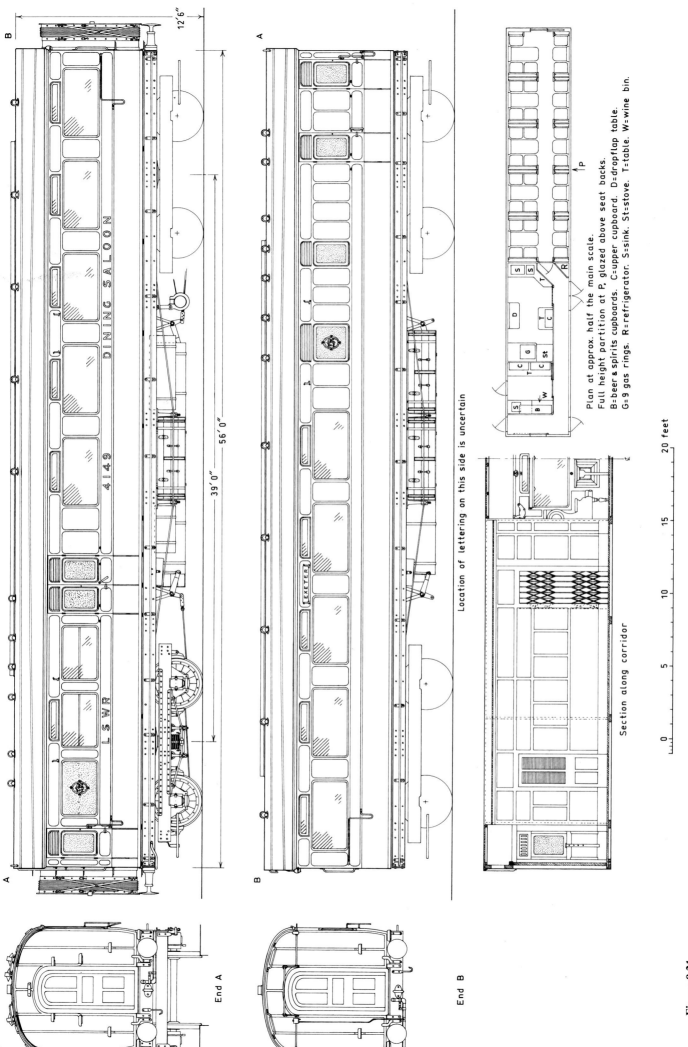

DINING SALOON

4149

L S W R

EXETER

12'6"

39'0"

56'0"

End A

End B

Location of lettering on this side is uncertain

Plan at approx. half the main scale.
Full height partition at P, glazed above seat backs.
B=beer & spirits cupboards. C=upper cupboard. D=dropflap table.
G=9 gas rings. R=refrigerator. S=sink. St=stove. T=table. W=wine bin.

D

T C

C T

G St

C

S B W

S S

T R

Section along corridor

0   5   10   15   20 feet

Figure 9.21
LSWR 56ft Dining Saloon of 1913.

Plate 9.21c 56ft Dining Saloon (LSWR No 4148, Drawing 2158) as SR No 7848. *F. Foote*

Plate 9.21d Former LSWR 56ft Dining Saloon No 4145 of 1913 (Drawing 2158), seen as Mess & Tool Van No 623s in 1951. *J. H. Aston*

time in the form of quite small sheet-steel affairs. The drawing was No 2207 (Figure 9.22) and the vehicles were all completed in October 1913, four having left-hand and four right-hand corridors. This might suggest that they were intended to be formed into set trains, but there is no mention of this, and the only other vehicles authorised at the same time were four Thirds to Drawing 1872, completed in July 1913. Corridor trains with solely Third class seem a little unlikely, so presumably some existing Composites were involved.

The Locomotive & Carriage Committee issued an instruction in March 1914 that 19 Brake Composites and four Dining Saloons used for through services were to be fitted with emergency apparatus. In the brake compartments this consisted of a case of various tools, two fire extincteurs (sic) and an ambulance box.

Only a fire extincteur was required in the Saloons. Later, in December 1915, this instruction was made to apply to all brake compartments in main-line service.

A further batch of six similar Brake Thirds, but to Drawing 2455, was authorised on 27 November 1913 for the 1914 renewals programme. However, only two were completed by December 1916 and the remaining four were deferred until after the war, to May 1919. As has been mentioned in the case of the Thirds, there were virtually no outward differences between these two batches, the main change being the use of steel panels on the later ones instead of wood. The main dimensions and placing of fascias were identical.

Also authorised on 27 November 1913 were six Brake Tri-Composites. None of these was completed until November 1918,

157

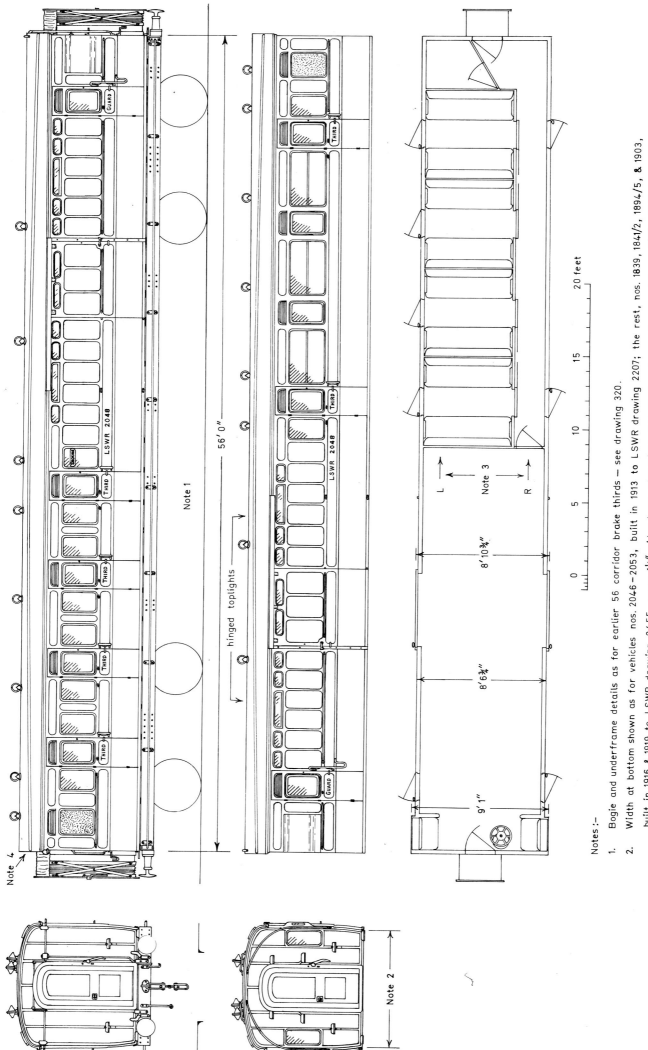

56' 0"

Note 1

hinged toplights

LSWR 2048

THIRD
THIRD
THIRD
THIRD
GUARD

Note 4

THIRD
THIRD
LSWR 2048
THIRD
GUARD

L
Note 3
R

8' 10¾"

8' 6¾"

9' 1"

0   5   10   15   20 feet

Note 2

Notes :-

1. Bogie and underframe details as for earlier 56 corridor brake thirds — see drawing 320.

2. Width at bottom shown as for vehicles nos. 2046-2053, built in 1913 to LSWR drawing 2207; the rest, nos. 1839, 1841/2, 1894/5, & 1903, built in 1916 & 1919 to LSWR drawing 2455, were 1¼" wider here, also width over stepboards was increased from 9'0"to 9'1."

3. Nos. 2046-9, 2053, 1839, 1841/2, 1894 had right hand corridor as drawn, rest had left hand corridor.

4. Lavatory ventilator replaced by hinged toplight on LSWR drawing 2455.

Figure 9.22
LSWR 50ft 0in Corridor
Brake Third.

Plate 9.22a 56ft Brake Third
(LSWR No 1841,
Drawing 2455) as BR S3143S,
in Micheldever sidings.
Lens of Sutton

Plate 9.22b 56ft Brake Third No 2052 (Drawing 2207)
A. E. West

Plate inside carriage advising on use of emergency chain

Plate 9.22c 56ft Brake Third (LSWR No 2046,
Drawing 2207) as DS 1549 in Stewarts Lane's breakdown
train in September 1949. *J. H. Aston*

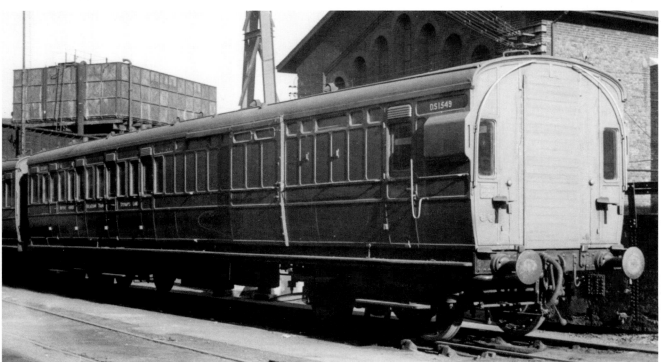

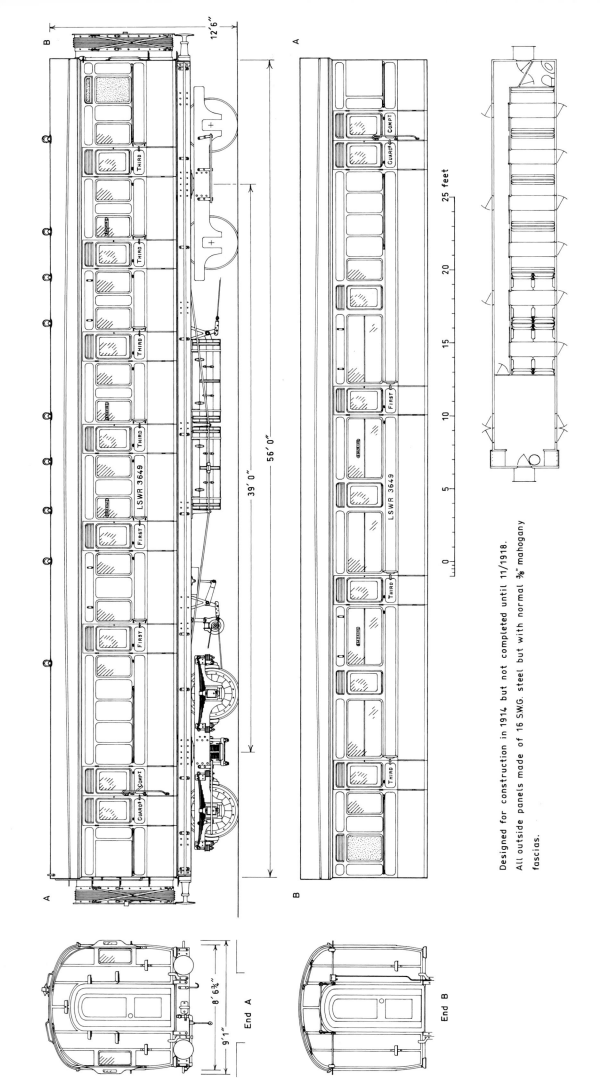

Designed for construction in 1914 but not completed until 11/1918.
All outside panels made of 16 S.W.G. steel but with normal ⅜" mahogany
fascias.

Figure 9.23
LSWR 56ft Brake Composite of 1908.

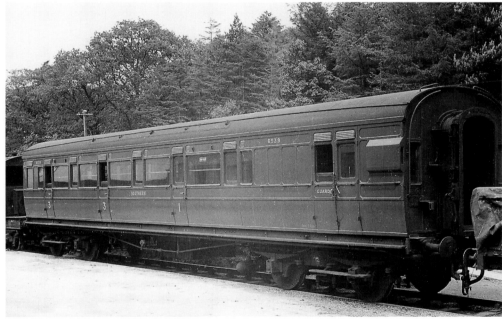

Plate 9.23a 'L12' class No 419 on a Portsmouth train. The leading carriage is a 56ft Brake Composite to Drawing 2362, followed by a 56ft Dining Saloon to Drawing 2158. *J. Tatchell collection*

Plate 9.23b 56ft Brake Composite (LSWR No 3652, Drawing 2362) as SR No 6539 at Petrockstow in July 1948. *J. H. Aston*

and by then the abolition of Second class was going ahead, so instead of the planned 2+2+2 compartments there were two First and four Third. The drawing, No 2362, appears from the sequence of numbers to have been prepared in 1914, preceding the steel-panelled Thirds and Brake Thirds mentioned earlier; thus it is the earliest drawing to specify the use of 16SWG (1⁄16 in) steel panels in place of the traditional 3⁄8 in mahogany ones. In many respects these carriages looked much like most of the other corridor stock, but they stood out because, as can be seen from Figure 9.23, they were given the same style of high elliptical roof as had been put on the 1913 Dining Saloons. Two not very obvious detail oddities were that the droplight between the First and Third doors on the corridor side did not precisely match the rest in position and frame fascias, and that instead of the usual ventilator in the top panel of the lavatory there was a hinged window, though with the normal ventilator in the matching position on the corridor side.

Apart from the increased wear and tear of war traffic, quite a few carriages had to be loaned or sold to the War Department. In general, the deficiencies could not be made good during the war, but of course the Locomotive, Carriage & Wagon Committee still had to review the position and make plans for renewals. Apart from those deferred vehicles already mentioned, they also ordered four five-car trains and five loose corridor Thirds on 20 May 1915, two 10-car boat trains on 29 March 1917 and 20 corridor Brake Thirds and 11 corridor Thirds on 21 March 1918, as well as substantial quantities of van and wagon stock.

In the Register entries for the Thirds that were eventually built in 1920, there are pencilled notes against the first five 'Rest of 5 Corr, Third 1916', and against the remainder 'Rest of 11 Third 12/18', which ties up with the authorisations, and shows them as built to Drawing 3128.

The whole of the body of these new 57ft Thirds was substantially identical to the earlier 56ft Thirds to Drawing 2390

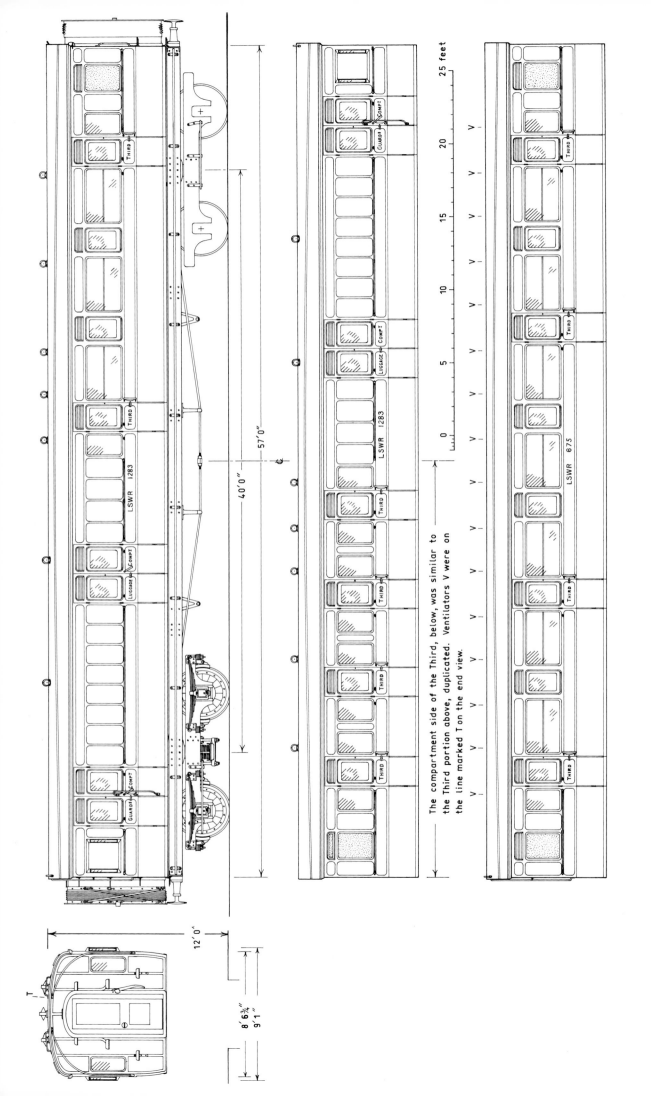

The compartment side of the Third, below, was similar to the Third portion above, duplicated. Ventilators V were on the line marked T on the end view.

Figure 9.24/9.25
LSWR 57ft Third and Brake Third of 1920 and 1921.

LSWR 1283

LSWR 675

57'0"

40'0"

12'0"

8'6¾"

9'1"

25 feet

GUARD'S COMPT

THIRD

LUGGAGE COMPT

LUGGAGE COMPT

GUARD'S COMPT

THIRD

(Figure 9.3), except that the two lavatories were each 6in wider, at 3ft 10¼in, and had hinged toplights like those on the Brake Composites of 1918. The bogies had the usual 8ft wheelbase, but were set at 40ft centres instead of the previous 39ft. There seems little point in producing a complete drawing with such small variations; therefore reference should be made to Figure 9.24/25 which combines sufficient of these Thirds with the succeeding very similar 57ft Brake Thirds.

When the 20 Brake Thirds were at last built, in November and December 1921, they also were constructed to the increased length of 57ft. The LSWR drawing was No 3151, and they are shown here in Figure 9.25. As with the entire Thirds, the compartments were as before; only the lavatory was altered, again by 6in. The luggage compartment was another variation of previous layouts, and the lookouts were also in a changed style, with hard-angled bends instead of the former ogee curves and with the glazing set at an angle. These carriages were the last to be built in the traditional, panelled style.

Plate 9.24a Former LSWR 57ft Third No 675 (Drawing 3128), later SR No 708, as No DS 3060 at Horley. *Author's collection*

Plate 9.24b The other side of former LSWR 57ft Third No DS 3060. *Lens of Sutton*

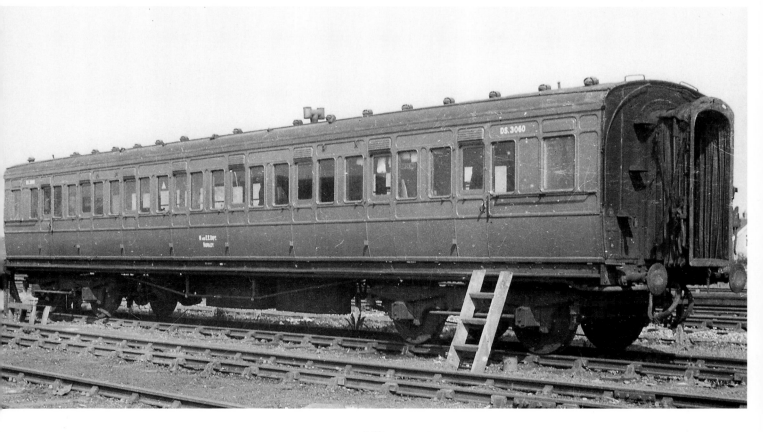

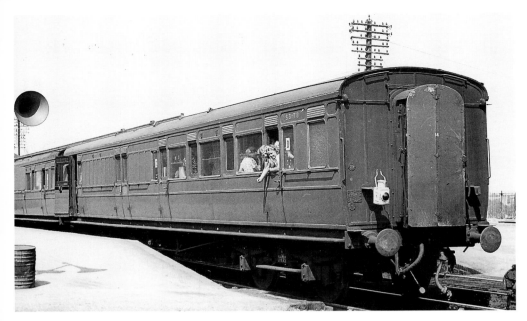

Plate 9.25a 57ft Brake Third (LSWR No 1349, Drawing 3151) seen at Okehampton in June 1949 as BR No S3178. *J. H. Aston*

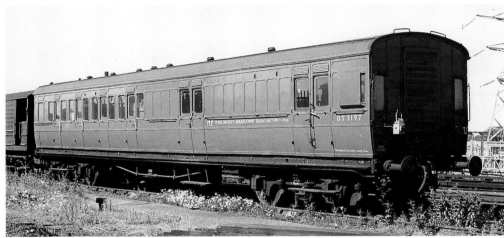

Plate 9.25b 57ft Brake Third (LSWR No 1283, Drawing 3151) in the Three Bridges breakdown train in August 1962 as BR No DS 3197. *J. H. Aston*

LSWR posters promoting travel to Paris or the West Country

Chapter 10

CORRIDOR CARRIAGES (57FT 'IRONCLAD')

The four five-car trains that were authorised in 1915 for the Bournemouth service were not completed until 1921, but then they completely changed the appearance of LSWR trains. The carriages were all 57ft long and 9ft wide, 12ft 5in high from rail to roof. Although built on teak and oak frames, they were clad with galvanised steel panels, the joints in which were protected by narrow metal strips in place of the conventional wooden mouldings. The windows were only slightly recessed behind the panel surface, with quite slender frames showing, so the overall appearance was thus of smooth flush sides. Because of this appearance of being all-metal, together with their use of 'Dreadnought'-type wide-framed bogies (Figure 9.5), they quickly earned another rather naval nickname — 'Ironclads'.

The new livery was a fairly dark green, as on the electric trains. Black and yellow lining was used to represent the pattern of the earlier panelling. The lettering was still in gold, shaded black. Some of the 1921 drawings and some further Southern Railway drawings of July and August 1925 show this imitation panelling with right-angled corners, this applying to steel-panelled stock on all three sections of the Southern Railway, but another drawing from mid-1925 shows the usual rounded corners with 2½in inside radius. Carriage ends were plain black.

The underframes were entirely of steel channel and angle sections and were painted black. The bodies were still mounted off the underframes on 1in wooden packing pieces. The tare weight had risen, in the case of Brake Thirds, for example, from around 26 tons for the earlier panelled stock to 33 tons for these

'Ironclads'. Disc wheels were now used instead of the former Mansell type in order to withstand the increased frictional heat arising from braking these heavier vehicles in faster trains.

Each train consisted of two Brake Thirds, a First, a Third and a Pantry Third. The Pantry Thirds were similar to the Thirds, but the space of one end compartment and lavatory was taken up by the pantry. This pantry was provided with a boiler for hot water, an egg-cooker and a grill; there was no intention of providing more than light snacks on this service. Portable tables were carried in each carriage and could readily be set up in the compartments. All compartments had electric-bell communication with the pantry. Total seating of the train was 42 First-class and 184 Third-class. These four trains were at first numbered as sets 1c to 4c, but later became SR sets 431 to 434.

The First-class compartments were finished in polished walnut and upholstered with blue figured moquette, whilst the Thirds were in polished mahogany and figured brown plush. All ceilings were fireproofed and painted flat white; in the Firsts they were also decorated in gold. All compartments were provided with mirrors and Photocrom scenic views of places on the LSWR.

The width of the carriages, at 9ft, prevented the provision of protruding lookouts for the guard, so on each Brake vehicle part of the body side tapered in until the width was 8ft 3in at a point 2ft 6in from the end. The last 2ft 6in were swelled to 9ft 1in wide on these first four trains, but on all later construction the width was kept to 9ft. This effectively created lookouts with very narrow windows giving a fair view along the train on anything but dead

Plate 10.1a 57ft First No 3867 in green livery with square-cornered panel lining. *J. Tatchell collection*

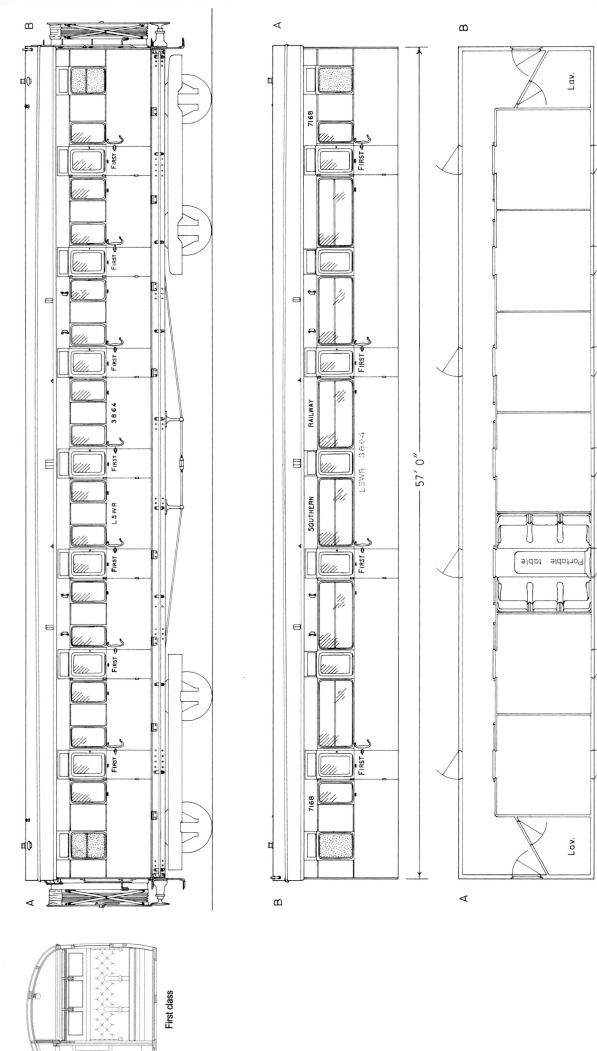

First class

Notes:-

1. All main dimensions, all underframe, bogie, end details, lining, etc., as for Third of 1921-1926.

2. Bogies type 1 fitted up until 3/1923 (LSWR 3938, SR 7178), type 2 from then on.

Figure 10.1
LSWR 57ft x 9ft First of 1921-1925.

166

straight track. The LSWR drawing numbers and the present figures are as follows:

First	Drawing 3194	Figure 10.1
Third	" 3251	" 10.2
Brake Third	" 3252	" 10.3
Pantry Third	" 3288	" 10.4

Incidentally, the works drawing for the Thirds that I have seen had been torn and the number was missing, but there was what appeared to be a later note 'E3128?' on it. This seems to be a mistake, as these vehicles are marked as 'Drawing 3251' in the Register, whilst '3128' is marked against the panelled 57ft Thirds mentioned earlier.

Following the earlier LSWR practice, the Brake Thirds were built in both left- and right-hand corridor versions — both types to the same drawing number but later being given different Southern diagram numbers. This was so that the five-car sets could be marshalled in the preferred LSWR manner with the corridor alternating from side to side along the train.

The wartime authorisations of March 1917 included two 10-car boat trains. Originally these were each to consist of two Brake Seconds, a Composite, seven Firsts and a 44ft Brake Van, but by the time they were built, in 1922, the plan had been changed to two trains each with two Kitchen Brake Firsts to Drawing 3665 (Figure 10.5) and eight Firsts to Drawing 3194 (Figure 10.1).

The Kitchen Brake Firsts had much the same catering facilities as the earlier Dining Saloons, but no fixed tables were provided;

Continued on page 177.

Plate 10.1b 9ft bogie on 57ft First (LSWR No 3924, Drawing 3194) seen as BR Third No S2323S at Axminster in 1957. *A. E. West*

Plate 10.1c 57ft First (LSWR No 3867, Drawing 3194) as BR No S7170S at Swanage in 1956. *J. H. Aston*

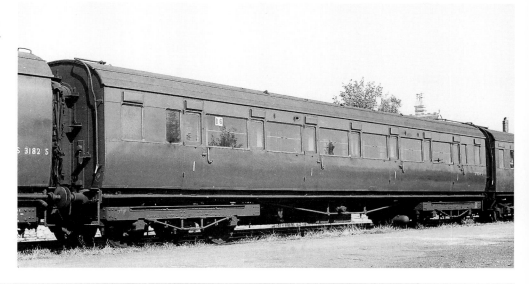

Plate 10.1d SR 57ft First No 7200 (Eastleigh Drawing 3708) on 9ft Ashford bogies, in LSWR-style green livery with square-cornered panel lining. *J. Tatchell collection*

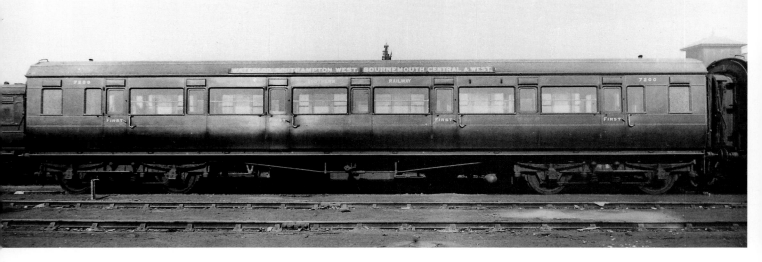

Plate 10.1e 57ft First (LSWR No 3924, Drawing 3194), altered to Third, seen as BR No S2323S at Axminster in June 1957. *A. E. West*

Plate 10.2a SR 57ft Third No 747 (Eastleigh Drawing 3709) on 9ft Ashford bogies. *R. A. Gilham collection*

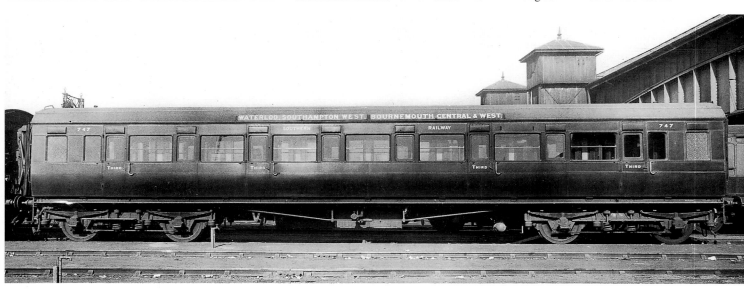

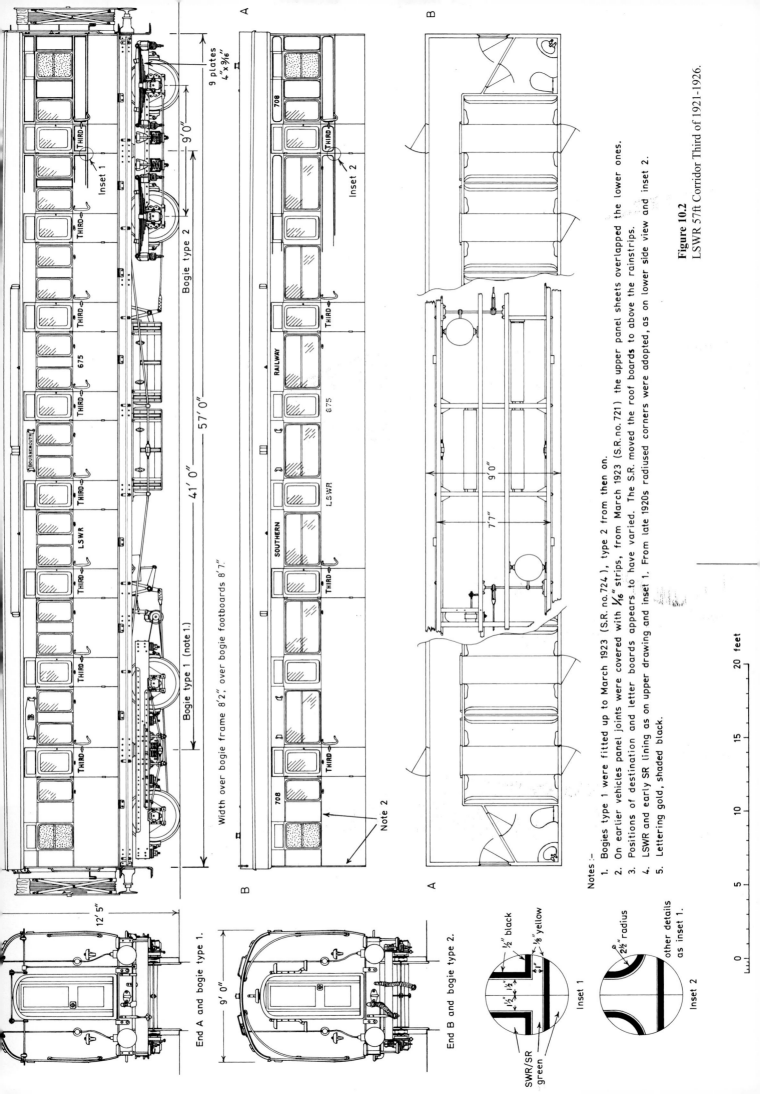

9 plates
4" x 9/16"

9'0"

Bogie type 2

Inset 1

THIRD   THIRD   THIRD   675   THIRD   THIRD   LSWR   THIRD   THIRD

BOURNEMOUTH

57'0"

41'0"

Bogie type 1 (note 1.)

Width over bogie frame 8'2", over bogie footboards 8'7".

708

Inset 2

THIRD

RAILWAY

675

SOUTHERN

LSWR

THIRD

708

Note 2

B

A

B

9'0"

7'7"

A

12'5"

End A and bogie type 1.

9'0"

End B and bogie type 2.

Notes :-

1. Bogies type 1 were fitted up to March 1923 (S.R. no.724), type 2 from then on.

2. On earlier vehicles panel joints were covered with 1/16" strips, from March 1923 (S.R.no.721) the upper panel sheets overlapped the lower ones.

3. Positions of destination and letter boards appears...to have varied. The S.R. moved the roof boards to above the rainstrips.

4. LSWR and early SR lining as on upper drawing and inset 1. From late 1920s radiused corners were adopted, as on lower side view and inset 2.

5. Lettering gold, shaded black.

1/2" black

1/8" yellow

1/2" 1/2"

1/2" 1/2"

SWR/SR
green

Inset 1

2½" radius

other details
as inset 1.

Inset 2

Figure 10.2
LSWR 57ft Corridor Third of 1921-1926.

0   5   10   15   20 feet

Plate 10.2b Detail of 1924 panel lining and Ashford bogie.

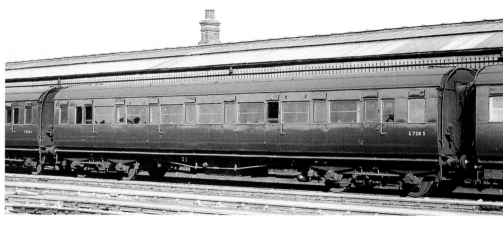

Plate 10.2c 57ft Third (LSWR NO 74) as BR No S728S at Clapham Junction, May 1958. *J. H. Aston*

Plate 10.2d 57ft Third (SR No 752, Eastleigh Drawing 3709) as BR S752S at Clapham Junction, May 1958. *J. H. Aston*

Plate 10.2e 57ft Third (LSWR No 774, Drawing 3251) as BR No DS 175 at Eastleigh, September 1959. *J. H. Aston*

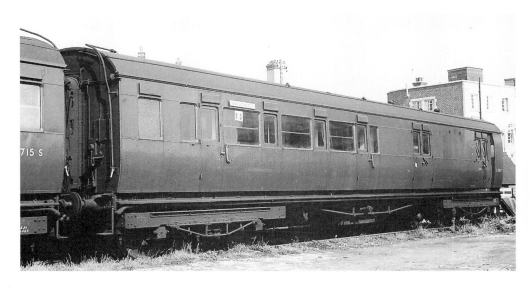

Plate 10.3a 57ft Brake Third (LSWR No 1276, Drawing 3252) as BR No S3181S in set 431, at Swanage in September 1956. *J. H. Aston*

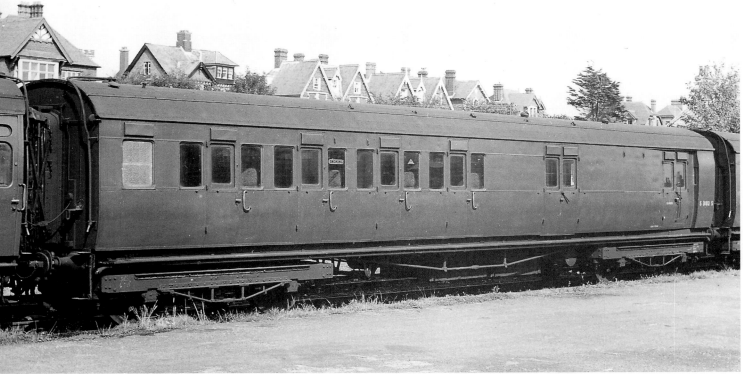

Plate 10.3b 57ft Brake Third (LSWR No 1277, Drawing 3252) as BR No S3182S in set 431, at Swanage in September 1956. *J. H. Aston*

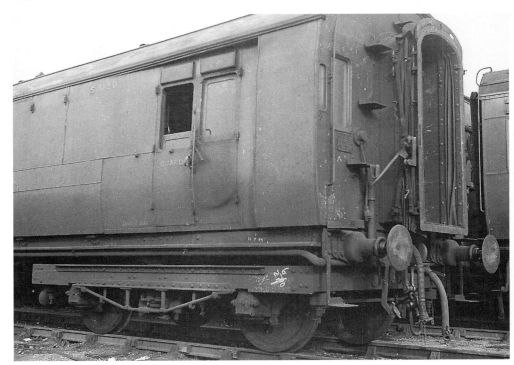

Plate 10.3c 57ft Brake Third (LSWR No 1353, Drawing 3252), later SR No 3190. *A. E. West*

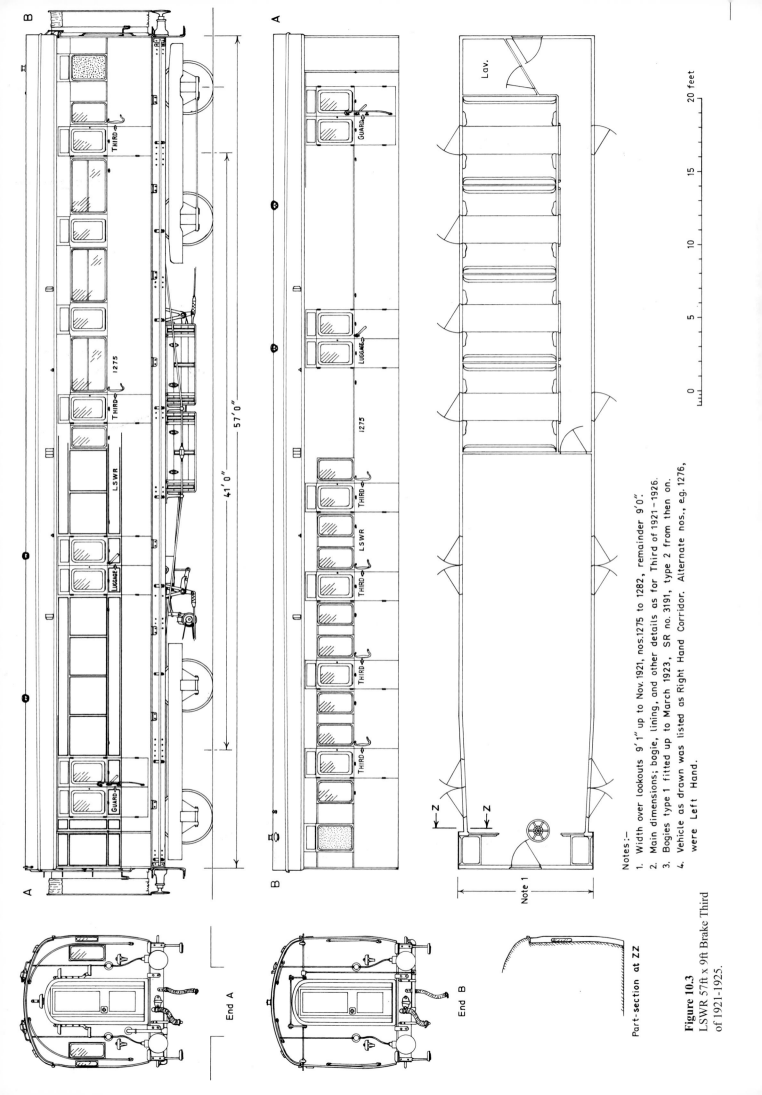

Notes:-

1. Width over lookouts 9'1" up to Nov.1921, nos.1275 to 1282, remainder 9'0".

2. Main dimensions; bogie, lining, and other details as for Third of 1921-1926.

3. Bogies type 1 fitted up to March 1923, SR no. 3191, type 2 from then on.

4. Vehicle as drawn was listed as Right Hand Corridor. Alternate nos., e.g. 1276, were Left Hand.

Figure 10.3
LSWR 57ft x 9ft Brake Third of 1921-1925.

Plate 10.3d 57ft Brake Third (LSWR No 1356, Drawing 3710), later SR No 3192, condemned as BR No S3192S at Micheldever c1959. *Lens of Sutton*

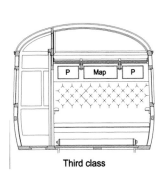

Third class

Plate 10.3e 57ft Brake Third (LSWR No 1357, Drawing 3710), later SR No 3193, as BR No DS 70133 on reinforced underframe at Eastleigh in May 1974. *G. R. Weddell*

Plate 10.3f 57ft Brake Third (LSWR No 1353, Drawing 3710), later SR No 3190. *A. E. West*

Plate 10.3g *(Below left)* Brake detail of 57ft Brake Third. *G. R. Weddell*

Plate 10.3g *(Below right)* Brake rigging of 57ft Brake Third. *G. R. Weddell*

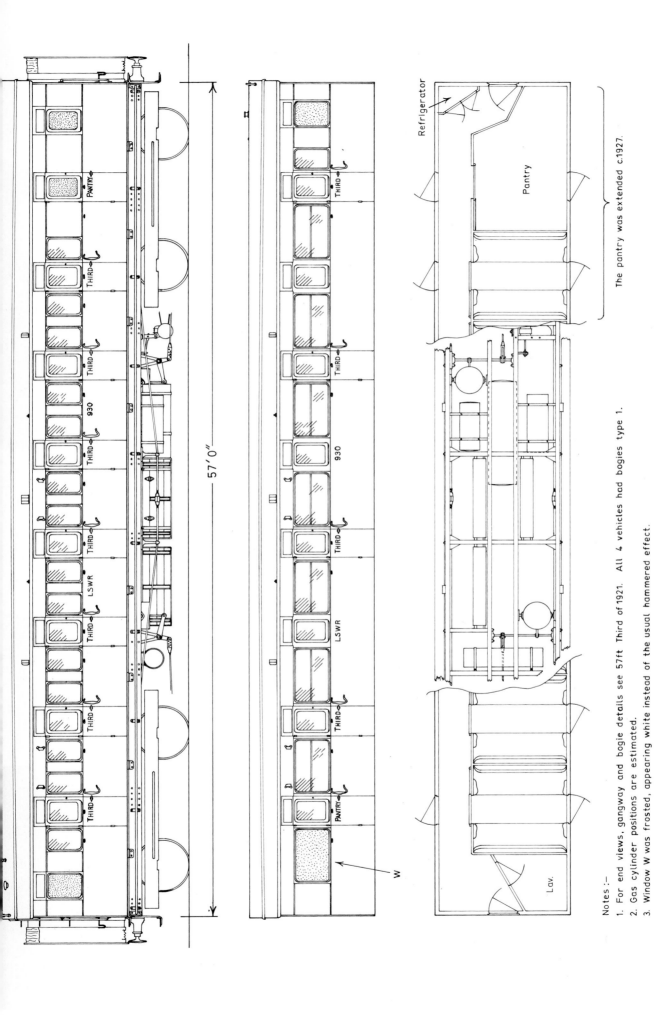

Notes :-

1. For end views, gangway and bogie details see 57ft Third of 1921. All 4 vehicles had bogies type 1.
2. Gas cylinder positions are estimated.
3. Window W was frosted, appearing white instead of the usual hammered effect.

The pantry was extended c.1927.

0   5   10   15   20 feet

Figure 10.4
LSWR 57ft x 9ft Pantry Third of 1921.

175

Plate 10.4a 57ft Pantry Third (LSWR No 930, Drawing 3288). *F. Foote*

Plate 10.4a 57ft Pantry Third (LSWR No 932, Drawing 3288) altered to all-Third, at Swanage in September 1956 as BR No S715S in set 431. *J. H. Aston*

on services when meals were to be served, portable tables could be fitted in the ordinary compartments — an arrangement which had its limitations. Gas cylinders for cooking were packed into all the available space on the underframe, necessitating a slight alteration to the usual positioning of the brake cylinders. The truss rods were again made of continuous flat strips, as for most of the previous 56ft Dining Saloons.

In May 1921 it was decided to order another four five-car sets for the Bournemouth service together with 10 loose full Firsts. Before they could be built, a further order was placed for two six-car sets, ostensibly for the Portsmouth service, but this was later amended to two five-car sets and two separate Dining Saloons. They were all completed in 1923 and 1924 under Southern Railway management, but as the SR numbering scheme was not completed until late 1923 the first four sets, numbered 5[c] to 8[c], and the two Dining Saloons appeared in LSWR sage green livery and numbering.

The Firsts, both in the sets and the loose ones, were built to Drawing 3708, which was very similar to the preceding Drawing 3194 (Figure 10.1), though after the first two, which had outside-framed bogies, the rest had 9ft-wheelbase bogies apparently of an Ashford Works design. The Thirds were to Drawing 3709, which again was very similar to Drawing 3251 (Figure 10.2), whilst the Brake Thirds were to the existing Drawing 3252 (Figure 10.3).

The new Dining Saloons, of which a further six were built in 1925, all to Drawing 3854 (Figure 10.6), were broadly similar in layout to those built in 1913, but were otherwise like the rest of the 'Ironclad' stock, except that, instead of the 'M.M.' ventilator bonnets over the windows, these carriages were fitted with Stone's glass louvre ventilators over the windows of the saloon, augmented by an extractor fan over the kitchen, drawing air from the saloon and kitchen through a trunking on the roof, as in the 1913 Dining Saloons. The Stone's ventilators consisted of vertical glass strips with a common pivoting arrangement operated by a

Plate 10.5a 57ft Pantry Brake First (LSWR No 4062, Drawing 3665) as SR No 7712 at Southampton Docks. *F. Foote*

Plate 10.5b 57ft Pantry Brake First (LSWR No 4063, Drawing 3665) as SR No 7713 at Southampton Docks. *F. Foote*

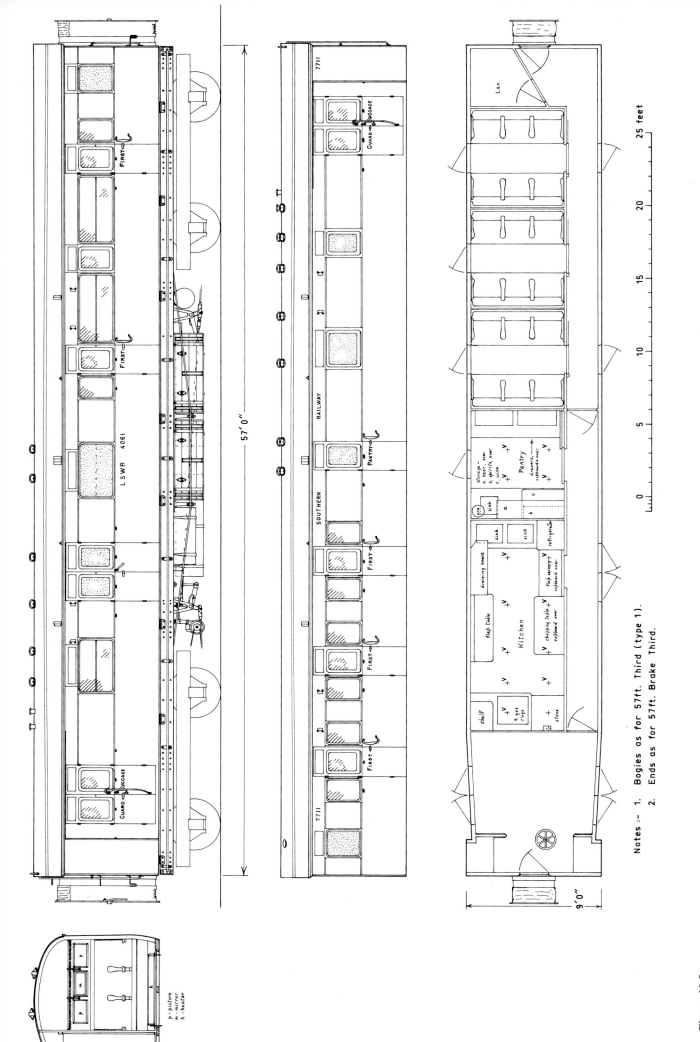

Figure 10.5
LSWR 57ft Kitchen Brake First.

Notes :- 1. Bogies as for 57ft. Third (type 1).
2. Ends as for 57ft. Brake Third.

25 feet

p : picture
m : mirror
h : heater

57' 0"

9' 0"

LSWR 4061

GUARD ← LUGGAGE

FIRST ←

FIRST →

7711

SOUTHERN   RAILWAY

FIRST ←

FIRST →

FIRST →

PANTRY →

GUARD ← LUGGAGE

Lav.

Pantry

Kitchen

storage -
a. beer, over
b. spirits, over
c. wine

drawers,
cupboards over

sink

sink

refrigerator

flap serving
cupboard over

chopping table
cupboard over

dressing board

flap table

shelf

4 gas rings

stove

urn

sink

a

b

c

Plate 10.5c 57ft Pantry Brake First (LSWR No 4064, Drawing 3665) altered to six-compartment Brake First in 1948 as BR No S7714S, at Clapham Junction in April 1954. *J. H. Aston*

lever on the inside so that they could either scoop or expel air, as desired. These were backed by inward-hinging windows to prevent rain entering. The saloon was divided into two sections by a glass partition, though without any door. Interior woodwork was polished mahogany, and the seats were upholstered with blue moquette. The underframes were similar to those of the Kitchen Brake Firsts as regards the truss rods and the provision of gas tanks.

No more LSWR-style Pantry cars were built. The original four Pantry Thirds were altered to entire Thirds (SR Diagram 23) in about 1936. The four Kitchen First Brakes were converted in 1944/5 — two as Ambulances and two as War Department Inspection cars — but shortly after that they were all restored to passenger service; then, in 1948, they had the former kitchen and dining area converted to make three more First-class compartments, making them plain Brake Firsts. They continued thus until withdrawal in 1959.

Post-Grouping, quite a lot more carriages to LSWR designs, and also to further LSWR-type designs as developments of the existing ones, were built at Eastleigh Works under the supervision of Surrey Warner. Many of these later vehicles were destined for use on other sections of the Southern, but they are included here to complete the 'Ironclad' story.

Altogether another 33 of the Firsts were built to a substantially identical drawing, No 3708, between March 1923 and March 1926. The first six were used in six more five-car sets (SR sets 435 to 440) for the Bournemouth service and, as mentioned earlier, were painted with LSWR numbers, 3937 to 3942.

Similarly, 30 more Thirds, to Drawing 3709 but virtually identical to the original four, were built, as well as another 20 Brake Thirds to the original drawing (No 3252), between March 1923 and September 1925. As with the Firsts, the first 12 of each were used for SR sets 435 to 440. It should be noted that there were now two full Thirds in these sets, instead of one Third and a Pantry Third in the original four sets.

So far, and perhaps surprisingly in view of past form, there had been no Composites in the new style, but May 1924 saw the introduction of four Composites, to Drawing 4115 (Figure 10.7),

Plate 10.6a SR 57ft Dining Saloon No 7854 (Eastleigh Drawing 3854). *F. Foote*

179

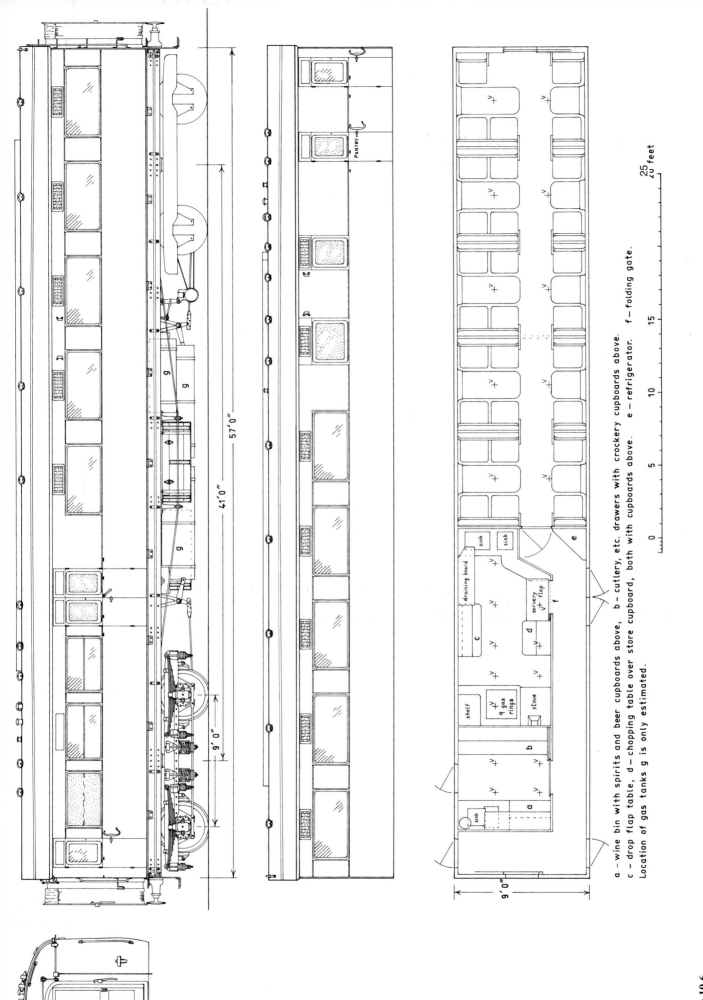

a – wine bin with spirits and beer cupboards above, b – cutlery, etc. drawers with crockery cupboards above.
c – drop flap table, d – chopping table over store cupboard, both with cupboards above. e – refrigerator. f – folding gate.
Location of gas tanks g is only estimated.

Figure 10.6
SR 57ft Dining Saloon of 1923/5.

Plate 10.6b SR 57ft Dining Saloon No 7854 (Eastleigh Drawing 3854) as Mess & Tool Van No 627s at Redhill in June 1949.
J. H. Aston

Plate 10.6c SR 57ft Dining Saloon No 7856 (Eastleigh Drawing 3854) as Mess & Tool Van No S629s at Padstow in July 1948.
J. H. Aston

having three First-class and four Third-class compartments. These appear to have been used as loose coaches, not regularly in sets.

Also in 1925 there were five Brake Composites that were used, together with five of the Brake Thirds mentioned in the next paragraph, to form two-coach sets 381 to 385 for the Waterloo to Lymington and Swanage through portions. The drawing number is not recorded in the Register, but they had two First- and four

Third-class compartments, and are depicted in Figure 10.8.

The last 'Ironclad' design was another version of Brake Third, to Drawing 4378 (Figure 10.9), which was produced in October 1925. These had six compartments, unlike the earlier series which had four. As already mentioned, the first five, which were completed in October 1925, were used to form two-car sets. These were attached to and detached from main-line trains in order to

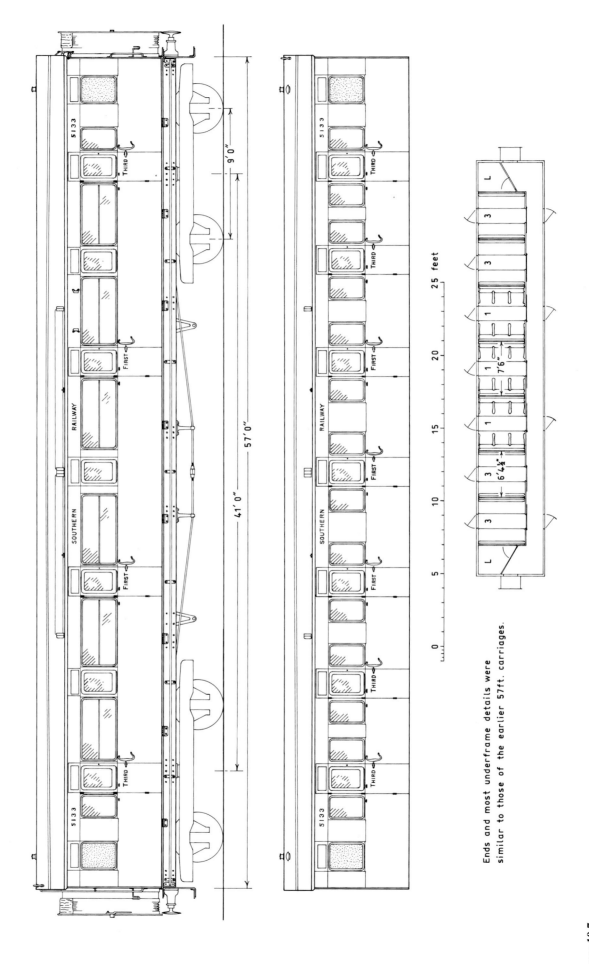

Ends and most underframe details were
similar to those of the earlier 57ft. carriages.

Figure 10.7
SR 57ft Composite of 1924.

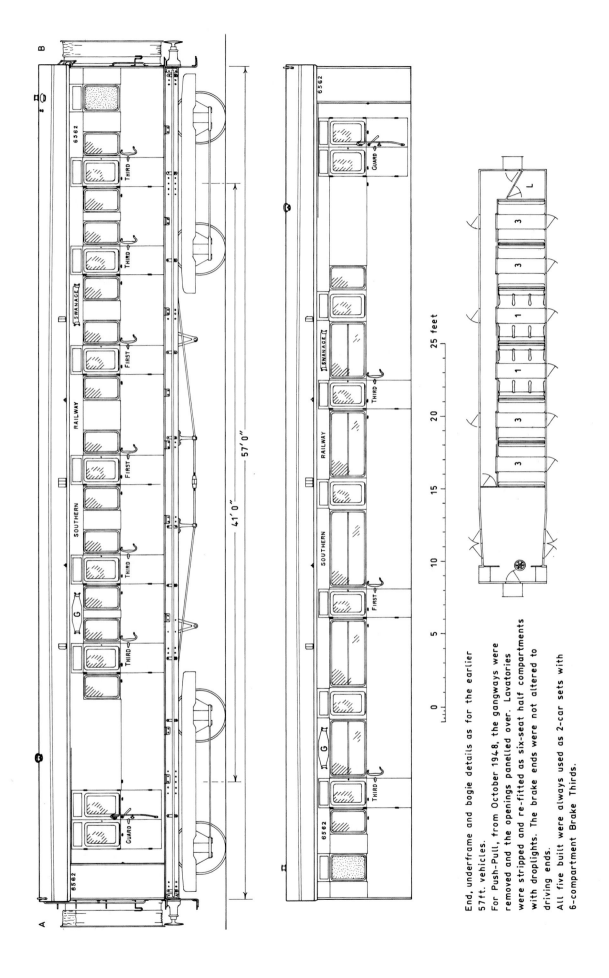

End, underframe and bogie details as for the earlier
57ft. vehicles.
For Push-Pull, from October 1948, the gangways were
removed and the openings panelled over. Lavatories
were stripped and re-fitted as six-seat half compartments
with droplights. The brake ends were not altered to
driving ends.
All five built were always used as 2-car sets with
6-compartment Brake Thirds.

Figure 10.8
SR 57ft Composite of 1924.

Plate 10.8a SR 57ft Brake Composite No 6564 in set 385 at Padstow in July 1948. *J. H. Aston*

Plate 10.8b 57ft Brake Composite (at left) and 57ft Brake Third altered for Push-Pull working (at right). *T. Wright*

provide through services between Waterloo and Lymington and between Waterloo and Swanage.

The five two-car sets continued to run in the London trains up until the end of 1948, when British Railways decided that it was more convenient to make passengers change trains so as to save management the bother of running through carriages. This was early in the era when the convenience of management became much more important than that of mere passengers. Thus at various dates between December 1948 and March 1952 all five sets were altered for Push-Pull auto working. For this conversion the gangway connections were removed; the lavatories in both types were stripped and fitted out as coupé compartments with six seats. The Brake Thirds were altered by having a seventh compartment created in the former luggage area, and the brake ends were altered to form driving ends, including the provision of droplights in the lookout sides. The sets were then used between Brockenhurst and Lymington, between Wareham and Swanage and between Seaton Junction and Seaton, until their withdrawal in 1962 (set 382 in 1959).

Apart from the set trains already mentioned, other sets were formed from the 1923 and later stock. An 11-car set, No 471, was built at Lancing in 1925, and was formed of two six-compartment Brake Thirds to Drawing 4378, seven Firsts, a Composite to Drawing 4115 and a Third. This train was used for the 'City Limited' on the Central Section.

The last full set to be built to these 'Ironclad'-style designs was also for the Central Section, for the Worthing and Bognor services, though the vehicles were built at Eastleigh, as the earlier Southern plan to build new carriages at Lancing was dropped. This was set 472, formed of two more six-compartment Brake Thirds to Drawing 4378, six Firsts and three Thirds. The balance of the stock authorised and built at this time does not appear to have been formed into specific sets, but was used as loose carriages for strengthening or replacement purposes.

All of the 'Ironclads' built before about April 1923 had the original Surrey Warner type of 9ft wheelbase 'Dreadnought' bogies, but most of those built from then until late 1925 had 9ft-wheelbase bogies designed at Ashford, whilst the final vehicles in this style, built in late 1925 and 1926, again had Ashford-designed bogies but of 8ft wheelbase that appeared very much like those which became the Southern Railway standard for quite a long time.

Immediately after the Grouping it was agreed that the Eastleigh Carriage & Wagon Works should produce about two thirds of the new carriage bodies for the Southern Railway and would take care of the maintenance of former LSWR carriages. Lancing Carriage Works would be responsible for the remaining one third of new carriage bodies and for all underframes for both Eastleigh and Lancing bodies, together with maintenance of ex-LBSCR carriages. Ashford Works took the responsibility for all wagon construction and the maintenance of ex-SECR carriages. In practice, by 1926 Lancing had ceased building new carriage bodies, leaving all of this work to the Eastleigh carriage shops.

There have been several references in this chapter, and in the previous one, to authorisations of batches of carriages to form particular train sets or for particular services. This may have been the true intention of the Committee at the time, or it may have been merely that the general stock needed to be increased by those quantities of vehicles to meet the overall service requirements.

Certainly, in the earlier cases, the sets specified were formed, but, as time went on, the formations appear to have varied, as can be seen in the Waterloo Train Summary for 1911/12. A rather odd feature of this is that, compared with the quantities of entire Thirds that were built (and are shown in the Appendix), relatively few appear in the timetable; trains were mainly formed of Brake Thirds, Composites and Firsts, leaving a slight question as to where and when all the Thirds were used! All vehicles shown in these examples are corridor unless otherwise noted.

6.10am   Brake Third, Compo, Brake Third for Plymouth, Dining Saloon for Exeter, Brake Compo and Brake Third for Torrington, one bogie van (non-corridor) for Pinhoe

8.50am   Brake Compo and Dining Saloon for Exeter, Brake Third, Compo, Brake Third for Plymouth, Brake Compo and Brake Third for Torrington

11am (after 30 October 1911)
              Brake Third, Third (Mon & Sat only), Compo, Brake Third for Plymouth, Brake Compo for Torrington, Brake Compo and Brake Third for Ilfracombe, Dining Saloon for Exeter, Brake Compo for Padstow, Brake Compo for Sidmouth

12.30pm   Brake Third, two Tri-Compos, Brake Third for Weymouth, Brake Third, Compo, Dining Saloon Tri-Compo, Brake Third for Bournemouth West, Dining Saloon (Sat only) and Brake Third (Sat only) for Bournemouth Central, Brake Compo for Lymington Pier

Then only one more corridor train between 1.05pm and 5.50pm

5.50pm   Brake Third, Compo, Brake Third for Plymouth, Dining Saloon, Brake Compo, Brake Third for Exeter, Brake Third, two Tri-Compos, Brake Third for Salisbury

6.55 pm   Brake Third, two Tri-Compos, Brake Third for Weymouth, Brake Third, Compo, Dining Saloon, Tri-Compo, Brake Third, Third (Wed & Fri only) for Bournemouth West, Dining Saloon (Fri only), Brake Compo (Fri only) for Eastleigh

A further volume will describe the passenger-rated vans, ie Luggage vans, Milk and Fruit vans, Travelling Post Offices, Horse Boxes and Carriage Trucks, as well as some 19th-century goods vehicles and a miscellany of other items.

Plate 10.9a SR 57ft Brake Third No 3213 in set 385 at Padstow in July 1948. *J. H. Aston*

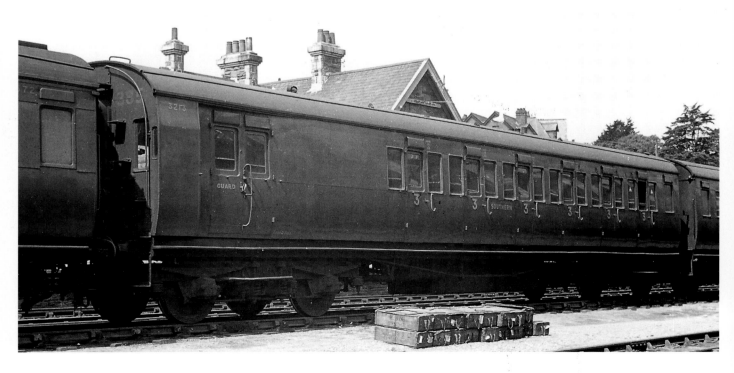

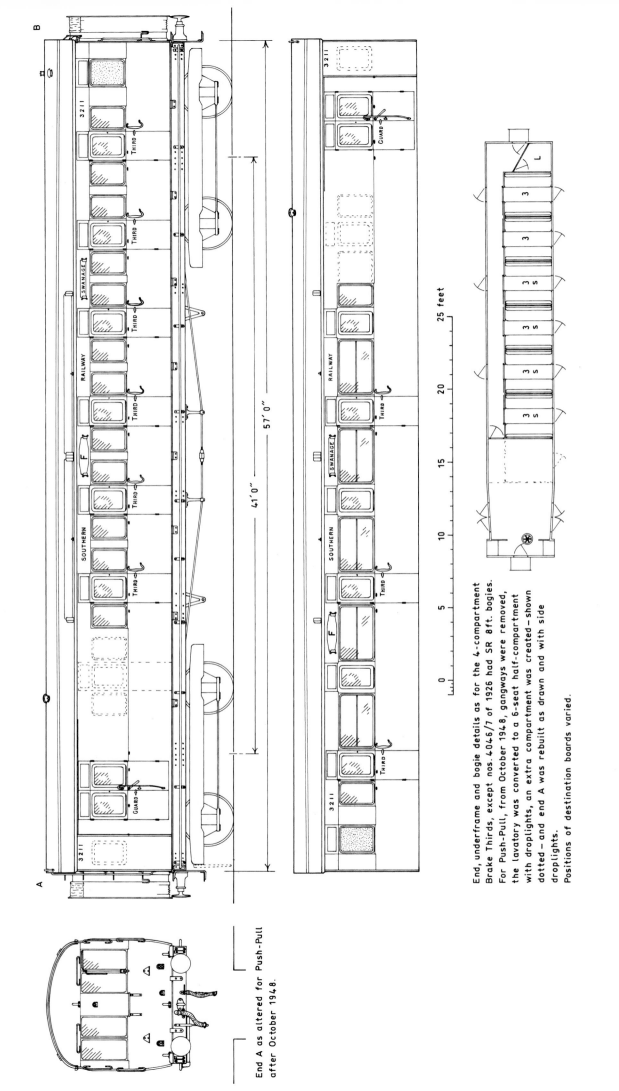

End, underframe and bogie details as for the 4-compartment
Brake Thirds, except nos. 4046/7 of 1926 had SR 8ft. bogies.
For Push-Pull, from October 1948, gangways were removed,
the lavatory was converted to a 6-seat half-compartment
with droplights, an extra compartment was created — shown
dotted — and end A was rebuilt as drawn and with side
droplights.
Positions of destination boards varied.

End A as altered for Push-Pull
after October 1948.

Figure 10.9
SR 57ft Brake Third of 1925.

Plate 10.9b SR 57ft Brake Third No 3211 (Eastleigh Drawing 4378) as altered to Push-Pull in 1948. *Author's collection*

Plate 10.9c Ex-SR 57ft Brake Third No 4052 and 57ft Brake Composite No 6560 at Seaton Junction in June 1959 as Nos S4052S and S6560S respectively. *J. H. Aston*

Appendix to Chapter 6

NON-CORRIDOR CARRIAGES, 1900-23

Any LSWR or SR number shown in brackets was allocated but probably not painted on before the next renumbering or withdrawal (Wdn). 'New No' is the post-1912 re-numbering scheme.

6.1   **50ft Double Saloon** of 1900. LSWR Drawing 919. SR Diagram 588.
Cost £1,086 each. Gangways and central connecting door provided in 4/1907 'for use with boat traffic'.

Built	No	New No	SR	Wdn
1900	57	4119	7818	7/34
1900	58	4120	7819	11/31

6.2   **50ft Composite** of 1901 (four lavatories). LSWR Drawing 980. SR Diagram 273.
Cost £983 14s 11d each. Most were wired for electric light, shown as EW, but had no equipment.

Built	No		New No	SR	Wdn	Remarks
6/01	115	EW	2359	5023	1939	to Camping Coach 14 5/36
6/01	141	EW	2384	5024	9/38	
6/01	145		2388	5025	12/35	
6/01	149	EW	2392	5026	1939	to Camping Coach 15 5/36
6/01	171	EW	2414	5027	1939	to Camping Coach 16 5/36
6/01	201	EW	2443	5028	11/35	
6/01	489	EW	2671	5031	11/35	
12/01	15	EW	2264	5014	11/35	
12/01	19	EW	2267	5015	11/35	
12/01	33	EW	2281	5016	11/35	
12/01	37		2285	5017	3/39	to Camping Coach 23 12/38
12/01	43	EW	2290	5018	10/35	
12/01	96	EW	2342	5019	1939	to Camping Coach 13 5/36
12/01	99	EW	2345	5020	9/36	
12/01	100	EW	2346	5021	9/34	LSWR set 134
12/01	107		2352	5022	1939	set 100 (Necropolis) c1936; to Camping Coach 24 12/38
12/01	481	EW	2668	5029	11/35	
12/01	482	EW	2669	5030	1939	to Camping Coach 17 4/36
12/01	498	EW	2674	5032	1939	to Camping Coach 18 6/36

6.3   **50ft Brake Third** of 1901. LSWR Drawing 982. SR Diagram 115.

Built	No	New No	SR	Wdn
6/01	35	1315	2724	9/36
6/01	177	1596	2725	10/33
6/01	178	1597	2726	2/35
6/01	554	1721	2727	2/39
6/01	563	1727	2728	6/36

6.4   **46ft Third** of 1901 (three lavatories). LSWR Drawing 993. SR Diagram 13.

Built	No	New No	SR	Wdn
6/01	16	16	543	2/39
6/01	110	110	544	1/39
6/01	198	198	546	2/35
6/01	383	383	550	2/39
6/01	400	400	552	2/39
6/01	501	501	553	1/39
6/01	511	511	554	3/35
6/01	1051	566	560	7/38
6/01	1052	565	559	2/39

Built	No	New No	SR	Wdn
12/01	185	185	545	2/39
12/01	300	300	547	11/39
12/01	356	356	548	1/39
12/01	368	368	549	1/39
12/01	392	392	551	7/38
12/01	519	519	555	2/39
12/01	521	521	556	2/39
12/01	534	534	557	1/39
12/01	545	545	558	11/39

6.5   **48ft Tri-Composite** of 1901 (three lavatories). LSWR Drawing 1051. SR Diagram 261. All electrically lit; cost £924 each.

Built	No	New No	SR	Wdn
12/01	119	2363	4556	12/38
12/01	139	2382	4557	10/35
12/01	174	2417	4559	8/36
12/01	177	2420	4560	6/38
12/01	188	2430	4562	11/36
12/01	212	2452	4563	6/35
6/02	25	2273	4555	6/33
6/02	146	2389	4558	2/34
6/02	182	2424	4561	2/39
6/02	228	2467	4564	2/39
6/02	229	2468	4565	12/38

6.6   **50ft Brake Third** of 1902. LSWR Drawing 1046. SR Diagram 117. All had electric light.

Built	No	New No	SR	Wdn	
2/02	311	1646	2729	12/35	
2/02	318	1650	2730	8/37	
3/02	324	1653	2731	12/38	
3/02	340	1661	2732	12/38	
3/02	342	1663	2733	9/36	
3/02	419	1678	2734	6/36	
3/02	490	1699	2735	6/35	
3/02	778	1878	2737	1/35	
3/02	822	1892	2739	11/35	
3/02	889	1915	2744	7/36	
3/02	890	1916	2745	6/38	
3/02	898	1918	2746	10/37	
3/02	902	1919	2747	9/35	
3/02	905	1921	2748	1/35	
3/02	927	1927	2749	6/37	
3/02	1002	1940	2750	8/35	
3/02	1003	1941	2751	5/37	
3/02	1008	1943	2752	10/36	
3/02	1011	1945	2753	12/38	to Camping Coach 21
4/02	515	1705	2736	11/36	
4/02	799	1887	2738	6/33	
4/02	824	1893	2740	2/38	
4/02	842	1899	2741	2/35	
4/02	866	1909	2742	10/35	
4/02	883	1912	2743	11/36	

6.7   **50ft Second** of 1902 (two lavatories). LSWR Drawing 1090. SR Diagram 16.

Built	No	New No	Third	SR	Wdn	
6/02	22	4071 (12/11)	833 in 1921	596	3/36	
6/02	48	4072 (11/13)	835	597	10/36	
6/02	49	4073 (12/13)	837	598	12/38	to Camping Coach 19
6/02	52	4074 (x/15)	838 in 7/19	599	12/38	to Camping Coach 20
6/02	54	4075 (11/13)	839	600	9/36	
6/02	55	4076 (5/15)	840 in 9/18	601	2/36	
6/02	116	4077	843 in 1918	602	12/37	
6/02	126	4078	844 in 11/19	603	8/34	

6.8 **48ft Third** of 1902 (two lavatories). LSWR Drawing 1093. SR Diagram 14.

Built	No	New No	SR	Wdn	
6/02	63	63	561	2/35	
6/02	735	735	563	2/35	
6/02	745 EW	745	564	3/35	
6/02	746	746	565	12/38	grounded at Brockenhurst 11/40
8/02	289	289	562	12/38	

6.9 **51ft Brake Tri-Composite** of 1902 (two lavatories). LSWR Drawing 1122. SR Diagram 405.

Built	No	New No	SR	Wdn	
11/02	16	3502	6464	9/38	set 97
11/02	179	3504	6465	7/38	(set 100 (Necropolis) in 1917/18)
11/02	208	3505	6466	10/35	set 59
11/02	211	3506	6467	8/38	set 60
11/02	218	3507	6468	7/38	(set 100 (Necropolis) in 1918)

6.10 **Suburban bogie block trains** of 1902.
Lighting: G = Gas, E = Electric complete with dynamos and batteries, EW = Electric but wired only.

(a) **51ft Composite.** LSWR Drawing 1127. SR Diagram 269.
Layout = 1 1 1 1 1 3 3 3. All shown as EW in the SR Register.
Note: the 7xxx range are conversions to electric trailers; the further history of these is in Chapter 7.

Built	No	New No	SW Elec.	SR & set	SR Elec.
12/02	781	2920		4938 184	9345 4/28
12/02	782	2921		4939 182	9340 3/29
12/02	783	2922		4940 183	9327 4/28
12/02	784	2923		4941 181	9314 2/28
12/02	785	2924		4942 185	9313 2/28
12/02	786	2925		4943 186	9337 5/28
12/02	787	2926		4944 188	9334 7/28
12/02	788	2927		4945 187	9346 4/28
2/03	797	2936		4946 189	9317 3/28
2/03	798	2937		4947 190	9310 2/28
2/03	801	2940		4948 191	9339 5/28
2/03	802	2941 P-P 9ᴾ		4949 360 (ex-set 12ᴮ; to P-P for Swanage [33333111] 1922) Wdn 5/36	
2/03	805	2944		4950 192	9342 3/29
2/03	809	2948		4952 194	9338 5/28
2/03	810	2949		4953 195	9312 2/28
5/03	806	2945		4951 193	9347 3/28
6/03	26	2274		4922 204	9307 x/28
6/03	152	2395 P-P 8ᴾ		4919 358 (to P-P for Claygate-Guildford 11/16) Wdn 3/38	
6/03	173	2416		4925 203	9349 4/28
6/03	175		7563 3/15		
6/03	190	2432		4927 205	9311 2/28
6/03	199		7583 6/15		
6/03	200		7587 7/15		
7/03	244	2483		4934 202	9324 3/28 u/f to van 2313
8/03	822		7567 3/15		
8/03	825		7555		
8/03	826		7571 4/15		
8/03	833	2972		4957 198	9316 3/28 u/f to van 2309
9/03	829		7575 5/15		
9/03	830		7579 5/15		
9/03	834		7559		
9/03	837		7611		
10/03	838	2977		4958 199	9331 4/28 u/f to van 2322
10/03	841	2980		4959 200	9319 3/28 u/f to van 2307
11/03	813	2952		4954 196	9330 4/28
11/03	814	2953		4955 197	9318 3/28
11/03	817	2956		4956 to P-P set 377 1927; Wdn 9/38	
11/03	842	2981		4960 201	9343 3/29 u/f to van 2308
12/03	29	2277		4923 206	9315 2/28 u/f to van 2298
12/03	157	2400		4924 208	9350 4/28 u/f to van 2299
12/03	232		7591		
12/03	818	2957 P-P 5ᴾ		4920 355 (to P-P for Claygate-Guildford 11/16) Wdn 6/37	
12/03	821		7607		

Built	No	New No	SW Elec.	SR & set	SR Elec.
1/04	776		7627		
2/04	176	2419		4926 207	9321 3/28 u/f to van 2289
2/04	856		7551 11/14		
3/04	207	2449		4931 210	9308 1/28 u/f to van 2296
3/04	236	2475	7440		8923
6/04	196	2438		4928 209	9322 3/28 u/f to van 2364
9/04	192		7623		
10/04	198	2440		4929 211	9333 4/28 u/f to van 2326
11/04	147		7619		
11/04	162		7599		
11/04	180		7603		
12/04	206	2448		4930 212	9335 7/28 u/f to van 2285
12/04	233	2472		4932 213	9336 5/28 u/f to van 2316
12/04	243	2482		4933 214	9329 4/28 u/f to van 2330
12/04	774		7615		
2/05	136		7631		
2/05	778	2917		4936 215	9328 4/28 u/f to van 2283
2/05	780	2919		4937 216	9320 3/28 u/f to van 2359
2/05	862	2991		4961 217	9325 3/28 u/f to van 2355
4/05	869	2998		4963 219	9341 3/29 u/f to van 2320
5/05	867	2996		4962 218	9326 4/28 u/f to van 2358
5/05	871	3000		4964 220	9323 3/28 u/f to van 2314
5/05	873	3002		4965 221	9332 4/28 u/f to van 2294
6/05	13	2263		4921 223	9348 3/28
6/05	479	2666		4935 227	to P-P set 380 7/30; Wdn 12/39
6/05	875	3004		4966 222	9309 1/28 u/f to van 2297
6/05	877		7595		
6/05	879	3008		4967 224	9301 1/31 u/f to van 2466
6/05	881	3010		4968 225	to P-P set 350 7/30; Wdn 12/37; to 1163s
6/05	893	3019		4969 226	to P-P set 379 7/30; Wdn 11/39

(b) **49ft Tri-Composite**. LSWR Drawing 1128. SR Diagram 265.
Layout = 1 1 1 2 2 2 3 3. All shown as EW in SR Register.
Note: the 7xxx range are conversions to electric trailers; the further history of these is in Chapter 7.

Built	No	New No	SW Elec.	SR & set	SR Elec.
12/02	98	2344		4849 183	8813 4/28
12/02	789	2928		4874 186	8823 5/28
12/02	790	2929		4875 182	8826 3/29
12/02	791	2930		4876 185	8799 2/28
12/02	792	2931		4877 181	8800 2/28
12/02	793	2932		4878 188	8820 7/28
12/02	794	2933		4879 187	8832 6/28
12/02	795	2934		4880 184	8831 6/28
12/02	796	2935		4881 189	8803 3/28
2/03	799	2938		4882 190	8796 2/28
2/03	800	2939		4883 191	8825 5/28
2/03	804	2943		4885 192	8828 3/29
2/03	807	2946		4886 193	8833 6/28
2/03	808	2947		4887 194	8824 5/28
2/03	811	2950		4888 195	8798 2/28
4/03	803	2942 P-P 10ᴾ		4884 359 (to P-P for Swanage 1922; ex-set 12ᴮ) Wdn 4/32	
6/03	23	2271 P-P 7ᴾ		4913 357 (to P-P for Claygate-Guildford 11/16) Wdn 2/37	
6/03	46	2293		4848 202	8810 3/28 u/f to van 2353
6/03	123	2367	7584 7/15		
6/03	129	2372		4851 203	8835 4/28
6/03	134	2377		4852 204	8793 x/28
6/03	217	2457		4857 205	8797 2/28
7/03	135	2378	7564 3/15		
7/03	158	2401	7588 7/15		
8/03	823	2962	7568 3/15		
8/03	824	2963	7556		
8/03	827	2966	7572 4/15		
8/03	828	2967	7576 5/15		
8/03	831	2970	7580 5/15		
8/03	832	2971		4892 198	8802 3/28 u/f to van 2342
8/03	835	2974	7560 2/15		
9/03	836	2975	7612		
10/03	839	2978		4893 199	8817 4/28 u/f to van 2341
10/03	840	2979		4894 200	8805 3/28 u/f to van 2336

Built	No	New No	SW Elec.	SR & set	SR Elec.
11/03	812	2951		4889 196	8816 4/28
11/03	815	2954		4890 197	8804 3/28
11/03	816	2955		4891	to P-P set 376 12/27; Wdn 11/39
11/03	843	2982		4895 201	8829 3/29 u/f to van 2349
12/03	172	2415	7594		
12/03	187	2429		4856 213	8836 4/28
12/03	240	2479		4860 206	8801 2/28
12/03	819	2958 P-P 6ᴾ		4914 356	(to P-P for Claygate-Guildford 11/16) Wdn 8/39
12/03	820	2959	7608		
2/04	854	2983		4896 208	8807 3/28 u/f to van 2334
2/04	855	2984	7552 12/14		
3/04	164	2407		4854 207	8794 1/28 u/f to van 2346
3/04	193	2435	7442		
3/04	246	2484		4861 209	8808 3/28 u/f to van 2332
10/04	113	2357		4850 211	8819 4/28 u/f to van 2331
11/04	224	2463	7624		
12/04	156	2399		4853 212	8821 7/28 u/f to van 2354
12/04	159	2402			
12/04	170	2413		4855 210	8822 5/28 u/f to van 2333
12/04	215	2455	7600		
12/04	238	2477		4859 214	8815 4/28 u/f to van 2352
12/04	773	2912	7616		
12/04	775	2914	7628		
2/05	777	2916		4872 215	8814 4/28 u/f to van 2344
2/05	779	2918		4873 216	8806 3/28 u/f to van 2337
2/05	863	2992		4897 217	8811 3/28 u/f to van 2338
2/05	864	2993	7632		
4/05	868	2997		4899 219	8827 2/29 u/f to van 2335
5/05	866	2995		4898 218	8812 4/28 u/f to van 2347
5/05	870	2999		4900 220	8809 3/28 u/f to van 2351
5/05	872	3001		4901 221	8818 4/28 u/f to van 2339
6/05	11	2261		4847 223	8834 3/28 u/f to van 2343
6/05	379	2599		4870 226	to P-P set 731 7/30; Wdn 8/39 after damage at Hoo Jct
6/05	874	3003		4902 222	8795 1/28 u/f to van 2348
6/05	876	3005	7596		
6/05	878	3007		4903 224	Wdn 1/31; u/f to van 2482
6/05	880	3009		4904 225	to P-P set 22 7/30; Wdn 12/39
6/05	892	3018		4905 227	to P-P set 378 7/30; Wdn 6/37
10/05	894	3020		4906 229	9816 8/30 u/f to van 2489
10/05	895	3021	7613		
10/05	897	3023		4907 228	9808 6/30 u/f to van 2487
10/05	900	3026		4908 230	9813 8/30 u/f to van 2484
11/05	902	3028		4909 231	9815 8/30
11/05	904	3030	7617		
11/05	905	3031		4910 232	9814 8/30
12/05	251	2489		4864 234	9817 8/30
12/05	264	2502		4866 236	9811 7/30 u/f to van 2483
12/05	318	2553	7444		
12/05	394	2611 P-P 2ᴾ		4916 352	(to P-P for Clapham Jct-Holborn 1915) Wdn 2/39
12/05	908	3034	7621		
12/05	910	3036	7622		
12/05	912	3038		4911 233	9809 6/30 u/f to van 2490
12/05	913	3039		4912 235	9824 1/31 u/f to van 2486
5/06	285	2520		4867 237	8830 2/29 u/f to van 2345
5/06	293	2528		4868 238	to P-P set 23 12/26; Wdn 11/39
6/06	290	2525	7625		
6/06	291	2526 P-P 3ᴾ		4915 353	(to P-P for Kensington-Richmond 1915) Wdn 12/39
6/06	918	3043	7448		
11/06	114	2358	7620		
12/06	247	2485		4862 240	(later 273)to P-P set 27 12/26; Wdn 12/39
12/06	249	2487		4863 241	to P-P set 29 12/26; Wdn 12/39
12/06	253	2491		4865 239	to P-P set 25 12/26; Wdn 11/39; to 1352s
12/07	298	2533	7561 2/15		
12/07	300	2535	7562 2/15		
1/08	302	2537	7565 3/15		
1/08	962	3081	7566 3/15		
5/08	4	2254	7553 11/14		
5/08	252	2490	7554 6/14		

Built	No	New No	SW Elec.	SR & set	SR Elec.
6/08	260	2498	7569 4/15		
6/08	261	2499	7557		
6/08	309	2544	7570 4/15		
6/08	974	3087	7558		
12/08	271	2507	7578 5/15		
12/08	283	2518	7573 6/15		
12/08	304	2539	7574 4/15		
12/08	306	2541	7577 5/15		
12/08	326	2561	7581 6/15		
3/09	296	2531	7582 6/15		
4/09	314	2549	7586 7/15		
4/09	316	2551	7589 7/15		
4/09	320	2555	7619		
5/09	328	2563	7593		
5/09	330	2565	7597		
6/09	2	2252	7601		
6/09	312	2547	7585 7/15		
6/09	332	2567	7598		
11/09	6	2256	7602		
11/09	9	2259	7592		
12/09	370	2590	7605		
12/09	372	2592	7606		
12/09	375	2595	7609		
12/09	378	2598	7610		
6/10	395	2612	7426 12/21		
9/10	1001	3103	7434		
7/10	400	2617	7432 12/21		
7/10	402	2619		4871 242	9823 1/31 u/f to van 2488
11/10	1012	3109	7626		
11/10	1014	3111	7629		
12/10	1016	3113	7614		
12/10	1018	3115	7618		
12/10	276	2512	7630 LSWR set 135[B]		
12/10	272	2508	7633		
12/10	274	2510	7406 Trailer Third 2/20		
12/11	351	2572	7411 Trailer Third		
12/11	353	2574	7422 Trailer Third		
1/12	355	2576	7415 Trailer Third		
1/12	357	2578	7634 Trailer Third		
8/12	225	2464		4858 243	9810 7/30 u/f to van 2340
8/12	226	2465	7419 Trailer Third		
9/12	333	2568		4869 244	9812 7/30 u/f to van 2485
9/12	334	2569	7403 Trailer Third		

(c) **51ft Brake Third**. LSWR Drawing 1129. SR Diagram 118.
MBT = conversion to electric Motor Brake Third, TT = Trailer Third.

Built	No		New No	SW Elec.	SR & set	SR Elec.
2/02?	67	EW	1395		2814 185	8185 2/28
3/02?	27	EW	1309		2787 187	9222 5/28
3/02?	741	E	1860		2882 188	8207 7/28
12/02	5	E	1299		2784 183	9246 3/29
12/02	31	EW	1311		2788 186	9235 3/29
12/02	32	EW	1312		2789 188	8206 7/28
12/02	37	E	1316		2791 187	9221 5/28
12/02	59		1369	MBT 6719 3/15		
12/02	260	EW	1622		2840 182	9215 4/28
12/02	266	E	1624		2841 182	9211 3/28
12/02	295	E	1636		2843 185	9225 4/28
12/02	310	EW	1645		2845 181	9217 4/28
12/02	335	EW	1660		2849 183	9254 3/29
12/02	452	EW	1682		2850 184	8218 4/28
12/02	541	E	1714		2851 184	8217 4/28
12/02	542	E	1715		2852 186	9236 3/29
12/02	555	E	1722		2857 181	9227 4/28
1/03	1251	EW	1251		2754 189	9214 4/28
1/03	1252	E	1252		2755 189	9230 5/28
2/03	1253	E	1253		2756 190	9231 5/28
2/03	1254	E	1254		2757 190	9226 4/28
2/03	1255	EW	1255		2758 191	8211 5/28
2/03	1256	E	1256		2759 191	8213 3/29
2/03	1257		1257 P-P 9[P]		2892 359	(to P-P for Swanage 1922, ex-set 12[B])
2/03	1258		1258 P-P 10[P]		2893 360	(to P-P for Swanage 1922, ex-set 12[B])

Built	No		New No	SW Elec.	SR & set	SR Elec.
5/03	163	E	1573 P-P 8[P]		2830 358	(to P-P for Claygate-Guildford 11/16)
6/03	20	E	1305		2785 203	9245 2/29
6/03	34	E	1314		2790 204	8179 3/28
6/03	70	E	1411		2816 205	8183 2/28
6/03	213	E	1611	P-P 7[P]	2839 357	(to P-P for Claygate-Guildford 11/16) Wdn 2/37
6/03	292	E	1635		2842 205	9223 5/28
6/03	750	E	1865		2883 204	9213 3/28
7/03	157		1514	MBT 6750 in 6/15		
7/03	175		1578	MBT 6749 in 6/15		
7/03	267		1625	MBT 6755 in 7/15		
7/03	299		1638	MBT 6756 in 7/15		
7/03	348		1666	MBT 6720 in 3/15		
7/03	562	E	1726		2858 202	8197 3/28 u/f to van 2327
7/03	728	EW	1853		2879 202	8196 3/28 u/f to van 2315
7/03	730	E	1855		2880 203	9255 3/29
7/03	1259	E	1259		2760 192	8214 3/29
7/03	1260	E	1260		2761 192	9297 7/30
7/03	1261	EW	1261		2762 193	8219 3/28
7/03	1262	E	1262		2763 193	8220 3/28
7/03	1263	E	1263		2764 194	8210 5/28
7/03	1264	EW	1264		2765 194	8212 3/29
7/03	1265	E	1265		2766 195	8184 2/28
7/03	1266	E	1266		2767 195	9216 4/28
8/03	1276		1276	MBT 6786 in 1915		
8/03	1277		1277	MBT 6726 in 3/15		
8/03	1278		1278	MBT 6725 in 3/15		
8/03	1279		1279	MBT 6707 in 1/15		
8/03	1280		1280	MBT 6708 in 1/15		
8/03	1281		1281	MBT 6732 in 4/15		
8/03	1282		1282	MBT 6731 in 4/15		
8/03	1283		1283	MBT 6737 in 5/15		
8/03	1284		1284	MBT 6738 in 5/15		
8/03	1285		1285	MBT 6744 in 5/15		
8/03	1286		1286	MBT 6743 in 5/15		
8/03	1287	E	1287		2776 198	8189 3/28 u/f to van 2311
8/03	1288	E	1288		2777 198	8188 3/28 u/f to van 2310
8/03	1289		1289	MBT 6714 in 1/15		
8/03	1290		1290	MBT 6713 in 1/15		
9/03	1291		1291	MBT 6791 in 1915		
9/03	1292		1291	MBT 6792 in 1915		
10/03	1293	E	1293		2778 199	8203 4/28 u/f to van 2317
10/03	1294	E	1294		2779 199	8202 4/28 u/f to van 2329
10/03	1295	E	1295		2780 200	9229 5/28 u/f to van 2368
10/03	1296	E	1296		2781 200	9218 5/28 u/f to van 2365
11/03	1267	E	1267		2768 196	9249 3/29
11/03	1268	EW	1268		2769 196	9251 3/29
11/03	1269	EW	1269		2770 197	8190 3/28
11/03	1270	E	1270		2771 197	8191 3/28
11/03	1271	E	1271		2772	to P-P set 376 x/27; Wdn 11/39
11/03	1272	E	1272		2773	to P-P set 377 x/27; Wdn 9/38
11/03	1297	E	1297		2782 201	8216 3/29 u/f to van 2370
11/03	1298	E	1298		2783 201	8215 3/29 u/f to van 2318
12/03	62	E	1392		2811 207	8221 4/28
12/03	75	E	1429		2824 207	8222 4/28 u/f to van 2287
12/03	296		1637	MBT 6761 in 1915		
12/03	302	E	1639		2844 206	8186 2/28 u/f to van 2325
12/03	304		1641	MBT 6762 in 1915		
12/03	546	E	1718		2855 206	8187 2/28 u/f to van 2306
12/03	1273	E	1273 P-P 6[P]		2774 356	(to P-P for Claygate-Guildford 11/16) Wdn 8/39
12/03	1274	E	1274 P-P 5[P]		2775 355	(to P-P for Claygate-Guildford 11/16) P-P removed 6/37; to 8033 11/37
12/03	1275		1275	MBT 6785 in 1915		
2/04	139	E	1505		2827 208	8193 3/28 u/f to van 2301
2/04	548	E	1719		2856 208	8192 3/28 u/f to van 2361
2/04	557		1724	MBT 6702 in 11/14		
2/04	727		1852	MBT 6701 in 11/14		
3/04	21	E	1306		2786 210	9220 5/28 u/f to van 2295
3/04	52	E	1321		2792 210	8180 1/28 u/f to van 2328
3/04	158		1526	TT 7441 12/21		
3/04	564	E	1728		2859 209	8195 3/28 u/f to van 2291
3/04	740	E	1859		2881 209	9243 3/29 u/f to van 2366
10/04	593	E	1756		2864 211	9239 ?

Built	No		New No	SW Elec.	SR & set	SR Elec.
10/04	607	E	1769		2866 211	9242 3/29
11/04	329		1655	TT 7439 c1921		
11/04	580		1743	MBT 6810 in 1915		
11/04	614		1776	MBT 6809 in 1915		
12/04	8		1300	MBT 6774 in 1915		
12/04	22		1307	MBT 6773 in 1915		
12/04	211		1609	MBT 6803 in 1915		
12/04	309		1644	MBT 6804 in 1915		
12/04	583		1746	MBT 6779 in 1915		
12/04	589	E	1752		2862 212	9237 9/28 u/f to van 2362
12/04	591	E	1754		2863 213	8208 7/29 u/f to van 2293
12/04	715		1846	MBT 6798 in 1915		
12/04	775		1877	MBT 6780 in 1915		
12/04	851	E	1902		2887 212	9234 3/29 u/f to van 2356
12/04	1024	E	1947		2889 214	9248 2/29 u/f to van 2288
12/04	1032	E	1948		2890 213	8209 5/28 u/f to van 2302
12/04	1035		1950	MBT 6797 in 1915		
12/04	1330	E	1330		2794 214	9247 2/29 u/f to van 2284
12/04	1331		1331	MBT 6815 in 1915		
12/04	1332		1332	MBT 6816 in 1915		
2/05	61	E	1370		2808 217	9238 1/29 u/f to van 2300
2/05	1044	E	1954		2891 216	9232 4/28 u/f to van 2360
2/05	1333	E	1333		2795 215	8201 7/28 u/f to van 2367
2/05	1334	E	1334		2796 215	8200 7/28 u/f to van 2290
2/05	1335	E	1335		2797 216	9219 5/28 u/f to van 2478
2/05	1336	E	1336		2798 217	9240 1/29 u/f to van 2282
2/05	1337		1337	MBT 6821 in 1915		
2/05	1338		1338	MBT 6822 in 1915		
4/05	186	E	1600		2836 219	9233 4/28
5/05	64	E	1393		2812 220	9241 3/29 u/f to van 2357
5/05	152	E	1511		2828 218	8199 4/28 u/f to van 2303
5/05	153	E	1512		2829 219	9212 3/28
5/05	665	E	1822		2872 218	8198 4/28 u/f to van 2305
5/05	1341	E	1341		2799 221	8205 4/28 u/f to van 2321
5/05	1342	E	1342		2800 220	8194 3/28 u/f to van 2363
5/05	1343	EW	1343		2801 221	8204 4/28 u/f to van 2369
6/05	66	E	1394		2813 224	8223 1/31 u/f to van 2471
6/05	73	E	1413		2817 226	to P-P set 379 7/30; Wdn 11/39
6/05	90		1444	MBT 6767 in 1915		
6/05	96	E	1481		2826 224	9163 2/31
6/05	171	E	1576		2831 222	8182 2/28
6/05	321	E	1651		2847 225	to P-P set 22 7/30; Wdn 12/39
6/05	576	E	1739		2860 227	to P-P set 378 7/30; Wdn 10/37; to 1151s
6/05	605	E	1767		2865 226	to P-P set 731 7/30; Wdn 7/39, accident damage at Hoo Jct
6/05	623	E	1784		2867 226	to P-P set 380 7/30; Wdn ?
6/05	684	E	1832		2874 223	9224 5/28 u/f to van 2304
6/05	686	EW	1833		2875 223	9228 5/28 u/f to van 2312
6/05	767		1875	MBT 6768 in 1915		
6/05	856	E	1904		2888 225	to P-P set 350 7/30; Wdn 3/38; to 1162s
6/05	1344	E	1344		2802 222	8181 1/28 u/f to van 2323
10/05	94	E	1447		2825 229	9159 2/31 u/f to van 2472
10/05	313	E	1647		2846 230	to P-P set 978 11/30; Wdn 11/37; to 1344s
10/05	330	E	1656		2848 230	8560 8/30 u/f to van 2479
10/05	543	E	1716		2853 228	to P-P set 977 11/30; Wdn 10/36
10/05	544	E	1717		2854 228	8555 6/30 u/f to van 2475
10/05	638	E	1798		2869 229	9165 3/31 u/f to van 2464
10/05	1348		1348	MBT 6795 in 1915		
10/05	1349		1349	MBT 6793 in 1915		
11/05	151		1510	MBT 6799 in 1915 (was in set 79[B] in 1908)		
11/05	209	E	1608		2838 231	9167 3/31 u/f to van 2467
11/05	1350	E	1350		2803 231	9157 3/31 u/f to van 2468
11/05	1351		1351	MBT 6801 in 1915		
11/05	1352	E	1352		2804 232	8562 8/30
11/05	1358	E	1358		2805 232	8561 8/30
12/05	57	E	1324		2793 235	9161 2/31 u/f to van 2477
12/05	69	E	1410		2815 235	8225 1/31 u/f to van 2461
12/05	74		1428	MBT 6807 in 1915		
12/05	179		1598	TT 7437 in 12/22		
12/05	582	E	1745		2861 236	8558 7/30 u/f to van 2480
12/05	640	E	1800 P-P 2[P]		2870 352	(to P-P for Clapham Jct-Holborn 1915) Wdn 2/39
12/05	671		1826	TT 7443 c1921		
12/05	681	E	1831		2873 233	8556 x/30 u/f to van 2474

Built	No		New No	SW Elec.	SR & set	SR Elec.
12/05	692	E	1836 P-P 1ᴾ		2876 351	(to P-P for Clapham Jct-Holborn 1915) Wdn 4/40; to 1454s
12/05	725	EW	1851		2878 236	9250 2/29 u/f to van 2324
12/05	786	E	1883		2884 234	8564 8/30
12/05	788	EW	1885		2885 233	9253 3/29 u/f to van 2281
12/05	848	E	1900		2886 234	8563 8/30
12/05	1364		1364	MBT 6805 in 1915		
12/05	1365		1365	MBT 6806 in 1915		
12/05	1366		1366	MBT 6808 in 1915		
5/06	654	E	1812		2871 238	to P-P set 23 12/26; Wdn 11/39
5/06	708	E	1844		2877 237	9210 3/28
5/06	1371	E	1371		2809 238	to P-P set 24 12/26; Wdn 9/39
5/06	1372	E	1372		2810 237	9209 3/28
6/06	756		1869	MBT 6811 in 1915		
6/06	1355		1355	TT 7445 in 12/22		
6/06	1359	E	1359 P-P 4ᴾ		2806 354	(to P-P for Kensington-Richmond 1915) Wdn 8/39
6/06	1360	E	1360 P-P 3ᴾ		2807 353	(to P-P for Kensington-Richmond 1915) Wdn 12/39
6/06	1361		1361	TT 7447 c1921		
6/06	1363		1363	MBT 6813 in 1915		
12/06	1414	E	1414		2818 239	to P-P set 26 12/26; Wdn 11/37
12/06	1415	E	1415		2819 239	to P-P set 25 12/26; Wdn 11/39; to 1351s
12/06	1416	E	1416		2820 240	to P-P set 28 12/26; Wdn 8/39
12/06	1417	E	1417		2821 240	to P-P set 27 12/26; Wdn 12/39
12/06	1418	E	1418		2822 241	to P-P set 30 12/26; Wdn 11/39
12/06	1419	E	1419		2823 241	to P-P set 29 12/26; Wdn 12/39
12/07	566	G	1730	MBT 6717 2/15		
12/07	567	G	1731	MBT 6716 2/15		
12/07	568	G	1732	MBT 6718 2/15		
12/07	569	G	1733	MBT 6715 2/15		
1/08	574	G	1737	MBT 6723 3/15		
1/08	575	G	1738	MBT 6721 3/15		
1/08	581		1744	MBT 6724 3/15		
1/08	1463		1463	MBT 6722 3/15		
5/08	584		1747	MBT 6704 12/14		
5/08	585		1748	MBT 6705 11/14		
5/08	586		1749	MBT 6703 11/14		
5/08	594		1757	MBT 6706 6/14		
6/08	590		1753	MBT 6711 1/15		
6/08	592		1755	MBT 6710 1/15		
6/08	597		1760	MBT 6712 1/15		
6/08	598		1761	MBT 6709 1/15		
6/08	599		1762	MBT 6729 4/15		
6/08	600		1763	MBT 6728 3/15		
6/08	1468		1468	MBT 6730 4/15		
6/08	1469		1469	MBT 6727 3/15		
12/08	601		1764	MBT 6735 6/15		
12/08	603		1765	MBT 6734 4/15		
12/08	606		1768	MBT 6736 4/15		
12/08	1489		1489	MBT 6733 4/15		
12/08	1490		1490	MBT 6741 5/15		
12/08	1491		1491	MBT 6745 5/15		
12/08	1492		1492	MBT 6742 5/15		
12/08	1493		1493	MBT 6739 5/15		
12/08	1494		1494	MBT 6747 6/15		
12/08	1495		1495	MBT 6746 5/15		
3/09	608		1770	MBT 6751 7/15		
3/09	1373		1373	MBT 6748 6/15		
3/09	1374		1374	MBT 6740 5/15		
3/09	1375		1375	MBT 6753 7/15		
4/09	609		1771	MBT 6754 7/15		
4/09	611		1773	MBT 6752 7/15		
4/09	613		1775	MBT 6759 7/15		
4/09	617		1779	MBT 6757 7/15		
4/09	620		1782	MBT 6760 in 1915		
4/09	622		1783	MBT 6758 7/15		
5/09	626		1787	MBT 6765 in 1915		
5/09	627		1788	MBT 6764 in 1915		
5/09	630		1790	MBT 6771 in 1915		
5/09	631		1791	MBT 6769 in 1915		
6/09	632		1792	MBT 6762 in 1915		
6/09	633		1793	MBT 6770 in 1915		
6/09	637		1797	MBT 6777 in 1915		
6/09	639		1799	MBT 6775 in 1915		

Built	No		New No	SW Elec.	SR & set	SR Elec.
11/09	87		1443	MBT 6763 in 1915		
11/09	92		1445	MBT 6766 in 1915		
11/09	642		1802	MBT 6778 in 1915		
11/09	643		1803	MBT 6776 in 1915		
12/09	93		1446	MBT 6783 in 1915		
12/09	95		1448	MBT 6782 in 1915		
12/09	97		1482	MBT 6784 in 1915		
12/09	100		1485	MBT 6781 in 1915		
12/09	595		1758	MBT 6789 in 1915		
12/09	596		1759	MBT 6788 in 1915		
12/09	1431		1431	MBT 6790 in 1915		
12/09	1441		1441	MBT 6787 in 1915		
6/10	103		1497	TT 7427 11/21		
6/10	106		1500	TT 7433 c1921		
6/10	107		1501	TT 7435 c1921		
6/10	781		1880	TT 7425 c1921		
7/10	108		1502	TT 7431 c1921		
7/10	143		1507	TT 7429 c1921		
7/10	189	EW	1602		2837 242	Wdn 10/31
7/10	635	E	1795		2868 242	8224 1/31 u/f to van 2463
11/10	659		1816	MBT 6814 in 1915		
11/10	660		1817	MBT 6812 in 1915		
11/10	662		1819	MBT 6819 in 1915		
11/10	663		1820	MBT 6817 in 1915		
12/10	277	EW	1630	MBT 6820 in 1915	LSWR set 135[B]	
12/10	646		1806	TT 7405 c1921		
12/10	653		1811	MBT 6818 in 1915		
12/10	658		1815	MBT 6825 in 1915		
12/10	664		1821	MBT 6796 in 1915		
12/10	667		1824	MBT 6824 in 1915		
12/10	674		1829	TT 7408 c1921		
12/10	782		1881	MBT 6794 in 1915		
12/10	836		1898	MBT 6802 in 1915		
12/10	860		1907	MBT 6800 in 1915		
12/11	787		1884	TT 7412 c1921		
12/11	804		1889	TT 7409 c1921		
12/11	887		1914	TT 7421 c1921		
12/11	1006		1942	TT 7423 c1921		
1/12	1009		1944	TT 7416 c1921		
1/12	1023		1946	TT 7413 c1921		
1/12	1434		1434	MBT 6826 in 1915		
1/12	1435		1435	MBT 6823 in 1915		
8/12	1588		1588	TT 7420 c1921		
8/12	1589		1589	TT 7417 c1921		
8/12	1590	EW	1590		2832 243	9244 2/29 u/f to van 2292
8/12	1591	E	1591		2833 243	8557 7/30 u/f to van 2465
9/12	1592	EW	1592		2834 244	9252 3/29 u/f to van 2286
9/12	1593	E	1593		2835 244	8559 7/30 u/f to van 2470
9/12	1594		1594	TT 7404 c1921		
9/12	1595		1595	TT 7401 c1921		

(d) **51ft Tri-Composite**. LSWR Drawing 1393. SR Diagram 271.
Layout = 1 1 1 1 2 2 2 3. All survivors shown as EW in SR Register.
Note: the 72xx range are conversions to electric Motor Brake Composites (MBC);
the 74xx range are conversions to electric trailers. For these see Chapter 7.

Built	No	New No	SW Elec.	SR & set	SR Elec.
10/05	131	2374		4971 230	9654 8/30 u/f to van 2473
10/05	896	3022	MBC 7231		
10/05	898	3024		4979 228	9649 6/30
10/05	899	3025		4980 229	9657 8/30
11/05	901	3027		4981 231	9656 8/30
11/05	903	3029	MBC 7233		
11/05	906	3032		4982 232	9655 8/30
12/05	250	2488		4973 234	9658 8/30; later DS 41
12/05	278	2513		4974 236	9652 7/30 u/f to van 2476
12/05	280	2515		4975 235	9303 1/31 u/f to van 2469
12/05	323	2558	P-P 1[P]	4917 351	(to P-P for Clapham Jct-Holborn 1915) Wdn 4/40; to 1453s
12/05	384	2604	to 7438 in trailer set T19		
12/05	907	3033	MBC 7235		
12/05	909	3035	MBC 7236		
12/05	911	3037		4983 233	9650 6/30

Built	No	New No	SW Elec.	SR & set	SR Elec.
5/06	282	2517		4976 238	to P-P set 24 12/26; Wdn 9/39; u/f to 1468sm
5/06	325	2560		4977 237	9344 3/29 u/f to van 2319
6/06	916	3041	MBC 7237		
6/06	917	3042	P-P 4ᴾ	4918 354	(to P-P for Kensington-Richmond 1915); Wdn 8/39
6/06	919	3044	to 7446 in trailer set T23		
12/06	938	3063		4984 239	to P-P set 26 12/26; Wdn 11/37
12/06	939	3064		4985 240	to P-P set 28 12/26; Wdn 8/39
12/06	940	3065		4986 241	to P-P set 30 12/26; Wdn 11/39
12/07	299	2534	MBC 7205 2/15		
1/08	301	2536	MBC 7206 2/15		
1/08	303	2538	MBC 7207 3/15		
1/08	963	3082	MBC 7208 3/15		
5/08	27	2275	MBC 7201		
5/08	256	2494	MBC 7202 6/14		
6/08	258	2496	MBC 7204		
6/08	267	2505	MBC 7203		
6/08	295	2530	MBC 7210 4/15		
6/08	307	2542	MBC 7209 4/15		
12/08	288	2523	MBC 7211 6/15		
12/08	305	2540	MBC 7212 4/15		
12/08	308	2543	MBC 7213 5/15		
12/08	324	2559	MBC 7214 5/15		
12/08	983	3096	MBC 7215 6/15		
4/09	315	2550	MBC 7218 7/15		
4/09	317	2552	MBC 7219 7/15		
4/09	327	2562	MBC 7220		
4/09	329	2564	MBC 7221		
5/09	331	2566	MBC 7223		
6/09	1	2251	MBC 7224		
6/09	311	2546	MBC 7216 6/15		
6/09	313	2548	MBC 7217 7/15		
11/09	7	2257	MBC 7226		
11/09	369	2589	MBC 7222		
12/09	371	2591	MBC 7227		
12/09	374	2594	MBC 7228		
12/09	376	2596	MBC 7229		
12/09	885	3012	MBC 7230		
6/10	396	2613	to 7428 in trailer set T14 12/21		
6/10	399	2616	to 7436 in trailer set T18 12/21		
7/10	401	2618	to 7430 in trailer set T15 12/21		
7/10	403	2620		4978 242	9302 1/31 u/f to van 2462 (to Bluebell Railway)
11/10	1013	3110	MBC 7238		
11/10	1015	3112	MBC 7239		
12/10	1017	3114	MBC 7232		
12/10	1019	3116	MBC 7234		
12/10	954	3074	MBC 7240 probably in LSWR set 135ᴮ		
12/10	273	2509	MBC 7241		
12/10	275	2511	to 7407 in trailer set T4		
12/11	352	2573	to 7410 in trailer set T5		
12/11	354	2575	to 7424 in trailer set T12		
1/12	356	2577	to 7414 in trailer set T7		
1/12	358	2579	MBC 7242		
8/12	51	2297		4970 243	9651 7/30
8/12	222	2461	to 7418 in trailer set T9		
9/12	151	2394		4972 244	9653 7/30 u/f to van 2481
9/12	169	2412	to 7402 in trailer set T1		

6.11   Pull-Push sets converted from bogie block sets.

Converted by LSWR

(Original LSWR and SR numbers of vehicles.)

Set No	Brake Third	(date)	Composite	(date)	(Drawing)	conv. date	SR set
1ᴾ	692/2876	(12/05)	323/4917	(12/05)	(1393)	1915	351
2ᴾ	640/2870	(12/05)	394/4916	(12/05)	(1128)	1915	352
3ᴾ	1360/2807	(6/06)	291/4915	(6/06)	(1128)	1915	353
4ᴾ	1359/2806	(6/06)	917/4918	(6/06)	(1393)	1915	354
5ᴾ	1274/2775	(12/03)	818/4920	(12/03)	(1127)	11/16	355
6ᴾ	1273/2774	(12/03)	819/4914	(12/03)	(1128)	11/16	356
7ᴾ	213/2839	(6/03)	23/4913	(6/03)	(1128)	11/16	357
8ᴾ	163/2830	(5/03)	152/4919	(6/03)	(1127)	11/16	358
9ᴾ ⎫ ex-	1257/2892	(2/03)	802/4949	(2/03)	(1127)	1922	360
10 ⎭ set 12ᴮ	1258/2893	(2/03)	803/4884	(4/03)	(1128)	1922	359

Converted by SR
(Paired to indicate probable original block sets.)

Set No	Brake Third	(date)	Composite	(date)	(Drawing)	conv. date
22	321/2847	(6/05)	880/4904	(6/05)	(1128)	7/30
379	73/2817	(6/05)	893/4969	(6/05)	(1127)	7/30
23	654/2871	(5/06)	293/4868	(5/06)	(1128)	12/26
24	1371/2809	(5/06)	282/4976	(5/06)	(1393)	12/26
25	1415/2819	(12/06)	253/4865	(12/06)	(1128)	12/26
26	1414/2818	(12/06)	938/4984	(12/06)	(1393)	12/26
27	1417/2821	(12/06)	247/4862	(12/06)	(1128)	12/26
28	1416/2820	(12/06)	939/4985	(12/06)	(1393)	12/26
29	1419/2823	(12/06)	249/4863	(12/06)	(1128)	12/26
30	1418/2822	(12/06)	940/4986	(12/06)	(1393)	12/26
376	1271/2772	(11/03)	816/4891	(11/03)	(1128)	1927
377	1272/2773	(11/03)	817/4956	(11/03)	(1127)	1927
350	856/2888	(6/05)	881/4968	(6/05)	(1127)	7/30
378	576/2860	(6/05)	892/4905	(6/05)	(1128)	7/30
380	623/2867	(6/05)	479/4935	(6/05)	(1127)	7/30
731	605/2865	(6/05)	379/4870	(6/05)	(1128)	7/30

This set was damaged and withdrawn in 7/39, replaced by 46ft 6in stock 1/43

978	313/2846	(10/05)	769/5010	(12/99)	50ft Compo*	11/30
977	543/2853	(10/05)	21/4988	(12/99)	50ft Compo*	11/30

*Drawing 861

6.12 **56ft x 8ft 6¾in Brake Tri-Composite** of 1903. LSWR Drawing 1190. SR Diagram 407.
(These carriages were not permitted on the SECR or Metropolitan Railway lines.)

Built	No	New No	SR & set		Wdn	
11/03	844	3595	6471	10	1/50	to 1572s
12/03	845	3596	6472	11	10/56	
12/03	846	3597	6473	56	10/47	
12/03	847	3598	6474	51	5/48	to National Railway Museum
3/04	848	3599	6475	98	5/52	to 3199s
3/04	849	3600	6476	52	5/50	
3/04	850	3601	6477	8	12/56	
3/04	851	3602	6478	12	3/57	
3/04	852	3603	6479	9	2/56	
3/04	853	3604	6480	54	9/57	

6.13 **Main-line bogie block sets.**
Like the suburban bogie block sets, only half the vehicles in a set had full electrical equipment;
those which were wired only, according to the 1923 renumbering register, are shown as EW.

(a) **56ft Brake Third.** LSWR Drawing 1303. SR Diagram 123.
Built for two four-car sets. Tare weight 25t. They were not allowed on the SECR or Metropolitan Railway lines.

Built	No		New No	SR	set (c1936)	Wdn	
12/04	104	EW	1498	2921	251	9/50	
12/04	588	EW	1751	2922	251	9/50	
12/04	612		1774	2923	252	7/44	to 102s
12/04	688		1834	2924	252	7/44	to 103s

(b) **56ft Brake Third.** LSWR Drawing 1446. SR Diagram 124.
Built for four-car sets. They were not allowed on the SECR or Metropolitan Railway lines.

Built	No		New No	SR	set (c1936)	Wdn	
6/06	1362	EW	1362	2925	253	2/53	
6/06	1379	EW	1379	2929	253	2/53	
6/06	1376		1376	2926	254	3/51	to DS 3169
6/06	1378		1378	2928	254	3/51	
6/06	570		1734	2980	255	2/51	
6/06	1377		1377	2927	255	2/51	

Built	No		New No	SR	set (c1936)	Wdn	
6/06	573		1736	2982	256	10/50	
6/06	610		1772	2985	256	10/50	
6/06	1380	EW	1380	2930	257	3/48	
6/06	1381	EW	1381	2931	257	5/56	
6/06	1382		1382	2932	258	12/56	
6/06	1383		1383	2933	258	12/56	
6/06	1384	EW	1384	2934	259	4/51	
6/06	1385	EW	1385	2935	259	4/51	
12/06	1386	EW	1386	2936	313	9/40	destroyed by enemy action
12/06	1387	EW	1387	2937	313	9/40	destroyed by enemy action
12/06	1388	EW	1388	2938	261	x/47	
12/06	1389	W	1389	2939	261	x/47	
12/06	1390	EW	1390	2940	262	5/51	
12/06	1391	EW	1391	2941	262	5/51	
5/07	1420	EW	1420	2942	263	x/48	
5/07	1421	EW	1421	2943	263	x/48	
6/07	1422	EW	1422	2944	311	1/43	to 1773s
6/07	1423	EW	1423	2945	311	1/43	to 1774s
6/07	1424	EW	1424	2946	312	x/46	
6/07	1425	EW	1425	2947	312	11/56	
6/07	1426	EW	1426	2948	260	2/51	
6/07	1427	EW	1427	2949	260	2/51	
11/07	565	EW	1729	2979	314	6/57	
11/07	571	EW	1735	2981	314	6/57	
11/07	577	EW	1740	2983	130	10/56	
12/07	1452	EW	1452	2953	130	10/56	
12/07	1453	EW	1453	2954	131	9/54	
12/07	1454	EW	1454	2955	131	9/54	
12/07	1455	EW	1455	2956	132	5/52	to DS 3210
12/07	1456	EW	1456	2957	132	5/42	damaged by enemy action
12/07	1457	EW	1457	2958	133	1/43	to 1906s
12/07	1458	EW	1458	2959	133	1/43	to 1905s
12/07	1459	EW	1459	2960	134	3/53	
12/07	1460	EW	1460	2961	134	/53	
12/07	1461	EW	1461	2962	135	1/51	to DS 3161
12/07	1462	EW	1462	2963	135	1/51	to DS 3162
6/08	1470		1470	2964	136	4/54	
6/08	1471		1471	2965	136	4/54	
6/08	1472	EW	1472	2966	137	4/50	to DS 1577
6/08	1473	EW	1473	2967	137	9/46	
9/09	604		1766	2984	138	1/55	
9/09	634		1794	2991	138	1/55	
9/09	615		1777	2986	139	1/57	
9/09	616		1778	2987	139	1/57	
10/09	624		1785	2988	140	9/49	to DS 1555
10/09	625		1786	2989	140	6/49	to DS 1553
10/09	629		1789	2990	141	5/56	(at some time in set 324)
10/09	101		1486	2968	141	5/56	(at some time in set 324)
10/09	102		1496	2969	142	8/54	
10/09	1432		1432	2950	142	8/54	u/f to DS 3235
1/10	1440		1440	2951	143	5/49	(may have joined 2966 in set 137 late 1946)
1/10	1442		1442	2952	143	x/46	
1/10	1515		1515	2970	144	12/56	LSWR set 61
1/10	1516		1516	2971	144	12/56	LSWR set 61
2/10	1517		1517	2972	145	8/53	to DS 1809
2/10	1518		1518	2973	145	8/53	
3/10	1519		1519	2974	146	8/48	LSWR set 63; destroyed at Vauxhall 29/8/12 but replaced
3/10	1520		1520	2975	146	8/48	LSWR set 63; to DS 1119; to Bluebell Railway 6/77
3/10	1521		1521	2976	147	3/51	
3/10	1522		1522	2977	147	3/51	
9/10	636		1796	2992	148	12/56	
9/10	641	EW	1801	2993	148	12/56	
9/10	644	EW	1804	2994	149	5/50	
9/10	645		1805	2995	149	5/50	
10/10	796	EW	1886	2996	150	2/51	
10/10	808		1890	2997	150	2/51	
10/10	832	EW	1896	2998	151	12/56	LSWR set 66
10/10	1547		1547	2978	151	12/56	LSWR set 66

(c)   **56ft Composite.** LSWR Drawing 1298. SR Diagram 274.

Built	No		New No	SR	set (c1936)	Wdn	
12/04	130		2373	5035	251	9/50	
12/04	143	EW	2386	5036	252	5/44	
6/06	921		3046	5056	253	2/53	to Camping Coach 38
6/06	675	EW	2814	5053	254	3/51	
6/06	265	EW	2503	5039	255	2/51	
6/06	10		2260	5033	256	10/50	
6/06	262		2500	5037	257	5/56	
6/06	32	EW	2280	5034	258	12/56	
6/06	263		2501	5038	259	4/51	
10/06	923		3048	5057	313	8/40	destroyed by enemy action at Portsmouth
12/06	925		3050	5058	261	8/47	
12/06	927		3052	5059	262	5/51	
5/07	944		3069	5060	263	1/48	
6/07	945		3070	5061	311	9/42	destroyed by enemy action at Lancing
6/07	946		3071	5062	312	11/56	
6/07	947		3072	5063	260	3/51	
11/07	281		2516	5040	130	10/56	
11/07	297		2532	5043	314	6/57	
12/07	289		2524	5041	131	9/54	
12/07	294		2529	5042	132	8/56	
12/07	957		3076	5064	133	9/43	grounded at Horsham
12/07	959		3078	5065	134	3/53	to Camping Coach 31; to K&ESR
12/07	961		3080	5066	135	12/49	
6/08	310	EW	2545	5044	136	4/54	
6/08	322		2557	5045	137	5/49	
9/09	887	EW	3014	5054	138	1/55	
9/09	889	EW	3016	5055	139	1/57	
10/09	377	EW	2597	5046	142	8/54	
10/09	990	EW	3097	5067	140	12/48	to DS 3236
10/09	991	EW	3098	5068	141	5/56	(at some time in set 324)
1/10	381	EW	2601	5047	143	9/46	
1/10	383	EW	2603	5048	144	12/56	LSWR set 61
2/10	387	EW	2607	5049	145	8/53	to Camping Coach 34
3/10	388	EW	2608	5050	146	8/47	LSWR set 63
3/10	390	EW	2610	5051	147	3/51	
8/10	406	EW	2623	5052	148	12/56	
9/10	1007	EW	3104	5069	149	5/50	
9/10	1009	EW	3106	5070	150	2/51	
9/10	1011	EW	3108	5071	151	12/56	LSWR set 66

(d)   **56ft Composite.** LSWR Drawing 1302. SR Diagram 17.

Built	No		New No	to Third (date)	SR	set (c1936)	Wdn	
12/04	132		2375	919 (5/16)	633	251		
12/04	140	EW	2383	920 (2/20)	634	252	12/49	
6/06	8	EW	2258	916 (3/19)	630	255	9/51	in set 475
6/06	47		2294	917	631	253	10/48	in set 301
6/06	254		2492	918 (5/16)	632	259	3/51	in set 302
6/06	257	EW	2495	921 (8/18)	635	258	1/54	in set 410
6/06	259		2497	922	636	257	2/54	in set 303
6/06	266	EW	2504	923	637	256	3/48	
6/06	920	EW	3045	928 (6/19)	642	254	8/50	in set 303; to Instruction car DS 3178
10/06	922		3047	830 (6/18)	606	313	12/53	in set 404
10/06	924		3049	925	639	261	2/57	in set 341
12/06	926		3051	926 (7/19)	640	262	3/52	to gasholder truck DS 2129
5/07	270		2506	924	638	263	4/55	in set 341
6/07	941		3066	827 (5/18)	604	311	3/51	
6/07	942		3067	829 (5/18)	605	312	3/51	in set 302
6/07	943		3068	927 (9/18)	641	260	2/54	in set 303
11/07	279		2514	845	608	130	7/54	to P-P set 37 in 8/41
11/07	284		2519	831	607	314	7/50	
12/07	287		2522	846	609	131	3/56	in set 410
12/07	292		2527	847 (9/18)	610	132	2/50	
12/07	956		3075	854 (8/19)	613	133	10/48	in set 301
12/07	958		3077	855 (12/18)	614	134	3/51	in set 302
12/07	960		3079	859 (5/19)	615	135	9/50	in set 414
6/08	319	EW	2554	849	611	136	3/51	
6/08	321		2556	853	612	137	5/50	
9/09	886	EW	3013	861	616	138	6/57	

Built	No		New No	to Third (date)	SR set (c1936)		Wdn	
9/09	888	EW	3015	862 (12/18)	617	139	3/56	in set 410
10/09	890	EW	3017	864 (9/18)	618	140	5/50	in set 413; to match truck DS 3234
10/09	168	EW	2411	865	619	141	1/47	damaged at London Bridge (sometime set 324)
10/09	373	EW	2593	867 (12/18)	620	142	12/53	in set 404
1/10	380	EW	2600	868 (5/19)	621	143	2/57	in set 341
1/10	382	EW	2602	869 (12/19)	622	144	11/53	LSWR set 61; to Camping Coach 37
2/10	386	EW	2606	871	624	145	4/55	in set 341
3/10	385	EW	2605	870	623	146	?	LSWR set 63
3/10	389	EW	2609	872 (9/19)	625	147	11/57	
9/10	404	EW	2621	874 (9/21)	626	149	3/56	
9/10	405	EW	2622	875 (1/20)	627	148	2/50	
9/10	1008	EW	3105	877 (11/19)	628	150	2/57	in set 341
9/10	1010	EW	3107	878 (9/18)	629	151	3/51	LSWR set 66

6.14 46ft 6in x 8ft 3³/₄in Invalid Saloon.

(a)   **Non-corridor version.** LSWR Drawing 1593. SR Diagram 580.

Built	No	New No	SR No	Wdn
1907	9	4103	7801	3/34
1907	10	4104	7802	4/34

(b)   **Corridor version.** LSWR Drawing 1906. SR Diagram 581.

Built	No	New No	SR No	Wdn	
1910	11	4105	7803		to Longmoor Military Railway 2/38; later to Severn Valley Railway; later to K&ESR
1910	12	4106	7804	11/39	u/f converted to LDV yard wagon 1579s in 11/40

6.15   **48ft Picnic Saloon.** LSWR Drawing 1746. SR Diagram 587.

Built	No	New No	SR No	Wdn
12/08	31	4115	7816	7/34
12/08	32	4116	7817	7/34

6.16   **51ft Double Family Saloon.** LSWR Drawing 1758. SR Diagram 589.

Built	No	New No	SR No	Wdn
12/08	37	4117	7820	5/34

6.17   **56ft Brake Third** of 1910. LSWR Drawing 1936. SR Diagram 125.
Double sliding doors. The first eight were intended for the Portsmouth-Cardiff service. Gas-lit before 10/11, electrically lit from then on but without dynamos or batteries. Some were formed up as LSWR sets 1 to 9 and 408 to 411, but there is no record of which vehicle was in which set. They were not allowed to run on the SECR or Metropolitan Railway lines.

Built	No	New No	SR	set	Wdn	
12/10	1527	1527	3002	159	6/51	
12/10	1528	1528	3003	159	6/51	
12/10	1529	1529	1504	160	4/57	
12/10	1530	1530	1505	160	4/57	
12/10	1531	1531	1506	161	6/57	
12/10	1532	1532	1507	161	6/57	
12/10	1533	1533	1508	162	9/55	
12/10	1534	1534	1509	162	11/55	
3/11	1535	1535	1510	101	10/56	
3/11	1536	1536	1511	101	10/56	to 080680 (internal use)
3/11	1537	1537	1512	102	9/51	to Dormitory DS 14
3/11	1538	1538	1513	102	9/51	
3/11	1539	1539	1514	103	5/44	sold to Admiralty
3/11	1540	1540	1515	103	5/44	to 1968s
3/11	1541	1541	1516	104	9/57	
3/11	1542	1542	1517	104	9/57	
4/11	1543	1543	1518	105	11/57	
4/11	1544	1544	1519	105	11/57	
4/11	1545	1545	1520	106	8/54	
4/11	1546	1546	1521	106	8/54	

Built	No	New No	SR	set	Wdn	
5/11	648	1807	1546	107	2/54	
5/11	649	1808	1547	107	2/54	
5/11	84	1439	1500	108	3/50	to Mess & Tool Van DS 1578
5/11	650	1809	1548	108	3/50	to Mess & Tool Van DS 1588
5/11	83	1438	2999	109	11/57	
5/11	99	1484	1501	108	11/57	
10/11	1548	1548	1522	110	5/56	
10/11	1549	1549	1523	110	5/56	
10/11	1550	1550	1524	111	4/51	to DS 3164
11/11	1551	1551	1525	111	4/51	to DS 3165
11/11	1552	1552	1526	112	5/56	
11/11	1553	1553	1527	112	5/56	
11/11	1554	1554	1528	113	6/51	to DS 3191
11/11	1555	1555	1529	113	6/51	to DS 3192
12/11	1556	1556	1530	115	8/57	
12/11	1559	1559	1533	115	8/57	
12/11	1557	1557	1531	114	10/57	
12/11	1558	1558	1532	114	10/57	
12/11	1560	1560	1534	116	11/57	
12/11	1561	1561	1535	116	11/57	
1/12	1562	1562	1536	117	9/55	(at some time was set 164)
1/12	1563	1563	1537	117	11/55	(at some time was set 164)
1/12	1564	1564	1538	118	6/57	(at some time was set 165)
1/12	1565	1565	1539	118	6/58	(at some time was set 165)
2/12	1566	1566	1540	119	12/54	(at some time was set 166)
2/12	1567	1567	1541	119	12/54	(at some time was set 166)
2/12	1568	1568	1542	120	3/48	
2/12	1569	1569	1543	120	3/48	
2/12	1570	1570	1544	121	10/54	
2/12	1571	1571	1545	121	10/54	

6.18 **56ft Brake Tri-Composite** of 1911. LSWR Drawing 1996. SR Diagram 408.
These carriages were not permitted on the SECR or Metropolitan Railway lines.

Built	No	New No	SR	Wdn	
9/11	1023	3639	6487	?	driving trailer, set 2 4/37
9/11	1024	3640	6488	7/62	driving trailer, set 1 6/37
9/11	1026	3642	6490	1/59	driving trailer, set 3 5/37
9/11	1027	3643	6491	11/58	driving trailer, set 4 6/37
9/11	1028	3644	6492	6/51	
9/11	1031	3647	6495	10/58	driving trailer, set 5 4/37
9/11	1032	3648	6496	4/59	driving trailer, set 6 5/37
12/11	1025	3641	6489	7/56	set 15
12/11	1029	3645	6493	4/51	set 13
12/11	1030	3646	6494	2/57	set 14
2/12	50	3503	6481	?	set 16; to Camping Coach 36 in 8/53
2/12	410	3522	6484	4/57	set 17
5/12	408	3520	6482	10/50	set 20
5/12	409	3521	6483	6/49	set 19; to 1554s
5/12	411	3523	6485	12/49	set 18; to DS 3167
5/12	412	3524	6486	2/48	set 21; grounded at Bricklayers Arms

6.19 **56ft Brake Third** of 1912. LSWR Drawing 2040. SR Diagram 126.
Single sliding doors. All with dynamo and batteries.
These carriages were not allowed on the SECR or Metropolitan Railway lines.

Built	No	New No	SR	set	Wdn	
5/12	670	1825	1559	122	9/57	
5/12	672	1827	1560	122	9/57	
5/12	673	1828	1561	123	1/53	to Dormitory DS 15
5/12	693	1837	1563	123	1/53	to Dormitory DS 16
5/12	690	1835	1562	124	10/56	
5/12	1577	1577	1549	124	10/56	
5/12	857	1905	1564	125	10/50	
5/12	920	1925	1565	125	10/50	
6/12	921	1926	1566	126	7/55	
6/12	1038	1952	1567	126	7/55	
7/12	1039	1953	1568	128	9/56	(at some time was set 163)
7/12	1579	1579	1550	128	9/56	(at some time was set 163)
7/12	1580	1580	1551	127	11/45	
7/12	1581	1581	1552	127	9/53	to DS 19

Built	No	New No	SR	set	Wdn	
7/12	1582	1582	1553	152	12/49	to P-P set 31 + 58ft Compo 4744; sliding doors removed 6/39
7/12	1583	1583	1554	152	9/58	to P-P set 34 + 58ft Compo 4747; sliding doors removed 6/39
7/12	1584	1584	1555	153	?	to P-P set 32 + 58ft Compo 4745; sliding doors removed 7/39
7/12	1585	1585	1556	153	11/57	to P-P set 35 + 58ft Compo 4748; sliding doors removed 7/39
7/12	1586	1586	1557	129	7/57	(at some time was set 167)
7/12	1587	1587	1558	129	7/57	(at some time was set 167)
3/13	2036	2036	1569	154	2/60	to P-P set 33 + 58ft Compo 4746; sliding doors removed 6/39
3/13	2037	2037	1570	154	6/59	to P-P set 36 + 58ft Compo 4749; sliding doors removed 6/39
3/13	2038	2038	1571	155	4/51	to two-car set 57 + 58ft Compo 4754 10/39; to DS 3166
3/13	2039	2039	1572	155	11/57	to two-car set 58 + 58ft Compo 4750 10/39
4/13	2040	2040	1573	156	7/48	to two-car set 59 + 58ft Compo 4755 3/40
4/13	2041	2041	1574	156	3/56	to two-car set 60 + 58ft Compo 4751 4/40; to DS 110
4/13	2042	2042	1575	157	10/54	to two-car set 61 + 58ft Compo 4753 7/39
4/13	2043	2043	1576	157	1/55	to two-car set 62 + 58ft Compo 4752 10/39
6/13	2044	2044	1577	158	8/57	
6/13	2045	2045	1578	158	8/57	

SR sets (mainly derived from Appendix to Carriage Working Notices, 16/6/47 and from photographs)

SR Push-Pull trains, sets 1-6, for use on Alton-Fareham, Bournemouth West-Wareham, Eastleigh-Alton and Gosport-Fareham services.

Set	58ft Lav Third Brake			56ft Lav Compo Brake (Driving)	
	(ex 48ft Compo Drawing 650)			(Drawing 1996)	
	LSWR	SR	SR(P-P)	LSWR	SR
1	2333	4746	2620	3640	6488
2	2744	4815	2604	3639	6487
3	2685	4756	2609	3642	6490
4	2806	4839	2605	3643	6491
5	2813	4846	2621	3647	6495
6	2763	4834	2612	3648	6496
7*	2804	4837	2603	3644	6492

*This set was the same formation but not Push-Pull

SR two-car sets (not Push-Pull)

Set	58ft Lav Third Brake			56ft Lav Compo Brake		
	(ex 48ft Compo Drawing 650)			(Drawing 1190 — 8ft 6¾in wide)		
	LSWR	SR	SR(BT)	LSWR	SR	
8	2689	4760	2614	3601	6477)	
9	2740	4811	2608	3603	6479)	These sets *might* have been Push-Pull
10	2751	4822	2613	3595	6471)	at some time; records are confusing
11	2702	4773	2615	3596	6472)	
12	2807	4840	2602	3602	6478)	
				(Drawing 1996)		
13	2809	4842	2601	3645	6493	
14	2761	4832	2617	3646	6494	
15	2679	4750	2616	3641	6489	2616 was alone as set 8 (or 19) at Meldon 6/59
16	2717	4788	2619	3503	6481	
17	2336	4747	2610	3522	6484	
18	2733	4804	2606	3523	6485	
19	2812	4845	2607	3521	6483	
20	2808	4841	2618	3520	6482	
21	2803	4836	2611	3524	6486	2611 was in three-car set 257 in 6/48

For sets 22 to 30 see ex-LSWR bogie block sets converted to P-P by SR.

SR Push-Pull sets

Set	56ft Lav Third Brake		58ft Lav Compo		
	(Drawing 2040 sliding doors removed)		(ex 48ft Compo Drawing 758)		
	LSWR	SR	LSWR	SR	SR(P-P)
31	1582	1553	2862	4726	4744
32	1584	1555	2838	4702	4745
33	2036	1569	2301	4615	4746

Set	56ft Lav Third Brake		58ft Lav Compo		
	(Drawing 2040 sliding doors removed)		(ex 48ft Compo Drawing 650)		
	LSWR	SR	LSWR	SR	SR(P-P)
34	1583	1554	2398	4749	4747
35	1585	1556	2719	4790	4748
36	2037	1570	2680	4751	4749

SR two-car sets (not Push-Pull)

Set	58ft Brake Third (ex 48ft Third Drawing 772)			58ft Brake Compo (ex 48ft Compo Drawing 758)			
	LSWR	SR(BT)		LSWR	SR(BC)	Wdn	
42	17	2636		701	6401	11/57	

Set	LSWR	SR(BT)		LSWR	SR(BC)	Wdn	
43	736	2637		137	6402	5/58	
44	517	2638		133	6403	4/58	
45	262	2639		508	6404	12/56	6404 alone at Lyme Regis 6/48;
							2639 also alone, same date
46	387	2640		689	6405	3/59	

Set	58ft Lav Third Brake (ex 48ft Compo Drawing 758)			56ft Lav Compo Brake (Drawing 1190)		
	LSWR	SR	SR(BT)	LSWR	SR	
51	2820	4684	2626	3598	6474	
52	2816	4680	2627	3600	6476	
53	2306	4619	2628	3599	6475	
54	2839	4703	2629	3604	6480	
56	2825	4689	2625	3597	6473	

Set	56ft Lav Third Brake (Drawing 2040)		58ft Lav Compo (ex 48ft Compo Drawing 758)		
	LSWR	SR	LSWR	SR(1)	SR(2)
57	2038	1571	2322	4634	4754
59	2040	1573	2818	4682	4755
61	2042	1575	2270	4608	4753

Set	56ft Lav Third Brake (Drawing 2040)		58ft Lav Compo (ex 48ft Compo Drawing 650)		
	LSWR	SR	LSWR	SR(1)	SR(2)
58	2039	1572	2738	4809	4750
60	2041	1574	2742	4813	4751
62	2043	1576	2698	4769	4752

The Composites in sets 57 to 62 were lengthened to 58ft c1936 retaining their 1923 SR numbers; they were then renumbered in 1939. Whether the sets then became P-P is not clear, but they were certainly not P-P by June 1947.

ELECTRIC TRAINS

Any LSWR or SR number shown in brackets was allocated but probably not painted on before the next renumbering or withdrawal, as shown.

7.1   **Waterloo & City Railway.**

(a)   **41ft x 8ft 6in Motor Car**

Nos 1-12, all built in 1898 at Wilmington, USA, by Jackson & Sharp but dismantled and re-erected at Eastleigh.

(b)   **41ft x 8ft 6in Trailer Car**

Nos 21-30, all built in 1898, as above.
Nos 31 & 32, built in 1904 by Electric Tramway Co of Preston
Nos 33-36, built in 1922 at Eastleigh (LSWR Drawing 3572)

7.2   **Waterloo & City Railway.**

45ft x 8ft 6in Motor Car (Single Unit)

Nos 13-17, all built in 1900 by Dick, Kerr & Co.

There is no record of any vehicles numbered 18, 19 or 20.
All the above carriages were withdrawn on 25 October 1940.

7.3   **Electric three-car sets, constructed from bogie block set vehicles c1915.**

MBT   Motor Brake Third, ex-block 51ft Brake Thirds, LSWR Drawing 1129.
MBC   Motor Brake Composite, LSWR Drawing 2253, ex-block 51ft Composites to Drawing 1393.
C49   49ft Composite, LSWR Drawing 1128.
C49S   49ft Composite with saloon, LSWR Drawing 2244 (ex-Drawing 1128).
C51   51ft Composite, LSWR Drawing 1127.

Set LSWR/SR	Motor LSWR/SR	Composite LSWR/SR	Motor LSWR/SR
E1 /1201	MBT 6701/8001 +	C51 7551/9414 +	MBT 6702/8002
E2 /1202	MBT 6703/8003 +	C49S 7552/9351 +	MBT 6704/8004
E3 /1203	MBT 6705/8005 +	C49 7553/9372 +	MBC 7201/8751
E4 /1204	MBT 6706/8006 +	C49 7554/9373 +	MBC 7202/8752
E5 /1205	MBT 6707/8007 +	C51 7555/9415 +	MBT 6708/8008
E6 /1206	MBT 6709/8009 +	C49S 7556/9352 +	MBT 6710/8010
E7 /1207	MBT 6711/8011 +	C49 7557/9374 +	MBC 7203/8753
E8 /1208	MBT 6712/8012 +	C49 7558/9375 +	MBC 7204/8754
E9 /1209	MBT 6713/8013 +	C51 7559/9416 +	MBT 6714/8014
E10/1210	MBT 6715/8015 +	C49S 7560/9353 +	MBT 6716/8016
E11/1211	MBT 6717/8017 +	C49 7561/9376 +	MBC 7205/8755
E12/1212	MBT 6718/8018 +	C49 7562/9377 +	MBC 7206/8756
E13/1213	MBT 6719/8019 +	C51 7563/9417 +	MBT 6720/8020
E14/1214	MBT 6721/8021 +	C49S 7564/9354 +	MBT 6722/8022
E15/1215	MBT 6723/8023 +	C49 7565/9378 +	MBC 7207/8757
E16/1216	MBT 6724/8024 +	C49 7566/9379 +	MBC 7208/8758
E17/1217	MBT 6725/8025 +	C51 7567/9418 +	MBT 6726/8026
E18/1218	MBT 6727/8027 +	C49S 7568/9355 +	MBT 6728/8028
E19/1219	MBT 6729/8029 +	C49 7569/9380 +	MBC 7209/8759

Set LSWR/SR	Motor LSWR/SR		Composite LSWR/SR		Motor LSWR/SR
E20/1220	MBT 6730/8030	+	C49 7570/9381	+	MBC 7210/8760
E21/1221	MBT 6731/8031	+	C51 7571/9419	+	MBT 6732/8032
E22/1222	MBT 6733/8033	+	C49S 7572/9356	+	MBT 6734/8034
E23/1223	MBT 6735/8035	+	C49 7573/9382	+	MBC 7211/8761
E24/1224	MBT 6736/8036	+	C49 7574/9383	+	MBC 7212/8762
E25/1225	MBT 6737/8037	+	C51 7575/9420	+	MBT 6738/8038
E26/1226	MBT 6739/8039	+	C49S 7576/9357	+	MBT 6740/8040
E27/1227	MBT 6741/8041	+	C49 7577/9384	+	MBC 7213/8763
E28/1228	MBT 6742/8042	+	C49 7578/9355	+	MBC 7214/8764
E29/1229	MBT 6743/8043	+	C51 7579/9421	+	MBT 6744/8044
E30/1230	MBT 6745/8045	+	C49S 7580/9358	+	MBT 6746/8046
E31/1231	MBT 6747/8047	+	C49 7581/9386	+	MBC 7215/8765
E32/1232	MBT 6748/8048	+	C49 7582/9387	+	MBC 7216/8766
E33/1233	MBT 6749/8049	+	C51 7583/9422	+	MBT 6750/8050
E34/1234	MBT 6751/8051	+	C49S 7584/9359	+	MBT 6752/8052
E35/1235	MBT 6753/8053	+	C49 7585/9388	+	MBC 7217/8767
E36/1236	MBT 6754/8054	+	C49 7586/9389	+	MBC 7218/8768
E37/1237	MBT 6755/8055	+	C51 7587/9423	+	MBT 6756/8056
E38/1238	MBT 6757/8057	+	C49S 7588/9360	+	MBT 6758/8058
E39/1239	MBT 6759/8059	+	C49 7589/9390	+	MBC 7219/8769
E40/1240	MBT 6760/8060	+	C49 7590/9391	+	MBC 7220/8770
E41/1241	MBT 6761/8061	+	C51 7591/9424	+	MBT 6762/8062
E42/1242	MBT 6763/8063	+	C49S 7592/9361	+	MBT 6764/8064
E43/1243	MBT 6765/8065	+	C49 7593/9392	+	MBC 7221/8771
E44/1244	MBT 6766/8066	+	C49 7594/9393	+	MBC 7222/8772
E45/1245	MBT 6767/8067	+	C51 7595/9425	+	MBT 6768/8068
E46/1246	MBT 6769/8069	+	C49S 7596/9362	+	MBT 6770/8070
E47/1247	MBT 6771/8071	+	C49 7597/9394	+	MBC 7223/8773
E48/1248	MBT 6772/8072	+	C49 7598/9395	+	MBC 7224/8774
E49/1249	MBT 6773/8073	+	C51 7599/9426	+	MBT 6774/8074
E50/1250	MBT 6775/8075	+	C49S 7600/9363	+	MBT 6776/8076
E51/1251	MBT 6777/8077	+	C49 7601/9396	+	MBC 7225/8775
E52/1252	MBT 6778/8078	+	C49 7602/9397	+	MBC 7226/8776
E53/1253	MBT 6779/8079	+	C51 7603/9427	+	MBT 6780/8080
E54/1254	MBT 6781/8081	+	C49S 7604/9364	+	MBT 6782/8082
E55/1255	MBT 6783/8083	+	C49 7605/9398	+	MBC 7227/8777
E56/1256	MBT 6784/8084	+	C49 7606/9399	+	MBC 7228/8778
E57/1257	MBT 6785/8085	+	C51 7607/9428	+	MBT 6786/8086
E58/1258	MBT 6787/8087	+	C49S 7608/9365	+	MBT 6788/8088
E59/1259	MBT 6789/8089	+	C49 7609/9400	+	MBC 7229/8779
E60/1260	MBT 6790/8090	+	C49 7610/9401	+	MBC 7230/8780
E61/1261	MBT 6791/8091	+	C51 7611/9429	+	MBT 6792/8092
E62/1262	MBT 6793/8093	+	C49S 7612/9366	+	MBT 6794/8094
E63/1263	MBT 6795/8095	+	C49 7613/9402	+	MBC 7231/8781
E64/1264	MBT 6796/8096	+	C49 7614/9403	+	MBC 7232/8782
E65/1265	MBT 6797/8097	+	C51 7615/9430	+	MBT 6798/8098
E66/1266	MBT 6799/8099	+	C49S 7616/9367	+	MBT 6800/8100
E67/1267	MBT 6801/8101	+	C49 7617/9404	+	MBC 7233/8783
E68/1268	MBT 6802/8102	+	C49 7618/9405	+	MBC 7234/8784
E69/1269	MBT 6803/8103	+	C51 7619/9431	+	MBT 6804/8104
E70/1270	MBT 6805/8105	+	C49S 7620/9368	+	MBT 6806/8106
E71/1271	MBT 6807/8107	+	C49 7621/9406	+	MBC 7235/8785
E72/1272	MBT 6808/8108	+	C49 7622/9407	+	MBC 7236/8786
E73/1273	MBT 6809/8109	+	C51 7623/9432	+	MBT 6810/8110
E74/1274	MBT 6811/8111	+	C49S 7624/9369	+	MBT 6812/8112
E75/1275	MBT 6813/8113	+	C49 7625/9408	+	MBC 7237/8787
E76/1276	MBT 6814/8114	+	C49 7626/9409	+	MBC 7238/8788
E77/1277	MBT 6815/8115	+	C51 7627/9433	+	MBT 6816/8116
E78/1278	MBT 6817/8117	+	C49S 7628/9370	+	MBT 6818/8118
E79/1279	MBT 6819/8119	+	C49 7629/9410	+	MBC 7239/8789
E80/1280	MBT 6820/8120	+	C49 7630/9411	+	MBC 7240/8790
E81/1281	MBT 6821/8121	+	C51 7631/9434	+	MBT 6822/8122
E82/1282	MBT 6823/8123	+	C49S 7632/9371	+	MBT 6824/8124
E83/1283	MBT 6825/8125	+	C49 7633/9412	+	MBC 7241/8791
E84/1284	MBT 6826/8126	+	C49 7634/9413	+	MBC 7242/8792

7.4   Electric Trailer Sets.

Formed by splitting four-car bogie block sets. Brake Thirds altered to nine-compartment full Thirds.
BT = Brake Third; C = Composite.

Set LSWR	SR	Origin	Elec No	SR No	length		Origin	Elec No	SR No	length
T1	1001	BT 1595	7401	8925	51ft	+	C 169	7402	8913	51ft
T2	1002	C 334	7403	8901	49ft	+	BT 1594	7404	8926	51ft
T3	1003	BT 646	7405	8927	51ft	+	C 275	7406	8914	51ft
T4	1004	C 274	7407	8902	49ft	+	BT 674	7408	8928	51ft
T5	1005	BT 804	7409	8915	51ft	+	C 352	7410	8915	51ft
T6	1006	C 351	7411	8903	49ft	+	BT 787	7412	8930	51ft
T7	1007	BT 1023	7413	8931	51ft	+	C 356	7414	8916	51ft
T8	1008	C 355	7415	8904	49ft	+	BT 1009	7416	8932	51ft
T9	1009	BT 1589	7417	8933	51ft	+	C 222	7418	8917	51ft
T10	1010	C 226	7419	8905	49ft	+	BT 1588	7420	8934	51ft
T11	1011	BT 887	7421	8935	51ft	+	C 353	7422	8906	49ft
T12	1012	BT 1006	7423	8936	51ft	+	C 354	7424	8918	51ft
T13	1013	BT 781	7425	8937	51ft	+	C 395	7426	8907	49ft
T14	1014	BT 103	7427	8938	51ft	+	C 396	7428	8919	51ft
T15	1015	BT 143	7429	8939	51ft	+	C 401	7430	8920	51ft
T16	1016	BT 108	7431	8940	51ft	+	C 400	7432	8908	49ft
T17	1017	BT 106	7433	8941	51ft	+	C 1001	7434	8909	49ft
T18	1018	BT 107	7435	8942	51ft	+	C 399	7436	8921	51ft
T19	1019	BT 179	7437	8943	51ft	+	C 384	7438	8922	51ft
T20	1020	BT 329	7439	8944	51ft	+	C 236	7440	8923	51ft
T21	1021	BT 158	7441	8945	51ft	+	C 193	7442	8910	49ft
T22	1022	BT 671	7443	8946	51ft	+	C 318	7444	8911	49ft
T23	1023	BT 1355	7445	8947	51ft	+	C 919	7446	8924	51ft
T24	1024	BT 1361	7447	8948	51ft	+	C 918	7448	8912	49ft

Appendix to Chapter 8

RAILMOTORS AND VESTIBULE CARS

N.B. The SR set numbers are quoted from an SR Register; variations may have occurred from time to time.

8.1   LSWR/LBSCR Joint railmotor, 'K11' class.
LSWR Drawing 1144 (Drawing 3353 for rebuild to 53ft 10¼in Trailer Third).

Built	No	Wdn	
4/03	1	8/14	Sent to Brighton for scrapping, 9/19
5/03	2	8/14	Body rebuilt as Trailer Third No 4261 in 9/19, SR 743; finally withdrawn 7/41 ex-set 370 after damage by bombing in 5/41.

Note: the 1914 disposals are according to the Register; however, other information is that it was No 1 that was rebuilt and No 2 that was sent to Brighton for scrapping.

8.2   Railmotor, 'H12' class.
LSWR Drawing 1273 (Drawing 3375 for rebuild to 48ft 3½in Trailer Third).

Built	No	New No	Wdn (as Railmotor)	Rebuild etc
5/04	1	4201	11/16	Body rebuilt as Trailer Third No 4258 in 6/22; SR 740, withdrawn 7/41 in set 371 after damage by bombing 5/41
6/04	2	4202	11/16	Body rebuilt as Trailer Third No 4259 in 10/22; SR 741, withdrawn 3/56 in set 361

8.3   Railmotor, 'H13', 'A14' & 'B14' classes.
LSWR Drawing 1415 (Drawings 2799, 2855 as Trailer Composite, Drawing 3357 as Trailer Third).
Gas-lit, converted to electric lighting when rebuilt.

Built	No	New No	Wdn	Renumbered to Brake Compo		SR No	Changes and withdrawal
10/05	3	4203	7/19	4314	x/x , set 16P	6556	Wdn 12/39 set 366
11/05	4	4204	7/19	4315	x/x , set 16P	6557	P-P removed 12/32; Wdn 4/56 set 366
12/05	5	4205	11/16	4306	10/19, set 14P	6548	P-P removed 2/33; Wdn 3/56
12/05	6	4206	11/16	4307	3/19, set 11P	6549	P-P removed 4/33; Wdn 10/47 set 362
1/06	7	4207	11/16	4308	3/19, set 12P	6550	Wdn 10/42 set 362; ex-set 364
1/06	8	4208	11/16	4309	3/19, set 11P	6551	P-P removed 5/33; Wdn 10/47 set 362
2/06	9	4209	11/16	4310	3/19, set 12P	6552	Wdn 10/42 set 362; ex-set 364
3/06	10	4210	7/19	Trailer Third 4260 c1919		742	Wdn 6/41 after bomb damage 5/41; ex-set 371
3/06	11	4211	11/16	4316	y/y , set 15P	6558	P-P removed 9/32; Wdn 4/56 set 365
5/06	12	4212	11/16	4311	10/19, set 14P	6553	Wdn 6/41 after bomb damage 5/41; set 370
5/06	13	4213	11/16	4312	5/19, set 13P	6554	Wdn 6/41 after bomb damage 5/41; set 371
6/06	14	4214	11/16	4313	5/19, set 13P	6555	Wdn 6/41 after bomb damage 5/41; set 371
6/06	15	4215	11/16	4317	y/y , set 15P	6559	P-P removed 4/32; Wdn 12/46 set 365

Later disposals:
SR 6556 grounded at Newhaven 1/40
SR 6549 and 6551 grounded at Gomshall
SR 6550 and 6552 grounded at Ashford
SR 6559 grounded at Eastleigh

Note: Dates x/x and y/y are given in the Register as 1919 and 12/16 respectively; in fact they should almost certainly be 11/19 or12/19.

8.4   48ft x 8ft 6in two-car Pull-Push sets.
Fitted with Drummond three-wire control equipment, converted to compressed air c1929.

(a)   Trailer Third. LSWR Drawing 1474 (20 tons).

Built	No	New No	Elec. light	Intended service	SR No	Wdn	
10/06	1	4251	4/16	Plymouth-St Budeaux	733	6/39	set 367
11/06	3	4252	2/17	Plymouth-St Budeaux	734	12/39	set 368
11/06	5	4253	7/20	Plymouth-Turnchapel	735	4/40	set 369

(b)   Brake Third (control). LSWR Drawing 1475 (22½ tons).

Built	No	New No	Elec. light	Intended service	SR No	Wdn	
10/06	2	4276	4/16	Plymouth-St Budeaux	3200	12/39	set 368
11/06	4	4277	2/17	Plymouth-St Budeaux	3201	6/39	set 367
11/06	6	4278	7/20	Plymouth-Turnchapel	3202	4/40	set 369

When built, the pairings were 1 & 2, 3 & 4, 5 & 6, but apparently the first two sets were cross-paired before or around 1916/17.

8.5   56ft x 8ft 6in Trailer set (1909).
Intended for Portland branch. Gas-lit; converted to electric 7/19. Fitted with Drummond three-wire control equipment.

(a)   Brake Composite (control). LSWR Drawing 1830 (24 tons).

Built	No	New No	SR	Wdn
12/09	7	4301	6543*	10/37 set 370
12/09	9	4302	6544*	destroyed by bombing 7/41; set 370

* P-P removed 10/33

(b)   Trailer Third. LSWR Drawing 1831 (22 tons).

Built	No	New No	SR	Wdn
12/09	8	4254	736	destroyed by bombing 7/41; set 370

8.6   56ft x 8ft 6in Trailer sets (1914).
Fitted with Drummond three-wire control equipment.

(a)   Trailer Third. LSWR Drawing 2295 (23 tons)

Built	No	Elec. light	Use in 11/18 (Register)	SR No	Wdn	
6/14	4255	11/19	Exeter-Honiton (not P-P)	737	11/58	set 363
6/14	4256	5/20	Fratton	738	10/60	set 373
6/14	4257	7/19	Lee-on-Solent	739	7/56	set 374

(b)   Brake Composite (control). LSWR Drawing 2296 (24 tons)

Built	No	Elec. light	Use in 11/18 (Register)	SR No	to Brake Third	Wdn	
6/14	4303	5/20	Fratton	6545	2622 in 8/39	10/60	set 373
6/14	4304	11/19	Exeter-Honiton (not P-P)	6546	2623 in 10/39	11/58	set 363
6/14	4305	7/19	Lee-on-Solent	6547	2624 in 11/39	7/56	set 374

Note: All three sets were sent to the Plymouth district in late 1939.
One set, later SR 363, augmented in 1916 with ex-'Eagle' Saloon Third No 72 for the Lee-on-Solent service.

Appendix to Chapter 9
CORRIDOR CARRIAGES (Panelled)

Any LSWR or SR number shown in brackets was allocated but probably not painted on before the next renumbering or withdrawal, as shown.

9.1 **56ft Brake Third**. LSWR Drawing 1227. SR Diagrams 138 (RH) and 130 (LH) with lookouts, Diagrams 139 (RH) and 131 (LH) without lookouts.

Built	No	Corr.	New No	SR No	
3/04	549	* R	1720	3120	Wdn 3/51 to Mess & Tool Van DS 1597
3/04	743	L	1861	3136	Wdn 11/43; grounded Gomshall
4/04	308	L	1643	3113	Wdn 1/47 set 326
4/04	558	R	1725	3121	Wdn 12/43 to K&ESR 6; Wdn 4/51
4/04	731	% L	1856	3133	Wdn 2/57 set 341
5/04	98	% L	1483	3107	Wdn 7/50 set 409
5/04	346	% R	1665	3115	Wdn 11/43 set 406
5/04	506	% R	1702	3118	Wdn 9/47
6/04	42	R	1318	3090	Wdn 12/53 set 404
6/04	54	* R	1322	3092	Wdn 9/50 set 403
6/04	333	% R	1659	3114	Wdn 9/50 set 414
6/04	416	R	1677	3117	Wdn 1/47 set 326
6/04	540	R	1713	3119	Wdn 3/51 to Mess & Tool Van DS 1595
6/04	619	R	1781	3125	Wdn 6/44 to Mess & Tool Van 101s
6/04	706	R	1843	3130	Wdn 12/49 set 412
6/04	729	* L	1854	3132	Wdn 10/50 set 303
6/04	732	% L	1857	3134	Wdn 3/51 set 303
6/04	737	* R	1858	3135	Wdn 8/47 set 402
6/04	744	% L	1862	3137	Wdn 2/57 set 341
6/04	747	L	1863	3138	Wdn 2/48 set 404
6/04	749	* L	1864	3139	Wdn 5/48 set 422
10/04	14	L	1304	3089	Wdn 2/51 set 408
10/04	51	L	1320	3091	Wdn 7/50 set 409
10/04	72	% L	1412	3098	Wdn 10/47 set 343
10/04	79	L	1430	3099	Wdn 6/47 set 418
10/04	105	L	1499	3108	Wdn 7/47 to Mess & Tool Van 1775s
10/04	306	R	1642	3112	Wdn 8/43 set 405; grounded Gomshall
10/04	618	* R	1780	3124	Wdn 6/45 set 401
10/04	676	* L	1830	3129	Wdn 8/47 set 303
10/04	716	% R	1847	3131	Wdn 6/44 set 415
10/04	771	L	1876	3140	Wdn 8/48 set 402
12/04	56	R	1323	3093	EKR 12/43, K&ESR No 1, returned 5/48; Wdn 4/51
12/04	212	% L	1610	3111	Wdn 8/47 set 407

Notes:
* these had the lookouts removed and brake-end gangways fitted in March 1907.
% these are shown in 1909 diagram book as without lookouts but with gangways (like Drawing 1568), date of alteration unknown.

9.2a **54ft Composite**. LSWR Drawing 1214. SR Diagram 282.

Built	No	New No	SR No	
12/03	857	2986	5116	Wdn 11/48 set 340; to DS 3159
12/03	858	2987	5117	Wdn 12/48 set 412
12/03	859	2988	5118	Wdn 7/43 set 339
3/04	860	2989	5119	Wdn 1/52
4/04	216	2456	5114	Wdn 12/43 set 421; grounded Woking
6/04	12	2262	5110	Wdn 6/47 set 418

Built	No	New No	SR No	
6/04	111	2355	5112	Wdn 5/48 set 422
6/04	160	2403	5113	Wdn 9/50 set 407
6/04	496	2672	5115	Wdn 8/55 set 406
10/04	34	2282	5111	Wdn 7/50 set 326
2/06	928	3053	5120	Wdn 9/56 set 326
2/06	929	3054	5121	Wdn 7/44 set 414
2/07	930	3055	5122	Wdn 12/49 set 309
2/07	931	3056	5123	Wdn 3/56 set 348
4/08	964	3083	5124	Wdn 3/47 set 419
4/08	965	3084	5125	Wdn 3/49 set 417
4/08	966	3085	5126	Wdn 2/46 set 403
4/08	967	3086	5127	Wdn 10/48 set 415

Note that Nos 857 to 859, at least, had a panel between the corridor side windows where a door divided the First-class from the Second-class section; this was not present on the later vehicles, and the SR diagram specifically mentions that Nos 964 to 967 did not have a door across the corridor.

9.2b   **54ft Composite**. LSWR Drawing 1225. SR Diagram 277.

Built	No	New No	SR No	
3/04	861	2990	5085	Wdn 9/51 set 409
4/04	104	2349	5078	Wdn 8/47 set 409
4/04	227	2466	5084	Wdn 7/50 set 416
5/04	5	2255	5075	Wdn 2/57 set 341
6/04	35	2283	5076	Wdn 7/50 set 339
6/04	41	2289	5077	Wdn 12/49 set 309
6/04	109	2353	5079	Wdn 4/47 set 340
6/04	112	2356	5080	Wdn 11/52 set 405
6/04	120	2364	5082	Wdn 1/52
6/04	150	2393	5083	Wdn 8/47 set 402
10/04	116	2360	5081	Wdn 12/55 set 421

9.3   **56ft Third**. LSWR Drawings 1226, 1872 and 2390. SR Diagram 21.

Drawing 1226

Built	No	New No	SR No	
3/04	738	738	680	Wdn 12/49 set 210
4/04	445	445	671	Wdn 12/49 set 210
4/04	734	734	679	Wdn 1/58 set 409 (used for Bertram Mills' Circus train)
5/04	726	726	678	Wdn 4/47 set 309
6/04	58	58	668	Wdn 7/50 set 408; to DS 23
6/04	451	451	672	Wdn 1/47 set 326
6/04	572	572	674	Wdn 6/57 set 379
6/04	668	668	–	4/18 to US Army Ambulance 6213, returned to be PBV 342, Wdn 3/46
6/04	742	742	681	Wdn 7/50 set 408
12/06	1393	143	–	10/17 to Continental Ambulance, Kitchen A, returned to be No 162, SR 669; Wdn 9/52
2/07	1392	144	–	10/17 to Continental Ambulance, returned as No 424, SR 670; Wdn 7/50
2/07	1394	142	–	4/18 to US Army Ambulance 6202 (did not return)
2/07	1395	139	–	10/17 to Continental Ambulance, Infectious P, returned to be SR 675; Wdn 9/54
3/07	1410	126	–	4/18 to US Army Ambulance 6211, returned to be PBV 340; Wdn 3/46
3/07	1411	125	–	4/18 to US Army Ambulance 6214, returned to be PBV 343; Wdn 3/46
3/07	1412	108	–	4/18 to US Army Ambulance 6203, returned to be PBV 332; destroyed by enemy action 10/42
3/07	1413	107	–	4/18 to US Army Ambulance 6210, returned to be PBV 339; Wdn 8/47; to 170s

Drawing 1872
These were as Drawing 1226, but the doors extended to the bottom of (and were recessed into) the bottomsides.

Built	No	New No	SR No	
5/10	669	669	676	Wdn 4/47 set 325
6/10	655	655	–	4/18 to US Army Ambulance 6209
10/11	205	205	–	4/18 to US Army Ambulance 6212 ?
10/11	494	494	673	Wdn 12/53 set 338; to Camping Coach 39; to Bluebell Railway 9/74
10/11	805	805	683	Wdn 3/51 set 409
10/11	864	758	682	Wdn 7/50 set 409
11/12	1605	14	667	Wdn 12/49 set 424

Built	No	New No	SR No	
11/12	1606	12	666	Wdn 9/56 set 309
11/12	1607	11	665	? set 378
11/12	1608	10	664	Wdn 12/46 set 408
11/12	1609	8	663	Wdn 1/58 set 409 (used for Bertram Mills' Circus train)
11/12	1610	5	662	Wdn 3/51 set 409
7/13	856	856	684	Wdn 7/50 set 409
7/13	857	857	685	Wdn 9/56 set 455
7/13	858	858	686	Wdn 12/46 set 475
7/13	860	860	687	Wdn 9/52 set 211

Drawing 2390

These were as Drawing 1872, but the panels were made of steel sheet instead of wood. Externally the same, the difference was in the sizes of frame members.

Built	No	SR No	
7/15	718	677	Wdn 12/49 set 210
7/15	863	688	Wdn 4/47 set 325
11/15	886	693	Wdn 6/51 set 342
11/15	887	694	Wdn 9/56 set 342
4/16	866	689	Wdn 4/47 set 325
4/16	873	690	Wdn 2/57 set 303
4/16	883	692	Wdn 8/47 set 342
5/16	876	691	Wdn 11/57 set 338 (used for Bertram Mills' Circus train)
7/16	889	695	Wdn 12/49 set 210
7/16	890	696	Wdn 12/57 set 99

9.4   **56ft Dining Saloon.** LSWR Drawings 1319, 1601, 1869 and 2077. SR Diagram 590.
All rebuilt with semi-elliptical roof in mid-1931.

Drawing 1319

Built	No	New No	SR No	
11/04	59	4121	7821	to Clean Dressing Van 1834s 6/43
3/05	61	4123	7823	to US Ambulance 204 11/43
4/05	60	4122	7822	to Clean Dressing Van 1837s 7/43
4/05	62	4124	7824	to US Ambulance 205 11/43
5/05	63	4125	7825	to US Ambulance 206 12/43
5/05	64	4126	7826	to US Ambulance 203 11/43
5/05	65	4127	7827	to WD 1642 10/43
5/05	66	4128	7828	used in Home Ambulance Train No 25 (otherwise of LNWR stock) in World War 1; altered to Naval Ambulance 6/43; to Camping Coach 25 3/48

Drawing 1601

Built	No	New No	SR No	
5/07	67	4129	7829	to Clean Dressing Van 1843s 8/43; Dormitory Set No 1
5/07	68	4130	7830	to Clean Dressing Van 1846s 9/43
5/07	69	4131	7831	to WD 1640 9/43
5/07	70	4132	7832	to WD 1641 9/43; to Mid-Hants Railway 1978
5/07	71	4133	7833	Wdn 3/45
5/07	72	4134	7834	to US Ambulance 201 9/43; later AD 3018
6/08	73	4135	7835	Wdn 11/44
6/08	74	4136	7836	Wdn 11/45
6/08	75	4137	7837	to Clean Dressing Van 1849s 10/43; Dormitory Set No 3 (Redhill)
8/08	76	4138	7838	to US Ambulance 202 10/43; to Mid-Hants Railway 1978
8/08	77	4139	7839	Wdn 11/45; to 622s 1948

Drawing 1869

Built	No	New No	SR No	
5/10	78	4140	7840	Wdn 5/46
5/10	79	4141	7841	to Clean Dressing Van 1823s 3/43

Drawing 2077

Built	No	Date	New No	SR No	
6/12	80		4142	7842	used in Ambulance Train No 38 (mainly LNWR stock) in World War 1; to Clean Dressing Van 1831s 6/43
6/12	81		4143	7843	to Clean Dressing Van 1840s 9/43

9.5 Note: there are no details — this number refers to the drawing of the outside-framed bogies.

9.6 'Emigrant' stock.

(a) **46ft 6in x 8ft 3¾in Brake Third.** LSWR Drawing 1348. SR Diagram 127.
Corridor, not gangwayed. Dual brake fitted.

Built	No	New No	SR		
3/05	1339	1339	3079	set 337	Wdn 9/37 in set 69
3/05	1340	1340	3080	set 337	Wdn 12/36

(b) **46ft 6in x 8ft 3¾in Third.** LSWR Drawing 1343. SR Diagram 18 (Diagram 403 as P-P BC).
Corridor, not gangwayed. Dual brake fitted.

Built	No	New No	SR			
3/05	602	602	643	set 337	to P-P Brake Compo 6428 2/35	Wdn 8/62 set 652
3/05	621	621	644	set 337	to P-P Brake Compo 6429 2/35	Wdn 2/61 set 653
3/05	628	628	645	set 337	to P-P Brake Compo 6430 2/35	Wdn 3/59 set 654
3/05	652	652	646	set 337	to P-P Brake Compo 6431 2/35	Wdn 11/60 set 655
3/05	710	710	647	set 337		Wdn 2/39

(The four conversions were paired with 58ft Thirds (ex-48ft Tri-Compo) SR Nos 1-4, for the All Hallows branch.)

(c) **46ft 6in x 8ft 3¾in Composite.** LSWR Drawing 1342. SR Diagram 275.
Corridor, not gangwayed. Dual brake fitted.

Built	No	New No	SR		
3/05	865	2994	5072	set 337	Wdn 2/39

(d) **46ft 6in x 8ft 3¾in Brake Third.** LSWR Drawing 1589. SR Diagram 128.
Corridor, gangwayed. Dual brake fitted.

Built	No	New No	SR			
6/07	1450	1450	3082	Wdn 11/33 used in Home Ambulance train No 21 (all LSWR stock) 2/16		
7/07	1449	1449	3081	new u/f 3/35 set 474	to P-P 2648 2/43	Wdn 6/60 set 738
7/07	1451	1451	3083	new u/f 3/35 set 473	to P-P 2646 3/43	Wdn 11/59 set 736
11/08	1487	1487	3084	new u/f 3/35 set 474	to P-P 2649 3/43	Wdn 1/60 set 739
11/08	1488	1488	3085	new u/f 3/35 set 473	to P-P 2647 2/43	Wdn 5/60 set 737

(e) **46ft 6in x 8ft 3¾in Third.** LSWR Drawing 1584. SR Diagram 20
(Diagram 101 as Brake Third, Diagram 288 as P-P Composite).
Corridor, gangwayed. Dual brake fitted.

Built	No	New No	SR	set		
6/07	1443	98	661	473	to P-P Brake Third 2645 4/43	Wdn 2/61 set 735
6/07	1444	97	660	474	to P-P Brake Third 2643 2/43	Wdn 10/60 set 734 or 733
6/07	1445	96	659	473	to P-P Brake Third 2644 4/43	Wdn 8/59 set 733 or 734
6/07	1446	95	658	474	to P-P Brake Third 2642 1/43	Wdn 12/60 set 732
7/07	1447	94	657	474	to P-P Brake Third 2641 1/43	Wdn 4/59 set 731
7/07	1448	93	656	474	to P-P Compo 4758 4/43	Wdn 9/60 set 733
11/08	1481	92	655	474	used in Home Ambulance train No 38 (mainly LNWR stock) in World War 1; to P-P Compo 4757 1/43	Wdn 7/59 set 732
11/08	1482	90	654	473	to P-P Compo 4760 4/43	Wdn 2/61 set 735
11/08	1483	87	653	474	to P-P Compo 4756 1/43	Wdn 10/59 set 731
11/08	1484	84	652	473	to P-P Compo 4759 2/43	Wdn 5/60 set 734
11/08	1485	83	651	473	to P-P Compo 4762 2/43	Wdn 5/60 set 737
11/08	1486	82	650	473	to P-P Compo 4761 3/43	Wdn 1/60 set 736

(f) **46ft 6in x 8ft 3¾ in Composite.** LSWR Drawing 1583. SR Diagram 276 (Diagram 289 as P-P).
Corridor, gangwayed. Dual brake fitted.

Built	No	New No	SR		
6/07	953	3073	5073	new u/f 2/35, set 473, P-P trailer 4763 2/43	Wdn 6/60 set 738
11/08	982	3095	5074	new u/f 3/35, set 474, P-P trailer 4764 3/43 ran in Ambulance train No 21, 2/16	Wdn 1/60 set 739;

Summary of SR Push-Pull sets using 46ft 6in carriages (from *Appendix to Carriage Working Notices*, dated 16/6/47).

Set	Brake Compo		58ft Third
652	6428	1	
653	6429	2	These four sets formed in 1935
654	6430	3	for All Hallows branch
655	6431	4	

Set	Brake Third	Compo	Allocation
731	2641	4756	C
732	2642	4757	C
733	2643	4758	C
734	2644	4759	W
735	2645	4760	W
736	2646	4761	E
737	2647	4762	C
738	2648	4763	E
739	2649	4764	E

C = LCD workings
E = LED workings
W = Western section (sets 734/5 allocated to Exeter Central as relief sets)

9.7   56ft Double-Brake Tri-Composite. LSWR Drawing 1363. SR Diagram 412.
(This carriage was not permitted to run on the SECR or Metropolitan Railway lines.)

Built	No	New No	SR	
6/05	891	3607	6542	Wdn 10/37 to Mess & Tool Van 1152s. Dual-braked 6/07 for Plymouth-Brighton service.

9.8   50ft Brake Composite. LSWR Drawing 1372. SR Diagram 406.
Intended for 'Paris, Havre and St Malo traffic'.

Built	No	New No	SR	
2/05	882	3605	6469	Wdn 9/36 to Mess & Tool Van 995s
6/05	883	3606	6470	Wdn 9/36 to Mess & Tool Van 996s

9.9   56ft Brake Third. LSWR Drawing 1487.
All these carriages retained their original numbers at 1912, and all were sold to the War Department 10/17 to form a Continental Ambulance Train. When they were returned they were all converted to Passenger Brake Vans (Drawing 3499) before being returned to service. They will be described under Vans.

Built	Nos
12/06	1396, 1397, 1398, 1399
3/07	1400, 1401, 1402, 1403

9.10   52ft Tri-Composite. LSWR Drawing 1488. SR Diagram 280.

Built	No	New No	SR No	
5/07	932	3057	5098	Wdn 3/49 set 418
5/07	933	3058	5099	Wdn 3/49 set 410
5/07	934	3059	5130	Wdn 12/48 set 412
5/07	935	3060	5131	Wdn 7/50 set 417
6/07	936	3061	5132	Wdn 9/50 set 414
6/07	937	3062	5103	Wdn 5/50 set 415

9.11   56ft Brake Tri-Composite. LSWR Drawings 1503, 1570 and 1736. SR Diagram 409.
At least some of these (it is not certain which) had LNWR sidelamps at the guard's compartment, probably for use on Bournemouth West-Manchester services.

Drawing 1503
(These had a door across the corridor with an LNWR private lock to separate Third-class passengers from their betters!)

Built	No	New No	SR No	
3/07	268	3508	6497	Wdn 9/52 set 211
3/07	269	3509	6498	Wdn 7/44 to 105s

Drawing 1570
(Did not have LNWR sidelamps.)

Built	No	New No	SR No	
10/07	955	3613	6504	Wdn 9/50 set 414

Drawing 1736
(This drawing shows LNWR sidelamps, but they were probably omitted on the final five.)

Built	No	New No	SR No	
5/08	968	3614	6505	Wdn 4/55 set 13
5/08	969	3615	6506	Wdn 2/57 set 15
5/08	970	3616	6507	Wdn 8/50 set 210 to 1602s
5/08	971	3617	6508	Wdn 12/46 set 475
5/08	972	3618	6509	Wdn 12/51 set 301 to DS 3195
5/08	973	3619	6510	Wdn 10/48 set 301
1/09	984	3620	6511	Wdn 10/48 set 8
1/09	985	3621	6512	Wdn 1/54 set 410
1/09	986	3622	6513	Wdn 9/54 set 211
2/09	987	3623	6514	Wdn 6/57 set 379
2/09	988	3624	6515	Wdn 3/56 set 10
2/09	989	3625	6516	Wdn 4/50 set 335 to 1573s
6/09	948	3608	6499	transferred to Brake Third 2650 in 6/45 for Midhurst and later for Hayling Island; Wdn 7/56
6/09	949	3609	6500	Wdn 9/49 to 1558s
6/09	950	3610	6501	Wdn 8/50 set 210 to 1599s
6/09	951	3611	6502	Wdn 11/44 set 378
6/09	952	3612	6503	Wdn 4/56 set 14

9.12   56ft First. LSWR Drawing 1527. SR Diagram 475 (Diagram 20 as Third).

Built	No	New No	SR No	
5/07	3	3753	7156	Wdn 8/50 set 408
5/07	4	3754	7157	Wdn 8/47 set 342
5/07	6	3756	7158	altered to Third 2301 in 6/55; Wdn 2/57
5/07	7	3757	7159	Wdn 2/57 set 457
5/07	15	3761	7160	Wdn 9/54 set 211
5/07	16	3762	7161	Wdn 3/51 set 408
5/07	81	3794	7164	Wdn 10/50 set 309
5/07	83	3795	7165	Wdn 4/47 set 325
8/07	20	3765	7162	Wdn 9/56 set 455
8/07	24	3769	7163	Wdn 12/49 set 210

9.13   56ft Brake Third. LSWR Drawing 1568. SR Diagrams 131 (LH) and 139 (RH).

Built	No	Corr.	New No	SR No	
9/07	1404	R	1404		to US Army Ambulance 6207 in 4/18, returned to be SR PBV 336; destroyed by enemy action 10/40 at Clapham Jct
9/07	1405	R	1405		to US Army Ambulance 6208 in 4/18; returned to be SR PBV 337; Wdn 4/46
9/07	1406	R	1406	3094	Wdn 8/43 set 405; grounded Gomshall
9/07	1407	R	1407	3095	Wdn 8/47 set 407
9/07	1408	R	1408	3096	Wdn 7/50 set 405
9/07	1409	R	1409	3097	destroyed 6/41 by enemy action
10/07	1525	R	1525	3109	to Mess & Tool Van DS 3201 10/51
8/08	578	R	1741		to US Army Ambulance 6205 4/18; returned to be SR PBV 334; Wdn 3/46
8/08	579	R	1742	3122	Wdn 2/48 set 411
8/08	1474	R	1474		to US Army Ambulance 6206 4/18; returned to be SR PBV 335; Wdn 5/40 after damage at Clapham Jct
9/08	587	R	1750	3123	Wdn 2/48 set 411
9/08	1475	R	1475		to Continental Ambulance train 10/17; returned to be SR PBV 330; Wdn 11/45
9/08	1476	R	1476	3103	Wdn 2/48 set 404
10/08	1477	R	1477	3104	Wdn 11/52 set 349
10/08	1478	R	1478	3105	Wdn 4/47 set 325
10/08	1479	R	1479		to US Army Ambulance 6215 4/18; returned to be SR PBV 344; Wdn 12/44
10/08	1480	R	1480	3106	Wdn 6/45 set 325
5/10	80	L	1433	3100	Wdn 10/56 set 309
5/10	81	R	1436	3101	Wdn 9/50 set 457
5/10	82	R	1437	3102	Wdn 7/50 set 405
5/10	1523	L	1523		to US Army Ambulance 6204 (?) 4/18; returned to be SR PBV 333; Wdn 3/46

Built	No	Corr.	New No	SR No	
5/10	1524	R	1524		LSWR set 401; to US Army Ambulance 6201 4/18;
					returned to be SR PBV 331; Wdn 11/46
7/11	180	L	1599	3110	Wdn 2/54 set 422
7/11	389	L	1675	3116	Wdn 4/47 set 325
7/11	656	L	1813	3126	to EKR No 5 2/46; Wdn 10/48
7/11	657	L	1814	3127	Wdn 8/47 (dual-braked 9/23 for Dover-Birkenhead service)
7/11	661	L	1818	3128	to EKR No 6 2/46; Wdn 10/48
7/11	863	L	1908	3141	Wdn 3/51 (dual-braked 9/23 for Dover-Birkenhead service)

9.14 **56ft Brake Third.** LSWR Drawing 1569.

Built	No	New No	SR No	
4/08	1464	1464		to US Army Ambulance 6216 in 4/18; returned as SR PBV 345; to Stores Van 447s 4/47
4/08	1465	1465		to Continental Ambulance train 10/17; later rebuilt as PBV 4367, SR 328; to wagon DS 3177 7/50
4/08	1466	1466		to Continental Ambulance train 10/17; later rebuilt as PBV 4366, SR 327; to M&T Van 223s 1/45
4/08	1467	1467		to Continental Ambulance train 10/17; later rebuilt as PBV 4382, SR 329; Wdn 11/46

9.15 **56ft Sleeping Saloon.** LSWR Drawing 1633.

Built	No	GWR No (in 1911)	
1908	39	9086	destroyed by fire c1912
1908	40	9087	destroyed by fire c1912
1908	41	9088	Wdn 5/28
1908	42	9089	Wdn 12/31

9.16 **54ft Tri-Composite.** LSWR Drawing 1690. SR Diagram 278.

Built	No	New No	SR No	
8/08	248	2486	5086	Wdn 4/51 set 343
8/08	255	2493	5087	Wdn 1/47 set 408
9/08	286	2521	5088	Wdn 3/48 set 407; grounded Ashford (Sports Club)
9/08	975	3088	5089	Wdn 2/48 set 404
9/08	976	3089	5090	Wdn 3/51 set 408
9/08	977	3090	5091	Wdn 6/45 set 401
10/08	978	3091	5092	Wdn 7/47 set 416
10/08	979	3092	5093	Wdn 8/47 set 404
10/08	980	3093	5094	Wdn 5/50 set 413
10/08	981	3094	5095	Wdn 8/43 set 405; grounded Gomshall

9.17 **56ft Brake Composite.** LSWR Drawing 1832. SR Diagram 410.

Built	No	New No	SR No	set	
4/10	391	3517	6519	335	Wdn 1/50; to Mess & Tool Van DS 1565
4/10	392	3518	6520		Wdn 6/49; to Mess & Tool Van DS 1552
4/10	393	3519	6521	99	Wdn 9/53
4/10	992	3626	6523	14	Wdn 4/57
4/10	993	3627	6524	413	Wdn 2/50
4/10	994	3628	6525		Wdn 1/52
4/10	995	3629	6526	17	Wdn 8/57
4/10	996	3630	6527	8	Wdn 5/56 (dual-braked 9/23 for Dover-Birkenhead service)
7/10	1002	3631	6528		Wdn 8/47
7/10	1003	3632	6529		Wdn 11/58 (lavatory and gangways removed 6/53 for Hayling Island service)
7/10	1004	3633	6530	309	Wdn 10/50
7/10	1005	3634	6531	338	Wdn 11/55 (dual-braked 9/23 for Dover-Birkenhead service)
7/10	1006	3635	6532	99	Wdn 9/53
7/11	14	3501	6517	422	Wdn 10/56
7/11	277	3510	6518		Wdn 3/53 (altered to Diagram 412 (12 First) 4/45 for Hayling Island service)
7/11	456	3537	6522	403	Wdn 10/51; to Mess & Tool Van DS 3200
7/11	1020	3636	6533		Wdn 6/53
7/11	1021	3637	6534	412	Wdn 1/51; to Mess & Tool Van DS 3163
7/11	1022	3638	6535	338	Wdn 11/55

9.18   56ft Composite. LSWR Drawing 1862. SR Diagram 283.

Built	No	New No	SR No	
5/10	998	3100	5128	Wdn 1/47 set 326
5/10	999	3101	5129	Wdn 4/49 set 420

9.19   54ft Tri-Composite. LSWR Drawing 1866. SR Diagram 279.

Built	No	New No	SR No	
5/10	997	3099	5096	Wdn 12/48 set 412
5/10	1000	3102	5097	Wdn 9/49 set 420; u/f shortened; used for rebuild of Directors' Saloon DS 1

9.20   52ft Tri-Composite. LSWR Drawing 2138. SR Diagram 280.

Built	No	SR No	
3/13	2266	5104	Wdn 5/50 set 406
3/13	2338	5105	Wdn 1/54 set 410
3/13	2408	5106	Wdn 12/48 set 99; to RME Instruction Car DS 3186 7/51
3/13	2445	5107	Wdn 9/49 set 99
3/13	2614	5108	Wdn 9/53 set 99; to Camping Coach 35
3/13	2652	5109	Wdn 12/53 set 338

9.21   56ft Dining Saloon. LSWR Drawing 2158. SR Diagram 591.

Built	No	SR No	
4/13	4144	7844	Wdn 6/45; grounded Wembley
6/13	4145	7845	Wdn 9/47; to Mess & Tool Van 623s
6/13	4146	7846	to US Ambulance 208 6/44
7/13	4147	7847	to US Ambulance 207 6/44
7/13	4148	7848	Wdn 6/45; grounded Wembley
7/13	4149	7849	Wdn 6/45; grounded Wembley

9.22   56ft Brake Third. LSWR Drawings 2207 and 2455. SR Diagrams 140 (RH) and 132 (LH).

Drawing 2207

Built	No	Corr.	SR No	
10/13	2046	R	3148	Wdn 6/49 set 403; to Mess & Tool Van DS 1549
10/13	2047	R	3149	Wdn 11/47 set 416; to Mess & Tool Van 1776s
10/13	2048	R	3154	Wdn 6/47 set 418
10/13	2049	R	3155	Wdn 4/49 set 420
10/13	2050	L	3156	Wdn 2/51 set 408; u/f shortened; 37ft 7in for Tunnel Inspection Vehicle DS 658
10/13	2051	L	3157	Wdn 4/49 set 420
10/13	2052	L	3158	Wdn 7/57 set 457
10/13	2053	L	3159	Wdn 8/55 set 406

Drawing 2455
(similar to Drawing 2207 but steel-panelled)

Built	No	Corr.	SR No	
12/16	1839	R	3142	Wdn 4/51 set 343
12/16	1841	R	3143	Wdn 1/57 set 403
5/19	1842	R	3144	Wdn 9/56 set 340
5/19	1894	R	3145	Wdn 3/47 set 419
5/19	1895	L	3146	Wdn 3/47 set 419
5/19	1903	L	3147	Wdn 3/56 set 410

9.23   56ft Brake Composite. LSWR Drawing 2362. SR Diagram 411.
(Note these had high elliptical roofs and 8ft bogies.)

Built	No	SR No	
11/18	3649	6536	Wdn 1/58 set 14
11/18	3650	6537	Wdn 7/50
11/18	3651	6538	Wdn 2/53; to Camping Coach 32; to DW 150383 11/66
11/18	3652	6539	Wdn 4/55 set 14
11/18	3653	6540	Wdn 6/58 set 20
11/18	3654	6541	Wdn 1/53

9.24   **57ft Third.** LSWR Drawing 3128. SR Diagram 22.
(Note these were 8ft 6¾in-wide panelled carriages.)

Built	No	SR No	
4/20	675	708	Wdn 12/48 set 99; to DS 3060
4/20	698	709	Wdn 12/57 set 99
5/20	699	710	Wdn 10/54 set 457
5/20	714	711	Wdn 2/57 set 457
8/20	768	712	Wdn 1/58 set 338 (used for Bertram Mills' Circus train)
12/20	107	697	Wdn 8/47 set 342
12/20	108	698	Wdn 12/48 set 99
12/20	125	699	Wdn 9/56 set 455
12/20	126	700	Wdn 9/56 set 455
12/20	139	701	Wdn 9/56 set 309
12/20	142	702	Wdn 11/55 set 20
12/20	143	703	Wdn 11/55 set 338
12/20	144	704	Wdn 9/53 set 99; to Camping Coach 33
12/20	205	705	Wdn 9/56 set 455
12/20	655	706	Wdn 2/51 set 309
12/20	668	707	Wdn 12/57 set 99

9.25   **57ft Brake Third.** LSWR Drawing 3151. SR Diagram 134.
(Note these were 8ft 6¾in-wide panelled carriages.) Tare weight 28 tons.

Built	No	SR No	
11/21	1283	3160	Wdn 1/52 set 339; to DS 3197
11/21	1286	3163	Wdn 11/52 set 349
11/21	1292	3167	Wdn 2/57 set 457
11/21	1300	3168	Wdn 8/55 set 406
11/21	1301	3169	Wdn 9/56 set 340
12/21	1284	3161	Wdn 1/52 set 339
12/21	1285	3162	Wdn 9/56 set 455 (used on K&ESR ?)
12/21	1289	3164	Wdn 5/47 set 342
12/21	1290	3165	Wdn 12/57 set 99
12/21	1291	3166	Wdn 3/56 set 455
12/21	1307	3170	Wdn 12/49 (used for Headcorn-Robertsbridge service from 8/48)
12/21	1317	3171	Wdn 9/50 (used for Headcorn-Robertsbridge service from 8/48)
12/21	1319	3172	Wdn 5/47 set 422
12/21	1331	3173	Wdn 5/56 set 421
12/21	1332	3174	Wdn 9/56 set 455: to DS 111 (used on K&ESR ?)
12/21	1337	3175	Wdn 12/57 set 99; to 080702 (internal use)
12/21	1338	3176	Wdn 4/56 set 421
12/21	1348	3177	Wdn 3/56 set 346
12/21	1349	3178	Wdn 3/56 set 410; to DS 112
12/21	1351	3179	Wdn 5/47

All of these were repainted with their SR numbers in 1927, except 1349 (2/28).

Appendix to Chapter 10
57FT 'IRONCLAD' CORRIDOR CARRIAGES

10.1   **57ft First.** LSWR Drawings 3194 and 3708. SR Diagram 476 (Diagram 25 as Third).

Drawing 3194
(all with outside-framed bogies)

The first four were used in five-car Bournemouth sets:

Built	No	SR No	
7/21	3864	7168	Wdn 10/57 set 431
7/21	3867	7170	Wdn 10/57 set 431
9/21	3922	7171	Wdn 10/57 set 433
11/21	3923	7172	Wdn 10/57 set 434

The next 16, to No 3936, were ordered with Brake Firsts (Pantry) (see 10.5) for two 10-car boat trains:

Built	No	SR No	
5/22	3854	7166	to Third 2320 6/54; Wdn 3/58 set 276
5/22	3858	7167	to Third 2321 7/54; Wdn 7/59 set 275
5/22	3866	7169	Wdn 12/37; u/f used to rebuild 50ft Compo 4992 to 57ft Brake Compo 6407
5/22	3924	7173	to Third 2323 6/54; Wdn 7/59 set 275
5/22	3925	7174	to Third 2324 7/54; Wdn 7/59 set 275
6/22	3926	7175	to Third 2325 6/54; Wdn 7/59 set 274
6/22	3927	7176	to Third 2326 6/54; Wdn 7/59 set 274
6/22	3928	7177	to Third 2327 6/54; Wdn 7/59 set 274
6/22	3929	7178	to Third 2328 6/54; Wdn 7/59 set 274
6/22	3930	7179	Wdn 10/58
8/22	3931	7180	destroyed by fire 1937; u/f used to rebuild 50ft Compo 4996 to 59ft Brake Compo 6406
8/22	3932	7181	Wdn 1/59
8/22	3933	7182	Wdn 10/56
8/22	3934	7183	to Third 2329 6/54; Wdn 3/58 set 276
8/22	3935	7184	Wdn 4/58
8/22	3936	7185	Wdn 1/58

Drawing 3708
(Bogies vary: O = outside-framed; 8 = Ashford-type 8ft; 9 = Ashford-type 9ft.)

The first six were used for five-car Bournemouth sets, SR 435-440.

Built	No	SR No	Bogie	
3/23	3937	7186	O	Wdn 10/58 set 436
3/23	3938	7187	O	to Third 2330 7/54; Wdn 8/59 set 275
6/23	3939	7188	9	Wdn 7/59 set 437
6/23	3940	7189	9	to Third 2322 10/54; Wdn 3/58 set 276
10/23	3941	7190	9	Wdn 2/59 set 439
10/23	3942	7191	9	Wdn 9/57 set 440
3/24		7192	9	Wdn 10/59 set 434
3/24		7193	9	Wdn 11/58
3/24		7194	9	Wdn 2/59 set 444
3/24		7195	9	to Third 2331 6/54; Wdn 7/59 set 276
3/24		7196	9	Wdn 1/59 set 442
3/24		7197	9	Wdn 11/59 set 201
3/24		7198	9	to Third 2332 6/54; Wdn 7/59 set 274
3/24		7199	9	Wdn 12/58 set 432
4/24		7200	9	Wdn 5/57; to Tool Van DS 227
4/24		7201	9	Wdn 11/59 set 443
7/25		7202	8	to Third 2333 7/54; Wdn 7/59 set 275
8/25		7203	8	to Third 2334 6/54; Wdn 7/59 set 274

Built	No	SR No	Bogie	
9/25		7204	8	Wdn 11/58 set 443
9/25		7205	8	Wdn 10/59 set 234

The next seven were built at Lancing with 9ft bogies and used for set 471, 'City Limited':

Built	SR No	
12/25	7652	Wdn 11/58 set 471
12/25	7653	Wdn 7/59 set 440
12/25	7654	to Third 2335 6/54; Wdn 7/59 set 276
12/25	7655	Wdn 7/59 set 435
12/25	7656	to Third 2336 6/54; Wdn 7/59 set 276
12/25	7657	Wdn 7/59
12/25	7658	Wdn 7/59 set 441

The rest were built for set 472 on the Worthing & Bognor service, using 8ft bogies:

Built	SR No	
3/26	7659	to Third 2337 7/54; Wdn 7/59
3/26	7660	Wdn 12/60; returned 3/61 for Bertram Mills' Circus train; Wdn 2/62
3/26	7661	to Third 2338 7/54; Wdn 7/59 set 275
3/26	7662	to Third 2339 6/54; Wdn 7/59 set 276
3/26	7663	to Third 2340 6/54; Wdn 7/59 set 274
3/26	7664	Wdn 12/60; returned 3/61 for Bertram Mills' Circus train; Wdn 2/62

10.2   57ft Third. LSWR Drawings 3251 and 3709. SR Diagram 24.

Drawing 3251

Built	No	SR No	
7/21	773	717	Wdn 10/57 set 433; to DS 226
7/21	774	718	Wdn 4/57 set 432; to DS 175
9/21	778	719	Wdn 6/57 set 436; to DS 176
11/21	929	720	Wdn 9/57 set 431; to Tool Van DS 177

Drawing 3709

The first 12, to No 103, were used in six five-car Bournemouth sets, SR 435-440.

Built	No	SR No	
3/23	62	721	Wdn 10/59 set 434 to 081272 (internal user)
3/23	64	722	Wdn 10/59 set 434 to 081274 (internal user)
3/23	66	723	Wdn 1/59 set 438
3/23	67	724	Wdn 10/57 set 438 to DS 225
6/23	69	725	Wdn 12/60 set 438; returned 3/61 for Bertram Mills' Circus train; Wdn 2/62
6/23	70	726	Wdn 7/59 set 435; to Tool Van DS 70127
6/23	73	727	Wdn 4/58 set 434
6/23	74	728	Wdn 7/59 set 435; to Riding Van DS 70011
10/23	75	729	Wdn 12/60 set 432; returned 3/61 for Bertram Mills' Circus train; Wdn 2/62
10/23	79	730	Wdn 10/57 set 432
10/23	81	731	Wdn 10/58 set 441
10/23	103	732	Wdn 10/58 set 436

The following were built with 9ft Ashford-type bogies:

Built	SR No	
4/24	745	Wdn 7/59 set 437; to Dormitory DS 70138
4/24	746	Wdn 7/59 set 441; to Riding Van DS 70012
4/24	747	Wdn 10/61 set 438; to Tool Van DS 70128
4/24	748	Wdn 7/59 set 437; to Motive Power Tool Van DS 229
4/24	749	Wdn 10/59 set 431; to Riding Van DS 70010
4/24	750	Wdn 7/59 set 440; to Staff Van DS 70123
5/24	751	Wdn 12/57 set 433
5/24	752	Wdn 7/59 set 435; to Tool Van DS 70014
5/24	753	Wdn 7/59 set 437; to Motive Power Riding Van DS 230
5/24	754	Wdn 10/61 set 433
7/25	755	Wdn 11/57 set 433
7/25	756	Wdn 7/59 set 441; to Tool Van DS 70015
8/25	757	Wdn 7/59 set 471
8/25	758	Wdn 12/60 set 438; returned 3/61 for Bertram Mills' Circus train; Wdn 2/62

Built	SR No	
9/25	759	Wdn 8/61 set 432
9/25	760	Wdn 11/59 set 440; to Tool Van DS 70013
9/25	761	Wdn 7/59 set 435; to Breakdown Staff Van DS 70124
9/25	762	Wdn 7/59 set 472
12/25	2341	Built at Lancing for set 471, 'City Limited'; Wdn 7/59

The following were built with 8ft bogies:

Built	SR No	
1/26	2346	Built for set 472, Worthing & Bognor; Wdn 12/61 set 436
1/26	2347	Built for set 472, Worthing & Bognor; Wdn 10/58 set 436
1/26	2348	Built for set 472, Worthing & Bognor; Wdn 7/59 set 472

10.3 **57ft Brake Third.** LSWR Drawings 3252 and 3710. SR Diagrams 135 (RH) and 213 (LH).
Tare weight 33 tons. (Drawing 3252 was 9ft 1in over lookouts; Drawing 3710 reduced to 9ft 0in.)

Drawing 3252
The first eight were built for four five-car Bournemouth sets:

Built	No	Corr.	SR No	
7/21	1275	R	3180	Wdn 10/57 set 432; to DS 70024
7/21	1276	L	3181	Wdn 10/57 set 431; to DS 70030; sold 6/69
7/21	1277	R	3182	Wdn 10/57 set 431; to Signal & Telegraph Van DS 231
7/21	1278	L	3183	Wdn 12/58 set 432; to Mess & Tool Van DS 70026
9/21	1279	R	3184	Wdn 11/57 set 433; to DS 178
7/21	1280	L	3185	Wdn 1/58 set 434
11/21	1281	R	3186	Wdn 1/58 set 434
11/21	1282	L	3187	Wdn 11/57 set 434; to DS 179; to Mid-Hants Railway 1979

Drawing 3710
The next twelve were built for six more five-car Bournemouth sets, 435-440:

Built	No	Corr.	SR No	
3/23	1310	R	3188	Wdn 10/58 set 436; to 081038 (internal user)
3/23	1325	L	3189	Wdn 10/57 set 436
3/23	1353	R	3190	Wdn 7/59 set 435; to DS 70016; to Mid-Hants Railway 8/78
3/23	1354	L	3191	Wdn 7/59 set 435; to Signal & Telegraph Van DS 70131; condemned 2/73

(Down to here had outside-framed bogies; the remainder had Ashford-type 9ft-wheelbase bogies.)

Built	No	Corr.	SR No	
6/23	1356	R	3192	Wdn 7/59 set 437
6/23	1357	L	3193	Wdn 7/59 set 437; to DS 70133
6/23	1365	L	3195	Wdn 1/59 set 438; to Mess & Tool Van DS 70027
6/23	1366	R	3196	Wdn 1/59 set 438; to Mess & Tool Van DS 70028
10/23	1361	R	3194	Wdn 10/59 set 439; to IV 081302
10/23	1367	L	3197	Wdn 10/59 set 439; to IV 081271
10/23	1369	R	3198	Wdn 10/57 set 440; to Signal & Telegraph Van DS 232
10/23	1373	L	3199	Wdn 10/57 set 440; to DS 70033
7/25		R	3203	Wdn 7/59 set 441; to DS 70017
7/25		L	3204	Wdn 7/59 set 441; to DS 70085; sold to S&DJR Museum 1973
8/25		L	3205	Wdn 10/61 set 442
8/25		R	3206	Wdn 6/61 set 442
9/25		R	3207	Wdn 11/59 set 443; to Lancing Workmen's train, DS 70068
9/25		L	3208	Wdn 11/59 set 443; to Lancing Workmen's train, DS 70061
9/25		R	3209	Wdn 11/59 set 444
9/25		L	3210	Wdn 11/59 set 444

10.4 **57ft Pantry Third.** LSWR Drawing 3288. SR Diagram 23.
Built for four five-car Bournemouth sets.

Built	No	SR No	
7/21	930	713	Wdn 4/57 set 437; to Riding Van DS 172
7/21	931	714	Wdn 6/57 set 432; to Riding Van DS 173
9/21	932	715	Wdn 9/57 set 433; to Riding Van DS 174
11/21	933	716	Wdn 10/57 set 434

10.5 **57ft Brake First (Pantry).** LSWR Drawing 3665. SR Diagram 542.
Built for two 10-car Southampton boat trains.

Built	No	SR No	
5/22	4062	7712	to Ambulance 6801 12/44, restored 9/45; to Brake First 1949; Wdn 9/58
6/22	4061	7711	to WD Inspection Coach 1643 9/44, restored 1/46; Wdn 11/58
8/22	4063	7713	to Ambulance 6701 2/45, restored 8/45; Wdn 5/59
8/22	4064	7714	to WD Inspection Coach 1647 in 1944, restored 1/46; Wdn 7/59

10.6 **57ft Dining Saloon.** Eastleigh Drawing 3854. SR Diagram 592.

Built	No	SR No	
10/23	4150	7850	Wdn 12/47; to Mess & Tool Van 624s
10/23	4151	7851	Wdn 12/47; to Mess & Tool Van 625s
7/25		7852	Wdn 12/47; grounded Widnes (Lancs)
7/25		7853	Wdn 12/47; to Mess & Tool Van 626s, to Restaurant Car 4/50, to Cafeteria Car 8/52; Wdn 1/63
7/25		7854	Wdn 12/47; to Mess & Tool Van 627s
8/25		7855	Wdn 10/44; to Mess & Tool Van 628s
8/25		7856	Wdn 10/44; to Mess & Tool Van 629s; condemned 6/70
8/25		7857	Wdn 10/44; to Mess & Tool Van 630s

Note records differ: those shown as withdrawn 12/47 might have been withdrawn in 1944.

10.7 **57ft Composite.** Eastleigh Drawing 4115. SR Diagram 284.

Built	SR No	
5/24	5133	Wdn 7/59 set 274
5/24	5134	Wdn 7/59 set 471
5/24	5135	Wdn 12/57 set 443
5/24	5136	Wdn 12/59 set 341
12/25	6287	built at Lancing for set 471, 'City Limited'; Wdn 6/59

The first four had Ashford-type 9ft bogies; No 6287 probably had 8ft ones.

10.8 **57ft Brake Composite.** SR Diagram 416 (Diagram 414 as P-P).

Built	SR No	Corr.	
10/25	6560	R	two-car set 381 with Brake Third 4052; to P-P 12/48; Wdn 12/62
10/25	6561	L	two-car set 382 with Brake Third 4053; to P-P 7/49; Wdn 10/59
10/25	6562	R	two-car set 383 with Brake Third 3211; to P-P 10/48; Wdn 12/62
10/25	6563	L	two-car set 384 with Brake Third 3212; to P-P 6/49; Wdn 12/62
10/25	6564	R	two-car set 385 with Brake Third 3213; to P-P 3/52; Wdn 8/62

All had 9ft bogies.

10.9 **57ft Brake Third.** Eastleigh Drawing 4378. SR Diagram 137
(Diagram 136 as P-P).

Built	SR No	
10/25	3211	two-car set 383 with Brake Compo 6562; to P-P 10/48; Wdn 12/62
10/25	3212	two-car set 384 with Brake Compo 6563; to P-P 6/49; Wdn 11/62
10/25	3213	two-car set 385 with Brake Compo 6564; to P-P 3/52; Wdn 8/62
10/25	4052	two-car set 381 with Brake Compo 6560; to P-P 12/48; Wdn 12/62
10/25	4053	two-car set 382 with Brake Compo 6561; to P-P 7/49; Wdn 10/59
12/25	4043	built at Lancing for set 471, 'City Limited'; Wdn 7/59 set 465
12/25	4044	built at Lancing for set 471, 'City Limited'; Wdn 7/59 set 471

The above had 9ft bogies; the following had 8ft ones:

Built	SR No		
1/26	4046	set 472, Worthing & Bognor service;	Wdn 7/59 set 472; to Dormitory DS 70089
1/26	4047	set 472, Worthing & Bognor service;	Wdn 7/59 set 472; to Mess & Tool Van DS 70112

Index